The Medici Wedding *of* 1589

Florentine Festival as *Theatrum Mundi*

YALE UNIVERSITY PRESS *New Haven & London*

The Medici Wedding *of* 1589

JAMES M. SASLOW

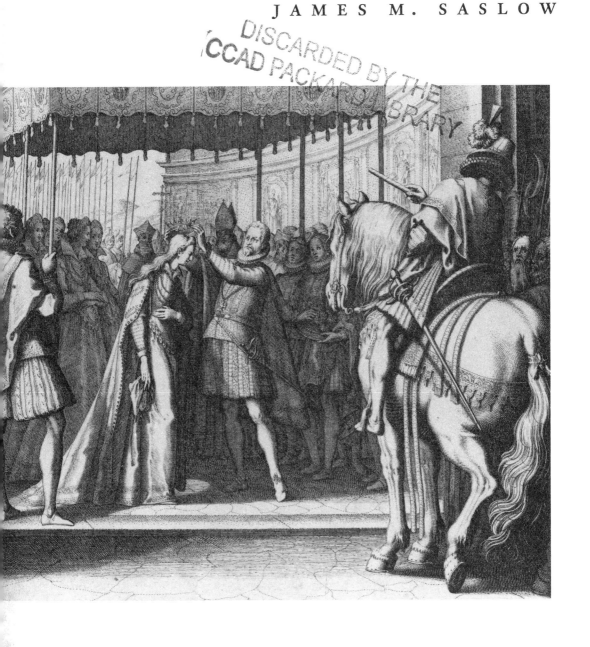

FRONTISPIECE

Ferdinando I crowns Christine of Lorraine, Porta al Prato, Florence. Jacques Callot. Metropolitan Museum of Art, no. 57.650.364(14).

Publication of this book has been aided by a grant from the Millard Meiss Publication Fund of the College Art Association.

MM

Designed by Richard Hendel
Set in Janson Text type by
The Composing Room of Michigan, Inc.
Printed in The United States of America by BookCrafters, Inc., Chelsea, Michigan.

Library of Congress Cataloging-in-Publication Data

Saslow, James M.
The Medici wedding of 1589 : Florentine festival as Theatrum Mundi / James M. Saslow.
p.   cm.
Includes bibliographical references and index.
ISBN 0-300-06447-0 (cloth : alk. paper)
1. Ferdinando I, Grand-Duke of Tuscany, 1549–1609 — Marriage.   2. Christine, of Lorraine, Grand Duchess, consort of Ferdinand I, Grand Duke of Tuscany, 1565–1636 — Marriage.   3. Marriage customs and rites — Italy — Florence — History — 16th century.   4. Pageants — Italy — Florence — History — 16th century.   5. Florence (Italy) — History — 1421–1737.   I. Title.
DG738.21.S37   1996
945'.5107'092 — dc20   95-32245   CIP

A catalogue record for this book is available from the British Library.

The paper in this book meets the guidelines for permanence and durability of the Committee on Production Guidelines for Book Longevity of the Council on Library Resources.

10 9 8 7 6 5 4 3 2 1

TO MY MOTHER

Terpsichore of South Orange

Contents

Acknowledgments, ix

Introduction, 1

1 SEPTEMBER & OCTOBER 1588

   The Creative, Management, and Public Relations Staffs, 21

2 NOVEMBER & DECEMBER 1588

   Casting, Costumes, and Rehearsals, 49

3 JANUARY & FEBRUARY 1589

   The Theater, the Scenery, the Artists, 75

4 MARCH 1589

   Artisans, Stagehands, Technical Rehearsals; Christine's Outbound Journey, 101

5 APRIL 1589

   Dress Rehearsals; Christine's Inbound Journey and Entry, 121

6 MAY 1589

   The Wedding As/In Performance, 148

7 JUNE 1589 AND BEYOND

   Aftermath and Later Influence, 174

CATALOGUE, 189

APPENDIX *Genealogical Tables, Valois-Habsburg, Medici,* 263

Notes, 267

Bibliography, 309

Sources of Illustrations, 315

Index, 317

Acknowledgments

Much of the archival research for this book was supported by two grants from the City University of New York PSC-CUNY Research Award Program in 1992 and 1993. The bulk of the writing was completed during my term as a J. Clawson Mills Fellow at the Metropolitan Museum of Art during 1993–94. In addition to my gratitude to the Museum for its financial support, I wish to thank the staff of the Department of Prints and Drawings for their helpful involvement in this project, especially Colta Ives, Catherine Bindman, and Suzanne Boorsch. I also profited during my year at the Museum from the advice of conservator Mindy Dubansky and of fellows Armin Kunz and Sarah McPhee.

Many friends and colleagues have read parts of this book in manuscript and have offered useful suggestions and welcome encouragement. William Wallace was, as always, a trusted and constructive critic, as well as a gracious host during my time in Florence. Wiley Hitchcock generously offered his expertise in music and theater history — and, with Janet Cox-Rearick, an enchanted dinner overlooking the Medici villa at Artimino. Victor Bumbalo's enthusiasm, as a theater professional, writer, and friend, buoyed my spirits at a crucial time. Members of the seminar on early modern material culture held in 1994 at Columbia University's Institute for Research on Women and Gender, particularly Jean Howard, Martha Howell, and Keith Moxey, were unstinting in their intellectual support. The Aston-Magna Academy, whose director Raymond Erickson invited me to speak about the Medici wedding in 1991, enabled me to appreciate the multimedia aspects of court ritual; among the many Academy participants who made that experience both delightful and educational I especially thank Ingrid Brainard, Barbara Russano Hanning, Robert Ketterer, Paula Elliot, Paul Ferrara, and Robert Rodini.

Many other individuals are due a debt of gratitude for their ongoing discussions about the project, suggestions for bibliography and research sources, and practical support. I especially thank Janet Cox-Rearick, David Rosand, Raymond Erickson, and Arthur Blumenthal, who was an inspiration both for his pioneering scholarship on Medici festivals and his unselfish enthusiasm for my incursions on his "turf"; also Pamela Askew, Konrad Eisenbichler, Michael Flack, James Middleton, Carolyn Valone, Elissa Weaver, and Susan Zimmerman. For facilitating my encounters with the original written and visual records, I thank the staffs of the Archivio di Stato Firenze, the Biblioteca

Nazionale Centrale Firenze, and the print and drawing departments of the Musée du Louvre, the Galleria degli Uffizi, and the Victoria and Albert Museum; Gino Corti graciously assisted with problems of paleography.

As always, my work would not be what it is without the support and affection of my companion, Steve Goldstein. I don't know which was harder to put up with: my prolonged absences for research, or my prolonged presence as a distracted writer. He comforts and heals both at the office and in the home.

The Medici Wedding *of* 1589

Introduction

In October of 1588, the Florentine delegate Orazio Rucellai formalized the engagement of Grand Duke Ferdinando I de' Medici to the French princess Christine de Lorraine, niece of King Henri III and granddaughter of Henri's mother, the formidable dowager Queen Catherine de' Medici, a distant cousin of Ferdinando. The union had been in negotiation for nearly a year, and plans were already well under way for an extravagant ceremonial reception of the bride. This monthlong sequence of public and courtly pageantry, which unfolded throughout April and May of the following year, began with Christine's progress through several major Tuscan cities, a passage that climaxed with her triumphal entry into the capital, Florence. Further celebrations proceeded through a series of banquets; performances in the Medici Theater at the Uffizi Palace; an allegorical-chivalric parade, tourney, and mock naval battle at the family's Pitti Palace; and a football game, animal-baiting, and a street masquerade.

The wedding *feste* of 1589 mobilized the combined intellectual, artistic, and administrative forces of Tuscany at the zenith of its wealth, power, and cultural prestige: "More events were planned, more lavish theatrical entertainments initiated, more money spent, and more visual and written records were executed than for any Medici wedding before or after."[1] Treated as a whole, the various components of this enormous *festa* constitute one of the outstanding late Renaissance landmarks of artistic creativity, encompassing art and architecture, theater, music, and political-religious ceremonial.

Some of the events, such as Christine's triumphal entry, were distinguished from their ancestors in a long tradition principally by their enlarged scale and greater complexity. Others, such as the naval battle, were innovative creations or novel re-creations of antique precedents. In particular, the spectacularly elaborate centerpiece of the state reception — several performances in the Medici Theater of a series of *intermedi*, inserted between the acts of varying comedies — occupies a seminal position in early modern stage history. A hybrid art form that fused instrumental music, song, dance, and splendid costumes and stage designs to glorify the ruling couple, intermedi were allegorical tableaux, in this case on a theme of the power of musical harmony, a topic with political overtones. The 1589 intermedi were replete with "marvels" and unprecedented technical effects of which one chronicler wrote,

"Their splendor cannot be described, and anyone who did not see it could not believe it."[2]

In theatrical and artistic terms, these presentations united humanist antiquarianism and far-reaching musical-dramatic innovation with important advances in architecture, mechanics, and stage design to lay the foundations for theater and opera as we know them today. The text and music for the intermedi were written by prominent members or associates of the progressive Camerata fiorentina, notably the programmer Giovanni de' Bardi and the composer Jacopo Peri, whose *Dafne* of 1598 is considered the first true opera. The three-year-old Medici Theater was remodeled for the occasion by its designer, the court architect-engineer Bernardo Buontalenti, as the first permanent indoor theater with a modern proscenium arch. Also the scenic designer, Buontalenti perfected here the sporadic development of illusionistic perspective stage settings and coordinated a vast team of artists and craftworkers, including the sculptor Giovanni Bologna and such painters as Alessandro Allori, Ludovico Cigoli, and Andrea Boscoli. The iconography of the events — characters and their actions, whether embodied by artistic images, by public figures on the urban stage, or by actors in frank impersonation — constitutes a revealing summation of the taste, imagery, and political-philosophical symbolism of an influential late mannerist court.

Alongside their importance as an artifact of culture in the narrowly artistic sense, the events of the 1589 wedding are also embedded in a matrix of cultural forces in the broader domains of economic, social, and political organization. The month of pageantry required a full year of preparations, from design and construction work involving numerous trades and industries, to organizing large groups of people from all classes for public ceremonies (and often providing them with livery or the fabrics to make it), to arranging lodging and food for several thousand international guests.

Because the logistics of such a complex event extended so far, both vertically (within Tuscan society) and horizontally (outward through the geography of the Mediterranean and beyond), they provide an index to many aspects of granducal administration and finance and connect these internal structures to the European and world context that the wedding aimed to impress. In these propagandistic displays by the emerging Renaissance nations — "the theater of triumphalism," as Loren Partridge and Randolph Starn characterized them — "art making was a product of the triumphalist state. It involved a large bureaucracy, an extensive division of labor, a careful allocation of resources, all controlled from the top to mobilize the display of intellectual, artistic, and material resources."[3] Although this formulation certainly captures the ideal envisioned by the state, no such monopoly of artistic production ever materialized in practice; there remained other institutions and classes, from clergy to villagers to the highest aristocrats, whose competing demands for time on the cultural stage had to be negotiated. Nor was the state's cultural apparatus, even within its own sphere, ever as efficient as it aspired to be, or able to guard completely against accidents either natural or human.

The goal of this book, therefore, is a reconstruction of the wedding events, as well as the preparations for them — a treatment of the total celebration as an episode in the creation of material culture. If, as Janet Wolff has put it, "the sociology of art is the study of the practices and institutions of artistic production," such an inquiry must take into account a range of interdependent aspects, among them the political and economic concerns of the patrons and the audience in front of the footlights; the creative and organizational activities of the writers, artists, and administrators; the backstage world of anonymous craftworkers and imperious sopranos; and the economic and manufacturing networks that supplied materials, equipment, and services.[4]

Though traditionally treated in isolation, all of these contributors to the 1589 feste are inextricably united. To arrive at a comprehensive iconology of the wedding, I examine three components of *meaning* in its broadest sense: the production of the physical objects (the performances), the objects themselves (form and content), and the multiple readings that various components of the audience made of this visual-verbal "text." I take as my guide in this endeavor Charles Wilson, who has written (in his study of Europe from 1558 to 1648), "In any age, art must reflect something of the nature of the society in which it is formed; but there is probably no other period in history in which its social content is so rich and varied, or so necessary an aid to an understanding of contemporary society."[5] In common with many contemporary historians, I would suggest only that the passive relation between art and society implied by "reflection" — in which art is figured only as a *product*, something produced by outside forces — should be reformulated as a more active and mutual *process*, in which both help to construct their shared reality. The following pages will reveal, I trust, artists and patrons in the process of creating society itself as much as they are creating works of art.

DOCUMENTARY SOURCES

In contrast to the ephemeral nature of much early theater, uniquely rich and extensive documentation survives for many of the events of 1589. Thanks to Medici policies of national and international cultural propaganda, as well as the dynasty's compulsive record keeping, Ferdinando and Christine's wedding is the best-documented of all such festivals, and was thus among the most influential for later developments in the genre. It is primarily this wealth of evidence, both visual and textual, that permits the detailed reconstruction of the 1589 feste that constitutes the core of this book.

Three types of documentation are available: published texts, visual records, and archival manuscript sources. These three forms of evidence reveal contrasting and complementary aspects of the event. The published accounts — both visual and verbal — that were produced under state auspices present the desired public face of the events, the official view from the audience and patron's standpoint; the administrative records and the sketches and other documents of the creative process, on the other hand, never having been meant for public scrutiny, offer informal and unofficial glimpses of the world "backstage" that was generally invisible to the audience. Taken together, these sources reveal the ideas, activities, and economic relations of a cross-section of Florentine society.

Printed texts. The text of Girolamo Bargagli's play *La pellegrina*, which accompanied the premiere of the intermedi, plus the libretto and music of the intermedi themselves, have come down to us intact, as have some details of their choreography. At least fifteen souvenir accounts of the major events were published — more than for any other such event — either as program books for use at the events themselves, or as memorials issued afterward. These festival books, or *descrizioni*, some of them richly illustrated, included Gualterotti for Christine's entry into the city; Rossi for the intermedi and comedy; Cavallino for the calendar of events; and Cavallino and Pavoni for the Pitti events (see Bibliography, *Contemporary Printed Sources*). All of these texts recount the "official" version of individual events: the plots, characters, and narrative structure and the symbolic meanings attached to them, along with a commentary meant to highlight and reinforce the virtues, magnificence, and political power of the Medici patrons and the Tuscan state.

Visual evidence. The sole original elements of the décor still extant are one arch painting (cat. 2), six stucco sculptures that adorned another entry arch (cat. 4), and a Roman warrior sculptured by Giovanni Bologna, probably for the Medici Theater. For the entry, intermedi, comedy, Pitti and Santa Croce events, some 88 individual drawings, paintings, and prints record the vanished temporary architecture, stage sets, and costume designs, either in original drawings by Buontalenti and his assistants or in copies by engravers. Also, Gualterotti's *descrizione* includes 65 plates that illustrate each entry arch and its individual paintings and sculptures; some are duplicated by the independently printed sheets. Finally, a handful of preliminary sketches survive for the paintings on the arches or drawn copies after them. These are described (in the order in which the wedding events took place) in the Catalogue.

Manuscript sources. The unusual wealth of documents consists largely of the administrative accounts of the Medici household, plus the summary of original sources (some now lost) that was prepared in the eighteenth century by Francesco Settimani. Of special utility to the present study are two lengthy codices pertaining to the Uffizi and Pitti events. The *Libro di conti*, a ledger containing detailed accounts for materials and labor, was kept by the the the staff of composer Emilio de' Cavalieri, who also served as the Medici superintendent of the fine arts and, in this capacity, as producer of these events; the *Memoriale e ricordi 1588–89* is a stage manager's daily production logbook kept by Cavalieri's and Buontalenti's principal executant, Girolamo Seriacopi.

These texts offer precise and detailed data about the identities and functions of some 50 tailors, 100 musicians and singers, and 250 general staff, as well as their work schedules and pay scales. They also indicate the materials and techniques used for the settings, costumes, and special effects; the cost and sources of materials; and the day-to-day processes of backstage work. Together with the costume and set designs, the texts give us a rare glimpse of the creative process in action, from the first conception through various changes and additions. Additional manuscript accounts detail other aspects of the event, from the logistics and artistic planning for Christine's journey to the provisioning of hundreds of guests at the Medici villas; others record, in the general context of employment rolls, the names and activities of artists connected with the feste.[6]

Unfortunately, there is one glaring lacuna in these otherwise so abundant records: they do not cover those elements of the 1589 feste that were organized by the Church, such as the bride's reception in the duomo or a procession celebrating the relics of St. Antoninus. Of necessity, therefore, the present study focuses on state patronage and imagery. This limitation should not lead us to overstate the distinction between secular and sacred, for the separation between the two spheres was not then anywhere near as sharp as it is today in the secularized West.[7]

STATE OF RESEARCH AND GOALS OF THIS STUDY

The intermedi especially, but also the other events of 1589, have long been a subject for art and theater historians. Research into the feste began a century ago with Aby Warburg, who first assembled and identified Buontalenti's set and costume designs for the intermedi in a long article, later reprinted with selected excerpts from Seriacopi's and Cavalieri's manuscripts.[8] This process of recovering the fundamental visual and documentary evidence continued with articles by Daddi Giovannozzi, Laver, and Massar that crystallized our knowledge about such individual events as the entry and the Pitti parade. Nonetheless, although further extracts from the graphic and written sources have been published sporadically, more than half of some 60 drawings by Buontalenti, as well as numerous prints and the bulk of the manuscript material, remain unavailable in print or largely unstudied.

I intend in this book to incorporate and extend, in three important respects, previous work on the 1589 feste. My goals are to provide a comprehensive chronological narrative, while at the same time ranging synchronically across a wide social and artistic terrain during a short time span, and to approach the totality of the event from an interdisciplinary standpoint that highlights the interplay between artistic and social analysis.

First, previous scholarship in this area has been characterized by a lack of chronological narrative coherence. The format of most research since the 1960s on the visual aspects of the wedding has been fragmented, often taking the form of brief exhibition catalogue entries on individual drawings or prints. The few attempts at a comprehensive narrative of the event (by Nagler, Strong, and the introductory essays to major catalogues between 1960 and 1980) are but brief summaries that suffer in varying degrees from incompleteness and a methodological emphasis on uncritical description.

Accordingly, Chapters 1 through 6 are organized to provide a month-to-month narrative of the events that unfolded largely between August 1588 and June 1589, from the marriage negotiations to the proxy wedding to Christine's voyage and the entry, performances, and further events in her honor. While dealing with traditional art-historical issues of style, sources, and content, this narrative will also include the preparations for all of these events, in order to examine the sociology of artistic production in the period when its organizational basis was shifting from small independent workshops to permanent state-supported administration of unprecedented scale and complexity.[9] In tandem with this artistic material, I hope to draw connections between the manifest content of the events and the wider forces that they embody and address.

Because contemporary literary theory has made academics chronically suspicious of narrative history, I freely admit that, as with all narratives, my account is in one sense merely a variation on an already familiar and available trope, the story of (in movie parlance) "putting on a show." In defense of this narrative mode, I would stress that such an overarching, contextual account is precisely what has been lacking in previous studies of the 1589 festival. Also unavoidably, the tale I have chosen to tell is selective and personalized. It is shaped by certain methodological interests and preferences — on one hand, for the broad dramatic sweep of history and geography; on the other, for the telling coincidence and the revealing anecdote, or what is often termed "journalistic" detail.

In particular, the direction of my research followed a growing curiosity about the "how-to" aspects of Renaissance theatrics. Previous research on the festivals' visual aspects has tended to focus on reconstructing their finished appearance and their official iconography, in part because much about the ephemeral processes of stage practice must remain conjectural. Notwithstanding these gaps in our knowledge, the following narrative pays special attention to backstage activities.

Much contemporary theory is concerned with cultural production, with what Michel Foucault called "the technologies of power," in the discursive sense — how images control and propagate ideologies. While New Historicist and related scholars usefully emphasize that the arts, in creating powerful representations and channeling discourse, help construct our very notions of *reality*, I confess to being at least as interested here in the more practical "technologies" of power: that is, the ways in which images and rituals are themselves quite literally constructed. To put it another way, I am interested here in *actual* as much as discursive "production," both in the everyday sense of physical fabrication and in its theatrical sense of "a production" — a performance or set of images that requires planning, labor, and matériel. The impact of such events in practical terms was significant; as Braudel reminds us, "war, public works, and state enterprises [arts included] were . . . more of an economic stimulus than might be supposed."[10]

This study might therefore be said to privilege reconstruction over deconstruction, at least to the extent that a comprehensive description must precede analysis. Its method is to combine the visual and textual evidence with the detailed manuscript accounts of planning, construction, payments, casting, and rehearsals to chart the processes of commission and design — from preliminary creative conception through execution of the physical setting and its actual use — as well as the complex logistics of the performance and of subsequent storage and reuse. These aspects of the production are inseparable from the parallel process of preparing the explanatory and commemorative texts and images. These "discursive interventions," along with finished visual-theatrical products, will provide a basis for understanding the iconography and iconology of the wedding events. At the same time, this investigation aims to deepen our understanding not only of the onstage images but also of the artistic and sociological aspects of the numerous backstage activities necessary to a complex multimedia project, from the sources and cost of materials to administrative and accounting procedures and technical experimentation. To draw a metaphor from the art of weaving that was so central to the Florentine economy, the ideal, finished face of this luxurious artistic fabric is but the reverse of what Edith Wharton called "the underside of the social tapestry, where the threads are knotted and the loose ends hang."

Because the art-historical prerequisite to any such narrative of artistic process is a firm base of visual documentation, the narrative chapters of this study are followed by an illustrated Catalogue of all the known materials — drawings, prints, and paintings — that record the wedding events, either from the design phase or retrospectively. In addition to providing basic data and references, my aim in the catalogue entries is to establish the attribution and sequence of the works (preliminary drawings, finished sketches, later copies) and to determine their relative reliability as records of the actual events.

The second methodological concern of this study is to be synchronic rather than diachronic — or, more accurately, synchronic across a very short time period, and across a very wide geographical and social space, centered on the Florentine base of preparations but showing how the tentacles of that controlling apparatus reached out, of necessity, to coordinate events elsewhere, from Pisa to Paris. By focusing on the narrow timespan, September 1588 to June 1589, documented almost day-to-day in the manuscripts kept by the principal organizers, this "microhistory" attempts to utilize those documentary sources to describe "a year in the life" of Florentine cultural activity.[11]

The study is also synchronic in the sense of cutting across all class and occupational lines. Monarchical society conceived of its own social organization as a series of concentric rings centered on the prince, with the other classes revolving around him (rarely, her) at various fixed distances — just as the twelve heavenly Sirens of the first intermedio propel their planetary spheres around the spindle, or *axis mundi*, of the goddess Necessity. The principal *audience* for the festival, as well as the instigating and directing minds and purses, may have been the court and the aristocracy, but street processions, sports events, and fireworks also had a broader appeal, attracting spectators with widely different habits of "reading" public events. Moreover, the celebrations were *created* by a far wider spectrum of people, moving outward from the directive elite attached to the court — authors, composers, designers — through the myriad occupations, of varying status and sophistication, that were responsible for executing these conceptions: visually, the craftworkers, carpenters, tailors, painters; theatrically, the singers, dancers, and instrumentalists and the stage crew. To see the event in its entirety thus requires taking in as wide a cross-section of the strands of Florentine cultural producers as the records permit, and (at the risk of superficiality) looking for clues to the socioeconomic aspects of Renaissance performance that were operating here, such as labor supply and working conditions, wages and hours, casting and rehearsals, and the differentials of class and gender.

Thirdly, therefore, an interdisciplinary methodology is necessary, one that will integrate the methods and insights of artistic history (art, music, literature) with those of the social and natural sciences. The Medici wedding is an episode not only in artistic, but also in social and economic history, and in the history of technology. Nor, as indexes to cultural meaning, are these episodes separate or distinct. As Heinrich Plett has insisted, "Cultural systems are manifested in specific forms of expression, such as literature, for example, painting, dress, architecture, eating habits, and so on. The totality of such expressions is . . . a complex text consisting of various linguistic and non-linguistic signs."[12]

It is this very interlocking complexity that underlies the widespread fascination with Renaissance festival and that provides the key to understanding it both as fine art and as a physical and social artifact: "As these multi-media events exploited the talents of impresarios and *maestri* of every variety, so today the processions and spectacles interest historians in diverse fields: art, architecture, literature, music, theater, dance, religion, diplomacy, anthropology, sociology, urbanism, hydraulic engineering and pyrotechnics."[13]

Most of this research to date, however, has proceeded within relatively watertight disciplinary compartments. Important studies of the intermedi by historians of music and drama (for example, Walker, Donington, Hanning), have understandably concentrated on the text and music, whereas the predominant interest of art historians has been on such formal and iconographic aspects of the *mise-en-scène* as attribution and stylistic development; social historians, for their part, may allude to the event as a political and fiscal landmark without addressing either its form or content. Furthermore, while all subsequent scholars have paid homage to Warburg's discovery of the Seriacopi and Cavalieri manuscripts, only Franco Berti has followed his lead by returning for a fresh look at those revealing documents; others have simply relied on the selected transcriptions appended to Warburg's article.[14]

In summary, then, this study proceeds from the belief that an artistic text like the 1589 festival can be most profitably read as a point of intersection between various worlds — cultural, social, technological — and, conversely, as a microhistorical index to all those realms. Such a text can simultaneously express official ideas and ideals, reveal gaps or inconsistencies in the realization of that ideal, and demonstrate precisely how, in practical terms, those in power attempted to enact their ideas on and through the body politic and artistic. Of course, I must here make the ritual confession of trepidation at trespassing in alien disciplinary waters. Much more could be made of this material, along differing axes, by specialists in economic and social history, science and technology, or the performing arts. Others will, I hope, flesh out the framework presented here in precisely those areas.

FERDINANDO DE' MEDICI

Many of the concerns of this study can be introduced through the two central actors who took the starring roles in the 1589 festivities. The bridal couple — in their political and family backgrounds, personal interests and professional pursuits — embody many of the themes that will run through the analysis of what was, after all, their wedding.

The second surviving son of Cosimo I, Ferdinando (1549–1609) was destined from an early age for the Church. Appointed to the rank of cardinal at age 14, he took up residence in Rome, where he gained a reputation as a religious reformer as well as a notable art patron, connoisseur, and collector. When his older brother Francesco died in 1587 leaving no eligible male heirs, Ferdinando renounced his vows and returned to Florence to rescue the fragile dynasty from extinction. Generally well-liked by the populace, he is credited with revitalizing the grand duchy after the decline of the 1570s and with bringing Tuscany to the acme of its power and prestige. In contrast to Francesco, whom he detested, Ferdinando was dutiful, even energetic in his pursuit of increased wealth and political independence, actively involving himself in economic development projects, scientific and technical experimentation (he was Galileo's patron), and international diplomacy.[15]

Ferdinando's ambitions and accomplishments, whether at home or abroad, focused on building up the economic and political security of both the Tuscan state and his own ruling family, and on presenting both to the world as commanding actors on the international stage. When the sea nymphs of the fifth wedding intermedio serenaded the newlywed couple with a prophecy of "a progeny of such brilliance that it will adorn the world from one pole to the other" (repeated in intermedio 6, that Ferdinand's own fame will fly "from one pole to the other"), the global metaphor was more than a mere literary conceit: Ferdinando was, in fact, involved in efforts to import goods from Africa and Persia, and he sent expeditions to explore the possibilities of trade and colonization as far off as Brazil and India.[16]

In foreign affairs, Ferdinando's overriding objective was to check the power of Habsburg Spain, which, while still the dominant power in Europe, was increasingly on the defensive, more noticeably so after the humiliation of the

Spanish Armada in the summer of 1588. Ferdinando's marriage to a princess of Valois France represented a pointed reversal of the pro-Habsburg policies of his father and brother; by marrying Christine he could ally himself with the country that had long been Spain's principal continental rival.

The wedding itself was Ferdinando's greatest example of an important Medici family tradition: extensive patronage of a court art whose goals were to aggrandize the dynasty and spread its reputation both at home and abroad. In supporting lavish entertainments and theater, Ferdinando was following not only precedents that had been set down by his father and brother, who were themselves elaborating an iconographic tradition stretching back even further in time.[17] A princely duty for *magnificence* — the ostentatious display of patronage in the service of propagandistic state goals — was a commonplace of political theory. Bastiano de' Rossi opens his official account of the intermedi and performance of *La pellegrina* with an homage to the classical virtue of *magnificenza*, which consists of "great expenditures, such as for building . . . [and] receiving foreign visitors with regal pomp" (pp. 1–2). At the same time, however, in a running counterpoint to this tradition, contemporary judgments and the evidence of the account books agree that, while Ferdinando could be generous with expenditures on projects that would contribute to his public prestige, he took after his banker-ancestors in being frugal to the point of parsimony over expenses that would not add directly to his public image, such as government salaries.[18]

Of course, much of the success of his court spectacle depended on precisely these less glamorous or visible components of Ferdinando's rule. What made the theatrical magnificence so impressive were advances in control over the physical resources, technology, and people needed to support such a complex and costly endeavor. Control over nature and culture went hand in hand: the higher the level of technological and economic resources that could be marshaled for public spectacles, the greater the effect the display could have on the spectators. Rossi and other commentators are fond of describing audience reaction with such adjectives as *stupiti* (astounded, overwhelmed), and the causes of their amazement are often termed *meraviglie*, marvels or wonders — a central term throughout Mannerist criticism to figure a fascination with all that pushes beyond the bounds of the normally possible.

The impulse toward increasing control is itself part of an even broader process, which accelerated throughout Europe in the early modern period: the development of absolute monarchy and the modern nation-state. This historic transition changed the basis of most societies from the medieval model of a feudal and agrarian world, small in geographic scope and tied by bonds of personal loyalty and custom, to the emerging national state: a territorially enlarged, centralized, and rationally administered regime, in which the impersonal efficiency of a permanent bureaucracy accompanied a marked expansion of the scope of government operations, both at a global scale (worldwide trade and colonization) and at local and internal levels. This strengthening of control over both physical nature and human society took place simultaneously in three overlapping spheres. Nature was altered and ordered through technology and economics; the human social realm through governmental administration; and art, the discursive-intellectual sphere, by instituting controls over *representations* of the monarch and the state.[19]

Technological control. Control and exploitation of material resources, the keys to the creation of the modern state and its art, increased markedly in the sixteenth and especially the seventeenth centuries. Before the early modern period, as Charles Wilson has written, "men were at the mercy of the elements"; although in comparison to later centuries "attempts to control the environment achieved only very limited success" before 1650, dominance of physical nature was being actively sought through scientific research and technological experimentation. Parallel to this effort and inextricable from it were the first steps toward economic rationalization of the processes of farming, mining, and manufacturing, as well as the control of local and international markets for goods and of the economic infrastructure to pay for them, which had been pioneered by Florentine bankers since the fourteenth century.[20]

This control and rationalization operated at several concentric levels, from the grand duchy down to the city and the theater. Large-scale engineering and architectural projects, many under the supervision of Bernardo Buontalenti, were aimed at draining swamps, enlarging the duchy's major international port, Livorno, and encouraging new crops. The engraving of Ferdinando directing the fortification of Livorno (fig. 1), from a posthumous series by Jacques Callot on the grand duke's accomplishments, emphasizes this prevailing theme of his reign.[21] The landscape around Florence was patterned by country villas built or refurbished for the Medici, while within the city itself major construction projects at the Pitti Palace, Palazzo Vecchio, Uffizi, and Fortezza da Basso continued the tradition of turning the entire city fabric into an extension of family power at a massive scale.

Social control. The sociopolitical goal of Ferdinando and his predecessors was to maximize control over all elements of the body politic, through a variety of institutions and practices, and thus to establish themselves as healers of social discord. The most visible aspect of this centralization was administrative control, which was continually tightened and rationalized. The begin-

1. *Ferdinando I fortifying the port of Livorno. Jacques Callot.*

nings of a permanent bureaucracy had been instituted by Cosimo I, who commissioned the Uffizi Palace — the word means *offices* — to house his growing administrative staff. Ferdinando maintained and expanded this corps of officials, while simultaneously increasing control of the populace through less benign methods: surveillance by a network of spies and informers, and a vigorous system of police, courts, and punishments. Although Florentine society continued to be menaced by endemic violence and brigandage, the bargain struck between the Tuscan populace and the grand dukes — to replace chronic factionalism and disorder with a strong authority — proved an effective trade-off, which demonstrated that an entire state could be governed from its metropolitan center "with a degree of uniformity remarkable for that time."[22]

In particular the court strove, again quite effectively, to domesticate the competitive and sometimes fractious patrician class, to co-opt them by involving them in court activities and patronage. In practical terms, this meant recruiting many officials for the bureaucracy from the older aristocracy.[23] More symbolically, the rigid and formal court etiquette adopted by Cosimo I under the influence of his Spanish wife, Eleonora of Toledo, with its niceties of hierarchical ranking and respectful rituals, was continued by Ferdinando as a way to sacralize the monarchy and the persons of the ruling family by surrounding them with an aura of mystery and pomp.

Elaborate public and courtly spectacles, from the wedding to similar festivities for baptisms, deaths, and military victories, were an integral part of this social integration. The festivals operated on several planes — ideological, sociological, and economic. Ferdinando demanded that all classes actively unite in creating, patronizing, and attending these ritualized celebrations of the ruling order. Aristocrats paid for and rode on some of the floats in the Pitti parade, and they acted as ushers and guards of honor at Christine's entry, thus garnering honor and status; lower classes were drawn into economic dependency on the court as paid performers, craftworkers, and laborers. On an overt iconographic level, such festivities exerted a powerful discursive function, as outlined by Clifford Geertz in his theory of the "theater state," by projecting an intensely dramatic and idealized image of collective order and hierarchical ideology. On a deeper structural level, they also served what Emile Durckheim, writing of religious rituals, termed a "latent function," that of bringing community members together in a collective affirmation of their social bond independent of any manifest content.[24]

The structural linkages between sacred ritual and the secular theater are the cue for the entrance of the phrase from my title, *theatrum mundi*. The Latin term for "theater of the world" was a favorite trope of sixteenth- and seventeenth-century authors and cultural theorists, from Shakespeare to Juan Vives. And if *theatrum mundi* was a basic metaphor underlying many plays and works of literary and plastic art in this period — which witnessed the rise of the great national dramatic traditions of England, Spain, and elsewhere — it was no less so for the festival of 1589, from the choice of activities to their iconography, visual style, and ideology. The term, which dates back to such antique writers as Pythagoras, grew to embrace multiple interlocking levels of application, from stage performance in the literal sense, to a metaphysical view of human life and action, to the entirety of the physical and social worlds.

At its most general, *theatrum mundi* conveys the belief that life itself is analogous to a theatrical performance. This sense is best known to English readers in the melancholy soliloquy of Shakespeare's Jaques, in *As You Like It* (2:7):

> . . . all the world's a stage,
> And all the men and women merely players:
> They have their exits and their entrances;
> And one man in his time plays many parts.

In this theatricalized view of human life, although God remains both director and prime audience, earthly mortals are the actors, the center of attention. The profound shift in human awareness and sense of increased potential that this metaphor embodied have been marked as the beginning of modern self-fashioning, or more broadly, of human self-consciousness, both as unique individuals and as heroic actors in the drama of history.[25]

Specifically of concern to the subject of courtly spectacle is one of the many corollaries of that general theory, namely that government, especially monarchy, is also a performance. Since Machiavelli, Italian political theorists had held that the prince's essential art is "looking the part" — that is, playing the public role of statecraft with conviction and splendor. To assure his success in this essential public relations matter, on which hung the dynasty's hopes for a "long run," whenever possible the public and court environments were structured with an eye toward dramatic self-presentation.

Two prongs to this weapon of statecraft particularly concern me here. First is the theatricalization of the whole spatial environment, in which the natural world was physically built (or rebuilt) in theatrical terms, as a stage set for human actions in the broadest sense. Such reworking took many forms, from the layout of rural villas to the relocation by Pope Sixtus V of an Egyptian obelisk. These efforts were concentrated in the capitals, in which restructuring and decoration of the urban fabric made the city a stage where the open spaces and buildings, including temporary festival architecture, became sets, and (in Trexler's phrase) "all urban dwellers were actors"; indeed, for the later sixteenth-century writer Jacopo Soldani, Florence was explicitly "a theater of the world."[26] Second is the construction of actual theater buildings, where the apparatus of state presentation could operate at a more contained and private — but correspondingly intensified — level. Performances in a space like the Medici Theater of the Uffizi might be a mere microcosm of the larger "world theater" outside its walls, but it was in this artificially controlled and esthetically concentrated space that the metaphor could come closest to a visual illusion of perfect order and its attendant splendor.

Artistic control. The development of the permanent palace theater brings us to the third level of control, over the entire artistic sphere. Art making in the broadest sense, including texts and images, was a central element of princely propaganda in the Renaissance and Baroque eras. Through the elaboration of intellectual and visual conceits Ferdinando, like most monarchs, sought to exercise control of political and social thought — of what we would now call the discourse about kingship, legitimacy, and other issues. The goals of such activity, once again, were order and uniformity — the intellectual equivalent of the striving for control in the political and technical spheres. This impulse can be seen in numerous cultural endeavors of the Medici regime, such as the founding in 1582 of the Accademia della Crusca (of which Bardi and Rossi were members) to standardize the Tuscan language and ensure uniformity of usage. Similarly, the establishment of a museum on the top floor of the new Uffizi, to house the Medici family collections, was a means toward appropriating cultural history and organizing it for dynastic glory.[27]

In parallel with his policies toward political and economic resources, Ferdinando used the occasion of the 1589 wedding to set artistic patronage on the same permanent, centralized, and rationalized footing as the rest of his administration. His changes marked a transition away from the social structure of earlier Renaissance arts, traditionally centered on the *bottega*, or workshop, maintained by each independent craftworker. As with the other governmental agencies, he instituted at the Uffizi a professional fine-arts bureaucracy, headed by Emilio de' Cavalieri, dedicated to centralized coordination in the name of efficiency and cost containment.

All three levels of control sought by Ferdinando's regime interacted and mutually reinforced one another. The wedding festival is thus a powerful example of the increasing scope and complexity of political economy in the Renaissance: both in its overt iconography, with its claims for world hegemony and universal order, and in its "esthetic economy," by which name might be designated the social, economic, technical, and managerial practices and institutions through which material culture was produced. The artistic sphere is inextricable from the practical realms that make it possible, in the senses both of paying for it and of physically enabling its creation. It follows that, if administrative control and rationalization of resources were improved, the same resources could be stretched to do even more. Ferdinando would probably have agreed with the English visitor Robert Dallington's tart comment, after observing Florence in 1596, "that the great Duke hath two Revenues whereby he groweth rich; that is, great impositions [taxes], and great sparing (for sparing is a great revenue)."[28]

CHRISTINE DE LORRAINE

Christine de Lorraine (1565–1636) was the daughter of Princess Claude de France, one of seven children of King Henri II and Catherine de' Medici, and of Claude's husband Charles III, Duke of Lorraine. Christine was the favorite granddaughter of Catherine, through whom she was a distant cousin of Ferdinando, and who raised her at court after the early death of her mother. Catherine's son King Henri III, who ruled from 1574 until shortly after Christine's marriage, was both Christine's uncle and her brother-in-law, hav-

2. *Christine of Lorraine. Anonymous, French School.*

ing married her sister Louise (important in the history of theater as the patron of the "Ballet Comique de la Reine" of 1581, a landmark in the French tradition of court spectacle). Twenty-four at the time of the marriage, Christine was little more than a pawn in a high-stakes game of dynastic marriages played by her powerful older relatives. The role played by the arts in these long-range dynastic alliances is clear from a portrait of Christine (fig.

2), which was made in 1588 to be shipped to Ferdinando during negotiations over the match.[29]

As part of the background to his account of Christine's entry into Florence, Raffaello Gualterotti tells us that Catherine "had always had a passionate desire to send back to her homeland, Florence . . . someone of her own blood," a desire that was satisfied when Ferdinando accepted the hand of Christine, "her granddaughter, whom she raised like her own daughter."[30] Catherine was no doubt sincere in wishing to preserve the longstanding family and cultural links between France and Tuscany, which dated back to the generations of Leonardo da Vinci and the School of Fontainebleau. At the same time, the political situation in France at this time suggests there was as much calculation to Catherine's desire as pure family feeling.

During the latter half of the sixteenth century, France was riven by factional fighting among several of the great noble families — Bourbon, Montmorency, and Guise-Lorraine — which amounted to a state of chronic civil and religious warfare. These social troubles, exacerbated by the failure of any of Catherine and Henri II's three weak sons to produce an heir, kept the state in continual political and economic distress, and made alliances against the encircling Habsburgs a pressing diplomatic concern.[31] Tuscan bankers were the main support of the Lyons financial markets and hence of the French economy. The crown's urgency over the Medici alliance can be judged from the size of Christine's dowry, which indicates how, as usual, the Medici drove a hard bargain: she was to bring with her the enormous sum of 600,000 scudi (half contributed by Catherine herself), as well as jewelry and other items.[32]

The wedding date was pushed back by successive family tragedies, the assassination of the Duke of Guise in December 1588 and the death of the aged queen mother in January 1589. The marriage by proxy finally took place in late February, after which the bride left immediately on her long ceremonial journey south. Political motivations notwithstanding, the marriage appears to have turned out remarkably well for such arranged affairs, and it became a genuine love match. Christine's personality and interests complemented Ferdinando's, particularly in matters of religion; in Tuscany she expended considerable energy on the foundation of monasteries and convents. Her reputation must have preceded her: the first play performed at her wedding, Bargagli's *La pellegrina*, whose heroine is a wise and pious pilgrim, was chosen as a homage to the bride's own religious devotion.

Because the narrative will necessarily jump back and forth among various events, the preparations for them, and Christine's itinerary, there follows a calendar of the events scheduled along Christine's route through Tuscany and following her entry to the city.[33]

April 24, 1589: Christine lands at Livorno; ceremonial welcome

April 24–26: ceremonial welcome to Pisa

April 28: arrival at Poggio a Caiano, the Medici villa outside Florence; first meeting with Ferdinando

April 30: triumphal entry into Florence (cat. 1–7)

May 1: citizens of Peretola bring a maypole into the city

May 2: performance in the Uffizi theater of the comedy *La pellegrina*, accompanied by first performance of the intermedi; banquet in Palazzo Vecchio (cat. 8–68)

May 3: Feast of Discovery of the True Cross; uncovering of the miraculous image of the Virgin Mary at the church of the Santissima Annunziata

May 4: football game (*giuoco di calcio*) played by teams of aristocrats in Piazza Santa Croce (cat. 69)

May 5 (Good Friday) and/or 6: performance in Uffizi theater of the comedy *La zingara*, accompanied by a repeat performance of the intermedi

May 7: Easter Sunday; solemn mass in San Lorenzo and knightly investiture

May 8: animal baiting, Piazza Santa Croce

May 9: translation of the relics of Saint Antoninus to a new chapel in the church of San Marco, with a religious procession throughout the city

May 10: joust, Piazza Santa Croce (cat. 70)

May 11: *sfila* (parade), *sbarra* (foot combat), and *naumachia* (naval battle) in the courtyard of the Pitti Palace (cat. 71–87)

May 13 and/or 15: performance in the Uffizi theater of the comedy *La pazzia* and repeat of the intermedi

May 23: tournament (*corso al saracino*)

May 28: allegorical parade staged by young nobles, starting from Pitti Palace (cat. 88)

June 8: repeat performance of a comedy and the intermedi.

When we add to this exhausting schedule the series of similar ceremonies staged at various port cities along Christine's earlier sea itinerary, it becomes evident just how broad a definition of *theater* is needed to encompass all these heterogeneous yet interrelated events. The common thread uniting them is not simply that they were all performances, in the narrowly theatrical sense, but that they were also acts in a larger drama which we, no less than the sixteenth century itself, might usefully term "the theater of the world."

As noted earlier, *theatrum mundi* means more than the philosophical and artistic conceit of the world as a stage and of people as playing a role in life. At its wider levels of meaning, it also implies that the entire physical and social world is a theater for action — in the military sense of the word, a *theater of operations*, a phrase whose dual meaning can also be seen in the term *staging ground* for the logistical epicenter of an event. In other words, the conception of world-as-theater unites actual theater with its social, economic, and political dimensions. Royal marriage ceremonies were not simply occasions for artistic display; they were also the fruit of diplomatic and economic operations. The painted decoration of Christine's private cabin on her sea voyage presupposed a network of navies, ports, and supply. And court players required not only an aristocratic audience but also the availability of a figurative army of socially humbler artists and craftworkers.

The Neoplatonic vision of a concentrically ordered universe, which was central to the semiotics of the wedding imagery, mirrored the Medici's systematic extension of technological and social organization outward, from granducal headquarters to the city of Florence, to Tuscany, and to the Mediterranean world. The metaphor of harmonious unity that was so compellingly presented onstage in symbolic and artistic language depended on, and developed in tandem with, the growth of state control over the larger theater of the physical and social world, particularly modern bureaucratic administration of people, land, and economic resources.

The story that follows oscillates continuously between these two sites of cultural production: the formal-symbolic level directed from the center, and the logistical-practical level located at varying distances around the periphery of palace and theater. It cannot do otherwise. Charles Rosen has commented about the opera, which is a near descendant of the 1589 events, that its "basis speciously appears to be an opposition between the ideal purity of the music and the gritty reality needed to produce it."[34] This apparent polarity is misleading because, as the following story demonstrates, the artifice of the theater was inseparable from the equally artificial manipulation of the world outside it. What I hope to reveal is some of both qualities: the fantastic and elevated imagery that so amazed and moved the spectators, and the "gritty reality" of the processes of making such an ideal conception concrete and perceptible.

CHAPTER ONE

September & October 1588

THE CREATIVE, MANAGEMENT,

AND PUBLIC RELATIONS STAFFS

Although the earliest systematic evidence for the Uffizi stage work, Seriacopi's logbook, begins in late August 1588, by then the various preparations had already been under way for some time. Scattered entries in earlier accounts record activities at the theater as early as January 1588, and it is clear from Seriacopi's first entries that the play *La pellegrina* had already been chosen and the libretto for the intermedi completed. Planning could have begun at any time after the commencement of marriage negotiations in late 1587 and was certainly moving ahead by February of 1588, when the author Scipione Bargagli mentioned in a letter that he had been approached about providing a comedy for the grand duke.

As with any performance, this first stage of preparations for the wedding festival called for assembling three parallel staffs: the creative team, the managerial or production staff, and what we would now call the public relations office. The personnel of these groups overlapped, as did their tasks, so efforts had to be coordinated through continuous consultation.

The creative group — embracing authors, lyricists, composers, visual designers, and stage directors — was responsible for what Renaissance theorists called the *concetto*, the underlying conception, of each event, and for developing these themes and imagery in text, music, iconography, and visual form. The following discussion of each event begins with the authors of the texts, for many current historians, whether of visual or social phenomena, have become aware of "the active role of language, texts, and narrative structures in the creation and description of historical reality."[1] As noted in the Introduction, however, because these textual creations are themselves also products, the focus here is less on epistemology than on praxis: how such texts were made, by whom, and how they were given physical form.

The production staff supervised praxis, that is, administrative and economic matters; it included the producer, and under him a principal stage manager or quartermaster, various assistants, and the technical crews. Public relations were handled by a third set of individuals, who were charged with producing the "secondary texts": the printed program books that directed the multiple audiences' contemporaneous *reading* of the events, and the later commemorative volumes that preserved and disseminated those texts. These documents were planned simultaneously with the events themselves and required both writers and, for illustrated volumes, visual artists.

Beyond the Uffizi, the wedding also employed several other teams, for various components were organized and paid for separately — by the court, the church, or individual patricians or groups of residents. Even those parts that were sponsored directly by the Medici were divided: work on the arches for Christine's triumphal entry was organized separately from the intermedi, and the physical workshops were located in different places. Two overlapping crews were responsible for the principal state events: an "entry team" created the procession of April 30 along the public streets of the city, while the better-documented team working out of the Uffizi and Pitti palaces organized those subsequent events that were physically located in the granducal household complex: the intermedi, comedies, and the parade–naval battle–tournament.

It is possible to follow the working methods and collaborations of these various crews in some detail, though the documents available differ somewhat from those of earlier and later festivals, leaving numerous gaps in our knowledge of specific procedures and schedules. But because the triumphal entry, intermedi, and tournament are all strongly conservative traditions, we can often fill these gaps with probable inferences drawn from the precedents set at other state festivals. The documents for 1589, besides laying bare the general structure of the artistic workplace, offer repeated anecdotal glimpses of frustration, rivalry, conflict, unforeseen difficulties, and forced alterations to work in progress.

THE TEAM FOR CHRISTINE'S ENTRY

The placement and design of the series of seven triumphal archways or facades that lined the route of Christine's entry to the city (cat. 1–7) were coordinated by Niccolò Gaddi, an art patron, collector, and officer of the Accademia del disegno, who devised the overall program; the Latin inscriptions identifying general themes and individual paintings and sculptures were the work of Pietro Angeli da Barga, who drew a granducal salary. Each arch had a distinct theme, and the overall scheme and sequence closely followed precedents set by the entries of previous Medici brides: that for Ferdinando's mother, Eleonora of Toledo, in 1539, and particularly for his brother Francesco's wife, Joanna (Giovanna) of Austria, in 1565.[2]

For the entry of Joanna, Cosimo I's literary advisor, Vincenzo Borghini, had exhaustively researched the long tradition of precedents for the proper form and imagery of a triumphal entry. His bound notes and correspondence with the artistic chief, Giorgio Vasari, indicate the continuous consultation and mutual adjustments that were necessary: for example, Borghini had use of a measured map of the city prepared by Vasari's assistants to estimate the number and size of possible pictorial locations. No such precise records of Gaddi's labors are known, but continuous consultation between artists and programmers would have been required because, as Borghini had explained, "the invention [of the program] had to accommodate itself to the spaces available."[3] Borghini sent his draft program to Cosimo in early April 1565, more than eight months before the event; if his practices were typical, Gaddi's program would have had to be roughed out by August 1588. It seems probable that Gaddi relied largely on Borghini's canonical report, since nearly the same route through the city was planned, and the iconography was fundamentally similar, varying only in emphasis, or where necessary to adapt to changes in international politics; themes were again civic, dynastic, marital, historical, and allegorical.

A large number of visual artists, meanwhile — indeed, virtually the entire roster of principal Florentines at this time — produced the architectural designs for these temporary decorations and the dozens of individual paintings and numerous stucco sculptures that adorned them. Reproductions of the principal works required 65 plates in Gualterotti's printed description. In each case, one architect, sculptor, or painter designed the structure itself, which was then covered with thematically related works by a team of assistants or collaborators. The busiest was the architect Giovannantonio Dosio, responsible for three of the seven decors; two more were by the sculptor Taddeo Landini, and each of the others by a single individual (for the themes of the arches and their principal designers, see cat. 1–7).[4]

The principal published description of Christine's entry was by Raffaello Gualterotti (1544–1618). Little is known about this self-described "Florentine gentleman," but, like Bardi and Buontalenti, he was a veteran of past court festivals, and the three had collaborated before. A frequent author for Francesco I, he may have also made the illustrations for his own text, though no visual works are attributed to him aside from his festival books (figs. 3, 8).[5]

Gualterotti's work forms part of an established genre of sumptuous festival books, known as *descrizioni*, which were published to describe almost all the royal festivals of the century; beginning with Gualterotti's joust book of 1579, some were illustrated with prints. These texts served two complementary purposes: as a record and a guide. The majority were published after the fact, serving mainly to fix these transitory events in permanent memory; they were a form of souvenir, to be distributed to those who had been present and, perhaps more importantly, sent abroad as propaganda for the magnificence and sophistication of the sponsoring court. Others were printed far enough in advance to be available at the events themselves, to serve as programs for privileged participants while they were actually attending the dynastic milestones — doubtless a useful service when the iconography and symbolism were, as so often, too complex to be readily grasped by any but the most pedantic scholar.[6]

Internal evidence from various exemplars suggests that Gualterotti's book was conceived in stages to fulfill both programmatic and commemorative functions. The more complete edition is in two distinct and separately numbered parts. Book 2 of this volume (which was also printed alone) seems to have been an actual guidebook: its dedication page bears the date of May 1, 1589, only a day after the entry; the introductory matter addresses the new grand duchess directly, as if intended for her own use; and the text provides sequential and detailed explanations, in the present tense, of the imagery of individual arches and their paintings. The much briefer Book 1 bears a separate dedication (to Ferdinando) dated June 4, more than a month later, and it lacks any illustrations, which would have needed longer to produce. Its form is not a catalogue/guide but a narrative, describing the procession chronologically, in the past tense, as it actually moved through the streets, and recounting the ceremonies performed at each arch. Most likely this addendum was written after the event, and then (in some cases) bound together with the earlier fascicule to round out the overall description for those who had not been present.[7]

Consultation with Gaddi and Angeli would have been necessary from the beginning, just as Borghini fed his notes continuously to the author Domenico Mellini in 1565. Gualterotti (and an artist he commissioned, if any) would also have had to be granted access to the artists' studios to observe and make engravings from their preliminary sketches or from paintings in progress. Gualterotti appears not to have been above taking sides in the rivalries that arose between the artists. His generally enthusiastic descriptions are noticeably less so for Dosio's contributions; in fact, the only attribution he omits entirely is that of Dosio for the duomo portal (cat. 4), perhaps out of subtle partisanship toward an old friend and collaborator, Buontalenti, who was then in competition with Dosio to design a permanent facade for the long-unfinished cathedral.[8]

The lead time necessary for preparing these complex guidebooks can be estimated from Gualterotti's reproduction of a painting for the second arch (cat. 2), which must have caused Christine an awkward pang of nostalgia (fig. 3). Giovanni Cosci's depiction of Christine taking leave of her family before heading south for Italy, which took place at the end of February, is centered on Christine's bow to her grandmother, identifiable by her distinctive widow's-peak veil. But no such tender moment actually occurred, for Catherine had died on January 5. This news reached Florence on January 17, so we can surmise that Cosci's painting must already have been completed at that time — or, at least, that the entire arch and its program were by then considered too far along to be altered — and that the process of engraving the pictures or sketches must also have been past correcting by this point, though the entry was still three months in the future.[9]

THE TEAM FOR THE UFFIZI-PITTI EVENTS

The most sophisticated and best-documented creative group is the team responsible for all the performances within the Medici's own official residences. This linked chain of palaces and administrative offices, which stretched from the Pitti over the Arno to the Uffizi and the Palazzo Vecchio, was the setting for the climactic events of the festival: the plays and intermedi with their following banquet, and the parade, tournament, and naumachia. As with Christine's entry, hundreds of individuals were involved; here the overall creative conception was entrusted to a triumvirate of experienced artists, closely coordinated with several equally experienced authors and artists for the secondary publicity materials.

Two members of the guiding trio, retained by Ferdinando from the reigns of his father and brother, were reprising their successful theatrical collaboration of 1585–86 on the wedding of Ferdinando's half-sister Virginia de' Medici and Cesare d'Este of Ferrara. Giovanni de' Bardi, of the family of the counts of Vernio, was again responsible for the program and iconography. Bernardo Buontalenti, who had created the Uffizi theater for its debut on that occasion, again took charge of all visual aspects, from redesign and lighting of the theater to the stage sets and costumes for both play and intermedi; he similarly supervised the Pitti preparations. The two were joined by a newcomer to Florence, the Roman patrician Emilio de' Cavalieri, who, in addition to his services as both a composer and stage director, also represented increased bureaucratic control over state patronage: he oversaw all expenditures, labor, and supplies from the newly created position of superintendent of the fine arts.

Being more closely tied than the entry team to the granducal household, managerially as well as physically, this group was organized in a strictly hier-

3. *Christine takes leave of her family. Raffaello Gualterotti (see cat. 2).*

archical structure. The chain of command embraced all classes and functions. At the apex of the pyramid was Ferdinando: though he is only recorded visiting the work site in person on a handful of occasions, he appears constantly in the records as the ultimate source of authority for various decisions large and small, a distant eminence referred to simply as "S.A.S." — *Sua Altezza Serenissima*, His Serene Highness. Next came his close advisors, who, like Bardi and Cavalieri, were often aristocrats. Below this level were two branches: the artistic staff (other authors and composers, plus the performers), who reported to Bardi and to Cavalieri-qua-director; and the technical support staff, corresponding to middle management (in theatrical terms, production stage managers), major segments of which were coordinated by Girolamo Seriacopi, the household's *provveditore* (quartermaster), who reported to Buontalenti and to Cavalieri-qua-administrator. Below Seriacopi were lower-level foremen, who dealt directly with the myriad manual workers: craftsmen, tailors, stagecrew, and outside contractors. Relations among the three principal organizers and with the others were necessarily closely collaborative; in spite of the supposedly orderly hierarchy, however, these interactions were not devoid of friction and rivalry. The conflicts were in part the result of a conscious transition effected by Ferdinando during the first two years of his reign: aiming to change policies from his brother's time, he gradually replaced key artistic personnel, often with friends or former employees imported from his long sojourn in Rome.

TEXTS AND AUTHORS

The numerous authors of the various theatrical texts, lyrics, and commemorative literature were coordinated by the theoretician and programmer Giovanni de' Bardi, who had primary conceptual responsibility for the largest single event, the intermedi, and seems to have been consulted about the Pitti events as well. A number of these authors, as well as several composers, were already linked to Bardi through his patronage and his central role in the musical society known as the Camerata fiorentina — though Cavalieri, as we shall see, was somewhat at odds with this group.

Giovanni de' Bardi

Although Bardi (1534–1612) is remembered as both a learned humanist and musician, he alternated these activities with periods of military duty appropriate to his aristocratic background. A prominent member of the literary-philosophical Accademia della Crusca, he was elected the group's archconsul from September 1588 through August 1589, while he was working on the intermedi. He had worked as author and composer with Buontalenti and the *descrizione* author Rossi on two previous Medici weddings, those of 1579 and 1586. But Ferdinando disliked Bardi and began to edge him out, in part because Bardi had approved and assisted Francesco's second marriage in 1579 to the hated Bianca Cappello.[10]

From 1576 to 1582, Bardi had led the circle of musical reformers known as the Camerata fiorentina — or, during his patronage, as the Camerata Bardi. Its membership included the poet Giovanni Battista Strozzi, the amateur musician Piero Strozzi, and the composers and musical theorists Vincenzo Galilei (father of Galileo) and Giulio Caccini. Although not formally members, the aristocratic poet Ottavio Rinuccini (1562–1621) and the composer-singer Jacopo Peri were apparently also sympathetic to the group. With the exception of Galilei, all of these figures contributed to the 1589 intermedi. Under Bardi's aegis, they pioneered the *riforma melodrammatica* of music and theater, part of a broader program for the revival of drama and music according to what could be reconstructed of the practices of classical antiquity.[11]

Although he himself composed one number (the madrigal sung to the shades in hell, "Miseri abitator," for intermedio 4), Bardi was not given personal control over the musical form of the intermedi; the post of musical director fell to Cavalieri, who was brought in by the grand duke to dilute Bardi's traditional authority. Nor did Bardi actually write the libretto, which was for the most part by Rinuccini, with additional verses by Giovanni Battista Strozzi (who also specified the sculptural program for the auditorium) and Laura Guidiccioni Lucchesini. Nonetheless, it is clear from Rossi and Seriacopi that Bardi was intended from the outset as the "master of ceremonies": he formulated the underlying conception, served as stage director, and coordinated all the intellectual and antiquarian aspects of the project, from the thematic structure and musical style to the classicizing details of the costumes.

Bardi had to work out these concepts in tandem with Buontalenti, however, in order to assure both their feasibility and their accurate execution. As Rossi records, the two men, whom he jointly honors as *pellegrini ingegni* (rare and questing minds), "having received the assignment . . . and having discussed and talked it over together . . . and agreed, each one devoted himself to thinking about what pertained to his own position." He goes on to tell us that Buontalenti, whom he calls *L'Artefice* (literally artificer, but figuratively author, implying visual creativity), "then received from the poet [his epithet for Bardi] specific and very detailed information."[12] Bardi proved a watchful and imperious supervisor, visiting the theater and workshops and not hesitating to ask for corrections. He is first mentioned in Seriacopi's logbook on October 5: "Signor Giovanni de' Bardi orders that work should be started on making the costumes for the intermedi, and declares that if there are any problems he should be told now, and that if he isn't, he doesn't want to hear about them later."[13]

As a theatrical genre, the intermedio (or intermezzo; French *intermède*, English *interlude* or *entr'acte*) can be traced back to the late fifteenth-century verse play with music, *L'Orfeo*, by the Medici poet Angelo Poliziano. The name derives from the tradition of performing brief musical tableaux between the acts of a prose comedy, but as the tradition developed in the sixteenth century the balance gradually shifted. In 1565 the intermedi were still performed within the same scenery used for the enveloping comedy, but by 1589 it had become axiomatic that each interlude would have its own spectacularly complex setting. Eventually the prose plays were so reduced in importance as to inspire a complaint by the playwright Il Lasca (A. F. Grazzini, 1503–84) that "the intermedi used to be made to serve the comedy, but nowadays comedies are made to serve the intermedi." At first each intermedio stood alone; although later authors sought to provide some unity of theme, this structural urge always had to be balanced against the desire for variety and surprise.[14] The theme for 1589 was the power of musical harmony, a loose umbrella that allowed for great diversity of individual scenes but nevertheless accommodated some overarching symbolic connections.

Bastiano de' Rossi

Before outlining this program, a short excursus into an important secondary source will clarify not only how we know so much about Bardi's imagery and intentions, but how that secondary source was itself created. Bastiano de' Rossi (fl. 1585–1605), author of the official *descrizione* for the intermedi and *La pellegrina*, fulfilled functions similar to Gualterotti's for the entry: to explain the complex symbolism in detail, and to laud the technical and artistic sophistication of the creators and the magnificence of their patron. In addition to being another veteran of the 1586 wedding, he was a close friend and ally of Bardi's at the Accademia della Crusca, of which Rossi was a cofounder and secretary. He evidently saw himself as a mouthpiece and propagandist for Bardi: the original edition of his *Descrizione* for 1589 was so pointedly slanted in favor of Bardi and against his rival, Cavalieri, that Ferdinando ordered it revised and reprinted.[15]

Rossi's timetable and working procedures, like those of Gualterotti, can be inferred from internal evidence. His text implies that he was privy to the early planning sessions between Bardi and Buontalenti: he tells us (p. 46) that Bardi specified that the costumes for intermedio 3 should be "tending to the Greek" style because the ancient sources specified that Apollo's battle with the python took place on a Greek isle; he goes on to reveal what was clearly a private decision, that "the colors [of these costumes] were left up to the discretion of the Artificer [Buontalenti]." Rossi must also have been granted advance access to Buontalenti's actual costume drawings, as his descriptions of many characters employ the same phrases to describe colors and materials as are written on the drawings themselves. For example, on the design for Arion in intermedio 5 (cat. 57; pl. 14), the fabric and color notes on the drawing are identical to the description in Rossi's text; Rossi says that the Apollo of intermedio 3 (cat. 35; pl. 9) is dressed "d'un abito resplendente di tela d'oro [cloth of gold]," and the drawing is marked, "vestita di tela d'oro."[16]

As for the schedule on which Rossi worked, his dedication is dated May 14, two weeks after the premiere of *La pellegrina*, so he must have been preparing his text for the printers for some months before the events. There are two significant discrepancies between his account and later sources, which may indicate that his text was past correcting by the time changes were made in the intended libretto. Arion's aria in intermedio 4 is given in a version prepared by Bardi, though Malvezzi's edition of the performance score indicates that Jacopo Peri, as Arion, sang a song of his own composition. Similarly, for the last intermedio Rossi reprints an original text by Bardi, but that finale was replaced by music of Cavalieri's and a new text. It is not known exactly at what point during rehearsals these substitutions were made, but apparently it was by then too late to change Rossi's text. Alternatively (or jointly), he may have resisted acknowledging these incursions on his friend Bardi's artistic authority.[17]

Plots and Characters of the Intermedi

According to Rossi's exposition, the six intermedi were unified by the theme of the power of music to influence both the human soul and the gods. The plots were derived from classical sources, especially Plato's *Republic*, but also Plutarch, Ovid, Virgil, and numerous lesser writers and scholiasts, often modified or conflated. Three of the series, nos. 1, 4, and 5, illustrated aspects of *musica mundana*, that is, the celestial "music of the spheres," while the other three represented *musica humana*, its more concrete influence in the affairs of gods and mortals. Interwoven with this philosophical conceit were symbolic allusions to, as well as direct praise of, the beneficence, permanence, and legitimacy of Medici rule. In particular, the first and last intermedi bracketed the self-contained inner episodes with more explicitly nuptial and personal accolades, constituting an introduction and a finale.

In this schema, the earthly microcosm — whether ancient Mediterranean lands or modern Tuscany — reflected in miniature the all-embracing heavenly macrocosm. As Rossi explains, the fixed and harmonious concentric order of the cosmos, which Plato and Pythagoras considered to be founded on the mathematical ratios underlying musical sounds, was to be read as a parallel to the earthly rule of the ideal prince, who could bring order and stability to the terrestrial universe of which he was the hub. The political cosmos of individuals and social classes revolved about the monarch just as the heavenly bodies revolved around the earth (or, metaphorically, the spindle of the goddess Necessity), each in a crystalline sphere propelled by the celestial Sirens who appear in the opening intermedio.

The relevance of this generic model to the present occasion was rendered explicit by references to another staple princely topos: the return to Earth of the Golden Age, a mythical time of peace and plenty presided over by the goddess Astraea, whose restoration was prophesied by Virgil in his Eclogue 4. The Medici had been particularly attached to this symbol since Lorenzo the Magnificent adopted the motto, "Le temps revient." The customary interpretation — that the prince would restore a paradisal realm that had been established by his worthy ancestors but interrupted by discordant opposition — may have held an additional personal meaning for Ferdinando, who upon his accession set out forcefully to eradicate problems that were left from the reign of his brother Francesco, of whose occult interests, reclusive personality, and scandalous second wife Ferdinando had intensely disapproved. Inseparable from the continuity with a glorious past was the prophecy of an equally glorious future, to be achieved by the "demigods," the dynastic offspring fervently wished upon the newlyweds in several songs and the concluding epithalamium.[18]

The following summary will serve as an outline for discussion of characters, actions, and stage designs of the intermedi; for further details see the catalogue entries.[19]

Intermedio 1. The Harmony of the Spheres (cat. 8–25). Above a perspective view of Rome, the heavenly messenger Harmony (figuring the Doric Mode of ancient music) descends to sing a prologue announcing blessings on the newly married royal couple. Rome then disappears, and the clouds open to reveal a starry firmament, in the center of which sits Necessity, who holds the diamond spindle that forms the axis of the universe. She is surrounded by her three daughters, the Parcae (Fates), eight gods and goddesses (seven representing the planets, plus Astraea), and the choir of Sirens, each of whom controls a celestial sphere, all seated on movable clouds. These sing nuptial blessings in various combinations as they are lowered to the earth and raised again.

Intermedio 2. The Contest of Muses and Pierides (cat. 26–32). In a lush grove, from beneath the ground slowly rises a mountain, on which are arrayed sixteen hamadryads (wood nymphs). They explain that they are to judge a contest: the nine Pierides, daughters of King Pierus, have challenged the nine immortal Muses to a test of musical skill. A pair of trellised garden bowers glide onstage and rotate to reveal the groups of competitors, each of whom sings a brief madrigal. The hamadryads declare the Muses victorious, where-upon the mortals are punished for their presumption by being transformed into magpies, who run chattering from the stage.

Intermedio 3. Apollo and the Python (cat. 33–50). In a forest clearing domi-nated by a rocky cave whose entrance is surrounded by blasted vegetation, eighteen couples enter, representing the citizens of Delos; as they lament how their island has been devastated by a monstrous winged dragon, the creature (known classically as the Python, actually a serpent) pokes its head out of the cave and spews fire from its mouth. Apollo descends from the sky in answer to their prayer; performing a five-part military dance (recalling an early Greek program piece recorded by the Roman scholar Julius Pollux), he challenges the beast, slays it (spilling its black inky blood), and dances in triumph, after which the Delphians hymn the god's praises.

Intermedio 4. Prophecy of the Golden Age (cat. 51–53). A sorceress flies in above the scene of Pisa that remains from the previous act of *La pellegrina.* Riding a chariot drawn by dragons, she conjures the heroic spirits of the air to foretell when the Golden Age will return. These spirits appear in a fiery cloud and announce that the present wedding of "two great souls" is the signal for such a revival of joy and goodness. As the spirits depart, Pisa is replaced by a stark rocky scene, representing Hell as described in canto 3 of Dante's *Inferno:* the floor opens to reveal an icy lake, from which rises a giant figure of three-headed Lucifer, devouring souls. Amid smoke and flames, devils prod the dead and taunt them that they will be alone for eternity, as the moral perfection of Ferdinando and Christine's reign will deprive them of further sinful company.

Intermedio 5. Arion and the Dolphin (cat. 54–62). Rocky cliffs frame an undulating sea over which dolphins pull a shell that bears Amphitrite, queen of the ocean, accompanied by tritons and nereids; they pronounce a marital blessing and predict for the royal pair "such a brilliant progeny that it will adorn the Earth from pole to pole." The sea creatures vanish as a giant galley approaches, bearing several dozen sailors and the poet-singer Arion, whose legendary musical prowess had been invoked earlier by the Pierides. The ship, bobbing realistically, turns forward and strikes its sails in reverence to the grand duke. Arion, who has been threatened with death by the sailors, cov-etous of his treasure, sings a farewell lament, then escapes their drawn knives by jumping overboard. The crew, presuming him drowned, merrily divide up the spoils; but Arion, saved by a dolphin who admires his song, is borne safely to shore.

Intermedio 6. The Gods Send Rhythm and Harmony to Earth (cat. 63–66). The scene returns to the cloud-filled heaven of intermedio 1, now crowned with a golden sunburst, beneath which sit all the Olympian gods in council, attended by the Graces and Muses. On the central cloud are Apollo and Bacchus, who descend to the stage to accompany Harmony and Rhythm in an enactment of a tale from Plato's *Laws*, in which the two allegorical figures were sent to Earth to provide some relief from mortal troubles. Jupiter announces his gift as golden rain falls and one by one the clouds lower to the ground, where the gods join a chorus of rejoicing nymphs and shepherds in a grand finale. Sung in alternation by the full cast and a trio of female singer-dancers, this lengthy epithalamium is again keyed to the returning Golden Age, in which "by Ferdinand shall be restored every virtue, every royal custom." The prophecy of "semidivine" children to come from the union harks back to Virgil's Eclogues and the epithalamia of Catullus.

The final element of the pageantry organized directly by the Bardi-Buontalenti-Cavalieri brigade was the tripartite evening at the Pitti Palace on May 11: chariot parade, joust, and naumachia. Here, Buontalenti was given a settled physical framework — the palace courtyard — into which he inserted temporary lighting, machinery, and decorative backdrops. The evening's themes were related in spirit to the intermedi, but more eclectic: classical gods and creatures on chariots for the parade continued the mythological-heroic vein, whereas the armed knights' foot tournament was a late example of the medieval chivalric tradition, with long roots in Florentine history and litera-ture; the naumachia was a novelty, though with antique precedent.

Bardi had somewhat less control here over iconographic details, because the participating nobility paid for their individual floats — an example of how Ferdinando cultivated involvement by the highest level of society in the socio-economic arts network of his *theatrum mundi*. Although asked to harmonize with the overall theme, these patricians were apparently free to invent their own projects and to hire outside artists and programmers. Perhaps due in part to this diffusion, two of the official diarists to whom we owe *descrizioni* of the Pitti events, Giuseppe Pavoni and Simone Cavallino, are at times vague about the iconography of these floats, or their analyses don't correspond exactly to the visual records (cat. 71–86).

Iconographic Structures: Sacred Space, Sacred Time

Although an iconographic analysis of all these state-sponsored events, from entry to theater to tournament, is beyond my scope here, one organizing principle requires comment in a study whose focus is the unprecedented social and technical complexity of these physical productions. There is a striking — and to modern eyes ironic — disjunction between the symbolic discourse of much of the festival and the pragmatic realities that supported it, indeed that made the regime itself possible. The wedding events were organized hierarchically into different levels of reality, graded from abstract, timeless allegory down through varying degrees of realism. The principal performances may be likened to the concentric universe they figured: the closer one approaches to the physical and symbolic center — the granducal theater, as the axis of sacred power expressed in purest fantasy — the less reference is made to mundane realities. Where such acknowledgments do intrude, they are restricted to the margins of this solar system, defined either discursively, physically, or socially.

At the center of the political-cultural sphere, within the sacred space and time of the Uffizi intermedi, the metaphorical language is overwhelmingly mythical, allegorical, and historical, and virtually ignores the manifold conscious and energetic policies — technological, administrative, military, and the like — on which Medici power and wealth were actually based. The texts of the intermedi make no mention of current affairs, and images like Ferdinando's fortification of Tuscany (fig. 1) are banished from the onstage picture; more typical is the first intermedio's apotheosis of the bridal couple as a "new Minerva and mighty Hercules," a paean framed in generic classical terms rather than concrete, individual qualities or deeds.

Such preferences are hardly unusual; throughout Renaissance court literature as a whole, "the transfer of contemporary events into a classical setting and the celebration of the patron as a mythical hero were common strategies." But the iconography of 1589, accentuating this cumulative process, made even fewer direct references to current practicalities than had its predecessors. Thus here, more acutely than ever before, the "transformation of historical events into poetic myth" points to a central problematic within courtly culture: "the conflict between poetry and history," that is, between the reality of increasing technical-social control that characterized early modern political economy and the fiction of a work-free, preindustrial Garden of the Hesperides as the ultimate source of spiritual and political legitimacy.[20]

That evolving contradiction marks a significant crossroads in European political ideology and symbolism. It was during Ferdinando's reign that the theory of divine right entered Florentine discourse. Its objective was to create legitimacy by assimilating the ruler to a sacred realm of meaning and fixed authority outside earthly space and time. An important effect of this doctrine was a shift in rhetoric: power and authority were figured, not as a product of deliberate manipulation, but as godlike and effortless. The insistence that power is of a higher order than mere exercise of technical and political skill served to forestall dissent, by occluding the often Machiavellian basis of social and economic relations: "In any society the dominant groups are the ones with the most to hide about the way society works."[21]

In semiotic terms, the overriding theme of the wedding, and especially the intermedi, is thus *return*, to an earlier Golden Age. This heroic, ideal past is figured partly through inherited medieval tropes of chivalry — the deeds of early Christian and Crusader ancestors — but most often through the Greco-Roman heritage whose revival led the period to consider itself a "rebirth." That this metaphor is both sung and embodied by heavenly powers who preside at the center of a concentrically rotating cosmos superimposes a second, complementary structure on the figure of return — of actual *turning*. In this discursive universe, all space is focused around a single fixed point (for 1589, the granducal palace complex, including the theater), and time is not linear and progressive but cyclical. Human history, in princely iconography, is a series of oscillations toward and away from that venerable fixed center, with the present always declared to be the perigee, or closest point.

Christine's entry sought to extend a similar iconography over the public cityscape, but there the aspiration of divine monarchy toward cyclical, timeless order conflicted with the earthly experience of time and space as linear: an entry is a parade, a line moving through social space. Notwithstanding the entry's inevitable accommodation to the physical and social setting, and indeed its exploitation of that setting to create processional drama, the imagery of the arches makes even less overt reference to that mundane terrestrial reality than had the earlier Medici weddings. The program of the official spectacle thus bears complex witness to a central metaphorical and epistemological characteristic of Renaissance court culture. In that culture's commitment to the humanist ideals of cyclicality and reverence for the past, it is profoundly retrospective: it seeks to exalt the present by establishing its pedigree as a continuation of an ideal and unchanging past. Discursively, therefore, it was all but prevented from consciously "seeing" or expressly celebrating the revolutionary actualities of its own time.[22]

Other events, while still under court aegis, were more open to contemporary reference as they moved farther from such quasi-sacred functions. For all its grandeur, the subsequent spectacle at the Pitti Palace took place in a domestic, not a public, space (the family home), whose location on the far bank of the Arno established the tone of an exceptionally splendid suburban garden party. Thus, although the parade and joust were still rooted in chivalric romance, the naval battle was staged between contemporary Christians and

Turks — at that time the great military adversaries of western Europeans in the Mediterranean — and the décor, including small porcelain admission tickets, was in part an advertisement for the Tuscan ceramics industry (see cat. 87). Rossi's published commentary on the intermedi, located at the margin of ritual performance by its posthumous and textual nature, is also permitted greater reference to "lower" realities: with propagandistic pride in Tuscan resources and technology, he records that Ferdinando aimed to produce a festival that, in its richness and variety as well as its "quantity of ingenious and imposing machines, would be inferior to none" (p. 5). And the sports and other secular entertainments in the Piazza Santa Croce, loosely under court auspices but held in a public space with broad participation and a mass audience, could descend to animal-baiting and other popular spectacles.

The Prose Comedies

One final element of the overall "script" of the wedding events, the series of three prose plays presented along with the intermedi, was located even farther toward the social margins of court culture, and was thus free to represent contemporary reality at the most earthy, even crass level of realistic comedy. The actors, lower-class intruders into the sacred space of the court theater, were framed by a genre that permitted the aristocratic audience to appreciate the bourgeois characters' squabbles over money, status, and social convention as comic relief, the implications of which were carefully walled off from the intermedi's idealized presentation of the higher orders and their contented mortal subjects. Although the acting companies were not under direct state control, sets and some costumes were supervised by Cavalieri and Buontalenti.

Many commentators have concurred with Lasca's judgment that the comedies performed on these occasions were increasingly a mere pretext, with little organic relation to the wider symbolism of their festivals. At least in the case of the first play, *La pellegrina*, however, Karen Newman has shown that this text was no more accidental than the rest of the carefully calculated celebration: its situation, characters, and narrative details were subtly revised to highlight the play's intrinsic relevance as a compliment to the bride. Ferdinando had commissioned *La pellegrina* from the Sienese academician Girolamo Bargagli in 1564, but it had never been performed. Bargagli having died in 1586, the comedy was adapted by his brother Scipione, who added touches of new symbolism fitted to the occasion.

The basic plot, a convoluted set of romantic dilemmas typical of the genre, remained unchanged: Drusilla, the eponymous heroine, arrives in Pisa on a religious pilgrimage whose true purpose is to seek Lucrezio, who had married her but then failed to return from a trip back to his native city. The frustrations and misunderstandings are resolved by the virtuous pilgrim, who can then reclaim the husband who mistakenly thought her dead. Besides the specific similarities between Drusilla and Christine — both were devoutly religious travelers passing into Italy from a foreign land — the heroine's near-miraculous qualities were precisely those that were idealized for women in general — piety, wisdom, and conscientious harmonizing of discord. Drusilla was originally Spanish, but in light of the pro-Valois shift, she was made a Frenchwoman; further highlighting the parallel with the bride, her sea voyage began, as Christine's had just done, in Marseilles. In deference to Ferdinando's ecclesiastical background, some of the humorous anticlerical remarks were expunged, and the pilgrim's destination changed from Loreto to Rome.[23]

The other two plays that were performed with the intermedi were popular pieces presented by an independent professional troupe, the Compagnia dei Gelosi. Here there was much less textual control than with the Bargagli; although Ferdinando naturally would have been concerned that the works suited the decorum of the occasion, the company was selected mainly for its celebrity and for the renown (and amusing rivalry) of its two leading actresses. *La zingara* (the gypsy woman), presented on May 5/6 with Vittoria Piissimi in the title role, and *La pazzia* (madness), starring its author Isabella Andreini the following week, were part of the flexible genre of the *commedia dell'arte*, performances semi-improvised on stock situations and characters by the developing profession of traveling players. For this occasion Andreini made a small but effective thematic gesture toward the bride. The tour de force of her *Pazzia* was the heroine's mad scene, in which she gibbered incoherently in a mix of languages; Andreini ended the soliloquy in a torrent of fractured French, which, Pavoni observed, gave Christine "so much delight that she could not express it."[24]

Emilio de' Cavalieri: Music and Administration

The second member of the organizing triumvirate, Emilio de' Cavalieri, served the wedding festival in two different professional capacities. As a musician, he composed part of the intermedi music and acted as the production's musical director and choreographer, complementing Bardi's role as stage director — a forced collaboration rife with potential for conflict. At the same time, as a high-ranking government official, the superintendent of fine arts, he acted in a capacity close to that of the modern producer, keeping the books and serving as a mediator between the worlds of the backers (the court, at the Pitti Palace) and the creative team and labor force located at the Uffizi.

Cavalieri (1545/53–1602) was a descendant of one of the oldest and most culturally prestigious Roman families: his father Tommaso, once the younger beloved of Michelangelo, had been instrumental as a city official in bringing to completion the architect's project for the Capitoline Hill civic complex after his death in 1564. Emilio had become close to Ferdinando during the latter's decades in the papal city, and the grand duke brought him to Florence almost immediately upon his accession (by January 1588) to develop the state arts program, as well as to travel on diplomatic missions. Cavalieri was granted a stipend of 25 ducats per month plus a horse and, unique among the wedding's senior staff, an apartment in the Pitti Palace. This physical proximity to Ferdinando signified his status and influence, which consisted in access to the "head of the pyramid." But he was no servile courtier; something of his proudly independent spirit, which contributed to prickly relations with Bardi, Rossi, and other staff members, is suggested by an early report of his tenure by the Venetian ambassador, who wrote that "he does not as attend as regularly upon the [grand duke's] person as others, since he loves his freedom; but he is in great favor with S.A. [His Highness]."[25]

Cavalieri composed only two or three numbers for the intermedi, but his ability to set aside the completed work of Bardi for the finale indicates his ultimate authority, as Ferdinando's chosen musical director, over the team of composers. Broadly, Cavalieri's advent signaled the influx of a whole new influence in Florentine culture, drawn from composers and performers whom Ferdinando imported from Rome, and who gradually supplanted the court artists he had inherited from his father and brother, though not without struggle and infighting.

As we have seen, the music for the intermedi was inspired, and for the most part executed, by the circle associated with Bardi's Camerata, who conducted research into the meager evidence about ancient musical principles. They sought a revival of music *all'antica* or *alla greca*, particularly the style of vocal music that they called *recitar cantando*: a form of monody, in which only one melody would be sung at one time, in polemic contrast to the prevailing polyphony of the madrigal. The text was to be paramount, the music subservient to its clarity and appropriate emotional expression; and melody and rhythm should follow the tones and accents of the spoken word. This theoretical program was not, however, fully realized in the intermedi compositions, many of which are written as traditional polyphony, with the solo voice taking one vocal line and the others assigned to instruments.[26]

The bulk of the music was by two established musicians who were also actively involved in musical preparations at the Uffizi. The prominent madrigalist and organist Luca Marenzio (1553–99) arrived in Florence by February 1588 among many musicians whom Ferdinando brought with him from

Rome, not only in anticipation of his wedding production but as part of an attempt to rival the famous musical establishment at the neighboring Este court of Ferrara. Cristofano Malvezzi (1547–99), a Florentine, was *maestro di cappella* of the cathedral; his edition of the text and music, printed at the grand duke's request in 1591, though not quite complete, is the basis for D. P. Walker's modern critical edition.[27]

In addition to Cavalieri's pieces and Bardi's chorus for intermedio 4, three other composers, all with strong Roman connections, contributed one number apiece, and several of them also performed. Jacopo Peri (1561–1633), known as Zazzerino for his curly hair, was born in Rome of Florentine parents; later a pupil of Malvezzi, he performed as Arion, singing an aria of his own invention to replace Bardi's. Giulio Caccini (1545–1618), a Florentine singer who had studied in Rome (he is often identified in the documents as "Giulio romano"), is frequently credited with inventing the *stile recitativo*, or speechlike musical declamation. He was the husband of Lucia Caccini, one of the principal female singers, and probably the brother of the sculptor Giovanni Caccini, who participated in the wedding decorations. And Antonio Archilei (ca. 1550–1612), husband of another soprano, Vittoria, may have written her opening solo as Harmony in intermedio 1; Cavalieri brought the couple from Rome, where they had been in the service of Ferdinando in the early 1580s.[28]

Rossi's description of intermedio 6, as noted earlier, differs from the printed score, indicating a change that occurred too late in the creative process to be incorporated, most likely within the month preceding the premiere. Ferdinando rejected the finale by Bardi and Rinuccini — a massive chorus accompanying the descent of Rhythm and Harmony — and had Cavalieri substitute new music, to which Laura Guidiccioni Lucchesini, an aristocratic poet from Lucca, crafted suitable words. In place of the more abstractly allegorical ending originally planned, Guidiccioni's dialogue between throngs of pastoral mortals and three celestial ladies is more explicitly focused on the bridal couple themselves, ending with the couplet, "Joyfully we sing in praise / Of Christine and Ferdinand." The bass line and harmonies of this piece, so intimately associated with the city and its ruling house, remained popular for more than a century as a standard base for improvisation, under the titles "Aria di Firenze" or "Ballo del Granduca."[29]

The haste with which this alteration was made, and the blatant reversal in its process of the humanist principle of musical subservience to text, raise the question of why change was deemed necessary at such a late date. Ferdinando's intervention seems calculated to increase the overtly ideological content of the evening, consistent with his assertion of divine right. If Bardi was being edged out, it was partly because, like his patron Francesco I, he was primarily an esoteric antiquarian, and he was insufficiently propagandistic for the new regime's intensified agenda. The shift is manifest in Ferdinando's forced revision of Rossi's text, in which the fulsome praise of Bardi and Buontalenti is shortened in order to allow space for this statement: "The grand duke, having at present in his service the Roman gentleman Emilio de' Cavalieri, in whose abilities he had great confidence, put him in charge, together with the aforementioned Giovanni Bardi, of the present comedy, with complete authority." Similarly, Caccini's aria for intermedio 4, "Io che dal ciel," was omitted from Malvezzi's printed score, possibly because of his intimacy with Bardi.[30]

Considerable instrumental music was also written for the intermedi, most of it accompanying such special scenic effects as the rising of the mountain in intermedio 2 or, like the lost sinfonia of intermedio 3, underscoring the dances. Cavalieri, who had a reputation as an excellent dancer, apparently worked out some of the choreography himself, at least (according to the printed score) for the concluding *ballo* that he composed. Some of the floor patterns for the choreography are reproduced in Malvezzi's edition of the music (see fig. 11, Chapter 6), and Rossi describes the five-part Pythian dance of Apollo from intermedio 3 in general outline but with no specifics about steps or movements.[31] Otherwise, unfortunately, little information survives about the form of these dances.

Cavalieri also played a second role for the wedding, as chief administrator and financial officer for the Uffizi-Pitti events. On September 3, 1588, he was appointed superintendent of the fine arts (*intendente generale delle belle arti*), a post that encompassed visual arts, crafts, and music.[32] Cavalieri's active role in labor management is in evidence beginning with the earliest entries in Seriacopi's logbook: on September 7, Cavalieri sent an order to the *provveditore* to bargain with the painter Giovanni di Pagolo on a price for the figures that he was then painting in the Uffizi theater.

This rationalization and centralization of management is merely one element in the broad process of systematizing and bureaucratizing all state functions. In a significant coincidence, during the same month that Cavalieri was appointed to his new post, the grand duke outlawed all private weapons in Tuscany, even down to potentially dangerous farming tools — a complementary attempt to extend the state's regulatory power over individual lives. The number of public officials increased markedly during this period; though still small by modern standards, it had reached about one thousand in the late sixteenth century. If the court staff was an instrument of control over the citizenry and resources, Ferdinando also sought to institute tight controls over the controllers: he set stringent rules for his staff, including precise work hours, fines for absence, and measures to prevent collusion or embezzlement. No one was immune from accountability: Cavalieri's own books for the wedding were audited in 1593 by an outside committee.[33]

Cavalieri set up his *Libro di conti*, or account book, soon after his appointment; its dated entries begin in the first week of November 1588, referring to materials received that must have been ordered during October. As later bound, it is in three parts. The first section, titled "Il taglio" (cuttings, or lengths of material), consists of 29 pairs of facing pages containing double-entry accounts for the fabrics, trimmings, shoes, and such props and equipment as instruments and garlands, ordered for the costumes for the intermedi and the comedies. This type of account book, called a *doppio* (double), was an example of the sophisticated advances in bookkeeping that had been introduced in Florence in the late thirteenth century.[34] The entries are grouped by individual material; quantities of a particular item received by the workshop are on the left pages, corresponding amounts sent out for use are opposite them on the right. Entries continue until some leftover amounts were reconsigned to the granducal Guardaroba (storehouse) in September 1589.

The second and third parts of the *Libro*, titled the "Quadernaccio" (scrapbook) and "Notizie e lettere," are not arranged by material, but in several precisely interlocked accounting systems that permit continuous tracking of locations, utilization, and costs. One unit lists all materials received, from any source, in chronological order, with cross-references to corresponding entries in the "Taglio"; another arranges the materials by individual costume, referenced to the performer's name and to identifying numbers on Buontalenti's sketches. Other units are concerned with tracking expenses: the tailors' weekly timesheets and payment records, extending into September 1589; total money amounts for each individual intermedio; totals spent on each material, across all six intermedi. As its name implies, the latter part of the third section comprises bound-in letters and other notes pertaining to supply and payment.[35]

Besides these rich specifics about costumes, materials, and casts, some general observations can be drawn from the *Libro di conti* about the economic scope and functions of the granducal administration. Geographically, entries refer to Tuscan agents and purchases in various towns of the grand duchy, in such nearby cities as Bologna, and as far afield as Naples, Venice, Rome, and Bavaria; this activity parallels the economic reach of the Tuscan economy as a whole, which during these years was attracting apprentice labor from Genoa, Bologna, and Mantua.[36] Also evident, however, is the clumsiness of doing business across the borders of so many small and independent states: lengths and prices of fabric frequently need to be converted from the vendors' units to the local Florentine system — even from Lucca, within the Tuscan economy, but whose unit of length differs by a small fraction (LC T13). Another complication regarding currency is that bookkeeping generally used "money of account" (*lire, soldi, denari*) whose units were not identical with the everyday denominations and actual coins used for cash payments (primarily *scudi*).

Bernardo Buontalenti and the Visual Arts Staff

More than any other single figure involved in 1589, Bernardo Buontalenti (1531?–1608) exemplified the artistic and technological ambitions of the Medici. Just as Cavalieri's appointment as superintendent was a step toward unified administration, Buontalenti's unprecedented degree of control over the visual and technical aspects of the wedding festival represented an increase in centralized creative direction. Although the 1589 events are often cited as a milestone for having one person in charge of all visual presentation, in fact Buontalenti's mentor and predecessor as chief court architect, Vasari, had had almost as much to do with the wedding of 1565; but the trend toward unification was nevertheless clear.[37] Vasari's own design for the Uffizi was still incomplete at his death, so the granducal workshops and agencies had not yet been concentrated there during his lifetime as they were in 1589. And Buontalenti's overall scope of operations was wider: he had more technological skills than Vasari, who was primarily a visual artist and theoretician, and he took on far more tasks, of a more diverse nature, than Vasari had.

Unlike Bardi and Cavalieri, Buontalenti was not an aristocrat, but a member of the artisan class. His father, Francesco, was also an artist, whose death in 1543/47 left Bernardo an orphan. The talented teenager came to the attention of Duke Cosimo, who made him a ward of the court and apprenticed him to its workshop, where his teachers were Vasari and, probably, the painters Salviati and Bronzino and the miniaturist Giulio Clovio. He was greatly appreciated by the Medici family, especially as a companion and tutor of then Prince Francesco, some ten years his junior; Buontalenti accompanied him on a trip to Spain in 1562–63, but traveled little otherwise. Devoting his entire professional life to court service, he took on a role of "artistic family retainer" somewhat like Mantegna's in Quattrocento Mantua, helping to theatricalize every dynastic occasion from baptism to funeral. At the same time, his respected position and his own efforts indicate the rise in status of his professions, both visual and technical, that was taking place at this time.

Buontalenti was a creative polymath, alternately (and sometimes simultaneously) scientific and whimsical, able to paint, to sculpt, and to design and build anything physical or mechanical, from fortresses to fountains to fireworks; his nickname, "Bernardo delle Girandole," refers to a type of rotating firecracker, the catherine-wheel (*girandola*), that he developed. After the death in 1574 of his predecessor and mentor, Vasari, he held what amounted to a bureaucratic management post as chief architect and engineer for the court. His major official duties had a double aspect. The first was large-scale and practical, as supervisor of military and civil building projects: as an engineer, he devoted much of his career to public works, ranging over all facets of technology and construction, from fortifications, port facilities, and city planning (Pistoia, Livorno) to roads, hydraulics, and bridges. But it has been suggested that, competent as he was in this arena, his true enthusiasm was reserved for smaller and more decorative projects that allowed greater scope for his distinctive creative fantasy, notably his theatrical work and his encouragement of the luxury craft industries, such as hardstone-carving, goldsmithing, porcelain and crystal, for which Florence is still renowned.[38]

As an architect, his extensive oeuvre is characterized by a structural simplicity and planarity harking back to local Quattrocento tradition, but enriched and varied by whimsical late mannerist details similar to the motifs of his decorative and theatrical work. He had commissions for all the principal building types of the period, mainly from the Medici but occasionally from independent institutions. He designed the facade and choir platform for the church of Santa Trinita, and he built or remodeled numerous Medici country villas, such as Castello, Magia, and Pratolino, where he installed gardens, waterworks, and automata. In Florence, behind the Pitti Palace, he completed his imitation grotto at the Boboli gardens in late 1588, using the same hydraulic skills he then applied to flooding the Pitti courtyard for the naumachia. He completed the Uffizi, and his expansion of the Palazzo Vecchio was going on simultaneously with the wedding. His last work, the enormous Cappella dei Principi at the church of San Lorenzo, a mausoleum for the granducal family, was begun in 1602. The nexus between architectural design and social control is most dramatically demonstrated in his systematization in 1571 of the Florentine ghetto, or Jewish quarter.[39]

Besides representing the centralization by the grand dukes of artistic control in a high-level civil servant, Buontalenti also typifies the emergence of several modern occupational roles. All the professions that overlapped in Buontalenti were undergoing a process of specialization and rising status at this time. The very term *ingegnere* (engineer), for example, was coming into common use and emerging as a respected profession with its own "college" (as distinct from a craft guild) — and increasing in status as its technical lore became more sophisticated, powerful, and essential to economic life. One requisite for elevation from craft to liberal art was to establish a corpus of canonical texts, both ancient and modern, a process in which Buontalenti actively participated: he acquired a translation of the *Pneumatics* by Hero of Alexandria, one of the few surviving antique treatises on mechanics, and himself wrote on sculpture and engineering.[40] Architects were similarly attempting to differentiate themselves from masons on one hand and painter-sculptors on the other; it was precisely those new areas of architectural knowledge involving sophisticated theory and technology, like fortifications and waterworks, that justified raising them above traditional builders.[41] In addition, Buontalenti contributed to the agenda of increasing visual artists' level of training: he kept an informal academy at his home, attended by such artists as his protégé and successor Giulio Parigi, Ludovico Cigoli, and Gherardo Silvani, to whom we owe a biography of his teacher.[42]

One index of prestige is, of course, salary, and on this scale he remained merely respectable: whereas Cavalieri received 25 scudi a month and free rent, Buontalenti got only 10 scudi a month in 1588 on top of a permanent grant of income from state property adjacent to the city walls.[43] Another such index is theoretical and definitional, which raises the complex issue of mannerist esthetics and artistic theory. On this scale Buontalenti was widely praised for possessing the quality most prized in sixteenth-century artists after Michelangelo: a unique and quasi-divine creative power that embraced invention, fantasy, and artistic license. Rossi lauds his "superhuman mind," and Vasari had earlier adjudged him "universally abundant in clever caprices."[44]

His "capricious" creativity was, of course, perfectly suited to the demands of theater and spectacle. Buontalenti cut his artistic teeth on festivals at the 1565 wedding play and intermedi, where he was already devising cloud machines and trapdoors. He was subsequently involved with every major dynastic festival, from Francesco's wedding in 1579, to 1586 when he designed the Uffizi theater, and down to the wedding of Francesco's daughter Maria to Henri IV of France in 1600.[45] For the 1589 festival, he began during the summer of 1588 by reconstructing the Uffizi theater (Rossi, *Descrizione dell'apparato*, 6); architectural work could presumably begin even before a clearly defined playscript or libretto. His main decisions were to construct a proscenium, which had been lacking in the original décor, and behind this façade to enhance the superstructure for flying machines and special effects; the first item in Seriacopi's log, on August 31, is a request from a carpenter for wooden planks "to make the waves of the sea" for intermedio 4 (MR 1r).

For the plays and intermedi to be performed in the theater on this occasion, Buontalenti designed the stage sets, costumes, lighting, and special effects. We can reconstruct some of his schedule and working methods from Rossi, who reveals that from the outset he was an intimate observer of the collaborative process between Buontalenti and Bardi. As we have seen, Buontalenti received detailed instructions about the form, iconography, and historical precedents of the costumes and sets from Bardi. He seems to have been allowed occasional creative leeway, for some of the costumes, such as those for the 20 pastoral couples in the finale of intermedio 6, "were left by the poet to the discretion of the Architect" (62) — though the fact that Rossi finds this worth reporting suggests how exceptional it was. For both men, technical limitations necessitated trial-and-error and compromise: describing the planetary gods on the clouds of intermedio 1, Rossi tells us that Buontalenti "would have liked each planet to appear on a [real] chariot," but when this proved impractical, "he decided that he would put them on painted seats" instead (see cat. 23, 24; pls. 2, 3).

Buontalenti supervised a staff of several hundred craftworkers, scene painters, and stagehands. In 1565, Vasari had toured the city on horseback to inspect the scattered workshops under his command; Buontalenti had the advantage that much artistic production had since then been centralized in the Uffizi, where the staff seems to have relied on his regular input, including rough sketches made in Seriacopi's logbook. He probably came in every day except when ill; early in the construction phase Cavalieri tells a painter to stop working on the auditorium candelabra until Buontalenti "is recovered" and returns to the shop (MR 2r, Sept. 7). A few experienced artists who were closest to him executed reproductive and detail drawings that fleshed out his conceptual *modelli* or sketches; Andrea Boscoli and Ludovico Cigoli were among the most important.

Buontalenti also supervised design work for the Pitti events of May 11, but this was less demanding and could begin later. Because the building already existed, the work was limited to construction of temporary decoration and lighting, costumes (some reused from the intermedi), and the mechanism for flooding the courtyard for the naval battle. Moreover, for the chariot parade patrician families like the Guicciardini paid for their individual floats and were apparently free to choose their own subjects and designers (who remain unknown). The only chariot for which we have an original drawing by Buontalenti and Boscoli is represented in cat. 73 (pl. 16), which carried Ferdinando's brother Don Pietro and his nephew Vincenzo Gonzaga; as high-ranking members of the ruling family, they could apparently commandeer the services of the official designer.

Girolamo Seriacopi: The "House Staff"

Girolamo Seriacopi, identified in the sources as *provveditore del castello*, was not one of the creative triumvirate, but the head of the next level down in the hierarchy, a business manager who executed requests from all three of the creative principals. His work, which like theirs began in the summer of 1588, was an essential part of setting up the administrative apparatus for the wedding; indeed, Seriacopi and his assistant Francesco Gorini are included with the triumvirate in the final audit of 1593 as the full team responsible for the event. His surviving record book provides a crucial element of the overall backstage documentation for the event.

Seriacopi's title, which translates as *purveyor* or *quartermaster*, comes from the building trades and refers to his permanent job in the Medici establishment as chief supply officer and engineer of fortresses. His functions included general administrative tasks related to military and technical construction, such as shipments of materials, foundry work, and labor supervision; from time to time, these duties would expand to cover the technical aspects of temporary commissions like the intermedi, comedy, and naumachia. In this theatrical role, his function combines aspects of today's production stage manager and assistant producer. Thanks to Borghini's correspondence, we know a lot about Seriacopi's predecessor, Giovanni Caccini, the *provveditore* for 1565, who was hired to "solicit, oversee, and check work, putting it into order and taking delivery, as well as keep order in the records and payments by type of work and have them at hand every day, even every hour." Seriacopi fulfilled all these tasks in regard to reconstruction of the theater, the construction of sets and costumes for the intermedi and *La pellegrina*, the Pitti events, and the banquet at the Palazzo Vecchio after the premiere of the intermedi. Though he generally served as the intermediary between ideators and executants, he also wrote to "S.A.S." directly on occasions of special urgency.[46]

Seriacopi's logbook, the *Memoriale e ricordi*, was set up on August 31, 1588, to fulfill precisely the functions outlined by Borghini. Entries touch on all practical aspects of design, construction, labor relations, supplies of equipment and personnel, rehearsals, even janitorial services; its final entries from June 1589 concern postperformance cleanup and dismantling and storage of the theatrical equipment. Some entries are meant as binding records of settlements of disputes, others are complaints or threats to workers; in addition, it contains numerous small working sketches, made on the spot by Buontalenti, of decorative details and practical devices. At first entries were made only every few days, but as the pace of work quickened — noticeably in November, after the marriage contract had been finalized — the problems noted and dealt with eventually required several pages a day.

The logbook was physically kept in or near the workshops and construction site at the Medici Theater itself: it refers to "going to the Pitti," and assumes that "here" is the Uffizi. It must have been open and accessible to various assistants and overseers, as it contains entries in many hands, often in question-and-answer or order-and-report format. Many of these are written by or addressed to Seriacopi's factotum, Gorini, who is identified as *provveditore alla commedia*. The subordinate position on the hierarchical chain of command occupied by Gorini, a combination of paymaster and labor foreman, is evident from the audit: "payments were made from orders and lists by Francesco Gorini . . . and endorsed by the abovementioned" major staff. When orders came from Cavalieri, Seriacopi wrote them in the *Memoriale* for Gorini to see to (or, if dictated by Cavalieri through Gorini, Seriacopi added a note such as "Accommodate him"); and when individual craftsmen or contractors had requests, it was Gorini who conveyed them to Seriacopi and Cavalieri via a note in the log.

Like Cavalieri's *Libro di conti*, the *Memoriale e ricordi* contrasts with the official focus of the *descrizioni*, allowing us a backstage view of day-to-day procedures and some sense of the larger economic world supporting and implied by the performances. Its geographic references extend to the entire grand duchy and beyond: houses were rented throughout Florence for the imported performers, agents were dispatched to outlying towns to procure lumber and old boats for the naumachia, and special materials were requested from Venice. The *Memoriale* also reveals the complexity of the granducal household in notes about transferring or borrowing materials from the *Guardaroba* (stores of goods) at the Pitti and elsewhere. One recurring theme is parsimony, manifested in frequent requests for economy and for competitive bidding that pitted artisans against one another.[47]

As expected for someone of less elevated social stature than Cavalieri or Bardi, we know little about Seriacopi's biography.[48] Although he is visible in the logbook only as a functionary, hints of his personality surface in a few surviving letters. He wrote to Ferdinando regarding a fire carelessly set by two stagehands, probably because he had received some criticism for incarcerating both men; although he apologizes if his response was too forceful, both that action and his defense, citing "the concerns of my position," suggest a streak of self-importance and authoritarian severity. (No doubt these were useful qualities in a labor supervisor, though they are no match for the suspicious malice of Vincenzo Borghini, who wrote to warn Seriacopi's counterpart in 1565 against greedy painters, whom he calls "certain ugly animals.") A series of testy exchanges extending from February through April 1589 records a continuing dispute between Seriacopi and Buontalenti over responsibilities for tardy work, during which Seriacopi again had recourse to Ferdinando to defend his veracity. The onus for this hostility may not rest entirely on Seriacopi, for Buontalenti was also squabbling with Cavalieri at the same time; in any case, the quartermaster's protestation that "if anything I've said is ever found to be other than the truth, may Your Lordship have me doubly and rigorously punished" accepts the same strain of strict accountability that he was willing to inflict on others.[49]

By the end of October, then, when the contract for Ferdinando and Christine's marriage was signed in France, the preparations for her reception in Florence were well under way. The administrative apparatus had been established, and the major creative teams, already at work for at least three and probably five months or more, had completed the program and at least some rough theatrical designs. Supplies had been ordered and architectural remodeling had begun. Tensions were evident between the old guard from the reigns of Cosimo and Franceso and the new blood being brought in by Ferdinando. As yet, however, they were all still only at the beginning of a long process.

CHAPTER TWO

November & December 1588

CASTING, COSTUMES, AND

REHEARSALS

Members of the staff, having determined the literary programs, set up their administrative apparatus, and made broad design decisions over the preceding several months, could now devote themselves in earnest to the various phases of execution. During the months of November and December, they began work on several interrelated tasks simultaneously: casting the performers, including singers, dancers, and musicians; fitting and sewing the costumes; and continuing to construct the sets and machinery in which these figures were to move. Cavalieri, Seriacopi, and their staffs coordinated supply and labor conditions between manufacturers, merchants, craftworkers, and subcontractors; entries in other account books indicate that the Medici household staff was beginning to plan for the lodging of hundreds of anticipated guests.

The numbers of people involved would have made the wedding, at least temporarily, among the largest economic enterprises of the city. Rossi marvels continually at the large forces, the splendor of the costumes, and the sonorous sound of the music, some of which he probably saw and heard in the early onstage rehearsals, which began in December. In his *descrizione* of the 1586 theatricals, he had recorded that more than 400 people worked to realize that event; his prologue for 1589 is less numerically specific, but he refers rhetorically to the city expending "all its resources" (pp. 2–4) and compares the event to an earlier festival organized by Lorenzo de' Medici, the Magnificent, "which kept the entire city busy working on it for several months." His earlier estimate is certainly inadequate for 1589, especially if we count the many related events at the Pitti Palace and Santa Croce. At the Uffizi alone we have the names of, or references to, some 100 theater performers, 150 soldiers and sailors for the naumachia, 50 tailors, and dozens of painters with their workshops, not to mention the hundred or so members of the stage crew that moved scenery, pulled winches, and lit lamps.

The Introduction focused on the royal and aristocratic class of patrons, and

Chapter 1 on the largely patrician or upper-level artist class responsible for the ideation of the entire festival. In practical terms, these relatively exclusive groups were far outnumbered by their employees and suppliers, who came from the artisan and laboring classes: actors and actresses, musicians, and dancers, as well as craftworkers, from carpenters, painters, and tailors to other skilled specialists in dyeing, hairdressing, and wigmaking. Although they were all at work at the same time, for clarity the following discussion will break these activities down into separate components: the present chapter focuses primarily on casting and costumes, Chapter 3 on scenic construction and stage equipment.

In general outline, a sequence can be inferred for the activities of the stage and costume workers. Buontalenti probably did the rough conceptual drawings for the stage sets for each of the six intermedi first, as the costumes shown in them are still vague and generic; in fact, as we have seen, the construction of stage pieces began well before the costumes. Next, he prepared the costume sketches that survive, which depict the basic concept of each outfit but are still far from detailed enough to serve as tailor's patterns; these were finished by October, when materials were ordered. Only after these costume designs were well under way were the roles they illustrated assigned to specific cast members: the cast names were written on the drawings for reference and measurements after the initial design, and these names are often crossed out or exchanged.

PERFORMERS

The performers in the wedding events, who totaled in the hundreds, can be differentiated into three categories. First there were the actors who performed the prose plays, who were grouped into independent acting companies. Second, the intermedi performers were not actors, but vocalists, instrumental musicians, and dancers; some were hired and supervised by Cavalieri's administration for this occasion only, while others were permanent employees of the granducal payroll or of the city's major churches. For the third type of wedding event — the outdoor public pageantry of the entry, the joust, the animal baiting, and the Pitti chariot parade, as well as the ecclesiastical rites — the "actors" were performing *ex officio* in their roles as aristocrats, public officials, and clerics, with their trains of attendants and pages.

Cast and Musicians

The two troupes of actors that performed the comedies had little in common: one was made up of aristocratic amateurs, the other of professionals in the still relatively new popular and commercial theater, which was not altogether socially respectable. Little is known about the cast members of Siena's Accademia degli Intronati who acted in *La pellegrina* except that they were members of a company of young Sienese patricians who staged plays, in the manner of the other learned academies of the time.[1] The Compagnia dei Gelosi, as an independent troupe, also has left no production documents, though the company's married leaders, Francesco (1548–1624) and Isabella Andreini (1562–1604), published some of their scenarios. About their 1589 production we have only the somewhat contradictory commentaries of the diarists. Pavoni, the source for Christine's delight in Isabella's French, also recounts with relish the rivalry between the two principal actresses, Andreini and Vittoria Piissimi, who fought over which was to perform first; Piissimi won out, starring in *La zingara* while Andreini had to wait to perform her own vehicle, *La pazzia*, a week later.[2]

The enormous cast of the intermedi, which were staged directly by the court, posed a logistical problem. Close to home, Ferdinando could draw on his own permanent musical establishment, the granducal chapel, as well as hire or borrow staff from religious institutions closely allied to the family (San Lorenzo) or the state (the cathedral); these employees worked on the intermedi either full-time, or part-time in addition to duties elsewhere. When these resources proved inadequate, they were supplemented by actors, singers, dancers, and instrumentalists — who often doubled in more than one of these capacities — from a wide range of locales and secular institutions, including individual freelancers who served for varying lengths of time. Bernardo Franciosino, nicknamed "della cornetta," was entered first on the granducal payroll (*ruolo*) in September 1588; a cornetto virtuoso who also operated a music school in the city, he provided numerous instrumentalists and other performers, probably his pupils, who are identified in the records as "del franciosino." Almost ten percent of the cast were ecclesiastics, ranging from one "priest Riccio" to seven *frati* (brothers) from the local churches of Santa Croce and the Santissima Annunziata, and even from Loreto and Venice — all presumably veteran sacred choristers or instrumentalists. Only two performers are explicitly identified as dancers, "Agostino ballerino" and Cecchino.

In addition to Loreto and Venice, singers were imported from Siena, Lucca, and Rome; a few independent artists identified as "da Roma" had probably already been brought in by Ferdinando and Cavalieri when they moved to Florence. A few names hint at non-Italian origins, such as one "Lorenzino tedescho" (German) and a page called "Francesco spagniuolo" (Spaniard), but they might have immigrated from their eponymous homelands at some earlier time. In any case, this converging Babel of international newcomers seems to have bred some confusion on the staff's part: in the most comprehensive cast list, which gives 82 names, the wardrobe master Benedetto Tornaquinci lists Antonio Archilei just after another Antonio, surnamed Naldi, whom Tornaquinci mistakenly identifies in Archilei's stead as "the husband of Sra. Vittoria [Archilei]."[3]

In spite of numerous changes of assigned roles during the rehearsal period, it is possible to assemble virtually complete cast lists for intermedi 1, 3, and 5.[4] We have already met several of the intermedi composers, who also performed onstage roles: Cristofano Malvezzi, Luca Marenzio, Jacopo Peri, Giulio Caccini, and Antonio Archilei. Malvezzi's brother Alberigo, the organist at the Medici's historic parish of San Lorenzo, also took part.[5] Because each intermedio was self-contained, most performers took different roles in more than one of the tableaux. Peri, for example, sang his own piece as Arion in intermedio 5, as well as a siren in intermedio 1; in intermedio 3, after first being assigned to play a bearded Delphian man (cat. 37; pl. 12), he ultimately played a Delphian woman (cat. 48).

Archilei, as noted, composed part of Doric Harmony's aria for his wife Vittoria, the *prima donna* of the occasion; primarily a lutenist and basso, he also appeared as a sea nymph in intermedio 5 (cat. 56; pl. 13). Vittoria, née Concarini (1550–ca. 1629), was a dancer and instrumentalist as well a celebrated vocalist, lauded by Peri as "the Euterpe of our time." Among the first women to achieve an independent performing career, she took the virtuoso roles of Harmony and of Amphitrite, queen of the sea, in intermedio 5. She probably studied under her husband, whom she married in 1578; the couple were protégés of Cavalieri's in Rome, entering Ferdinando's service there and moving to Florence with the change of regime as permanent court employees.[6]

Vittoria was one of three principal women in the cast. The next member of this trio was Lucia Caccini, Giulio's pupil and first wife. As *seconda donna* of the production, she sang a siren in intermedio 1 and the sorceress in intermedio 4, whose aria her husband composed. The third, a younger singer named Margherita who lived with the Archileis, was most likely their pupil and perhaps also their adopted daughter; she is listed as Antonio's *putta* (young girl). Margherita sang one of the sea nymphs in intermedio 5 (cat. 56) and a Delphian woman in intermedio 3; she may be identical with the Margherita who later became the second wife of Giulio Caccini.[7]

Male performers varied widely in age and voice. Onofrio Gualfreducci from Pistoia was one of several castrati, identified as such in the payment lists. Young boys were recruited to play the souls devoured in the mouth of Lucifer in intermedio 4, and the magpies into which the presumptuous Pierides are transformed in 2. Their principal qualifications were being small, agile, and energetic; these parts needed no vocal skills, as the characters made only squawking or moaning noises.[8]

Unfortunately, as is typical of Renaissance musical practice, we lack precise information about the total forces and distribution of the orchestral instrumentalists. Like many temporary orchestras today, this one dressed up a core of available local personnel with a few celebrities of prestigious reputation. In addition to the various players hired from Franciosino's academy or from Siena and other Tuscan cities, several well-known figures of the day can be identified, among them Antonio Naldi (also known as Bardella) and Giovanni Battista Jacomelli, nicknamed "il violino," who was among the earliest virtuoso performers on the violin. The versatile Giulio Caccini played the harp, and also sang a siren in intermedio 1. Also recorded are Alessandro Striggio father and son; the elder was a virtuoso instrumentalist and composer and the younger, who played the viol, later penned the libretto for Monteverdi's earliest opera, *L'Orfeo* (1607).

Something of the relative social status and lifestyles of these performers can be gleaned from their salaries, partially listed in the household payroll drawn up on September 1, 1588 — at the same time that Cavalieri was setting up the accounts for arts administration. Cavalieri, it will be recalled, received 25 ducats per month plus lodging and horse; the compensation for his employees ranges downward from his by a third or more. The maximum fee of 20 ducats per month for Franciosino probably included amounts to be paid to the students he provided, seven of whom are listed for intermedio 5 and four for intermedio 3. The other high salaries were 15 ducats for Marenzio, who of course also served as a composer; 16 for the violinist Jacomelli; 18 for Antonio Archilei, which included expenses for his girl Margherita, her nurse, and house rent; and a separate 10 for his wife Vittoria, indicating that she was employed independently of her husband. Others earned from 9 down to 4 ducats per month, but often had other duties or forms of income. According to the records, a basso, Don Giovanni, "still serve[d] at the duomo," and Antonio Naldi received only 6 ducats but was further named as "guardaroba della musica" (duties unspecified), with a note that he also received meals (*mangia in tinello*).[9]

Gender, Transvestism, and Homosexuality

The casting practices for the intermedi and comedies provide a case study of the conventions attached to gender in the Renaissance theater, revealing a transitional landmark in the increasing role of women. Up to this time, as one manifestation of long historical restrictions on public speaking and public appearance, women had been rare as either authors or performers. This situation was just beginning to change: we have already met Laura Guidiccione, the only female author invited to contribute verses to the intermedi. The commedia dell'arte, first documented about 1545, included women as cast members by about 1560 and had reached the point where Isabella Andreini wrote her own vehicles. At this juncture women were still seen as a theatrical novelty, and support of them as proof of cultural sophistication: the duke of Ferrara had recently established a three-member *concerto di donne*, and the three main women singers who were brought in for 1589 may have represented Ferdinando's bid to rival his Este relations, who were considered a model of aristocratic patronage. In addition to that trio, two girls and their brother were reportedly added to the cast of intermedio 2 at a late point and given the madrigal "Bella ne fe' natura," which, because it declares their role as judges, more logically belongs to the chorus of hamadryad nymphs (all played by men).[10]

In spite of this increase in opportunity, exclusion persisted even on the naturalistic stage. Two concurrent examples exemplify the transitional situation at this time and the factors of class and economics that were at work. Although the play *La pellegrina* has many female characters, including the eponymous heroine, its cast must have been all men, as the Intronati was restricted to aristocratic male amateurs. By contrast, although the tradition of female impersonation survived from the founding phase of commedia dell'arte, in the public theater women could now play women and men generally played men, and professional companies like that of Piissimi and Andreini offered the first opportunities for women on the commercial stage. The intense jockeying for precedence between the Gelosi's two prima donnas amused the court, but it should also be viewed, in context, as a necessary part of their larger battle for professional advancement in a competitive industry only recently, and still incompletely, opened to them.[11]

Progress duly noted, nevertheless virtually all the female roles in the intermedi were taken by men, and this established custom was still institutionalized through long-standing practices and conventions that provided modes of substituting for the absent female. Here, as in the all-male *Pellegrina*, two methods helped to overcome some of the gender disparity between the character and the physiognomy and voice of the actor. One traditional expedient was the castrato; the other, less drastic and more temporary, was transvestism (which castrati also practiced).

The emasculation of young boys to preserve their prepubertal treble voices owed its origins to the Catholic Church's prohibition on women singing in church. The resultant soprano (or alto) register, combined with the physical capacity of a grown male chest, combined the ethereal and the stentorian to captivate audiences and create early modern celebrities. Onofrio Gualfreducci, the most important castrato of 1589, was near the top of the salary range at 15 ducats per month. Along with him, the cast also included "Pierino castrato, . . . Niccolò Bartolini da Pistoia eunuco," and the more ambiguously identified "Tommaso contralto" (which could also mean a falsettist). Like the rest of the male cast, including the *frati*, these singers might play roles of either gender: Gualfreducci sang the goddess Necessity in intermedio 1, then Jupiter in 6. Bartolini's known parts are all female (a siren in 1, a Delphian woman in 3, and a marine nymph in 5), but Pierino played a male sailor in the latter.[12]

The vast majority of male vocalists, however, impersonated females simply by cross-dressing, without benefit of hormonal modification; many are identified as bass voices, which must have produced a more earthbound tessitura than ideally appropriate to, for example, the chorus of heavenly sirens in intermedio 1. Earlier scholars, well aware of the visual and auditory disjunction between female role and male performer, tended to approach the costuming from a common-sense assumption that the designers did all they could to disguise it. As the sketches and materials orders make clear, many of the female costumes were fitted with cardboard (or perhaps papier-mâché) "chests with breasts," which Nagler sees as intended "to rid the singers of their masculine appearance." This traditional interpretation views such artificial body parts and masks as an expedient, their goal to make male performers look physically more "realistic."[13] And of course, as Rossi's comments testify, Buontalenti was much occupied with maximizing verisimilitude, an essential element in creating and maintaining any theatrical fantasy.

Mere cardboard, however, can hardly have overcome the visible facts very convincingly. As an example, the female role of siren 9 in the first intermedio was taken by one "Ceserone basso"; as the suffix to his name suggests, Ceserone was a large man, and even attached breasts would not make his frame seem feminine. Moreover, although all of the characters wore masks, these covered only part of the face and would not have concealed the full beards worn by almost all men in the late sixteenth century (except, in most cases, castrati).

What the costumes lacked in illusionistic power they made up for in symbolic power, which was of much greater concern to designers and audience alike than the "problem" of verisimilitude that so puzzles many modern scholars. Cardboard breasts and masks were, after all, also attached to the costumes of female characters played by female performers, who presumably did not need them: no distinction is made, for example, between the design for the siren played by Lucia Caccini and those of her eleven male cohorts.

Exaggerated in form and decoration, applied to performers of both genders, artificial breasts were not so much *trompe-l'oeil* expedients as symbolic breast-plates, functioning more as semiotic signifiers for "woman" than as cosmetic appendages.

Onstage no less than off, male and female identities were clearly defined, and clothing, as an essential social vehicle for enforcing and communicating those constructs, was invested with a degree of absolute reality far beyond its status in a later world more conscious of fashion as artifice. The Cinquecento audience was more willing to accept signs as transparent, to believe that clothes make the man (or woman). Sumptuary laws literally embodied a minute code of social rank, and at a time when most ordinary people owned only one suit of clothes, a change of identity was hard to practice or suspect.[14] Thus disguise and mistaken identity are a stock element of period comedy and literature: Drusilla, the heroine of *La pellegrina*, meets frequently with her lost husband Lucrezio, but because she is "disguised" as a pilgrim, he never recognizes her until she reveals herself. Parallel to this convention is the expectation that, because the man playing Drusilla is officially disguised as a woman, the audience will primarily register the external signs of "her" identity, disregarding any dissonance with the figure beneath.[15]

The sexual ambiguity of onstage cross-dressers intersected with the symbolism of the androgyne, and more specifically the hermaphrodite, an image principally derived from Plato that was current throughout Renaissance culture in the occult sciences, visual arts, and even statecraft. On the highest plane, this ideal fusion of qualities normally split between two contrasting genders symbolized the positive combination in "the body politic" of the ruler of all desirable virtues, as in the elaborately propagandistic self-portrayals of England's androgynous Virgin Queen, Elizabeth I, and the image of Christine's great-grandfather, François I of France, dressed simultaneously as Minerva and Mars, War and Civilization (fig. 4).

At the same time, this inherently unstable and multivalent symbol was beginning to be associated more literally with less elevated or socially acceptable sexual ambiguities: François's grandson Henri III, an effeminate homosexual who was notorious for his male favorites and for appearing at court functions in women's garb, was caricatured in printed satire as the leader of an "Isle of Hermaphrodites." And although Isabella Andreini's exact dialogue in 1589 is not recorded, in a variant script of similar title that has survived, the mad scene, protected from *lèse-majesté* by the character's insanity, made crude jokes about the rumored physical abnormalities of Queen Elizabeth, whose failure to marry was suspected in contemporary anti-Tudor sentiment to be due to "monstrous" hermaphroditism.[16]

F Rancoys en guerre est vn Mars furieux
En paix Minerue & diane a la chasse
A bien parler Mercure copieux
A bien aymer. vray Amour. plein de grace
O france heureuse honore donc la face
De ton grand Roy qui surpasse Nature
Car lhonorant tu sers en mesme place
Minerue Mars Diane Amour. Mercure.

4. *François I as a composite deity. Attributed to Niccolò da Modena.*

The discursive nexus that joined transvestism, androgyny, effeminacy, and homosexuality as vices particularly prevalent in the marginalized theatrical world began to crystallize at about this time, also in Elizabethan England, notably around the playwright Christopher Marlowe, who died in 1594. These connections mark the gradual emergence of a changed, early modern paradigm for sexual and social identity, in which the fluidity of roles in the theater (especially the boys in drag) came to be considered psychologically resonant with, and attractive to, a recognized personality type of homosexually inclined males, who at least in London had begun to gather in their own urban subcultural milieus by the 1590s. The documents of 1589 offer no evidence of such networks in Florence, though it is suggestive that in contemporary Venice, music schools — like that of Franciosino, who provided so many of the artistic young men for the court orchestra — were notorious as meeting places for what were then generally condemned as "sodomites."[17]

COSTUMES

Counting the costumes and ceremonial outfits necessary for Christine's entry, for the intermedi and their associated plays, and for the events at the Pitti and Piazza Santa Croce, the total must have reached well over a thousand. Taken as a whole, as Anna Maria Testaverde concluded in her important survey of the wedding costumes, these outfits "represent a remarkable repertory of theatrical costumes, which . . . provides a mirror image of the division of roles and categories within contemporary society."[18]

Design and Construction

Three distinct types of costumes were prepared, by designers and tailors working in at least two separate crews. Each costume type was appropriate in style and materials to the nature of the event(s) for which it was made, and each descended from a specific tradition of theatrical and aristocratic spectacle. In the intermedi, the allegorical characters and style were drawn from the tradition of the pastorale, associated with the realm of mythic fantasy. The comedies were costumed in a more realistic register, its style derived from the world of contemporary fashion that its characters inhabited. And for the quasi-military or processional outdoor events — encompassing Christine's entry, the tourney in Piazza Santa Croce, and the Pitti sbarra and naumachia — the liveries provided to participants (sewn by a team largely separate from that which provided purely "theatrical" costumes) recalled the antique and medieval tradition of court ceremonial and mock-combat, combining elements of chivalric fantasy with recognizable aspects of contemporary uniforms.

As we have seen, the costume designs for the first two modes of dress must already have been at least schematically complete by October 5, when Bardi ordered work to begin on outfits for the intermedi and *La pellegrina*, and Cavalieri's account book was opened in early November to receive goods already ordered. Unfortunately, no drawings for the thirteen personages of *Pellegrina* itself survive (with the possible exception of cat. 67), though some idea of their substance can be found in the *Libro di conti*, which lists materials for each character's costume along with those for the intermedi.[19] The elaborate sumptuousness of all the costumes is Rossi's constant refrain; typical is his marvel (*Descrizione dell'apparato*, 20) at the appearance of the opening tableau of Necessity and the planetary gods: "Such were the splendor . . . and the costumes of the gods and heroes who displayed themselves in this heaven, rich with gold, and with brilliant attire, that it might well have seemed to everyone that Paradise had opened up, and become the entire stage and setting."

Two hundred eighty-six costumes were designed and built for the intermedi. Forty-three sheets of watercolor sketches attributed to Buontalenti, illustrating almost half the costumes with notes on casting and materials, are preserved in the Biblioteca Nazionale Centrale, Florence; a few more are scattered or unlocated. In addition, several drawings by other hands seem related to 1589, either as elaborations or copies by assistants. For some intermedi, almost all the drawings survive; for others, few or none. The number of costumes for each intermedio, and the catalogue numbers of the known sketches, are as follows:[20]

Int. 1	45 costumes	cat.	11–25
2	34		28–32
3	38		35–50
4	42		none
5	37		56–62
6	90		65–66
La pellegrina (?)	1		67

Sketches for both sets and costumes were organized into six separate portfolios, one for each tableau (Seriacopi's notes refer to *il libro del terzo intemedio*, MR 24r). All the sheets are roughly the same size; when larger drawings are called for, they are made up of two of these folios (cat. 28, 49–50; pls. 5, 10–11). The idea of composing such folders must have come only after Buontalenti's first schematic drawings for the stage sets were already finished. Being much larger, these could not fit the portfolios' format; apparently, at least in the case of cat. 51, an assistant made a reference copy of the earlier design at a reduced scale which, when folded in half, would exactly match the size of the single costume sheets.

The costume drawings are further organized and amplified by written texts. Most of them bear an identifying number in the upper right corner, in a separate sequence for each intermedio, to keep the unbound drawings in order (the present Catalogue is arranged following these sequences). Also, individual figure sketches were given reference numbers for the tailors and accountants, and sheets often bear captions or notes on character names, casting, materials, and colors; the three distinct hands have not been identified. Occasional notes written on the blank verso of a drawing may represent additional later suggestions referring to the drawing on the facing recto page (see cat. 23–25; pls. 2–4).[21]

Buontalenti and his crew were working within an established tradition for the style and visual sources of costumes, codified for theater professionals in treatises by Leone de' Sommi, the influential designer and author from the court theater at Mantua (*Dialoghi*, ca. 1565), and later writers.[22] These manuals identify three aspects of design — style and cut, color and texture, and applied decoration. A fourth aspect, to which they devote little attention, is symbolism, precisely the aspect so central to Bardi and other humanist programmers. This discrepancy in needs and interests between theoreticians and practitioners in the theater is not unique to that time: a costume designer, tailor, or purveyor need not understand the philosophical significance of a costume in order to create it physically. And in fact the working documents of the Uffizi-Pitti staff are often generic in their language: the sirens are simply called "nymphs," a term adequate for the craftworkers' practical purposes, and the heroine Drusilla is continually referred to as the "French gentlewoman" (*gentildonna franzese*). One wonders whether Bardi, who had lavished so much of his antiquarian minutiae on the precise individualized attributes of each siren, ever saw the entry in Cavalieri's accounts describing siren 6 matter-of-factly as "one [character] who goes on a cloud" (LC Q291).

The style of the intermedi costumes follows in the tradition of allegorical masque and festival costumes dating back to the fifteenth-century pastorales of Poliziano at Mantua and Leonardo at Milan. For female characters, the classical nymph was the most common source and ideal: long tresses plaited with fluttering veils, a long, supple skirt and shorter overskirt (*sottana* and *sottanella*), and floral or woodland decorative trimmings, all familiar from such works as Botticelli's *Primavera*. Within this general stylistic mode, every effort was made to differentiate individual characters by details of costume and accessories; as de' Sommi had advised, "I strive as much as possible to dress the performers differently . . . so that as soon as one sees them . . . one recognizes them, without having to wait for them to declare themselves in words."[23]

Fabrics and colors were also conventionalized to accommodate a complex symbolism of hue and texture. Colors were brighter and more varied than those of contemporary everyday clothes, in part for practical motives of visibility and impact under conditions of stage lighting and distance. Costume linings were constructed of coarse, inexpensive fabrics like *tela* (linen, canvas) and *perpignano* (wool), but the outer layers of skirts and bodices were covered in materials — silk, satin, taffeta, and *ermisino* (sarsenet, a light silk) — that were thinner and more fragile than ordinary street wear.[24] The single largest acquisition was some 1,200 *braccia* of *velo di bologna*, a Bolognese import used for the thin, gauzy veils of various colors that hang from the headdresses of most female characters (LC T6; one braccio equals 58 centimeters or 23 inches). This fabric was much prized for theatricals because it would ripple elegantly when the loose ends of the veils were held in the hands of dancing or gesturing characters (for example, cat. 32, pl. 7). Rossi calls attention to this quality in his description of the floor-length veils of the hamadryads in intermedio 2 (p. 40), "which, swelling [*gonfiando*] with each puff of breeze, made that noble and rich costume more magnificently embellished" (cat. 28; pl. 5). He is echoing the established judgment of theater theoreticians, such as de' Sommi's praise of "the fluttering veil that comes before all of a woman's other head ornaments."[25]

The intermedio costumes were also differentiated by material from one act to the next, to correspond with the varying levels of reality depicted. The costumes for intermedi 2, 3, and 5, which primarily portray mortals, demigods, and nymphs, are described as made simply of *drappi*, a generic term for cloth; those for intermedi 1 and 6, however, in which the major gods and cosmological figures appear, are specified as *drappo di perpignano*, a more substantial woolen material. The costume drawings for six sirens, those of the ninth and tenth spheres and the Empyrean (cat. 19–21), are all labeled that the skirts should be "transparent like diamond," as they represent the spirit of the uppermost, airiest heavens. And for the central intermedio 4, which takes place in the antimasque world of animalistic hell, devils, and monsters, the costumes are made of *drappo e pelle*, fabric supplemented with more evocative skins or furs (LC T26). Nudity, when required for such figures as Apollo, Mercury, Bacchus, and Amphitrite, was simulated by close-fitting, flesh-colored silk (Rossi, 55, 66, 67).

Green velvet (*velluto verde*) is a good example of a fabric with highly specific uses and associations. It is referred to frequently in the documents and evidently held some measure of extra dignity, no doubt in part due to its cost; de' Sommi associates both velvet and satin costumes exclusively with aristocratic characters, and in 1589 it was worn only by characters of divine or supernatural essence. Altogether, some 168 braccia (106 yards) were used. Characters dressed in this fabric begin with Doric Harmony in intermedio 1 (cat. 11); Rossi (p. 22) invokes the authority of both Plato and Aristotle for Bardi's prescriptions for her, saying that she was dressed in dark green velvet "because it seemed to [Bardi] that this color, more than any other, suited the purpose of her costume," to represent the musical Dorian mode's attributes of virility and strength. The length of velvet for her costume amounted to 18½ braccia, or 12 yards; given the weight of velvet, and the numerous other fabrics and headdress Archilei wore, it is fortunate that her character did not have to walk about. Also so cloaked were, probably, the Muses of intermedio 2, the sorceress of intermedio 4 with her "22 angels on the cloud that passes through the center" of the stage, and 11 nymphs for intermedio 6. By contrast, the only green velvet listed specifically for the more plebeian characters of *La pellegrina* are trimmings on three costumes, totaling about 6½ braccia.[26]

The decorative vocabulary applied to all these fabrics throughout is rich and complex, conveying splendor and allegorical significance through standardized classical motifs. Rossi's description of Doric Harmony explains that "to make it more majestic, [her dress] was adorned with a fine supply of solid gold, and a belt . . . all covered with jewels" (p. 22). Other descriptions and costume notes refer to sequins, rosettes, imitation flowers, lionhead and other masks, and bells; and numerous fabrics were sent out to be printed (*stampato*) or handpainted with overlaid patterns. The accounts list hundreds of braccia of tinsel (*orpello*), fringes (*frangie*), and lace edging (*trina*), plus assorted ribbons and buttons. Trimmings were adjusted to the geographical location of each intermedio: marine motifs for 3 and 5, which take place on an island or at sea, included pearl, mother-of-pearl, shells, and coral branches, while the celestial sirens of 1 were to be covered in feathers and their headdresses varied to indicate their individual planetary or zodiacal associations. Frequent notes in Seriacopi's log refer to similar woodland, serpent, or marine motifs, real or cardboard, that were attached to the musical instruments carried onstage to make them, too, suit the changing themes (for example, MR 45r, Apr. 9).

Many of these details do not appear in Buontalenti's costume sketches, which are somewhat schematic and simplified. There must have been more detailed intermediate drawings for the tailors and scene painters, as well as patterns for cutting, almost all now lost. For example, one of Buontalenti's assistants traced and amplified his original conceptual sketch for the sirens (cat. 12–22). A drawing by his collaborator Andrea Boscoli (cat. 32; pl. 7) may be the only other surviving example of such secondary drawings; although it does not exactly correspond to any of Buontalenti's surviving designs, it generally conveys the texture and density of detail of a finished costume. The existence of additional detail drawings can also be surmised from such sketches as cat. 25 (pl. 4), for Necessity and the Fates. Rossi goes into detail about the painted designs on Necessity's throne, but the sides of her seat are invisible in this drawing; another *modello* must have provided instructions for the prop painters. (That such decorative details would have been nearly as invisible to the audience as they are to a viewer of the drawing seems not to have deterred Bardi's desire for iconographic elaboration.)[27]

Although no sketches survive (with the possible exception of cat. 67) for the second mode of costume, that for the three comedies, some idea of their materials and style can be gleaned from Cavalieri's account book, which lists amounts and types of fabric and accessories for each costume by the name of the character. (The number next to each name suggests that, like the intermedio costumes, these sketches were serially numbered for reference.) In contrast to the complex mythic style of the intermedi outfits, these were closely modeled on everyday street wear; contemporary treatise writers stressed the need for realism in such costumes. Because the genre of comedy dealt with more familiar settings, its humor resided in the characters' similarity to recognizable social types and classes, ranging from the bawdy innkeeper Violante to the dignified matron Drusilla; as Strozzi's motto beneath the allegorical statue of New Comedy in the Uffizi theater put it, "I describe the manners of man."[28]

The orders for *Pellegrina* costumes alternately describe them as *alla fiorentina* or *alla franzese*, indicating that clearly understood fashion conventions would enable the audience to identify the characters as either Tuscan (the play is set in Pisa) or, like Drusilla (alluding to Christine), French. In contrast to this verisimilitude in design, however, the fabrics specified are often, like those of the intermedi, lightweight and sheer. This incongruity was apparent to a representative of the Sienese acting company, who asked Cavalieri repeatedly for an actual street dress for the character of the young *innamorata*, Lepida (who acts insane to avoid an unwanted marriage): "The girl who feigns madness should be dressed, not in imitation materials, but in something solid, noble and seemly clothes, as has been said many times; but we've never been able to obtain them, even though they could be gotten on loan without cost." The implication is that Lepida is no ethereal, imaginary nymph, but the daughter of the Pisan bourgeois gentleman Cassandro, and the interest of her dilemma is inextricable from that "solid" social reality that produces conflicts between private passion and arranged marriage. Cavalieri seems to have agreed; his response suggested that such a dress be borrowed either from the wardrobe of the Medici princesses or, should they be unwilling, from the patrician woman Camilla Rucellai, whose family were high court officials. Even such attempts at realism were limited along another axis, of course; as will be recalled, the part of Lepida was taken by a young man.[29]

System of Production

For these first two types of costumes, as well as for construction of the stage sets and decorations, an overlapping hierarchy supervised the complex procurement of materials, their consignment to tailors, painters, carpenters and other craftworkers, and accounting and payments. The tiered chain of command was overseen ultimately by Cavalieri, but his bureau was itself a part of the Guardaroba, the larger administration of all court storehouses and supply networks, which preserved his records. He negotiated with and coordinated the efforts of various other administrators, among them household officials like Napoleone Cambi, Benedetto Fedini, and Enea Vaini, as well as the group at the Uffizi under Seriacopi and Gorini.

The first entry in the *Libro di conti* for materials given to a specific tailor is dated November 4 (LC Q1). As indicated on the credit side of the ledger, many of these supplies were sent over from the *Depositeria generale*, the general stores and payroll at the Pitti Palace, headed by Cambi as treasurer. Seriacopi wrote to Cambi on November 26, addressing him as *depositario grande per S.A.S.*, to request supplies of ropes, metalwork, and tinsel for the theater but also for the naumachia, tournament, and other events to be staged in the palace itself. Most of the time, however, the principal intermediary was Seriacopi's assistant, Francesco Gorini, who had responsibility for the continual movement of fabrics and other materials. Many items are listed as "received from Gorini" (*havuta da Gorini*): for example, he was issued cloth that he then consigned to painters or dyers, received back from them, and delivered to tailors.[30]

The crew of tailors and assistants was captained by Maestro Oreto Berardi, the principal tailor, and Niccolò Serlori. Although existing records show that about a dozen individually named tailors were paid directly on a daily wage basis, Oreto and Niccolò seem also to have operated as independent subcontractors for the bulk of the work: Oreto received a set sum for each completed costume, out of which he was to pay his own staff of "circa 50" unnamed *laboranti*. Labor for the 286 intermedi costumes was billed at the rate of 2 lire, 17 soldi, and 6 denari per costume, for a total fee of 822 lire, 5 soldi. Oreto was earning additional amounts simultaneously for sewing the outdoor festival costumes and household livery, working with another crew under separate artistic and administrative control more directly tied to the granducal household.[31]

The *Libro* provides some informative details about salary rates and work conditions. Pay records, kept by the week, begin in early November, but continue only through the end of December; the tailors kept working, so perhaps all labor in the later months was under contract through Oreto and Niccolò. The November–December work force varied weekly, from 15 between November 20 and 26 to only 7 in later December; wages ranged from 3 lire a day for Oreto down to 1⅔ per day for some assistants. This compares favorably with the well-documented wages for skilled laborers in construction, whose daily pay at this time was about 35–40 soldi (as much as 2 lire); unskilled workers earned about half as much, 15–18 soldi per day.[32]

At these rates, the maximum wage would be 18 lire for a full six-day week (most of the tailors worked less than full-time at the Uffizi, sometimes only one day a week, but they may have been employed at other workshops on days off, as Oreto himself was). At 7 lire to the ducat (earlier called a *fiorino*, and by this time often *scudo*), this would amount to a maximum monthly pay of about 10 ducats, roughly comparable to the middle salaries for singers and musicians. But money earned could be slow in coming. Payments were made to the tailors by Seriacopi, countersigned by Benedetto Fedini, the granducal *guardaroba maggiore*; after the first few weeks, the paymaster authorized less than the full amount due, and Oreto and Niccolò only received a final installment four months after the performances.[33]

In addition to tailors, the Uffizi workshops employed or patronized additional craftworkers in ancillary theater trades. Some costumes, once sewn, were then consigned to the principal theater painters, Lorenzo Francini and Francesco Rosselli, who hand-painted additional details on them, embellishing the naval attire for the naumachia, for example, and the costumes of the nine magpies of intermedio 2 (MR 42r, 48r). One name that crops up repeatedly is Tonino (Antonio) di Chelino, a wigmaker or milliner, who was responsible for numerous hats (*berrette*) and at least 320 headdresses (*acconciature*). His was a major task, as each headdress could require several braccia of fabric, plus attached veils and the requisite decorative symbols (shells, coral, feathers, and jewels, among others).[34]

Benedetto Tornaquinci, the wardrobe master, dictated an order on December 11 for 43 masks — one for every performer of the first intermedio. Characters were masked throughout the intermedi, and his descriptions here of each mask indicate that an attempt was made to differentiate and signify the type of character, in at least a generic way, by details of age, sex, personality, and (for male characters) length or absence of beard. Later he placed the orders for some 150 pairs of gold and silver shoes, listing performers' names so they could have their feet measured; additional orders for shoes, socks, and belts imply an elaborate network of craft suppliers.[35]

Sources and Types of Fabrics

Fabric orders in the *Libro di conti* were placed through December 12 for the costumes of individually named actors; these materials continued arriving through February 1589. The accounts yield extensive information about the materials used in the costumes and props: quantities, costs, and something of the geography and economics of supply. The amount of all fabrics ordered for the intermedi and *Pellegrina* costumes is staggering. Roughly 12,300 braccia (7,800 yards) were received; subtracting leftover amounts reconsigned to the Guardaroba, material actually consumed was close to 8,300 braccia (5,300 yards). Dividing this figure by some 300 costumes (including those for *Pellegrina*) yields a rough average of 18 yards per costume, which includes shoes and headdresses. Major characters' outfits required much more: Drusilla in *Pellegrina*, for example, accounts for 69½ braccia of material (LC N397–99), and for the sirens the total is about 58. Less important characters range upward from 10 to 13 or 17 braccia, close to the overall average.

In the sixteenth century textiles, along with many other consumer goods, were increasingly procured through the extensive and growing network of long-distance trade in cloth, metalwares, dyes, leather, and ornaments organized by patrician merchants. The intermedi and household accounts reveal fabrics imported from Lucca, Bologna, and Venice, and from Flanders and England; some of the ceremonial weapons are described as Bavarian.[36] Here again, green velvet is a revealing index, as its far-flung sources required special attention. Some, already on hand, came from the Guardaroba, the rest via Cavalieri's personal exertions. At the end of his *Libro* are a series of letters between him and members of Ferdinando's personal staff who remained in Rome, arranging for them to purchase lengths of this material for him between January and March 1589.[37]

Increased international trade notwithstanding, the lion's share of the necessary cloth was produced locally. At the end of the sixteenth century, Florence had just passed its peak after several centuries as one of the premier European centers of cloth manufacturing, producing largely wool but also silk (whose manufacture Ferdinando encouraged by planting mulberry trees) and other luxury goods. The woolen industry, which directly or indirectly employed perhaps 20,000 in a total population of about 70,000, imported its raw materials from as far away as Spain and was the engine of the city's protoindustrial economy. Its presence fostered precisely those allied trades and services useful to the nascent theater: skilled designers and tailors; subcontractors like dyers, printers, and embroiderers; and artists who, by this time, had long experience painting cloth banners and temporary decorations.[38]

Another local manufacture important to supplying the wedding production was the paper industry, then concentrated in central and north Italy (and still a Florentine specialty). Many properties and set pieces for the intermedi, like the harp held by Arion in intermedio 5, are specified as made of cardboard (*cartone*) or papier-mâché (*carta pesta*), which was then painted in gold or silver, or covered with fabric; others include masks, shoulder ornaments (*spallace*), floral rosettes, ruffs or collars (*lettughe*), and the female breastplates discussed earlier.[39]

The fabrication of many decorative materials and trimmings was "farmed out" to hundreds of subcontractors throughout the city and surrounding areas. Most of these remain mere names, but the names alone are revealing in one respect: among these contractors, the wedding and household documents list payments to a significant number of women artisans for materials and services. Recent historians of women and work have marked the Renaissance as a period in which medieval women's comparatively widespread participation in the public economy was consciously, if gradually, curtailed. There were, indeed, few women at this time in such well-documented trades as construction, but in the cloth industry women and children were extensively utilized because the lower wages they commanded could help trim costs in hard times; in the silk sector, which suffered severe contraction beginning in the late sixteenth century, women represented an exceptionally high percentage of employees by the early 1600s. Moreover, decorative needlework remained a traditionally female accomplishment among all classes, and wives, widows, and nuns were all eager to satisfy the court's ample needs in exchange for piecework income.[40]

Most of the work contracted to women for the intermedi and *La pellegrina* was in decorative crafts such as embroidery and button making; all the costume tailors named are men, although at least one woman was responsible for an important element of the celestial stage sets: payment was made to "Margherita, wife of the late footman Ottavio . . . for having sewn the canvas of the heavens." Women also did general sewing for the Guardaroba, mostly of bedding, tableware, and clothing, some of which was destined for the liveried events. Many of the orders went to women religious; the nuns at the convent of Santa Caterina, for example, were paid for making garlands of artificial flowers for the intermedi (LC Q188, May 24). Convents were the sole centers of independent female economic and cultural activity, and needlework provided a steady supplemental revenue whose relative importance needs further study. More than a dozen such institutions are listed in the payments; typical of these enterprises, another group of nuns from Fuligno were paid in February 1589 for general sewing, and again in June for embroidery relating to the state livery provided for the public wedding events.[41]

A Sample Costume

It is instructive for matters of design process, materials, casting, and technique to follow in detail the construction of one costume. Catalogue 22 (pl. 1), now identified as the Siren of the Eighth Sphere, was made early in the campaign as a test sample for the twelve nearly identical outfits for the sirens of intermedio 1. Work on it began on November 4, when Maestro Oreto received 16 braccia of fabric to make a costume "for one [character] who goes on a cloud"; "the said costume" was to "serve as a model for the first intermedio" (LC T1, Q291). After this sample was completed, Buontalenti's sketch was reproduced eleven times, probably by Boscoli or another assistant, and the attributes varied slightly to represent each of the other spheres and their symbols.

Buontalenti's drawing seems originally to have borne the roman numeral *VI* at the top; the account books assign the role of the sixth siren to Giovanni Lapi (who also played a sailor in intermedio 5). At some point in the autumn, however, more sirens were added and the costume drawings shuffled and renumbered: Lapi remained the sixth siren, but the outfit originally designed for that role was assigned to siren 9 (the number *VIIII* is written over the original *VI*), and the actual outfit eventually worn by Lapi was made from the copyist's sketch in cat. 16, which bears his name and the number *VI*. The sample costume already built with Lapi in mind, cat. 22, was reassigned to "Ceserone basso," whose problems resembling a female in this role were discussed above.[42]

Typically, the attributes of Lapi's original siren are precise and based on various literary authorities: a zodiacal bear and stars on her head, a bodice covered with feathers of sky blue to suggest the ethereal realm, and a turquoise skirt embroidered with stars (Rossi, 25). Shoes, headdress, and drape are all painted pink, and she wears a necklace of coral-colored beads. As often with these preliminary sketches, by the time the actual materials were ordered many changes had been made in the colors and additional decoration added (perhaps specified in another, lost detail drawing); the sketch instructions do not always match the fabric orders, which are more variegated in hue and texture, or the descriptions by Rossi.

The costume seems to have been completed by November 17, when a list in the *Libro* sums up all the various materials used for "costume no. 6 for Giovanni Lapi"; another listing of materials for this same costume, with minor differences, provides a few more details. Combining them permits a close estimate of the amounts and purposes of each fabric.[43] The total of materials, some 58 braccia, or 35 yards, is staggering — literally so, for the weight of this much fabric and trim would have limited the speed and complexity of movement possible for Lapi or the other actors (they did not, in fact, move very much, often remaining on their cloud platforms):

Red silk for armlets, skirt and underskirt	$11\frac{1}{3}$ br
Turquoise taffeta for lining of hanging hair-veils [*bendoni*]	$1\frac{1}{8}$
Yellow veiling [*velo*] for around armlets and lapels	8
White veiling for ruffled collars, hose, etc.	5
Striped veiling, green with gold, for belts etc.	$4\frac{1}{3}$
Rolled cloth for making bust, sleeves and sashes	$7\frac{3}{5}$
Rough canvas [*tela di quadrone*] painted with feathers, for the feathers of bust, sleeves and sashes	8
Decorative strips of cloth with tin dyeing [*stagnaiulo, stagnato,* to imitate silver] of gold and green, both wide and narrow, to trim skirt and underskirt	14
4 small masks for the front and 2 large cardboard ones to put on the shoulders	
Pink cloth for the ruffled collars	$\frac{3}{4}$

The constant concern for economy can be traced through the account records for this costume and its companion series. In October, Bardi had listed among his requirements for various costumes and props "a very large quantity of goose feathers" for 22 costumes, 13 in the first intermedio and nine in the second (MR 3r). These encompassed Harmony and the twelve sirens in 1 and the nine muses in 2, for both of which groups bird motifs would suggest something of their airy, celestial character; in fact Rossi makes the connection between feathered muses and the sirens explicit (p. 41). The muse designs are problematic (see cat. 29), but the sketch for Lapi's siren modello bears the inscription on the finely textured bodice and sleeves, "of feathers, as shown" (*come si vede di penna*), and the *Libro di conti* describes the sirens' outfits as having "little wings" (*aliette*, Q291). But real feathers were very expensive, and in fact already by October 5, 53 braccia of cloth had been consigned to Francesco Gorini to have them painted with feather designs for 14 costumes of the first intermedio.[44] This simulation took until November 26, when the painted fabric was again recorded as received from Gorini (LC T18), but some of it must have been completed by the 17th, when it entered the calculations for Lapi's sample costume.

Ceremonial Livery

The third category of costumes was produced for the public or quasi-public events that directly involved court officials and their aristocratic guests, including Christine's entry, the Pitti festival, and the various outdoor events held in Piazza Santa Croce (including the *giuoco di calcio* on May 4, animal baiting on the 8th, and jousting on the 10th). Being more closely tied to court ceremonial, these events fell under the medieval tradition of "livery," or household uniforms: as with his foot soldiers, attendants, and palace employees, the grand duke was expected to provide clothing not only for the members of his own household but also for guests who were required to participate in wedding events, including aristocrats and their personal attendants, numbering in the hundreds. The enormous expense was amply justified in political terms, both as a conspicuous display of wealth and as a visible expression of control over the participants, whose physical appearance would be set by court designers: Gualterotti (1:14) exults over a group of women in Genoa who greeted Christine in dresses so uniform that "everything seemed made by the same hand and by the same will."

As noted earlier, the conventions of this mode of costume combined references to actual military uniforms — classical, knightly, and contemporary — with a heightened splendor of material and decoration. Although no sketches for these outfits survive, some general idea of their appearance can be gained from images of the *calcio*, the tournament, and the Pitti evening, supplemented by account books and *descrizioni* (see cat. 69–88).[45]

Production of liveries fell directly under the Guardaroba, supervised by Benedetto Fedini as *guardaroba maggiore* and Enea Vaini, the grand duke's majordomo. Cavalieri was in continuous contact with them over costumes related to events he was supervising, from the Pitti joust to the musicians on board Christine's galley; a letter to Fedini notes that the grand duke had left such matters to their joint discretion. The Guardaroba had a broad scope, and it is difficult to separate wedding production proper from the simultaneous accounts for everyday household uniforms (for slaves, coachmen, cooks) and military outfits, domestic equipment (saddles, linens, tableware), and the personal wardrobe for Ferdinand and his family and their retainers. Further complicating the abundant records, some items in all categories were bought ready-made from merchants and artisans, whereas others were sewn "in-house" with purchased raw materials. Nevertheless, a few general observations can be made concerning the design, supply, and execution of the wedding liveries.[46]

These costumes were designed by artists on the court payroll and made by an assemblage of court tailors and outside contractors largely separate from the Uffizi theatrical staff, though with some overlap. (As we have seen, Seri-acopi's crew prepared some of the Pitti costumes, which fell under this category of martial events; others were ordered from Milan.)[47] Those artists who are named in direct connection to the wedding livery were also designing and executing various other projects simultaneously, indicating how inextricable the production of the festival was from the whole range of officially supported cultural manufactures. The most prominent designer, who acted as a kind of senior artistic advisor for the household, was the painter Alessandro Allori (1535–1607), often identified in the accounts as Bronzino, after the earlier court artist who had adopted him as a pupil and a son; he also contributed paintings to the entry arches and the galley decorations. Allori's collaborator Giovanmaria Butteri (ca. 1540–1606), another pupil of Bronzino active on the street and ship décors, was paid during this same period for designing patterns to be embroidered on altar textiles by the nuns at Santa Felicità.[48]

Some half-dozen household tailors can be identified, from Ferdinando's personal tailor, Andrea del Marinaro, to Ghottardo and Matteo tedesco ("German"), Domenico spagnuolo (Spanish fashions being prevalent in much of Italy), and Maestro Domenico, "tailor for the princesses"; Giovanni Balbi and Marchino made costumes for the May 8 animal hunt. In addition to his work for the intermedi and *La pellegrina*, Maestro Oreto worked regularly for the Guardaroba; he constructed personal outfits for the grand duke, the uniforms for the staff of the galley that sailed to bring Christine to Italy, and masquerade outfits for the young pages of Don Pietro de' Medici and for Cesare d'Este of Ferrara, Ferdinando's brother-in-law, on designs by Allori (which included more of the frugal "cloth feathers" used in the intermedi).[49]

Although Marchino was paid for 11 of the animal-hunt costumes for May 8 (out of 15 principal knights), as with the Pitti parade chariots a few of the noble participants, such as the Marchese of Cetona (captain of the guard), had their costumes designed and built by their own personal tailors. The Duke of Mantua, along with several other participants in the animal-baiting, was dressed in a jacket of green velvet with gold trim — another indication of the association of that fabric and color with noble dress, perhaps more specifically with the hunt. For his companions, Balbi made 29 liveries in green challis (wool) from Pisa; other outfits were of green silk.[50] These same tailors produced the hundreds of livery outfits needed to dress participants, pages, and eight of Franciosino's musicians for Christine's greeting in Livorno, her progress through Tuscany, and her Florentine entry (though some of these may have been refurbished existing outfits conserved by the Guardaroba).[51]

The material supply and labor network for the Guardaroba covered the entire Tuscan region and encompassed the humble, the bourgeois, and the noble, from "Mona Brigida the widow at San Niccolò," who was sent gold thread to decorate two coats, to the family's favorite haberdasher (*merciaio*), Alessandro Chelini, who was paid 12,272 ducats (half the cost of the entire intermedi) in December 1589 for various clothing and accessories supplied since the previous January. It included many more women than are noted for the Uffizi theatricals, including members of some dozen convents, who sewed and embroidered, as well as piecework employees, usually identified as wives or daughters of artisans, who worked on livery, everyday clothing, and household linens. A few women, called *rivenditori* (resellers), acted as cloth merchants, perhaps for used goods.[52]

Far more significant, both numerically and socially, were the cloth purchases made from the numerous wealthy families who still maintained their traditional activities in the fabric industry. The list of patrician suppliers, each due between 250 and 750 ducats for the year 1589, is a veritable who's who of patrician names: Strozzi, Guicciardini, Salviati, Rinuccini, and many more.[53] These commercial dealings illuminate the full range of motivations behind such acts of wedding patronage as the float for the Pitti parade provided by the Guicciardini (cat. 76) or the endowment by the Medici's cousins the Salviati family of the new mortuary chapel for Saint Antoninus, which Christine visited at San Marco. In part, these ritual exchanges still functioned in what anthropologists term a "gift economy," a reciprocal web of obligations expressing support for the Medici as their feudal superiors. At the same time, the strong economic links between the elite families constituted the emerging "market economy," in which such gestures also served to cement good relations with a cash customer.

STAGE SETS AND REHEARSALS

While all this activity relating to costumes and livery was getting under way, other aspects of the wedding preparations continued, and formal structures were set up to oversee the projected activities for the remaining six months. The stage designs and equipment plans had already been set for several months, and construction at the Uffizi theater, both of the auditorium itself and the sets and props, proceeded at an increasing pace, followed after November 22 by work at the Pitti, also supervised by Seriacopi (see Chapters 3, 4). Plans were roughed out for a temporary bridge to connect the theater with the Palazzo Vecchio for the banquet following the premier, and for decorations in the great Salone dei Cinquecento of the palazzo, which was being remodeled and extended throughout 1588–89. And some time in December, Ferdinando appointed a committee to oversee all wedding preparations and hospitality for foreign guests, including his treasurer Cambi, Vaini, Orazio Rucellai (his *maggiordomo maggiore*), the Marchese di Cetona, and about ten other gentlemen.[54]

Seriacopi's notes for November and December deal primarily with procurement of supplies and skilled labor. On November 12 the painters ordered materials; on the 22nd, orders were placed for fabric and lumber for the Pitti naumachia and joust; in December, Seriacopi outlined staffing plans for the artists who were soon to work on the arches for Christine's entry, contracted for Pitti carpenters, and listed provisional crews of stagehands. On December 11 the principal scene painter, Francesco Rosselli, ordered a scaffolding to be erected on the Uffizi stage so he could work on "the garden," probably some element of the wooded grotto for intermedio 2. A few weeks later, the cast was sufficiently fixed to permit initial rehearsals; the stage must have been a beehive of overlapping activities by Christmas day, when mounting time pressure resulted in Cavalieri's ordering the carpenters and scene painters to vacate the theater during his rehearsals — they shifted to the Palazzo Vecchio — then return to work late at night by candlelight. Bardi, as usual, exercised tight control, ordering on December 10 that "no intermedi should ever be rehearsed unless His Lordship [Bardi] is there, and unless he orders it himself, since he wants everything to be up to his standards [*passino per suo segno*]."[55]

Apparently the stepped-up pace and overtime beginning to wear on the workers. On December 21, a fire broke out in the theater — a constant fear, against which Buontalenti had earlier ordered buckets of water kept onstage — and the matter was serious enough that the next day Seriacopi wrote directly to the grand duke to report what had happened and to justify his own rather severe reprisals. His letter says he narrowly averted a conflagration after two workers had carelessly left a candle on some wood (doubtless during one of the night sessions decreed by Cavalieri), and it had burned down and begun to set fire to the planks. Seriacopi sent both of them to the Bargello (police headquarters), not only because of their dangerous negligence but also to set an example to others and encourage greater watchfulness. If he was wrong to lock them up, he writes, "I ask forgiveness," but he insists rather sententiously that he did so to impress upon them "the gravity of their acts and the interests of my position; and that if such dangers are anticipated, no one gets punished; and that there's no cure once an accident has happened."[56]

Even as the theatrical preparations in the center of Florence were reaching this already advanced phase, other components of the total festival welcome, spread over the whole Tuscan landscape, were beginning to intensify. On December 22, nuns were sewing shirts at San Clemente; on the 23rd, eight embroidered wool shirts were delivered to Franciosino's musicians. During

the fire and rehearsals of Christmas week, Seriacopi had to write to Ferdinando because the grand duke was in Pisa, where the court traditionally spent
the holiday. Four days after the Uffizi fire, on Christmas day, a letter was
written from Livorno by one Alfonso to Fedini, listing supplies required to
staff and decorate the galleys of the granducal fleet that would be departing
from the giant Tuscan port in late winter to meet Christine in Marseilles. The
request for furnishings and linens, as well as for gold and damask cloth to be
draped over the stern of the newly built flagship, referred to as *La Capitana*,
indicates that artistic and practical planning for this triumphal journey was
already advanced.[57]

The day following Christmas, St. Stephen's Day, Ferdinando ceremonially
took the habit of the seafaring knights of Santo Stefano, of which as grand
duke he was now patron; on the same day, in Florence, the Guardaroba
responded to one of Alfonso's requests by consigning 367 braccia of rose-pink
damask to Alessandro Chelini to be sewn into pennants, door curtains, and
swaggings for the Capitana. On November 30, Ferdinando had performed
the public ritual of officially laying aside his cardinal's robes, and buckling on a
temporal sword; this phallic regalia nicely symbolized his release from clerical
celibacy, more specifically his availability for the impending marriage. December's Santo Stefano ceremony again declared through a new costume his
change of status, from prince of the church to prince of a well-coordinated
economic and technical realm, with a naval force prepared to assert its interests throughout the Mediterranean — whether by repelling infidel pirates or
escorting homeward a new grand duchess. The broader stage for the wedding
was set, and Ferdinando was already acting out the prologue of his *theatrum
mundi*.[58]

CHAPTER THREE

January & February 1589

THE THEATER, THE SCENERY,

THE ARTISTS

Throughout the course of an unusually long and harsh winter — from the busy Christmas week until early March of 1589 — preparations for the wedding, now steadily under way, continued to expand in scope and intensity. At the Uffizi, the daily number of pages in Seriacopi's logbook increased from early February onward; beyond this epicenter of costume, set, and rehearsal work, activity extended outward in concentric rings. Throughout the city and its satellite towns, agents were searching for lumber, ships, and other materials. Farther out in the countryside, the family villas were being decorated to receive the bride and accommodate wedding guests. And at the gateway to the Tuscan region, the port at Livorno, provisioning and decorating the fleet went on steadily from December on; many of the furnishings were made in Florence, then transported to the coastal city, where naval overseers installed them.

At its outermost edges, this sociocultural sphere increasingly intersected with the neighboring cultural orbit of Christine's homeland. Curiously, Seriacopi's logbook is blank for the entire month of January, though it is clear when his notes resume on February 4 that work had been progressing during that time. This dated entry uniquely specifies "in Firenze," implying that the quartermaster had been out of town; perhaps his attention was partially commandeered for several weeks by an unforeseen development in France that momentarily interfered with the wedding plans. On January 5, the 70-year-old Catherine de' Medici died, and news of her passing reached her native city on the 17th. Preparation for her obsequies, which took place in the family church of San Lorenzo on February 6, must have demanded a considerable diversion of artists and resources. Following established tradition, such a state funeral required on short notice scores of livery and mourning costumes, elaborate temporary decorations at the family palace and the church, and a canopied catafalque.[1] Once the initial mourning period ended and the proxy wedding could take place on February 20, the bride began her journey south to meet Ferdinando's fleet at Marseilles, each leg of the journey propelling her farther toward the periphery of her French birthplace and simultaneously drawing her closer to the focal center of her future domain.

Ceremonially and administratively, that center was the interconnected aggregation of buildings that stretched like an irregular dumbbell through the center of Florence: from the family residence, the Pitti Palace, across the Arno River via the elevated and enclosed corridor built by Vasari, to the Uffizi and the Palazzo Vecchio (fig. 5). Begun long before the wedding preparations but rushed to completion along with them, this developing megastructure was enlarged or rebuilt in overlapping campaigns aimed at increasing security, efficiency, and royal mystique. At the Pitti, Buontalenti was still overseeing installation of the grotto, waterworks, and garden statuary. At the Uffizi, in addition to remodeling the theater, work was progressing on the gallery, the semipublic display space for Medici artistic treasures, including Buontalenti's octagonal Tribune. Major additions and renovations at the Palazzo Vecchio occupied the whole of 1588 and 1589, during which Buontalenti doubled the size of the ancient town hall to improve facilities for the granducal government. In order to permit guests at the intermedi premiere in the Uffizi to pass directly to the ensuing banquet in the palazzo's great hall, an aerial bridge was thrown over the street separating the two buildings; this structure forged the final link in a continuous chain of interior spaces first conceived by Duke Cosimo as a unified setting for the state apparatus.[2]

As Richard Goldthwaite has observed, the Medici's manifold building projects did not produce the kind of wholesale urban alteration carried out more ruthlessly by other princes of the time (the Savoy rulers in Turin, Sixtus V in Rome). Nevertheless, their works not only embellished many streets and squares with a new scale of enterprise, they also stamped upon the city's face a physical reminder of the dynasty's authority: "Architecture became a means of communicating the new [power] arrangements to the city."[3] The temporary street architecture of the entry, which served a parallel purpose, compensated for its impermanence by the greater decorative complexity affordable in ephemeral plaster and paint.

A similar urge for controlled display motivated the integration into the palace complex of two buildings less directly related to government function: a church and a theater. The Baldracca Theater, situated directly behind the Uffizi to the east, was active from 1576. Extensively restructured by Buontalenti in 1588, it was designed to be Italy's first public — that is, commercial — theater; *commedia dell'arte* troupes such as the Andreini's usually performed here. It was less ornate than the court theater next door, as befitted its lower social status; its entrance street was a somewhat risqué milieu of inns and

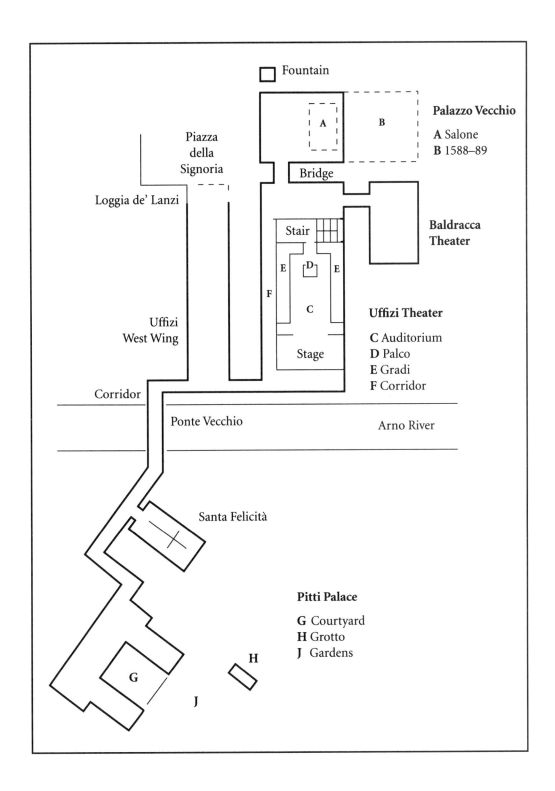

Fountain

Palazzo Vecchio

A Salone
B 1588–89

A

B

Piazza
della
Signoria

Bridge

Loggia de' Lanzi

**Baldracca
Theater**

Stair

E D E

F

C

Uffizi
West Wing

Stage

Uffizi Theater

C Auditorium
D Palco
E Gradi
F Corridor

Corridor

Ponte Vecchio

Arno River

Santa Felicità

Pitti Palace

G Courtyard
H Grotto
J Gardens

H

G

J

5. *Central Florence, Medici palace complex.*

brothels, popularly associated with theater professionals. The building was owned by the customs authorities, and it has been suggested that the theater was located there, and linked to the Uffizi, to preserve public control over its activities. The grand duke had Buontalenti install a private balcony, concealed by a grille, which could be reached by another bridge from the Uffizi. Like a similar balcony opening from Vasari's corridor onto the Pitti parish church of Santa Felicità, this space allowed the rulers to attend a public event while retaining, for reasons of both security and protocol, the distance from their subjects necessary to preserve a sacral aura of aloof mystery.[4]

ACTIVITIES IN THE THEATER

As we have seen, already in November and December activities at the Uffizi theater related to architecture, stage construction, sets, and technical equipment (machinery and lighting) had been proceeding simultaneously with costume work, casting, and the first rehearsals. Indeed, the large-scale reconceptualization of the theater interior was the prerequisite for any further work on the intermedi and *La pellegrina* innovations; this reconstruction was well along by August 31, 1588, when the opening page of Seriacopi's logbook records Buontalenti's instructions for installing completed statues in niches along the theater walls.[5]

The Auditorium

The interior of the Uffizi theater was of a different formal type from that of the Baldracca. Specifically theatrical settings and structures began to be constructed only in the late fifteenth century and underwent a variety of experiments at the hands of such influential designers as Serlio, Peruzzi, and Vasari. At first, most were temporary additions or modifications to existing buildings, like banqueting or meeting halls or outdoor loggias; the occasional custombuilt interiors were subsequently destroyed. By the 1580s, a clear typology of three modes of fixed theater had emerged: court (the Uffizi), public-commercial (the Baldracca), and academic. Palladio's Teatro Olimpico, completed in 1584 in Vicenza, was the closest example of the private and antiquarian academic setting; it differed from the Uffizi in recreating a Roman amphitheater, with a fixed backdrop behind a playing area extending into the auditorium, where no wings or flies were possible.[6]

An imposing ceremonial space was planned and set aside within the Uffizi by Vasari as early as 1572, with a monumental access stair (still used for museum entry); although not perhaps intended at the outset as a theater, the space was roughly equal to that of the enormous Salone dei Cinquecento in the Palazzo Vecchio, where Vasari had staged the theatricals for Francesco I's wedding in 1565. In any case, Francesco soon did develop this space as a dedicated theater to provide his court with a fixed ritual setting. Buontalenti finally fitted it out for the wedding of Virginia de' Medici in 1586, as a kind of "interior garden" with no proscenium; he then remodeled his own design in 1589 into a more revolutionary prototype, the first permanent indoor theater with a proscenium arch.[7]

The long-disused theater served as the seat of the national senate during Florence's brief term as the nineteenth-century capital of united Italy but was subsequently dismantled and subdivided, leaving only faint traces of its original form or decoration.[8] There are some guides to its appearance, however: breathlessly detailed descriptions from Rossi and other chroniclers for both 1586 and 1589; a Callot engraving from a later performance of 1617, showing some changes from 1589 (fig. 6); and the precise if fragmentary notes in Seriacopi's log.[9] On the basis of these sources, numerous attempts have been made to reconstruct the theater and stage in conjectural, but probably reasonably approximate, drawings and models.[10]

Rossi gives the dimensions of the theater as length 95 braccia, width 35, height 24, or roughly 180 by 65 by 45 feet (55 by 20 by 14 meters). He also tells us that the floor slopes downward toward the stage, to allow better vision from the rear, a total drop of 2⅛ braccia (about 4 feet; the stage also sloped toward the audience). His dimensions apparently included both the floor area of the auditorium (*platea*) and the backstage area (*palcoscenico*). The latter took up 25 braccia (48 feet or 15 meters) of the overall length of the space, leaving an auditorium length of about 70 braccia (130 feet).[11]

In its 1589 incarnation, the auditorium had two long side walls, each composed of nine bays articulated by Corinthian pilasters; these framed four windows on the house left and, mirroring these on the right, interior openings leading to the upper, or gallery, level. The architectural elements were richly decorated, some gilded, others imitating stone (lapis lazuli, jasper); the walls were painted in perspective wherever they were not covered with carved figures, cartouches, and masks. The ten bays without windowed openings held statues in niches, on a program by Giovanni Battista Strozzi, representing various aspects of comedy and poetry; one by Giambologna survives in a fragmented state. The vast carved wooden ceiling, coordinated with the wall bays, was nine panels long and five wide. Each painted soffit was decorated with a large gilded rosette, and from 16 of the 45 panels hung large chandeliers, each with six sculpted figures representing the coat of arms of the bride and groom and surmounted by a crown.[12]

Seating comprised three distinct areas, differentiated by gender and rank.

PRIMO INTERMEDIO DELLA VEGLIA DELLA LIBERATIONE DI TIRRENO, FATTA NELLA SALA DELLE COM
DIE DEL SER.^mo GRAN DVCA DI TOSCANA IL CARNOVALE DEL 1616. DOVE SI RAP.^re IL MONTE D'ISCHIA CON IL GIGANTE
TIFEO SOTTO.

6. *Interior of Uffizi theater:* La liberazione di Tirreno e Arnea, *1617. Jacques Callot.*

Women sat on the *gradi*, tiered benchlike platforms arranged around three sides of the perimeter in an elongated, squared-off U shape (figs. 5, 6); men sat on chairs in the center of the floor. The granducal party occupied a slightly raised platform in the middle of that floor; here, in contrast to their condescendingly secluded position at the Baldracca, the Medici were the unabashed centerpiece of their own social and cultural circle. This general disposition set the standard for later court theaters from the Farnese at Parma (1618) to others in Venice, Rome, and Paris. The five tiers of seats were reached by narrow scroll-like stairs set into the front and side facings of their raised area, which were also painted in chiaroscuro. The gradi stayed level despite the sloping floor, starting from the rear at a height of six braccia (11 feet). A list of materials for the theater made up on November 25 includes "60 gradi for the salone" to be procured from Vieri de' Medici, "who has them in the Palazzo Medici"; these may have been prefabricated modular elements developed by Buontalenti for the first use of the hall in 1586 and then put into storage, following the precedent of Vasari's dismountable seating for 1565.[13]

At the front of the house was the most innovative and influential feature, the framed proscenium; given the consistency of architectural articulation, its opening was probably three bays wide, or 21 braccia (39 feet). Flanking the opening were two bays, each about 7 braccia (13 feet) wide, with niches containing statues of the Arno and Moselle rivers, symbolizing Tuscany and Lorraine; these bearded men, who spouted perfumed water from their hair and from the artificial shells and sponges surrounding them, must have resembled the familiar giant river-god fountain recently constructed by Giambologna at the Medici villa of Pratolino (1580–82). These side elements served to visually define the stage area and mask the complex machinery and movements of performers and crew. The stage floor was raised some 4 braccia (7 feet) above the auditorium, and the gap was bridged by a stair with a central landing.[14]

Perspective Scenery

The view from the audience into this proscenium revealed two distinct types of stage set, each representing a milestone in its tradition: the static architectural scene of *La pellegrina* and the variable, fantastic locales of the intermedi. The technical author Nicola Sabbattini codified the difference by dividing his theatrical treatise on set design and construction (1638) into two books, on fixed comedy and movable intermedi. The modes shared some goals — verisimilitude and perspective — but only the intermedi exploited technology for astounding supernatural effects.

The shared contribution of both types to illusionistic perspective — what

Rossi calls the "sweet deception" (*dolce inganno*, 33) — marked the culmination of a long, slow evolution that began with the single backdrop at Ferrara for an Ariosto play in 1508. The basic components were exterior scenes, composed symmetrically about a central axis, with depth created by a series of planar scenic units that extended back from the proscenium. The convergence of all lines of sight on a single vanishing point was derived and extended from painting, and indeed the proscenium was conceived as a picture frame, the space within which replicated in three dimensions the mathematical schema of perspectival pictorial recession codified by Alberti. The epistemological link between such a system of universally extensive and monocularly determined spatial arrangement and the political ideal of a single all-powerful sovereign was manifested architecturally by the location of the vanishing point on the same privileged central axis as the seat of the ruler, who alone could appreciate it fully.[15]

Of the three theatrical modes codified by Serlio, following Vitruvius — tragic, comic, satyric — two are represented here. The set used for *La pellegrina* and the other plays (cat. 68) — the fixed urban locale prescribed for comedy — constructed its perspective grid by canvas units that simulated architectural elements, plus various painted backdrops, further diminishing in scale, to extend the cityscape's fictive depth.[16] In the intermedi, whose pastoral settings (if not their ethical tone) drew on the satyric-woodland tradition, the parallel and receding lines were approximated by the less mathematical contours of natural forms — trees, rocks, or heavenly clouds — which also converged and diminished in scale toward the rear (fig. 7).

Although the specific play depicted in cat. 68 is unclear, the print gives a general idea of the scenery used for all three comedies. In the foreground are a series of building façades in a mix of classical orders, beginning at a height of 20 braccia (38 feet) near the proscenium, then diminishing as they recede at oblique angles toward a central point. For *La pellegrina*, the principal buildings in the foreground represented Violante's inn (where Drusilla, the female pilgrim, lodged) and the home of Cassandro, father of the distressed Lepida. Not unlike the more archeological setting at Palladio's Olimpico theater, three narrow streets radiate away from the central playing area, their linear perspectives simulated on a painted backcloth.

Opinions differ about the design and construction of the cityscape, principally over the question of how it was physically alternated with the intermedi. Broadly, two methods of set change were current at this time: rotating prisms, and sliding shutters in grooves. *Periaktoi*, a Greek term usually rendered in Italian as *telari*, were triangular or quadrilateral vertical shafts, their faces each painted with a different scene, that could be pivoted on a central axis to present successive faces to the audience, one of which could have represented Pisa.[17] On balance, their use here seems unlikely: Seriacopi's log often refers to the "houses" (*case*) of the set, implying immobile objects, and Rossi writes almost exclusively that the *Pellegrina* sets "were changed" (*si mutavano*, 34, 49) or its "houses were covered up" (*ricoperte*, 35, 37, 51, 55); Pavoni follows his language. None of Seriacopi's notes mentions periaktoi, but his log frequently refers to grooves (*canali*) in the floor, implying sliding flat panels, probably parallel to the proscenium and pushed in from the sidestage areas to overlap and conceal the fixed *Pellegrina* architecture. Such a system would require gaps between the "houses," and in fact cat. 68 shows light falling through cracks between what could be several rows of separated buildings, each an open L-shape with a deep return to block oblique views backstage (fig. 7).[18]

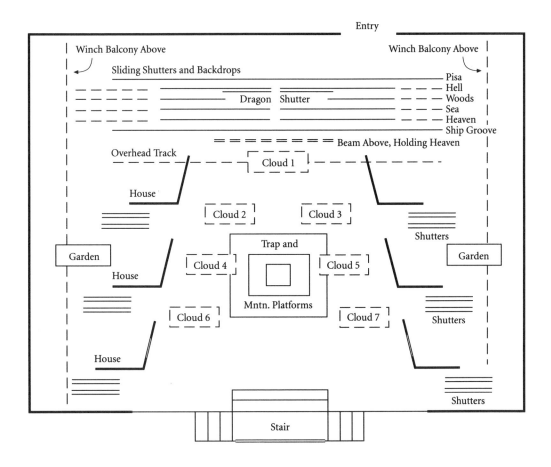

7. *Uffizi theater, schematic stage plan.*

Stage Space and Machinery

Backstage, sophisticated machinery and technical devices permitted the scene to alternate repeatedly and smoothly between the comedy buildings and a half-dozen diverse other settings, as well as facilitating the numerous special effects, from a fire-breathing dragon to a flying Apollo. Rossi places repeated emphasis on the rapidity of the scene changes, which occurred "like lightning" and left the spectators feeling "as if they were dreaming," and he remarks on their delight at seeing "lifelike" motion and actions from mechanical contrivances that "seemed to exceed human powers" (34).

Notwithstanding the ambitiousness and achievement of the occasion, much theatrical practice remained in an early, experimental phase. There were still no terms for upstage, downstage, stage right, or stage left, for example. For the hanging platform farthest downstage right, Seriacopi uses the rather clumsy (and localized) locution "the first cloud toward the rooms of the *zanni* and comedians"; *zanni* refers to commedia dell'arte players at the Baldracca, which was next door to the east. For the corresponding stage left platform he says "toward the corridor" — the hallway running along the court side of the Uffizi.[19]

Though the stage and its equipment are long lost, references in Seriacopi, stagecraft manuals, and the surviving court theater at Parma (modeled after the Uffizi theater some two decades later) permit a hypothetical reconstruction (fig. 7). The basic repertory of mechanical equipment included, above the stage, a flyloft, or grid of beams from which clouds and other aerial platforms as well as painted figures could hang or descend on ropes; on the stage floor, grooves and other devices for sliding or moving both scenic backdrops and side shutters, plus mobile set pieces; and underneath, a trapdoor in the stage floor with platforms that could rise from the ground.[20]

Prototypes for the overhead apparatus had been developed in the earlier Renaissance, both in church pageants (Brunelleschi's angels on wires) and in temporary aerial riggings at previous intermedi. Buontalenti's permanent overhead grid of wooden trusses and beams, with catwalks atop them for crew access, supported a series of winches and pulleys; their magnitude can be glimpsed in an order for the rigging placed in late October, which requisitioned 1,000 braccia of heavy ropes and 1,600 braccia of lighter ones. This apparatus accommodated fixed units in the upper zone of the stage, as well as seven rising and falling platforms disguised as clouds, and the sorceress's chariot (which traveled from side to side in the air). The front curtain was also suspended from the flyloft, though unlike modern practice it was lowered at the beginning of the performance, possibly into a trench in the floor; according to Pavoni, other curtains, really scene drops, were raised into the flyloft.

The complex potentials of the aerial grid were realized most fully in the heavenly apparitions of the first and last intermedi, in which the suspended upper backdrop of fixed clouds behind the seven movable ones split open to reveal massed heavenly choirs (probably painted) and a radiant sunburst, and later descended into twinkling starlit night.[21]

The exact placement of this elaborate machinery cannot be determined, but its general structure and the number of stagehands needed to operate it are clear from two lists of the crews for each mechanical unit; drawn up in December and again in March, they differ in details but agree on the overall system of machines and their relative sizes. Approximately a hundred names are listed, with many individuals assigned to a different crew for each successive intermedio.[22] Each of the two clouds farthest downstage (fig. 7, nos. 6, 7) required its own crew of ten to twelve men, two of whom let out the coiled ropes (*anguille*, "eels"); another single winch or capstan (*argano*) with five more men was jointly connected to both clouds. The next pair (nos. 4, 5), apparently smaller, were manipulated by a single common windlass (*verricello*) needing eleven men; each had two additional men to "fold them up" (*ripiegarsi*), suggesting that they expanded in some way. The three central clouds farthest upstage were for the most important gods and allegories, all of which "came out of the heavens" of the upper background. Of these, the two flanking clouds (nos. 2, 3) did not descend to earth and seem to have required only six men between them, while the central cloud (no. 1), for Doric Harmony and others, required twelve men plus a "windlass in the sky" — set above the grid — with six staff. Perhaps this mechanism also permitted the central cloud, when used for the sorceress of intermedio 4, to travel from side to side; that motion required four men.[23] The heavenly backdrop also opened, by means of a rising dropcloth (*tenda*), to reveal the uppermost choir of intermedio 1.

On the stage floor, each intermedio's setting was established at the sides by pairs of wood-framed canvas flats or shutters sliding in grooves, each side requiring two stagehands as "guides for the canvases." The various scene changes would have required a minimum of four pairs of shutters in front of each Pisa house: the Roman amphitheater for the prologue to intermedio 1, clouds (1 and 6), rocks (4 and 5), and trees (2 and 3). Six related backcloths were needed, all movable except for the one farthest to the rear (logically the *Pellegrina* view of Pisa, which could then stay in place throughout). As with the side wings, some scenes could reuse the same backdrop; views included Rome (prologue), clouds (1 and 6), trees (2 and 3), a burning city in hell (4), and a seascape (5).[24]

Trapdoors had been used earlier, but Buontalenti's underfloor winches and nesting platforms allowed illusions of unprecedented size to rise from the earth. The trap required six to eight men to open it, and below were several machines to lift the hamadryads' mountain of intermedio 2 and the grotesque giant Lucifer of 4, shown in Cigoli's drawing issuing from a hole in the floor (cat. 52–53). The understage being only 9 feet (5 braccia) high, the mountain had to rise in telescoping stages: a main section raised by an eight-man winch, then a nested upper section raised by two more at a smaller windlass. Two additional men were assigned understage to insert wooden struts (*puntelli*) under the raised sections "for security," indicating Buontalenti's doubts about his machinery's reliability.[25]

Other floor equipment included a wave machine for intermedio 5, a standard feature of nautical scenes, set on the floor and simulating the rhythmic rocking of the sea.[26] In addition, several intermedi made use of "practical" — free-moving — set pieces, like the two woodsy grottoes of intermedio 2 (referred to as "gardens" or "houses"), which required a crew to slide or (more probably) wheel them into place and rotate them on cue; the mobile dragon of 3 (cat. 50); and in 5, the shell of Amphitrite, the sympathetic dolphin, and Arion's great ship, all gliding between the wave segments.

The constricted stage space forced certain limitations on the placement of all this machinery. Taking the opening of the proscenium at some 39 feet, the width of the backstage space was only 13 feet on each side. Such a narrow clearance, which would hardly allow for one hundred stagehands and another hundred cast members and musicians to maneuver simultaneously on stage level, must have necessitated some complex multitiered arrangement. As noted, at least one of the winches is "in the heavens"; possibly others were positioned on balconies along the side walls (as at the Farnese Theater), and/or in the understage area, with ropes passing through slots in the floor. While the total depth of the stage area was about 47 feet, the actual playing area would have been much shallower to leave space upstage for the numerous shutters and drops, for crew behind to push them, and for a passageway across the rear of the stage for entrances and exits and hidden crossings (the only known door to the stage area was in the back wall).[27]

Lighting and Ventilation

As important as the sets and machinery was the technical and logistic feat of illuminating both the large enclosed space of the audience and the stage itself with its special effects. Although the available technology was limited to open flames in a variety of containers, theatrical lighting had grown increasingly sophisticated and lavish in tandem with the elaboration of theatrical spaces, including outdoor nocturnal settings like the Pitti courtyard. The same architects were responsible: where Vasari, in 1565, had developed colored spotlights by shining torches through glass jars filled with tinted water, Buontalenti far surpassed his master in technical experimentation, inventing such mechanical marvels as lamps that lit without visible touch. This occasion was distinguished as well by sheer quantity: the total number of lights referred to for the Uffizi and Pitti events reaches into the thousands, and they were "mass-produced" by metalsmiths and carpenters following a few basic models. Not surprisingly, given the magnitude of production, construction was under way from late August 1588, when Buontalenti ordered a lathe-worker (*torniaio*) to finish the spindles for the large standing candelabra by the following Saturday.[28]

Principal illumination of the Uffizi theater's audience area included 18 standing torchères on the front parapets of the gradi (one per architectural bay) and 16 chandeliers hanging from the ceiling, with 18 lights each. The former were composed of elaborate triangular pedestals on lion's paws supporting imposing freestanding sculptures, each consisting of a columnar stand topped by numerous candle holders and ornamented with carved garlands, masks, artificial fruit, and pedestaled vases. These components were ready to attach to the lathed posts by October 4; later, swags of cloth of gold were attached, and the whole assembly was painted in imitation of gold, enamel, and stone. The ceiling lamps were equally complex, each comprising the coats of arms of the newlyweds above six scrolled metal brackets, on which sat putti and heraldic birds that supported the armorial balls (*palle*) of the Medici; in the center was a jeweled and gilded crown. In mid-February, additional lamps were hung along the walls, between the windows.[29]

Within the stage area, hundreds of more utilitarian lamps, each holding two or four lights, were positioned at the sides and front of the stage platform for general lighting, and more were concealed behind the scenery and in the flyloft to simulate heavenly radiance.[30] Footlights were hidden behind the balusters of the stair landing, midway between stage and house floor. Another set of lights was attached to the rear of the houses of *La pellegrina*, each lighting the architectural unit next upstage; these could be swiveled to cast light on the sliding flats of the intermedi as those were pushed farther onstage. Rossi particularly praises the profusion of lamps shining through holes in the painted sky (which could be opened and closed by movable shutters) to suggest the starry firmament of intermedi 1 and 6, producing throughout the stage area "such a unified light, that it seemed like that of the sun at midday."[31]

Although most of the lamps are described as candlesticks (*candelliere*), others are called torch holders (*torciere*) or "little ovens" (*fornoli*, enclosed tin lanterns). Plain candles were supplemented by more powerful oil lamps and chemical torches (more suitable for outdoor use at the Pitti), and some at the

Uffizi were surrounded by metal boxes or cylinders to permit adjustable light levels. The list of supplies drawn up for the Pitti on November 22 includes 30 barrels of oil "for the joust and for the comedy," and large quantities of cotton wool for wicks. For the candelabra, the list specifies about 1,100 pounds (1,400 Florentine *libbra*) of ordinary candles and 400 pounds of spiral ones (*candele di seno*) for each performance of the intermedi and comedy. Seriacopi, immediately aware of the enormity of this order, wrote to the grand duke's treasurer, Napoleone Cambi, on November 26 to suggest that the candles be manufactured in Arezzo to specifications by Buontalenti. Two days later, in a characteristic attempt at thrift, Seriacopi noted that "some old lamps from the previous comedy" (perhaps 1586) were being refurbished "to be put in the corners of the courtyard" of the Pitti.[32]

Rossi notes the manifold problems associated with candles and torchlight for which Buontalenti had to find solutions: smell, smoke, heat, and ventilation (and, as seen earlier, fire). These problems were compounded by the device of making the chimneys of the Pisa set seem to puff realistically, using incense that perfumed the auditorium "like Arabia itself." To enhance ventilation of the hall, holes were carved in the ceiling, concealed by bosses (*rosoni*) suspended below them, and provision was made to leave the windows open during performance, camouflaged by trellises of artificial foliage to block intruding light from outside. Backstage, the "starlight" perforations in the heaven dropcloths served the second purpose of releasing accumulated smoke from the stage below.[33]

ARTISTS AND CRAFTWORKERS

All of this elaborate equipment required a large complement of both designers and executants; hundreds of artists and craftworkers were deployed in a hierarchy with overlapping assignments. There was only minor duplication between the entry staff and the theatrical équipe, but the crews for the Pitti Palace were substantially the same as those for the Uffizi, assigned alternately under the same administrative apparatus. There was also much shuttling back and forth to the opposite ends of the corridor by Buontalenti, Cavalieri, and their factotums; on one occasion, Seriacopi wrote to Ferdinando that he needed to resolve some matters regarding the Pitti tournament with Cavalieri, "with whom I'll be tomorrow."[34]

For the Uffizi and Pitti, as well as at the Palazzo Vecchio, Buontalenti was the overall supervisor of both architectural design and applied décors. Creative authority then descended to his principal associates, who fleshed out his conceptions in more detailed drawings to be realized by the numerous professional painters and sculptors. Straddling the border between artists and crafts-men, a lower level of what we might call today "scenic artists" may have had some discretion for elements of this work but were basically carrying out the conceptions of these superiors; the two mentioned most often are Francesco Rosselli and Lorenzo Francini (Rossi, 8).

Below those of artist status were the craft employees: the masons, carpenters, metalworkers, and lampmakers who built the machinery, lights, and set pieces. Drawn from the same class were the stage crew, supervised by Alfonso Parigi, and various workers involved in the maintenance of the physical plant, who reported to Seriacopi. All of these groups worked together and simultaneously, though their economic and social organization varied considerably across a complex spectrum from independent contractors to state employees, with varying combinations of salaries, hourly wages, and reimbursement for materials. This section will concentrate on the artists; the activities and conditions of the craftworkers are treated more fully in Chapter 4.

Three generations of Florentine painters and sculptors intersected here, encompassing those whose stylistic roots were in high and late Mannerism as well as the first stirrings of the more naturalistic reform movement of the Cinquecento's closing decades. Most of the first generation of Mannerist court artists (born ca. 1500–10), who had developed and codified the Medici court style under Cosimo and Francesco — Bronzino, Vasari, Cellini — had died in the previous decade. One "old-timer" still active in 1589 seems to have enjoyed the status of a senior advisor: the sculptor-architect Bartolommeo Ammannati (1511–92), who had added the wings that defined the great court-yard of the Pitti Palace where the naumachia was to take place, was still on the grand duke's household payroll in September 1588, and he was consulted, along with Valerio Cioli and Giambologna, to estimate the value of sculptural work completed at the Medici Theater in December.[35]

The second generation, those born ca. 1525–35, were the dominant figures in prestige, if no longer in numbers. Many of them, like Buontalenti himself, had trained under Vasari and Bronzino, playing important roles in the earlier wedding of 1565. Others included the two sculptors chosen along with Ammannati to evaluate finished work: Valerio Cioli (1529–99), whose marbles adorn the Boboli Gardens (for his entry work, see cat. 6), and Giovanni Bologna (1529?–1608), whose colossal statue for the interior of the theater survives, though not his figures for the second entry arch (cat. 2). Like many of the wedding artists, Giambologna — who had recently adorned the Medici villa at Pratolino with a colossal fountain sculpture fitted with grotto machinery by Buontalenti — was simultaneously active at other sites, both those peripherally related to the festival and additional public and ecclesiastical projects, including the Palazzo Vecchio and the equestrian monument to Cosimo I for the adjacent Piazza della Signoria.[36]

The principal painters of this second generation included Alessandro Allori (1535–1607) and Santi di Tito (1536–1603). Allori, the pupil and adopted son of Bronzino, cut his festival teeth on the funeral of Michelangelo in 1564 and the wedding of Francesco the following year. With the deaths of Bronzino (1572) and Vasari (1574), he became the senior painter in the city. Although his direct contribution to the 1589 wedding was limited to the design for the entry arch at Porta al Prato (cat. 1), his larger role was administrative. As overseer for the granducal workshops at the Uffizi gallery, he was charged with evaluating commissioned work, such as Cigoli's painting for the Prato arch.[37] His contemporary and fellow Bronzino student Santi also worked only on the entry (cat. 3), but both artists indirectly shaped the entire event as the teachers of many third-generation painters, among them Cigoli, Boscoli, Ciampelli, and Pagani.[38]

Alfonso Parigi the Elder (ca. 1535–90) was less a designer than a technician and foreman of architectural projects. First referred to as a mason (*muratore*), later as a "practical architect" (*pratico architetto*), he rose through experience from craft employee to administrator. After the death of Vasari, he managed the construction site (*fabbrica*) at the Uffizi from 1575–80; during the wedding preparations he held several important jobs concurrently as Buontalenti's technical assistant. He oversaw the construction and decoration at the Palazzo Vecchio; in the theater log Seriacopi refers to him as one of the "principal officers [*caporali*] in charge of everything," mainly recruiting and supervising the stagehands and backstage staff; and he helped with the Pitti tournament. Typical of Florentine artisans, his skills were a family tradition: Ammannati was his maternal uncle, and his son Giulio Parigi (1571–1635), who in 1589 worked for him as a young apprentice, became an architect and Buontalenti's eventual successor.[39]

The largest cohort of wedding artists was from a third generation, most born between 1550 and 1560; many were touched at some point in their careers by the anti-Mannerist, naturalistic and classicizing impulses of the late century, particularly through the example of Santi. Though the majority — including Cavalori, Poppi, and the sculptor Giovanni Bandini — were involved solely with the entry arches (see Introduction and cat. 1–7), a few also played a wider role: Jacopo Ligozzi (1547–1627), for example, also received a permanent salary as superintendent of the Uffizi gallery and its associated painting workshop, as well as for designing for luxury crafts such as decorative stone inlay-work (*pietra dura*), tapestry, and glass.[40]

Among members of this generation who figure prominently in the theatri-

cal documents, Andrea Boscoli (ca. 1560–1607) was Buontalenti's main artistic assistant (cat. 9, 32, 51, 54, 73) and also worked on the entry (cat. 3). A pupil
of Santi, he collaborated on the cupola frescoes of the Florence Duomo, but is
best known as a draftsman; many of his works were engraved, and he served as
the intermediary between Buontalenti's original designs and the engravers of
the commemorative books.[41] Ludovico Cardi, known as Cigoli (1559–1613),
was also an important figure on Buontalenti's team and contributed as well to
other projects related to the wedding, from the duomo to frescoes at the Villa
Petraia. His skills straddled genres: he first studied painting with Allori and
Santi, becoming one of the leading naturalists, and was subsequently trained
as an architect by Buontalenti, for whom he conceived, in Baldinucci's account, "an extraordinary friendship" (he was also a close friend of Galileo).
Although he operated in part independently, he had a special niche in Buontalenti's shop because he was a painter, whereas most of that staff specialized in
scenography or architectural decoration. His extremely emotional, sometimes gruesome style made him a suitable choice to detail the grotesque
Lucifer of intermedio 4; as noted, he also painted on the arch at Porta al Prato
(cat. 1, 53).[42]

The overlapping of three generations of men connected by ties of family as
well as by continuous local tradition ensured a considerable consistency of
style, technique, and iconography. Scholarship has tended to dismiss these
later sixteenth-century Florentines as derivative, dry, and formulaic; these
charges are not without validity, though hard to assess fairly for the wedding
itself, for which almost the only visual evidence is the often crude engravings.
In their defense, it should be noted that the reliance by these artists upon
standardization and canonical poses was a necessary practical virtue in the
milieu of state production. As seen with the interruption due to Catherine's
funeral, their most prominent and steady patron, the court, required frequent
projects of vast scope, often on short notice, with a consistent program of
conventionalized iconography that was enthusiastically (even pedantically)
supervised by professional academicians like Borghini, Bardi, and Gaddi.

Their reliance on revered models and convention also had a theoretical
basis: the codification of art-historical precedents was part of the attempt to
elevate the professional status of artists. Previously ranked as members of a
mechanical craft, they now aspired to the category of liberal arts, the criteria
for which demanded intellectual content — recall Rossi's praise of Buontalenti
as a "questing mind" (*pellegrino ingegno*) — that could be transmitted as a
coherent body of learned and venerable rules. With its emphasis on organized
teaching and literary content, the Florentine Academy of Design, founded by
Vasari and others in 1563, constituted a polemical alternative to artists' tradi-

tional corporate structure, the craft guild. Many wedding artists were members of this academy, among them Cigoli, Boscoli, Ligozzi, and Cosci; Niccolò Gaddi was an officer, by virtue of his excellence in the higher-ranked verbal skills (knowledge of Latin, symbolism, history) needed to invent the literary program for the entry.[43]

This period was also witnessing a parallel transition in the socioeconomic organization of artistic production. In earlier times, production was based on the craft model: the independent, often family-based workshop (*bottega*) performed all work on commission for an agreed total price, sometimes including payment for special materials. State production was more centralized, specialized, and bureaucratized, with the principal artists and artisans paid fixed monthly wages — under varying conditions, but usually with the understanding that the Fabbrica provided the materials, the employee only his or her labor and tools. In practice it is hard to draw a precise line between the two overlapping systems: although some artists were salaried and others still supervised their own workshops, most of the wedding artists did both, in varying proportions and degrees of independence.[44]

Allori provides a typical example: he received a salary as supervisor of the Uffizi workshops but by February 1589 was also receiving a separate state payment of 35 ducats per week. This amount, six to ten times the average individual wage, indicates that he was simultaneously a subcontractor, responsible for his private crew of employees (a similar mixed mode characterized the tailors). The 35 ducats are expressly intended for various members of his own workshop (including his associate Butteri and his son, Cristofano Allori), who are named in the account books for such work as the galley decorations, and are also "lent" to the Pitti to gild the grand duke's furniture. Allori's situation was a delicate one, for as supervisor at the Uffizi he was himself responsible for fixing the price that Benedetto Fedini was to pay to Allori's own partner Butteri.[45]

Giambologna presents an even more complicated case of interlocking patronage. As we have seen, he was salaried for his state work, but at the same time, he maintained a workshop (apparently in the Palazzo Vecchio) to assist him on such large projects as the equestrian statue of Cosimo I — payment for which came through the Fabbrica, not the Seriacopi administration, and (as with Allori) included amounts designated for Giambologna to pay his own subordinates. As an independent entrepreneur, he was simultaneously putting the finishing touches on the Salviati Chapel in San Marco, constructed 1579–88 — the receptacle for the relics of Saint Antoninus that was to be ceremonially dedicated during the wedding celebrations on May 9, in the presence of the new grand duchess, and which was paid for by the Medici cousins mentioned earlier as suppliers of cloth for the theatricals. In order to accept the Salviati commission, Giambologna had to be released part-time from his extensive duties for Grand Duke Francesco and his wife, "with Their Highnesses' consent."[46]

THE FEBRUARY "PUNCH LIST"

The construction of stage sets, props, and lighting for the Uffizi went on simultaneously with the Pitti and Santa Croce preparations, though each of these individual projects was subject to frequent technical delays and troublesome labor disputes. We can follow the progress of the whole series of endeavors by looking at the "punch list" prepared in the second half of February. This "list of jobs that remain to be done for the carpenters' job contract [*cottimo*] for the comedy" was drawn up by Buontalenti at the request of Seriacopi.[47] As a means of taking stock of progress and planning the next stage of work, the Uffizi-Pitti administrators made up roughly one such list a month: Francesco Gorini had written an earlier one in December (MR 14v–15r), then another was dictated by Bardi on March 11, and a final one on April 9. Each provides a cross-section of the multiple activities under way at a specific moment, as well as useful clues to working methods, accounting procedures, the organization and coordination of labor, and labor-management relations; they also expose an ongoing squabble between Buontalenti and Seriacopi that reveals much about each man's personality and management style.

The punch list, though dated February 13, is inserted in Seriacopi's log at the date of March 2, with a note labeling it as a "copy of a list given to Messer Girolamo Provveditore by Messer Bernardo this day." The February date indicates when Buontalenti began to compile the list, but according to Seriacopi, who had asked for it some days before then, Buontalenti was tardy and incomplete. Seriacopi's nagging reminders, complaints, and rejection of an early draft led to such ill feeling between the two that on March 2, the same day he finally accepted the finished list, Seriacopi wrote to Ferdinando to justify his view of the dispute, which he feared might have been reported to Ferdinando one-sidedly.

His letter explains that he had asked Buontalenti for the promised list three weeks earlier but that Buontalenti had barely begun compiling it, so Seriacopi had handed the paper back to him with a sharp reproof for its "not being even a quarter [of the necessary items] and not being done the right way." Buontalenti was offended and had apparently said so on several occasions; fearing that "Bernardo may have brought this up with S.A.S., being something of a confidant of yours," the quartermaster insists that "if anything I said is found to be other than the truth, let me be doubly and severely punished." His legalistic insistence on "justice" and threats of punishment shows that he is willing to bear himself the same kind of strict reprisal for wrongdoing that he had earlier meted out to the hapless carpenters who almost burned down the theater.

A final note on unrelated matters unwittingly reveals more of Seriacopi's combativeness and stubborn pride, suggesting that Buontalenti, though far from blameless, was reacting to more than customary abuse: one Don Cesare had also disagreed with Seriacopi concerning some arrangements at one of the fortresses under his administration, and "I told him in return how things looked to me, so that at least he would realize he wasn't dealing with ghosts [*ombre*]." When Cesare attempted to justify his own position, "I demolished him with sharp thinking, in such a way that I don't think he'll speak so freely any more, having been beaten back by convincing arguments."[48]

As finally compiled, the list reveals numerous instructive details about the auditorium, stage, sets, props, and rehearsals. In the house, the walls were being covered with rose-pink hangings, which needed to be adjusted so that they could drop to reveal the wall décor behind and "be hidden under the gradi," which must therefore have stood slightly forward of the actual walls. It was also time, Buontalenti notes, to begin constructing the raised platform in the center of the hall for the granducal family, to be surrounded by a balustrade; and he ordered "many benches with backs" for the men's seating on the main floor. Several notices about the *Pellegrina* set, which was by this time basically in place, include requests to attach lamps to "the houses of the stage set" and to "make doors in the two first [downstage] houses so the actors can enter and exit" (MR 25v). Both specifications are consistent with flat, fixed sidewings and not with impermeable periaktoi.

Some glimpses of the basic stage machinery and lighting are also given. Buontalenti commands, for example: "Make the slots [*canali*] on the stage where painted [*dintornate*] figures and the ship have to move" in intermedio 5. The large ship wheeled about in the foreground, but there must have been an upstage groove in the floor for sliding distant cardboard ships, which would increase perspective depth by their relatively tiny scale (MR 26r, Mar. 9; Warburg, 401). Further, he directs the crew to "make [holes in] the clouds of the heaven . . . to draw off the smoke" and to trim the edges of the openings. Such holes were also required for the hidden lights and the flyropes; Rossi's claim that the movable cloud platforms rose and fell with no visible support (49–50, 62) is explained (with some allowance for enthusiasm) by Buontalenti's note to "touch up the first two [downstage] clouds with cloth and felt to cover the ropes." He also calls for construction of "balusters and small pilasters on the parapet [*risalto*] of the stage, to put lights behind" for footlighting.

As to the individual intermedi, there is no mention of number 2, apparently more or less finished by this time; and for the heaven set of intermedi 1 and 6, only such refinements were ordered as adding the stars in the sky and adjusting the size of the clouds. Intermedio 3, however, was late getting started: Buontalenti repeats an earlier call for construction of the wooden framework (*ossatura*) for the dragon, and of separate pieces made of papier-mâché for its head and claws (so they could be moved realistically, probably by a person hidden inside), and notes that the wire for the flying Apollo has yet to be installed.[49]

Intermedio 4 was half complete: the giant figure of Lucifer still needed its head and wings, and it remained "to draw [*dintornare*] the figures of hell," probably painted shapes of suffering souls that the devil is shown gobbling alive (cat. 53). But "the chariot of Donna Lucia," the flying sorceress, still needed to be made, along with the dragons who carry it across the sky. By contrast, intermedio 5 seemed nearly finished: the wave machine had been among the first stage components worked on, and the huge ship needed only to be fitted with its mast and some painted figures. Buontalenti asks for a dolphin four braccia (seven feet) long, to be made of papier-mâché; the larger practical sea-transport, Amphitrite's shell, is never mentioned, so it was presumably already completed.

Above many items in the punch list, Seriacopi recorded the disposition of Buontalenti's requests, which were parceled out to the lower-ranking artists and craftsmen. Many carpentry items, like the skeleton for the serpent, were assigned to Orazio Graziadio, a principal carpenter, with a note that "Messer Bernardo will make a drawing of it," necessarily something more detailed than the dragon sketch of cat. 50. Painting tasks were given to Francesco Rosselli, one of the two main scenic painters, and work on the lights and wall hangings of the auditorium to Piero Pagolini, a jack-of-all-trades who was to find builders (*muratori*) and carpenters to help him. These and other craftworkers, their labor conditions and creative organization, will be examined in more detail in Chapter 4.

OTHER SITES

If much remained to be accomplished at the Uffizi and Pitti, the same was true at the other sites that claimed a share of the organizers' overstretched attention. Besides coping with unforeseen delays and personality conflicts in the theater, Seriacopi continued to bear his general responsibilities for many other palaces and fortifications, and Buontalenti for construction and decoration elsewhere in the Uffizi, at the Palazzo Vecchio, and beyond.

Developments at the Pitti Palace most closely paralleled those in the theater, because both sites were under the same direction. Beginning in late November and continuing through the first of January, the documents provide many details of design, construction, and technology not visible in Gualterotti's engravings of the courtyard (cat. 71, 87). Work seems to have begun all at once on a wide variety of temporary construction (the painted castle backdrop, seating, waterworks), decoration and lighting, chariots for the procession, and livery and uniforms. A platform was built within the fountain grotto that tunneled into the hill on the court's open side, to serve as a staging area for the ships and chariots; its entrances are visible as arches at left and right of the rear wall (cat. 87). The court was covered with a single huge awning in red cloth, suspended on ropes held with pulleys. As at the Uffizi theater, seating was tripartite: tiered risers (gradi) under the portico for the women, men on the balconies above, and a raised platform on the floor of the court for the granducal party, again covered with rose-pink cloth. The exteriors that faced the court were hung with window ornaments, chiaroscuro paintings over each pilaster, papier-mâché cartouches, and draped swags of fabric, and the arch openings were filled with garlands made of straw, greenery, and tinsel. The whole arena was illuminated by hundreds of lamps and torches, both freestanding and fixed to the walls.

Technologically, the most complex task was hydraulic: flooding the court while holding the water back from the seating under the arcade. The "ocean" was pumped in via the grotto piping, and two river gods were modeled in clay, each eight braccia high, with working spouts; painted fountains continued the motif. Barricades were erected within each of the 18 ground-floor arches, topped by balustrades refitted from "the old comedy" (probably the 1586 performance); built of a double wall of used planks, they were filled with fuller's earth, an absorbent powder. About the planks Seriacopi notes pragmatically that, for such rough construction, "any kind will do."[50]

The logistical problems posed by the enormous quantities of materials required various agents to comb the city as well as the country towns for 10 to 20 miles outside both Florence and Siena. Some lumber was purchased in town, and some from the agent of a convent called "del paradiso." It proved especially difficult to find sufficient planking longer than six braccia (11 feet) for the benches of the gradi; one Battista del Cascha made a scouting trip on which he arranged to purchase and dismantle six disused towers, from Ponte a Grieve and from a miller at Montelupo (possibly a windmill). The naumachia, requiring 18 ships, each with a capacity of eight to ten men, was supplied by Francesco di Jacopo Rabattini, a ships' caulker (*calfatore*) from Lastra a Signa, apparently the administration's "boat consultant." He estimated the price of building new boats at 93–99 lire each; Cavalieri, with the usual eye for savings, also ordered the purchase of used boats. Rabattini undertook the week before Christmas to contact and negotiate with shipwrights in Brucianese, Ponte a Signa, and La Pineta, reporting back by January 1 the availability and the asking prices of seven small boats (one new, several broken apart).[51]

The parallel work at the Palazzo Vecchio operated independently of the theatrical team, for it was a larger architectural project not limited to the ephemeral wedding decorations and requiring the many trades of new construction and water supply. There was, however, considerable overlap of supervisory staff: the building was designed by Buontalenti; construction was managed by Alfonso Parigi, who also oversaw the Uffizi stage crew; and some of the decoration was painted by Francesco Rosselli, also from the Uffizi. The workshop at the Palazzo Vecchio had its own paymaster, but he operated under the general authority of Seriacopi, who checked the weekly payroll and expense settlements almost every Saturday from September 17 through at least March 18. Among artists here, those also active at other wedding sites include Jacopo Ligozzi and Giambologna; the latter was responsible for a fountain and possibly a new well, alongside ongoing work on the statue of Cosimo I.[52]

Throughout summer and fall of 1588, a large force of workers were in the great hall of the palazzo, the Salone dei Cinquecento, constructing and decorating *la testata del salone*, probably the raised platform, with carved wooden capitals, for the bridal table. In October, Parigi assessed the value of work completed by some of the carpenters; on December 6, he and Buontalenti estimated materials needed for the overhead bridge to the Uffizi. From January to March the kitchens and pantry were expanded, initially to serve the great banquet into which the opening-night guests at the intermedi would arrive over that bridge; some of these rooms were reconstructed by February, when a crew of whitewashers began putting a final coat on them.[53]

Work on the arches for Christine's entry procession had been well under way by November, when Allori assessed Cigoli's Prato arch painting (cat. 1); it continued during the early months of the new year, though little is documented.[54] As already observed, this work must have reached an irreversibly advanced stage by January 17, when news of Catherine de' Medici's death arrived too late to permit alteration of scenes on the second arch (and in Gualterotti's book). The costume work also continued: a meeting about liveries for the entry was convened on February 16 in Ferdinando's Pitti chambers between the grand duke; his brother Don Pietro, the fleet commander; Cavalieri; and Benedetto Fedini, who recorded the decisions and was responsible for carrying them out. Fedini's notes include detailed lists of the names of pages, equestrian knights, and other attendants, and of the amounts of fabric and decorations, including outfits for the company that was to ride to Livorno in April to meet Christine and escort her back as far as Florence.[55]

Although that meeting touched on a few matters concerning the Livorno end of Christine's journey, preparations for the fleet and its crew seem to have been well in hand by this point. In December orders had been sent to equip the fleet, especially the flagship (La Capitana), newly constructed at Pisa; costumes for eight musicians from Franciosino's school, who were to sail with the fleet to entertain Christine, were first mentioned in December and January (though not fully ready until March 15, when the fleet was about to set sail). Much of the decorative work was done in Florence: during Christmas week, red damask for manufacturing pennants for the flagship was consigned to the haberdasher Chelini and the tailors; by January 7, Giovanmaria Butteri had begun painting these ship's standards and other draped hangings. By January 24, embroidered sheets for the grand duchess's bed were complete; other fabrics were delivered through late February. As these sumptuous fittings arrived one after another at the docks of the bustling port, the sense of anticipation must have mounted, especially after January 12, when four galleys of the Knights of Malta sailed into the harbor to join forces in the northbound international flotilla that Ferdinando was assembling.[56]

REHEARSALS

Rehearsals, first mentioned in late December, became more frequent in February, providing further details on the cast and their activities. Their dates, and something of their specific activities, can be gleaned from preparatory orders and from notes written afterward by Buontalenti, Cavalieri, or Bardi, obviously derived from experiences at a rehearsal they had just attended. This record testifies to the incremental completion of sets and props, as well as to the continuing process of experimentation, problem solving, and empirical adjustment as individual units were put into practice.

One ongoing problem indicates the difficulty of translating the perspective system developed for the relatively intimate, two-dimensional art of painting to three dimensions at a vast scale. In keeping with the construction of theatrical space to focus flatteringly on the centralized prince, Buontalenti's original sketches assume the ideal vanishing point, centrally located opposite the ruler's unique position in the raised center of the hall; but his olympian calculations could seriously misfire from the less exalted angles physically consigned to the lower orders in the audience. In the March punch list he asks, "Enlarge the cloud of the first intermedio so that it goes higher than Signora Vittoria, as ordered by Signor Emilio." Evidently Archilei had been up on this machine already in rehearsal, and Cavalieri (seated in the house, as director) had noticed that, from the audience viewpoint largely underneath her, the cloud was too foreshortened to provide the seraphic surrounding halo effect contemplated in Buontalenti's sketch (cat. 11). Such discrepancies surfaced in both directions: after a later rehearsal in March, Cavalieri complained that the foreground houses of the *Pellegrina* set were too high, and were blocking the view of the clouds during the intermedi (being far downstage, they loomed higher in the audience's foreshortened view than would have been foreseen).[57]

On March 3, the day after Buontalenti submitted his long-contested punch list, he recorded via Francesco Gorini that "the intermedio of the ship having been rehearsed, he didn't see the novice gunners," so the ship looked "as if there was no one there." This lack of military splendor had distressed Ferdinando himself, for Buontalenti adds that he has ordered more sailors "so as not to disobey the commands of S.A.S." As with his inflated signature on the punch list, this remark seems calculated to overawe the presumptuous Seriacopi, by insisting on Buontalenti's own importance as an intermediary with the grand duke.[58]

Other practical matters relating to performance also arose at the same time. Thinking ahead about how to light and extinguish the numerous chandeliers being installed in the auditorium, Buontalenti notes that he will need a crew of 32 apprentices (*novizzi*), adding (yet another dig at Seriacopi), "as he says he said to the *provveditore* some time ago." Alluding, perhaps sarcastically, to Seriacopi's punitive approach toward employees, the architect specially requests that those charged with the sensitive lamps directly over the heads of the granducal party "should be trusted and experienced people, lest, should any problems arise, the *provveditore* punish and reprimand them."[59]

CHRISTINE IN FRANCE

On February 20, four days after the meeting in Ferdinando's presence to plan for her arrival, he and Christine were officially married. The proxy wedding took place in the royal chapel at Blois, in the presence of King Henri III, Queen Louise, and the entire court. On the 27th, Christine left Blois to begin her three-week journey south to Marseilles, where she would be met by Don Pietro de' Medici and the Tuscan fleet.[60] Preparations for her escort and reception had by now been proceeding for several months. The vaunted organizational capabilities of the Medici were well on their way to producing a spectacle worthy of the grand duchy and its new royal mistress. Of course, the wheels of that great state machine did not turn without a few squeaks: Buontalenti and Seriacopi were in the midst of their three-week spat, and on February 25, conceding that his edict from the previous September disarming all Tuscan citizens had had little effect in controlling outlaws, Ferdinando reaffirmed similar legislation.[61]

But the petty squabbles and unrest in and around Florence were minor compared to the political and social discord rending France, which must have made Tuscany seem a distant Eden. Marseilles had briefly declared itself a republic, and the death of the queen mother had removed any lingering force, however ineffectual, still working diplomatically to stem the internecine bloodshed that was typified by Henri III's order to assassinate Christine's cousin, the Duke of Guise, on December 23. When Christine departed his palace, with her personal attendants and an armed escort to ensure her safe conduct through rebellious territory, Henri's parting words were, "Happy are you, my niece, for you will be in a peaceful land and will not see the ruin of my poor kingdom."[62]

Giovanni Cosci's painting on the second entry arch (cat. 2; fig. 3), imagining this sad farewell between three generations headed by the benevolent queen-grandmother, became, with Catherine's death, an ironic fiction. But its very status as an artificial construction underscores how acutely it maps the meanings and ritual caliber of a state festival: an homage to the familial links between the two realms expressed in terms of personal affections, coupled with pragmatic politics, and the whole acted out over vast distances as splendid theatrical ceremonial. Ferdinando's gift of jewelry for the bride had been sent to France in December; now her enormous dowry, including clothes and jewels, began to arrive in Florence, where Ferdinando's tailors were also sewing her new garments in the local fashion and preparing her gaily decked transport home, including her first marriage bed.

Like her new husband in his solemn December ceremonies of investiture, Christine was being costumed in symbolic garments and readied to assume her new role as Grand Duchess of Tuscany. As the bride moved closer, the groom's cultural arms opened outward to embrace her. From late February through late April, when she would finally arrive in Tuscany, her progress through France and Italy would mesh ever more tightly with the progress in preparations for her arrival.

CHAPTER FOUR

March 1589

ARTISANS, STAGEHANDS, TECHNICAL REHEARSALS; CHRISTINE'S OUTBOUND JOURNEY

In March and early April, the artistic, technical, and political spheres of Ferdinando's theatrical universe began to converge, as preparations for the wedding festival built toward their dénouement and preliminary ceremonies took place along Christine's route through France. This chapter and the two following narrow increasingly in their geographic scope as the bride approaches ever closer to her new home: the first deals with preparations in March, while Christine was still traveling through her home country; Chapter 5 with April, encompassing her sea voyage and her overland approach through Tuscany; and Chapter 6 with events within the city of Florence during May.

On March 11, Giovanni de' Bardi prepared a new theatrical "punch list" for the Uffizi that superseded the one Bernardo Buontalenti had finally submitted on March 2; this chapter focuses primarily on events between Bardi's progress report and the next and near-final lists drawn up on April 7–9, when dress rehearsals were scheduled. The records of the Uffizi-Pitti-Palazzo Vecchio workshops during this period reveal a phase of creative production which, at the risk of anachronism, will be recognizable to scholars or enthusiasts of modern "show business" films. As the date of performance drew nearer, frenetic exasperation increased among the senior staff — but not, apparently, on the part of their individual subcontractors and craftworkers, about whose lateness and steep price demands they complained constantly, and whom they alternately threatened, cajoled, or dismissed. The tension and delays also pitted the principal organizers against one another: the feud between Buontalenti and Girolamo Seriacopi continued from mid-February into early March and erupted again later.[1]

Meanwhile, along the Tyrrhenian riviera from Livorno to Genoa to Marseilles, and inland to Lyons, preparations were being finalized for Christine's triumphal passage. As noted earlier, she left Blois on her southward journey on February 27, accompanied by an unusually large suite to protect against civil unrest. The ceremonial welcomes along her route were modeled on the tradition of the royal progress, like the heavily allegorized travels of Christine's older contemporary Elizabeth I. As Christine was nearing Marseilles on March 22, the Medici fleet under Ferdinando's brother Don Pietro left Livorno to sail north toward that rendezvous point.

At the same time, peripheral centers within the Tuscan domain were beginning their own plans to contribute to the bride's imminent arrival. The officers of Siena's municipal council, the Balia, wrote to the grand duke on March 18 to inquire whether they might be permitted to make some suitably noble representation of their "great devotion" before the new grand duchess.[2] Just how spontaneously the subject cities of Ferdinando's still recently consolidated realm offered these aesthetic protestations of loyalty is an open question.

CONSTRUCTION AND REHEARSALS AT THE MEDICI THEATER

To begin at the center of activity, the Uffizi theater in March was the site of more frequent and comprehensive rehearsals, now involving not only singers and musicians but also the large stage crew for technical run-throughs; the schedule tightened as craftworkers and artists rushed the physical setting toward completion. Bardi, Cavalieri, and Buontalenti conferred frequently with one another and with Cristofano Malvezzi, who besides being the principal composer served as musical conductor. On March 18, Seriacopi instructed his subordinate Cialle Fabbri, the chief of physical plant, to find out daily from all four of these men "which intermedi are to be rehearsed, so that he'll know in advance how many men he should call . . . to operate the machines."[3]

A useful index to the status of stage construction and rehearsals is provided by Bardi's March 11 punch list, which preceded the first complete run-through, on Thursday, March 16.[4] With only six weeks left before the opening performance, much of the basic stage machinery and many of the set pieces were operational, and Bardi's attention could be devoted almost entirely to matters of smaller props and supplementary decoration. Intermedio 1, for example, lacked only such items as Necessity's diamond spindle and the haloes (*mandorle*) behind the eight planetary gods; the wind gods on the large cloud for intermedio 4 needed wings. A few of the larger mobile assemblies, however, still remained incomplete, including the rising Lucifer for the hell sequence and the python for Intermedio 3 (cat. 50, 53; pl. 11). Both of these complex constructions were chronically delayed: although the fire-breathing dragon had been ordered in early February, later that month Buontalenti was still calling for construction to begin, and Bardi's mid-March notes indicate that little had yet been accomplished — a foretaste of continuing difficulties with this piece.[5]

Much of Bardi's attention throughout the month was taken up with "finishing touches" to costumes, sets, and props, such as disguising the musical instruments with cardboard and fabric to suit the motif of each intermedio. On March 11, he asked for those in intermedio 1 to be covered with celestial rays, in 2 with "something woodsy" (*qualche cosa boscareccia*), and in 5 "so that they look like sea shells"; the descending clouds of intermedio 6 were to be adorned with artificial flowers. (Buontalenti had already ordered "a large quantity" of paper flowers two days earlier; a week later, he ordered 100 more branches for intermedi 2 and 6 — perhaps from the nuns of Santa Caterina whose payment was noted earlier.) With characteristic concern for economical reuse, Bardi noted that the instruments on the heavenly cloud in intermedio 4 "can be decorated with the rays from the first intermedio." In what was to become a leitmotif of frustration and increasing tension between supervisors and workers, Bardi had to repeat his instructions about the instruments more than two weeks later, at which time nothing yet seems to have been carried out, and Seriacopi's marginal reply notes that a design for the instruments in the first intermedio is still needed from Buontalenti. By this time Bardi had developed his doubling plan in more detail, and spelled out that "the ones for the second can also serve for the third, and those for the first will serve for the fourth and sixth."[6]

Some alterations or additions were deemed necessary, based on experience during rehearsals. We have already seen the first empirical adjustments to the perspective scenery; later changes were generally more subtle. For example, regarding the Delphic couples of intermedio 3, on March 11 Bardi requested, "add more decoration [*riadornare*] to the costumes for the dancers, which look skimpy [*povere*]." And apparently unsatisfied with the lighting effect for the heavenly apparition of intermedio 6, but needing advice on what to do, he listed, "Think about the sunbursts [*splendori*]."

Much of the inventorying of existing stocks and ordering additional décors was handled by Benedetto Tornaquinci, the property and wardrobe master. On March 18, responding to Bardi's request of the previous week to enhance the marine motifs of the instruments, Seriacopi convened a brief meeting with Tornaquinci and Gorini. The quartermaster himself recorded in his log that the wardrobe master "has looked over the [artificial] coral branches we have, and says they're all satisfactory, but we need to have some more provided, as follows"; Gorini then took over as scribe for the details (30 small and 30 large branches, 200 buttons or beads).[7]

As these various refinements were added to existing constructions already being used in rehearsal, unforeseen technical difficulties multiplied, necessitating frequent test runs. In regard to the traveling platform that carried the sorceress's airborne chariot, one note suggests, "move the cloud that goes across, in order to see if certain additions that have been made to it cause any trouble"; and similarly, "let down the cloud in the middle to see if the movable shutters [*sportelli*] turn properly." The complexity of the equipment also raised questions of safety and solidity: a note on March 18 asks the crew to "nail some planks under the stairway that leads to the heavens, for the satisfaction of the ladies who have to perform there"; another on March 28 commands, "Pull up the cloud that Vittoria goes on, and have someone go up on it to see if it shakes [*scuote*]."[8]

This caution about stability was presumably instigated, at least in part, by the performers' unnerving experiences during rehearsals. The risks of riding unpredictable aerial apparatus are attested by the chronicler Baldinucci's anecdote about the singer-composer Giulio Caccini, whose nickname "Benedetto" was supposedly bestowed on him after a mishap during performance of a *sacra rappresentazione* at Santo Spirito. As part of a chorus of angelic singers on a movable cloud, he alone kept his head when the machine's rapid descent and expansion struck "so much fear in the hearts of the musicians . . . that suddenly they all lost their wits [and] fell dumb for some while." By continually repeating the music's refrain, "O benedetto giorno," Caccini ostensibly managed to fill the awkward interval until his associates recovered. As there is no independent record of Caccini's involvement in that performance, however, Baldinucci's story is often assumed to be a conflated memory of some accident that actually occurred during intermedio 6, in which the similar lyric "O fortunato giorno" was sung while the clouds moved.[9]

WORKING METHODS

A question that arose earlier in this chronology, and which comes into sharper and more useful focus in the records for the spring of 1589, addresses the organization of labor for the many practical tasks evident in these rehearsal preparations. The identities of the principal visual artists, and the varieties of their economic and social arrangements during a prolonged transition from independent workshops to permanent state employment, were discussed in Chapter 3. Here we can extend that analysis to their numerous co-workers — among them carpenters, metalsmiths, and scenery painters — whose contribution to the physical production was considered more craft than art.

Drawings and the Creative Hierarchy

Two distinct but mutually implicated aspects of artistic production have thus far been outlined: the creative system for disseminating images down the "assembly line" from Buontalenti to many artisans, and the socioeconomic system of labor conditions, payments, and personal relations. For craft-workers as for artists, both of these structures shared three characteristics: the separation of design from execution, now involving a hierarchical chain of intermediaries; the division of labor among both designers and artisans, with increasing specialization; and the resultant growing need for record keeping and coordination by an administrative bureaucracy.[10]

Turning first to the artistic processes: How were the conceptual requirements of Bardi, and their visual and technical specifications by Buontalenti, transmitted and enforced down a long chain of executants, often remote in physical or social location? The documents attest to a variety of overlapping methods; the visual included diagrams, sketches, and three-dimensional models, supplemented by written descriptions and on-site demonstrations.

We have already seen how one of Buontalenti's close associates, Andrea Boscoli, worked up more detailed variations on his original schematic drawings for the costumes and a similar process of elaboration for the stage sets; many other less elaborate sketches are mentioned for and/or by a variety of artisan occupations. When produced at the ideational summit of originality, such designs came to share in the increasing prestige assigned by Renaissance aesthetics to drawings as a form: Buontalenti's will bequeathed some of the sketches he had prepared for various productions to his Medici employer, suggesting that they were considered to have historical and/or practical value for the guidance of future production designers.[11]

At the secondary and tertiary tiers, however, except for a few drawings (cat. 32, 53; pl. 7) and occasional thumbnail sketches in Seriacopi's and Cavalieri's notebooks, virtually all traces of intermediate drawings, which were doubtless "used to death," have vanished. But there must have been scores of them, as the large crew and fragmentation of tasks required precise physical coordination as well as centralized stylistic and iconographic control: for example, Seriacopi's note telling Gorini to discuss some features of the stage lights with a lanternmaker "according to the enclosed sheet" testifies to their circulation through the design workshops. These sketches, often termed *modelli*, could also be an integral part of contracts: artisans agreed to do certain jobs at fixed prices based on written specifications that often alluded to an accompanying *modello*.[12]

A variety of terms, principally *modello* and *mostra*, are used to refer to these visual guides. Although the words are ambiguous and overlapping, each suggests a somewhat different role in the creative sequence, implying a staged series of refinements of initial concepts. The most generic term is *modello*, which is less often the three-dimensional object implied in our English "model" than a two-dimensional sketch (alternatively called a *disegno*, or drawing) to serve as the original guide for construction of woodwork, set pieces, lamps, and other elements. One group of these survives: Buontalenti's rudimentary sketches in Seriacopi's log, some hardly more than doodles, specifying the basic form and dimensions of pulleys, greenery swags, or the platform in the center of the theater. All others by him, prepared independently and more finished, are lost; at least one of the lost modelli — for the head of the dragon — was on canvas, suggesting a large, quickly brushed sketch, perhaps at actual size.[13] These first-order conceptual drawings were then worked up into one of a variety of more detailed prototypes, most often called a *mostra* — a term that has dual meanings, both from the root "to show." As a noun it usually means a physical model or sample, but in verb form it implies that Buontalenti will also make a "demonstration" in the performative sense: "as he will show [*mostera*] on the spot, and is seen in the drawing [*disegno*]."[14]

Intermediate modelli were also made by subsidiary designers and craft-workers. Some were functioning as independent consultants in their own specialties: when the stonecutter Niccolò di Michelangelo Boscoli was asked about the construction of the awning over the Pitti courtyard, he advised that it should be reinforced "as is shown in the drawing made and written by him." This design was then passed on to Giovanni di Lorenzo, a mattress maker (*materassaio*) who gave his opinion on the project "having received the drawing which remains in his hands." More often, a lesser artist or artisan worked up Buontalenti's sketches into a prototype which, once approved, could be copied by others. His conceptual sketch for the Pitti garlands was drawn in Seriacopi's log on March 13, and the first mostra, a full-scale sample for the guidance of bidders, was delegated to one of the principal scene painters, Lorenzo Francini (who was paid for this single unit, but lost the commission for the remaining replicas to another bidder).[15]

Craft Contracts and Supervision

As with the fine artists, the economic and social organization of the production crews encompassed a mosaic of different arrangements for labor and materials, most of which were coordinated by Seriacopi. We have already encountered several eruptions of his prickly temper and legalistic authoritarianism; subsequent events confirm and extend this impression of the quartermaster's character. By late March, responding nervously to mounting time pressure and repeated failures to meet deadlines, he began to repeat the phrase "as soon as possible" (*quanto prima*), and a week later he threatened the painters Bernardino Poccetti and Alessandro dal Impruneta: "If they haven't gotten a start . . . by tomorrow morning, let me know . . . wherever I am, so I can do what their excessive lateness deserves."[16]

If Seriacopi's fault was an excess of conscientiousness, the positive by-product of his zeal was a well-organized and carefully documented administration. He kept numerous account books, each detailing a different aspect of the preparations; by mid-March, the sheer complexity of these diverse interlocked ledgers must have threatened to escape Seriacopi's mental grasp, for he ordered Gorini to count up and list all the notebooks pertaining to the theater. Scrupulous record keeping was a longstanding Medici practice: on several occasions when the quartermaster wished to compare current expenditures for the Pitti tournament with the one held there previously for Francesco's wedding, he could take it for granted that these decade-old accounts were preserved and accessible.[17]

These documents are replete with details of the modes of labor-management relations customary on such projects: Seriacopi's log records a variety of contracts and estimates, terms of employment, resolutions of disputes, warnings and threats to workers, as well as the familiar concern for cost control. Contracts contained detailed lists of items to be made (*capitoli*), which, as seen earlier, might also include visual specifications. In some cases, Seriacopi insisted on face-to-face contact, perhaps for haste or to show a subcontractor the framework into which his smaller unit had to fit: on March 27 he notes, "Maestro Nellio has been ordered to come and get in person [*in voce*] the order for the eyes" of Lucifer. Usually, as was frequent practice for outside contractors in, for example, the construction industry, agreements reached verbally were transcribed in the log or separately and the parties asked to sign directly on the page. Labor arrangements at the Palazzo Vecchio and Uffizi gallery, which more closely approximated a traditional construction site, were equally detailed.[18]

Among identifiable contracting artisans, two carpenters (*legnaioli*) who appear repeatedly will illustrate customary procedures. Orazio di Zanobi Graziadio and Domenico di Bartolo Atticiato were partners (*compagni*). The first worker named in Seriacopi's log is Domenico: on Aug. 31 he had already requested lumber to construct the wave machine for intermedio 5, and he helped build elements of the ship and clouds. Orazio was at work from mid-September on projects in the theater ranging from stairs for the tiered gradi to candelabra, pilasters flanking the proscenium, and the mechanism (perhaps like drapery rods) that would lower the fabric hangings to reveal the wall décor, "according to what the architect [Buontalenti] says." In March, both associates were working on the elements of hell visible through the trapdoor, and on April 7 the sorceress's airborne chariot for that scene as well as the dragons that pulled it were still awaited from Orazio, who was also busy at the Pitti. Finally, like many such craftsmen, both doubled as stagehands.[19]

The contracts with these and other workers stipulate two methods of setting prices. One, a stima — on estimate — relied on mutually acceptable experts (periti) in the appropriate crafts to assess fair amounts for work upon completion and to arbitrate unforeseen expenditures or alterations; such evaluations were carried out by the likes of the painter Allori and the sculptors Giambologna and Ammannati. In late December, for example, interior construction in the salone of the Palazzo Vecchio was given to Orazio and Domenico a stima, and the painting of their construction to Lorenzo Francini and his partner Francesco Rosselli on the same basis. Alternatively, many jobs were assigned a cottimo — by the job contract — a system of written contracts with articles (capi or capitoli) that detailed each item and a preset total price. Such precise division of labor required careful coordination of the work sequence: whereas "the body and all the rest [of the dragon's frame were] included in the carpenter's cottimo," its movable papier-mâché head and claws were to be added by a sculptor.[20]

Both sides were meticulous about hewing to the terms of written contracts and ceremoniously referred to the documents when necessary. In September the carpenters "of the cottimo" insisted that they were not responsible for nailing canvases onto the wooden frames they were making for the painters, who in turn appealed to Cavalieri that having to do such work violated the terms of their cottimo. To resolve the matter, "the capitoli were read to [the carpenters], which say that the Fabbrica is to give the painters all the canvases nailed to the frames and gessoed [interrettate]"; Cavalieri ordered the woodworkers to observe these terms, and Seriacopi added that "in many places of the [carpenters'] capitoli it says 'nailed canvases' . . . and in this matter it's necessary to follow not the capitoli of the painters, but those of the carpenters." Orazio and Domenico precipitated a similar dispute in March, prompting Seriacopi to instruct Gorini, "Call Orazio and Atticiato and read them all the tasks that were commissioned to Orazio on March 10 in Messer Bernardo

Buontalenti's presence." For good measure, he threatens, "Admonish them to hurry, otherwise I'll get seriously angry with them."[21]

The contracts also alternate two methods of calculating payment: with or without supplies, or what we would now call time and materials, versus a flat-fee basis. Although arrangements were flexible, the two systems mark differing economic modes and roles: the independent contractor, who has his own access to resources of production, as against the salaried employee, who is only exchanging labor for wages. Those instances where the total price includes materials use variants of the phrase *a tutte sue spese*, "entirely at his expense."[22] Elsewhere, materials are supplied by the administration. Frequent lists beginning "Pietro Pagolini has asked for . . ." are resolved by notes to the Guardaroba or other supply depots; Pagolo Delli, for example, who made the garlands for the Pitti, was supplied by the Guardaroba with branches, straw, twine, and vinegar (perhaps to preserve the greenery). Some arrangements were mixed: on March 16, the carpenter making covers for the smoke holes in the theater ceiling was given "only wood and nails" but had to cut his own canvas; two days before, a painting commission for *La pellegrina* had specified *a tutte spese del pittore* but then added that "for the pennants [*banderuole*] he'll be given precut pieces of taffetta" to finish. When Domenico the carpenter requested planks, he was told to go buy them himself and promised quick repayment.[23]

In arriving at these contracts, the administration frequently sought to keep costs down, both by individual negotiations and by competitive bidding. Cavalieri instructed Seriacopi that he "should bargain" (*pattuisca*) with the painter-gilder Giovanni di Pagolo for finishing the sculptures in the theater "for the greatest advantage possible."[24] More often bids, usually three, were taken from artisans. Sometimes these were based on verbal descriptions, but on many occasions a physical sample was provided: when a number of lamps were to be made according to Buontalenti's prototype, "Jacopo di Lessandro was sent to the workshops of the following [smiths] with the mostra to find out each one's prices." An ironworker who had been asked to make a sample torch bracket completed it to Buontalenti's satisfaction in February, but because his cost estimate to continue the job "seems an exorbitant price" (*parendo pregio di sorbitante*), his completed mostra was shown to two other smiths, who offered lower fees. Although the primary concern was economic, competition could also be a means of quality control, as when Seriacopi solicited samples of tournament swords from three cutlers, "so that once we've seen how they succeed, and whether they're satisfactory, we can determine the price with whoever makes them best."[25]

The process of soliciting bids was usually straightforward but could also be used to play one artisan against another or otherwise minimize expenses. On April 5 three bids were recorded from lathe workers (*torniai*) for wooden components of the theater candelabra. Although Piero di Pandolfo's initial bids came in highest, he was vulnerable to further pressure, "seeing as he has no work left," and he agreed to match the lowest individual bid for each separate item, as well as absorb all expenses for the wood. On another occasion, Seriacopi rejected both bids for the dragon's claws and head "because they seem too high," and gave the job to Valerio Cioli. Although, as one of the senior sculptors on the site, Cioli would have commanded even higher rates, his regular monthly stipend from the Guardaroba presumably included such tasks, so Seriacopi was saving money by using "in-house" staff.[26]

Finally, workers' attendance on a fixed schedule was vigilantly enforced. On December 10 one Battista di Alessandro reported his fruitless efforts to track down the painter Stefano Pieri the previous day. When Pieri did not answer a summons to the work site, Battista "went to his house, but didn't find him there, and his wife and his mother-in-law told [Battista] that [Pieri] was with the sheep, so he went there, but didn't find him there [either]." What happened next remains unknown, but the ultimate penalty was dismissal, as decreed by an irritated Seriacopi on March 26: "Since Lessandro di Casentino has abandoned the *salone*, and I couldn't get in the two or three times that I came back, have him dismissed, as we don't need someone who's absent so much." He added, in typical self-righteous fashion, "If that displeases him, let him consider that it displeased me much more not to be able to fulfill my responsibilities because of him." Short of firing, an overdue worker might find that Seriacopi had hired someone else to complete the assignment at the laggard's expense.[27]

In common with their fellow craftworkers, Orazio and Domenico were taken to task by Seriacopi for their slow pace. In their case he took the unusual step of appealing for enforcement to an unnamed authority ("honored chancellor") to whom he wrote on December 10, perhaps driven by the specter of disorder raised by that day's report on Pieri's absence. His letter complained that the pair's delay on numerous tasks was holding up the painters Rosselli and Francini, who had to decorate what they were making. Seriacopi asked this official to order the carpenters to finish by Christmas and to further threaten that if they continued their "usual tardiness" for more than another week, other workers would be hired to finish the job at their expense, and that they might be assessed for additional damages or jailed if all was not completed by the end of the month (MR 10v).

FRANCESCO ROSSELLI AND LORENZO FRANCINI, ARTISAN-PAINTERS

Like the carpenters whose work they decorated, the two principal technical painters, Francesco di Stefano Rosselli and Lorenzo Francini, also offer a detailed glimpse of patterns of craft employment. In spite of the annoyance they chronically provoked in the administrators and even in Ferdinando, these contentious and dilatory partners assumed the bulk of responsibility for decorative painting throughout the Medici complex. They created most of the Pitti décors and temporary embellishments to the salone in the Palazzo Vecchio, as well as working at the Uffizi on both the architectural chiaroscuro and on the stage sets and props, from the Muses' grotto to the giant Lucifer. Their handiwork, which covered most of the visible surface of the theater and stage, was prominent enough to attract brief praise from Rossi, who opines that "the great hope" invested in them was rewarded with "great results."[28]

Not otherwise known to art history as independent personalities, Rosselli and Francini occupied a professional rank midway between the artists aspiring to academic standing and artisans like the carpenters. Rossi's remarks indicate that they enjoyed some leeway for designing their own "inventions," a crucial term in defining the high artist as a creative intellectual, but his flattering implication overstated their artistic freedom. For much of their work at the Pitti — backdrop paintings for the castle, costume decoration, garlands and hangings — Buontalenti provided the modelli. Francini's role was that of a trusted but subordinate intermediary, as in the incident noted earlier where he assembled a mostra for the garlands from Buontalenti's sketch but lost the bid for the balance of the job (March 13).[29]

Labor conditions for these men, generally similar to those of other craftworkers, can be examined in unique detail: for their Pitti work, specifications for a full cottimo survive, along with an agreement that resolves disputes over its interpretation. The administrators' compulsion to specify everything, out of their legitimate concern to obviate just such disputes as did arise, also affords a richer description of the courtyard décor than could be accommodated in the print of this area (cat. 87).

On November 28 Buontalenti provided the list of work items (*capi di lavori*) for the court decoration, "so that they can be given out to be done *a stima*, or *a cottimo*, depending on which is determined to provide better savings"; all of these items were to be made following his various samples. The list, which formed the basis of a cottimo with Rosselli and Francini, comprises three categories, by ascending architectural level of the courtyard: items to go around and under each large arch of the ground level (gradi for seating, painted fabric panels and swags, garlands, cartouches of painted cardboard); second-story elements "on the large cornice between the arches and the windows" (more gilded swags, paintings, and garlands); and "on the large windows above, and at the top" (third floor), in addition to more of the same, painted coats of arms, torches, and candlesticks. In the court itself, he also asks for two clay river gods for ground level eight braccia (15 feet) high and the actual barrier for the joust, two braccia high and covered with narrative paintings "as is seen in the *modello*, and will be shown better in the *esemplo* and *mostra* that are to be made."[30]

Problems with Rosselli and Francini's execution of this contract must have begun almost immediately, because on December 16 Cavalieri dictated the terms that he was willing to accept "for final resolution" of their complaints regarding the scope of the original contract, costs of materials, and the relation of this contract to separate additional commissions. Applying pressure by indicating that the two artisans were already on shaky ground, Cavalieri begins tartly that Ferdinando "has been unsatisfied with the last cottimo given to them, as the painters and others have heard many times," which had given rise to the "danger that the cottimo may not move forward." He then makes an offer, sweetened by an inducement: "If they are content to do all the tasks that are in the modello, and in addition the lamps for the hall of the comedy, for 2,000 scudi," they will also be awarded *a stima* "the painting work to be done in the Salone [dei Cinquecento]." If they reject these terms, not only will they forfeit the salone job, but they will be removed from the Pitti work in progress and paid off proportionately for whatever they have already done. He stipulates that, should they agree to these terms and it later become necessary to substitute less costly tinsel or tinning (*stagniuoli*) for the specified gilding, their fee will be reduced by an amount to be determined "by two expert and experienced people."

The partners counteroffered with two qualifications. They would acquiesce if, first, they could have *a stima* not only the salone job but also those elements of the expanding Pitti job that were not specified in the original modello. Second, they firmly insisted on additional payment for the lamps, for "at the time when the contract items were read, Messer Bernardo Buontalenti added the narrative paintings in oil to go over the grotto, entirely at their expense, which up until then they had thought were to be in tempera." Although they asked for 180 scudi extra, Seriacopi got them to settle for 73, with an additional proviso that, if the four paintings were changed back to tempera, they would abide by another cost reduction by the two expert assessors. Perhaps because of the complexity of the negotiated settlement, Seriacopi took the precaution of having both men sign the bottom of his lengthy memorandum. Five days later, to verify their claims and keep an eye on their progress, he had Gorini inventory the items that the painters had already completed "before they were given the contract" and "up to now."[31]

Such acrimonious haggling notwithstanding, both Rosselli and Francini continued to work on various jobs right up until the wedding events took place. At the theater, Rosselli was assigned to paint the starry backdrop of intermedi 1 and 6 and part of the giant Lucifer, neither of which was completed by April 5. Trying a new management style, perhaps to defuse chronic tension, Seriacopi was uncharacteristically mollifying in his request that, if these weren't finished soon, Gorini should notify him [Seriacopi] about it, "but let [Rosselli] be reminded kindly [*amorevolmente*]." In this case, it should be noted, part of the delay was Bardi's fault: the iconographer only provided the necessary description of Lucifer and other monsters on April 7. The Pitti work was also running behind by this time, and on the 8th a frustrated and again insistent Seriacopi, relapsing into his legalistic mode, forced Rosselli to sign a written pledge to finish all the jobs outstanding there by April 28. In a now-familiar threat, Seriacopi added that "if he does not promise to have them finished entirely and well by that date, then we'll start to give his tasks to others to do at his expense."[32]

PIERO PAGOLINI, JACK-OF-ALL-TRADES

Rosselli and Francini's Uffizi activities are often cited in tandem with those of Piero Pagolini, whose tasks intersect and complement theirs. Less than an artist but more versatile and trusted than an ordinary carpenter, he was a sort of universal craftsman or theater technician, whose multiple responsibilities surfaced in the March 2 punch list. Pagolini built and installed sets and executed other general work on the stage carpentry, furniture, canvas, lighting, and costume storage facilities. In some of these capacities, such as when he was assigned to set torches in the auditorium windows and authorized to find masons and carpenters to assist, his work was quasi-supervisory; at other times he bid for work like any outside craftworker — his was one of the estimates rejected as "exorbitant" in the account above. Finally, like the carpenters and many other artisans, he doubled as a stagehand.[33]

During the month of March, Pagolini shouldered so many tasks that they progressively overwhelmed him. In addition to his work on the theater and equipment, he was simultaneously fashioning the Lucifer, the dolphin for intermedio 5 (plus three sea monster companions molded on the same frame), and "all the branches of [artificial] coral as well as the coral beads [*paternostri*]" to decorate this and the other nautical-themed scenes.[34] The complex Lucifer unit (cat. 53) proved a chronic headache for all concerned. Construction of its main trunk was already advanced by the March 2 order for its movable head, horns, and wings, which were to be painted by Rosselli; it also needed hands, which fell to Pagolini. A month later, on April 5, Rosselli had not finished, and one hand remained behind schedule: regarding Pagolini, Seriacopi told Gorini ominously to "remind him, and if by Thursday he hasn't finished it, let me know, so that he won't need to be reminded again." The craftsmen were not the only staff falling seriously behind: their delay was extenuated by Bardi, who, working between daily rehearsals, was late with a description of Lucifer.[35]

With so many tasks falling due at once, Pagolini was increasingly harried and irritable. The next day, Thursday, April 6, was particularly difficult. Seriacopi was expecting all the coral pieces "by Saturday at the latest . . . by Sunday at the very latest." Pagolini managed to hand in a first installment of 54 small branches but also reported a snag in putting up the stage canvases because Rosselli and his crew hadn't finished painting them. When simultaneously reminded about the unfinished sea monsters, Piero finally snapped that "he'll do everything as soon as he possibly can" (*quanto prima potrà*). Seriacopi learned of the coral delivery only on Friday, April 7; no doubt relieved to find anything coming in near schedule, he promptly consigned these to be added to the costume headdresses, then reminded Pagolini to finish all the stools for the theater by a week from Saturday.[36]

Amid all of these conflicting demands, it is hardly surprising that work on the Lucifer continued down to the wire: only on April 25, a week before the premiere, did Gorini finally order green taffeta "to make the wings of the devil." The giant's hand was no further along on April 13 than on the 8th, and an impatient Seriacopi demanded that Pagolini be reminded "heatedly" (*caldamente*) to finish by Saturday or "I'll complain about him" to unnamed authorities. Nor by that same day had he finished the remaining coral still due, and Seriacopi, observing that that project was impeding more pressing items still awaited from the obviously overburdened Pagolini, decided to cut his losses: he simply took the coral assignment away from the technician, noting with resigned annoyance that "we'll find a way to do without them."[37]

STAGE CREW

By March 18, the machinery and stage equipment were sufficiently operational that Seriacopi, anticipating frequent technical rehearsals, ordered the custodian Fabbri to ascertain daily which intermedi would be rehearsed and to notify the appropriate members of the sprawling crew. Over the past three days, Seriacopi had drawn up a complete personnel list of these stagehands, to be supervised by Alfonso Parigi as "foreman [*caporale*] over all those written below." State performances being widely intermittent, only Parigi was retained as a permanent expert on theatrical practice, and then only alongside his related technical responsibilities at the Palazzo Vecchio and the Pitti (where on March 14 he was consulting about tent ropes). In this embryonic stage of the theater, without the permanent industry to support specialized full-time workers, the rest of Parigi's crew were hired temporarily, though often from the ranks of artisans and builders already familiar with the state workshops in their everyday capacities.

The ultimate crew list names some 95 individual stagehands, plus another 50 assigned to kindle, extinguish, and adjust the lights. The most technically complex intermedi, 1 and 6, required 12 simultaneous teams, totaling 82 members, while intermedio 3, which involved no major set change, needed only seven men. The stagehands were organized into squads of varying size, each assigned to a fixed task or piece of equipment: the winches for major clouds and the hamadryads' mountain required up to a dozen men, headed by their own foreman, whereas pairs of men were sufficient to insert struts under the mountain or rotate the mobile garden houses. Many of the stagehands doubled or tripled in different assignments for successive intermedi, but their task for each act was fixed, so that they could get accustomed to timings and teamwork; one rehearsal order makes sure to specify that the men called for a particular act "should be the same" (*sieno medesimi*) each time.[38]

Although systematic practice was necessary, the basic operations of this still rudimentary technical apparatus required little specialized ability beyond physical strength. The crew was thus recruited from various trades, supplemented by household staff from the Pitti and state buildings and from the church of Santa Croce. Among the numerous occupations noted, the largest group are masons or carpenters, including Orazio and his partner Domenico. Other occupations include smiths or ironworkers, lamp makers, a stonecutter, a cooper, and a ship's caulker. The more specialized technician Piero Pagolini assisted with the sophisticated novelty of intermedio 3, assigned to the overhead catwalk "to make the Apollo fly." At least some of these hands received overtime pay; such temporary supplementary income was doubtless as welcome to them as embroidering to nuns or second jobs to the tailors.[39]

Because so many of these stagehands were also employed at the Uffizi, Pitti, and Palazzo Vecchio workshops, the increasing time required of them onstage conflicted with looming craft deadlines to create staff shortages. Personnel allocation had to become more precise: on April 5, laying out staff

needs for the following day, Seriacopi told Gorini to determine which intermedi were to be rehearsed, and "summon only those [crew members] who are
called for, without taking away more people than are needed, both so as to
avoid any unnecessary costs, and not to decimate [*sinistrare*] the Fabbrica and
other places" (MR 39v).

LOGISTICS AND PHYSICAL PLANT

Cialle Fabbri, who called these crew members to daily rehearsals, fulfilled
the responsibilities of a head custodian, supplying and maintaining everything
concerned with physical needs: water, fire, dirt, food, shelter, and body functions. Buontalenti had requested someone to sleep in the theater as a fire
watch in November; apparently Fabbri filled this post, and was provided with
at least some food or other necessities, for in April Cavalieri requested that
Cialle's room in the Uffizi be supplied with "ten or twelve flasks . . . of water
and wine." Among his other duties laid out in March, Fabbri supervised
weekly cleaning at the Uffizi and Palazzo Vecchio, taking care to swab the
floors of the workshops to avoid raising dust on the painters' work in progress.
In an era before indoor plumbing, water supply required constant attention to
large numbers of barrels and pails provided not only for washing but for safety,
drinking, or toilet purposes. Fabbri reported that "it's necessary to have all the
water buckets emptied, because they stink, and have them refilled quickly with
fresh water," and Seriacopi ordered him to inspect and empty "the many tubs
[*bigonci*] where people urinate since, being full, they're rank and smelly [*infet-
tono e appuzzono*]." In addition Fabbri, whose tall elegant handwriting appears
increasingly in the log from March onward (a welcome relief from Gorini's
spidery, sometimes illegible script), acted as a clerk, transcribing Buontalenti's
punch list of February–March and various other lists and contracts.[40]

Beyond the theater, Fabbri also journeyed throughout Tuscany on various
missions, such as reconnoitering outlying areas for housing and equipment. In
Florence, where accommodations were needed for "the Sienese players and
Roman musicians who are to perform in the comedy," he supervised the
repairing, cleaning, and furnishing of two houses, one a former inn, borrowed
from nearby residents in mid-March. For one house, supplies were shipped
over from "the castle"; for the other quarters, on March 18 Fabbri copied out
Seriacopi's agreement with one Vincenzo Bonmattei to deliver bedding,
linens, and tableware over the ensuing ten days. Lodging and supplies must
barely have been ready in time for the arriving players: the Intronati troupe
were already at work in the theater by April 7, when "the Sienese gentlemen"
ordered props, makeup, and set changes.[41]

DON PIETRO AND CHRISTINE

Meanwhile, preparations for the outbound voyage from Livorno to meet Christine had been proceeding for several months. Aboard the Capitana, already being richly caparisoned, various colors were consigned to "Bortolo, Venetian miniaturist," to paint the interiors of individual rooms. In addition to artistic preparations, the four ships had to be outfitted with linens, tableware, and other household goods to accommodate the crew, aristocratic passengers, and Christine's retinue. Benedetto Fedini, the granducal *guardaroba*, oversaw these arrangements, which he listed in chronological order for each stage of her projected itinerary: "coming by sea," "once arrived in Livorno," and so on. For the ships he ordered 140 tablecloths, 500 additional linens, and four dozen assorted basins, plus clothing, bedding, furniture, and carpets. Tailoring of liveries for the attendants, including eight musicians from Franciosino's school and a gentlewoman, continued throughout March.[42]

On March 8, a naval officer wrote to Ferdinando from the port, saying he would soon be submitting the ships to a final inspection and was awaiting the order to set sail; he passed along the news, undoubtedly seaborne, that Christine had left Blois on February 27. Although much of the administrative correspondence throughout March pertaining to Livorno and the fleet concerns artistic matters, the logistical difficulties and risks of long-distance travel are a constant counterpoint. The same letters are full of reports from around the Mediterranean of ships kept in port by bad weather and of ambassadors and messengers delayed on land by weather or by civil unrest in France, an index of the limited ability of both political institutions and communications and transport technology of the time to control either human or natural upheavals.[43]

On Sunday, March 19, Don Pietro de' Medici arrived in Livorno, and the following Wednesday his fleet, staffed by Ferdinando's Order of Santo Stefano, left the harbor carrying many nobles and patrician pages, all richly costumed. On board to attend the bride were Francesca Orsini, who was to administer Christine's household; her husband Francesco; and two women of the Rucellai family, whose leader Orazio, Ferdinando's ambassador, also traveled to facilitate the bridal journey. Ferdinando, his nephew Don Virginio Orsini, and assembled notables waved from the dock as the Florentine ships, plus the quartet contributed by the Knights of Malta, sailed for Genoa to join up with four galleys from that city and together await a final four dispatched by the Pope. On March 25 this fully assembled flotilla headed north from Genoa.

Once Christine left Blois, she traveled south for two weeks to reach Lyons, a hospitable city with strong financial ties to Medici bankers, in mid-March. Beyond that outpost her journey, including receptions in Avignon and Aix, was increasingly troubled by local political strife. About April 1 Don Pietro sailed into Marseilles, whence he sent a letter reporting that the city councilors were eager to have Christine embark there, and not elsewhere along the coast. Presumably some change of venue had been suggested due to the power struggles in the port city, and then rejected. The royal faction, accepting the risks of a public festival for the sake of a symbolic demonstration of political supremacy, turned Marseilles into "a city everywhere filled with arches, statues, paintings, and lovely ornaments," and welcomed their princess with fireworks, trumpet blasts, and balls that lasted several days. Don Pietro's cannons joined in the tumultuous greeting on April 9, but this splendid bravado was counterbalanced by pragmatic caution: his ships remained offshore, and his letter had already observed that Christine's departure must be carried out in secrecy and tight security, and had detailed his plans to set out several thousand troops around the harbor and the city.[44]

On the morning of April 11, Christine stepped aboard the Capitana. An engraving from Gualterotti's souvenir book, after Giovanni Cosci's painting for the entry arch at the Ponte alla Carraia (cat. 2; fig. 8), imagines how she was welcomed by Don Pietro, who took her arm in a familial gesture. This crude image of an image unfortunately conveys little of the sumptuous decorative backdrops that set the proper tone of magnificence for this ceremonial prologue to the theatricalization of Tuscan dominion over the bride and the world. The artists' labors were discussed earlier; suffice it here to give two examples. The haberdasher Alessandro Chelini provided a large awning (*tendale*) for the stern of the flagship, consisting of 20 braccia (38 feet) of cloth of gold lined with rose-pink damask and trimmed with 160 braccia (300 feet) of red silk fringes and ribbons. The "principal chamber" of the ship, Christine's rear bedroom, was outfitted with ceiling curtains, wall-hangings, portières, and bedding all in cloth of gold and green silk; the records evocatively refer to it as "the jewelbox" (*scrignietto*).[45]

No doubt it was in this room that Christine, finally alone after the public welcome, soon composed her first known letter to Ferdinando. This soliloquy, the overture to their marital masque, is at once touchingly honest and formulaic (and orthographically inconsistent):

> I felt great joy and honor upon seeing my lord your brother and your
> galleys, which are very lovely, especially mine: when I entered it I
> thought I was entering paradise. I also thought that, it being so
> beautiful, the sea could do me no harm; however, I'm distressed to find

8. *Don Pietro de' Medici and Christine embark at Marseilles.*
Raffaello Gualterotti (see cat. 2).

myself a little indisposed. . . . I beg you to believe my eagerness to have
the honor of receiving your commands, which I will maintain as
carefully as the very life of
Your very humble and obedient fiancée and servant,
Christine de Lorraine[46]

Back on Florentine soil, on April 5 Averardo de' Medici assured the Florentine administration that various units of cavalry were awaiting the order to
march to preassigned places within the grand duchy to await the bride's
imminent arrival.[47] And at the Uffizi theater on April 9 — the same day
Christine arrived in Marseilles — the final punch list was completed, an exhaustive progress report before the dress rehearsals that would dominate until
her arrival three weeks later. While still showing much to be done, this list
implies that all but the few troublesome items discussed above were nearing
completion. For example, Bardi's request a month earlier to "think about the
sunbursts" had been resolved: Seriacopi notes that "the sunbursts have to be
half-gilded" to increase their brilliance (MR 42v). By this time, the wear and
tear of frequent rehearsals was already taking some of the freshness off the
settings; Buontalenti's list including the sunburst is headed, "Note about
things that remain behind schedule due to damage," such as canvases that
needed to be renailed to their frames. With an eye toward avoiding any further
touch-up work, he suggests, "It's best not to get started on these [*mettere prima
mano*] until Her Highness is in Livorno, since that will leave adequate time to
finish them, and then they'll be new and nice."[48]

By this first week of April, the princess's expectant hosts could just make her
out on their watery horizon, and she in turn had met and joined their advance
party. If not quite everything was ready, it was too late for either side to turn
back. The curtain was about to rise.

CHAPTER FIVE

April 1589

DRESS REHEARSALS;

CHRISTINE'S INBOUND

JOURNEY AND ENTRY

Throughout April, preparations within the theater, at other palaces, and across the city all meshed more tightly as they entered the final production stages of dress rehearsal and performance. And the theater staff now worked under an additional pressure: the audience was approaching and could, both figuratively and later literally, be heard gathering in the lobby. That approaching audience was personified by Christine and her travels, paralleled by the gradual convergence of thousands of wedding guests on the Tuscan capital. This second phase of Christine's trip lasted from April 11, when she left Marseilles, to April 30, the day of her triumphant entry into Florence. In contrast to her outbound route through France — a path of farewell — as she stepped aboard the Tuscan flagship the semiotic was reversed: she was no longer moving away from the center of her old existence, but centripetally, into ever-tightening circles of Medici organization and symbolic density. She reached Livorno on the 24th, then proceeded through the Tuscan landscape from Pisa to Poggio a Caiano; the date chosen for her entry, Palm Sunday, seems calculated to underscore the parallel to Christ's entry into Jerusalem, with its twin themes of triumphant acclamation and irreversible absorption into the bastion of civil and religious authority.

In tandem with these secular preparations, the ecclesiastical establishment was organizing its own series of solemn events, which, while not directly controlled by the civic authorities, nevertheless had to be coordinated with them. The duomo shut its doors on April 4, allowing almost four weeks to decorate and furnish its vast interior: the priests' procession carrying the host to its temporary home in the church of San Michele Visdomini marked the ritual beginning of the religious reception, which, like the state's, would claim the streets and buildings of the city with enfilades of costumed employees in ceremonial movement. In exchange for these expressions of their sacred legitimacy, the secular authorities offered both practical assistance and symbolic support. Logistics and aesthetics were channeled through the arts and supply bureaucracy: as early as February 7, Francesco Gorini had recorded a request from the Opera del Duomo, the cathedral works office, to borrow 100 *libbre* (70 pounds) of building materials, probably in connection with the ceremonial platform for the bride. Ferdinando personally supervised his symbolically significant gifts, which cemented the interlocking relationships between church, state, and aristocracy: the Archbishop of Florence, it will be recalled, was his cousin Alessandro de' Medici.[1]

What emerges most strikingly in these events is the theme, first remarked in the Introduction, of control. The two overarching goals of the Medici, in common with most early modern governments, were control of the physical world of natural resources and social control over the body politic, including the artistic discourses of public life. Realization of these twin agendas went hand-in-hand and can be seen at three geographical levels through which Christine passed on her Tuscan journey: subordinate cities and towns, the rural countryside, and the capital. The grand duchy's physical and social landscape was turned into a stage set for her arrival, its people and resources mobilized to produce displays of beneficent power over sea, land, and citizens. All of these trajectories converged on and culminated in the theater, where a bravura display of technical artifice was directed at an elite audience who were offered sumptuous clothing, honors, and gifts in exchange for their patronage of, and performance in, these elaborately choreographed public figurations of their subordination to a worthy, wise, and powerful ruler.

In terms of social policy, Ferdinando continued the project of consolidating the various city-states absorbed by Florence into a single political-economic-military entity, controlled and policed from the center with increasing scope and efficiency. Technologically, nature and its resources were harnessed by large-scale interventions informed by scientific developments, parallel to similar efforts elsewhere: while still a cardinal in Rome in 1586, Ferdinando would have witnessed Pope Sixtus V's logistical feat, unprecedented since the ancient Empire, of moving the Egyptian obelisk from the imperial Circus into the new St. Peter's Square. Modes of this physical dominion, many of them with an artistic component, ranged from large-scale construction and fortifications in both cities and villas to land reclamation and hydraulics.[2]

In the arts, various new means were developed to represent this ideal of control, to register it in and through artistic discourse — whose growing importance as a tool of public policy was typified by the appointment of Emilio de' Cavalieri as the first state administrator of fine arts. From painted maps to colossal sculptures to the conspicuous display of technical sophistication in stage machines and the fountains of the Pitti naumachia, these projects embody a primary concern of mannerist esthetics, in which such terms as *meraviglie* — marvels — and *Wunderkammer* — chamber of curiosities — epitomize the fascination with artifice, that is, with creative ingenuity that transcends the limits of the ordinarily possible. Rossi, in his *Descrizione* of the 1586 performance at the Uffizi theater, wrote that "nature was, by common agreement, practically overcome [*quasi superata*] by art." By 1589, this theoretical commonplace — art improves on nature — had progressed from a purely esthetic conceit to a technological one. Art, in its broadest sense of all practical skills that transform the material environment, had made the first of its early modern "quantum leaps" in its ability to manipulate the physical world.[3]

All the same, a tension remained between the regime's aspirations to universal dominion, admired as unusually successful, and the constraints persisting in both social and technical spheres. Social control was never absolute, scientific knowledge was but in infancy, and nature was still an unpredictable and formidable obstacle. The monument in the Pitti Palace courtyard commemorating a mule that labored in its construction is quaintly humorous, but it also bespeaks the dependence of human builders, still small-scale and largely pretechnological, on such limited sources of energy, with whom they lived in close symbiotic contact.

The Tuscan winter of 1588–89 had been unusually harsh and long, resulting in much deprivation and disease: exceptional numbers of people died of a severe respiratory infection that took most victims in less than four days, many others from smallpox. As Christine rode across the greening Tuscan landscape in late April, the citizens would truly have been rejoicing in the final arrival of benign spring weather, relief from a ceaseless and often futile struggle. In such circumstances, displays of effective control over the physical and social environment, even when confined to the interior of a theater, must have seemed to contemporary eyes all the more wondrously promising.[4]

PREPARATIONS IN THE THEATER, APRIL 7–15

In the first weeks of April, while Christine was still wending her way south toward Marseilles, preparations for the most elaborate, kinetic *Wunderkammer* of the wedding, the intermedi and comedies, had reached the final stages. On April 7, the same day that the Intronati company from Siena was onstage rehearsing *La pellegrina*, the conductor Cristofano Malvezzi scheduled a rehearsal for the following day of four of the six intermedi, and a note from Cavalieri informed the theater staff that the grand duke would be attending a run-through on Wednesday the 12th, for which S.A.S. wished to see "the entire comedy with costumes . . . and all the machines, and with the first intermedio of Vittoria [Archilei]."[5]

In the event, Ferdinando's first inspection was put off until Sunday, April 16. The postponement must have come as a relief, for the punch list that Bardi and Buontalenti were immediately asked to compile between April 7 and 9 recorded delays on the part of Piero Pagolini, Francesco Rosselli and Lorenzo Francini, among others, on numerous set, costume, and lighting tasks. Obviously under great pressure, the crew worked overtime on Sunday the 9th: on that day Benedetto Tornaquinci made up his list of cast to be assigned shoes, and the painter Pieroni was threatened with replacement if he did not complete the stair on the stage parapet by Tuesday, the day before the grand duke was expected.[6]

For the theater itself, some final architectural modifications and seating provisions remained. Buontalenti was going to supervise during performances from an observation desk concealed beneath the tiered seats; he asked for a small door to be cut into the side parapet of the gradi, near the main entrance, "to get to the booth unseen." This carrel must have had a view of both auditorium and stage, probably a window cut into the front parapet.[7] The most crucial item still lacking was the platform (*palco*) for the granducal party, which was to be the centerpiece of the auditorium. Although it had been requested as early as the March 2 punch list, Buontalenti only sketched a rough modello on April 5, for a dais about 22 feet wide and 18 deep, to be surrounded with a richly draped balustrade. This princely precinct, from whose elevated viewpoint the stage perspective was calculated, would also dominate the hall by sheer size, occupying more than half the width of the floor between the two side tiers.[8]

CHRISTINE AT SEA, APRIL 11–23

When we left Christine at the end of Chapter 4, she had boarded the Capitana, welcomed by Don Pietro de' Medici, and sailed east toward Monaco. Like her earlier land journey, her sea voyage over the ensuing two weeks illustrates both the great physical and political resources that could be marshaled for princely travel and receptions, and the degree to which such concentrated efforts remained circumscribed by uncontrollable nature (map, fig. 9). Expanding networks of international trade and transport notwithstanding, her journeys exemplify the observation of Fernand Braudel that, in this period, "every activity had to overcome the obstacle of physical distance." The fleet's forced two-day stopover in Monaco is a case in point. On this

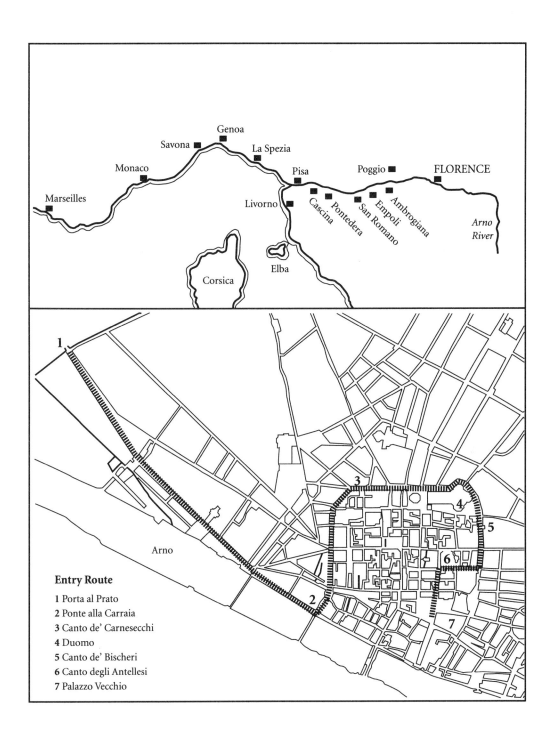

Marseilles

Monaco

Savona

Genoa

La Spezia

Pisa

Poggio

FLORENCE

Livorno

Cascina

Pontedera

San Romano

Empoli

Ambrogiana

Arno River

Corsica

Elba

Arno

Entry Route

1 Porta al Prato
2 Ponte alla Carraia
3 Canto de' Carnesecchi
4 Duomo
5 Canto de' Bischeri
6 Canto degli Antellesi
7 Palazzo Vecchio

9. *Christine's sea voyage and entry route.*

occasion the cause was bad weather, but even under the best conditions water travel was slow and unpredictable. Piracy and shipwreck were common risks, leading ships to sail close to shore, which allowed the Duke of Monaco to exact a toll from all vessels passing his coastline. Direct routes across open sea were impractical in any case; limited by small capacity and the lack of preservation techniques, boats had to go into port at least every second day to replenish stocks of water, fuel, and food.[9]

At last able to leave Monaco on April 17, the fleet arrived the next day in Genoa, which provided an elaborate reception befitting its status as the Mediterranean's paramount trade crossroads and financial center.[10] On her arrival, Christine was received by the city's doge and councilors amid the customary welcoming ships, artillery salutes, and music, plus "portable bridges" (*ponti portatili*), probably waterborne floats. Passing through streets "which seemed to have become theaters" via their splendid temporary décors, she lodged in the Palazzo Doria, where the next day civic officials called on her in the vast salone, "which along with the whole palace was covered with cloth of gold and silk." The fleet was again forced to delay its departure for several days, this time by the rising of unfavorable sirocco winds; it finally left on the last leg of the voyage, probably on April 23, reaching Livorno on the 24th.[11]

FIRST DRESS REHEARSAL, APRIL 16

While Christine was en route from Marseilles to Genoa, preparations in Florence were expanding and intensifying. At the church of San Marco, where she was to attend the dedication of the Salviati family's new mortuary chapel for Saint Antoninus, the Quattrocento archbishop's body was removed from its original resting place on April 15 to prepare it for a ceremonial procession through the streets before reinterment in the sepulcher designed by Giovanni Bologna; on April 19 the church, like the duomo before it, was closed to the public for decoration. At the Uffizi theater, the dress rehearsal originally planned for April 12 took place on Sunday the 16th; orders for it began on Thursday the 13th, when the custodian Cialle Fabbri was told to clean up the dressing rooms by Saturday.[12]

For the first time, rehearsal plans included food; because a full run-through would last five or six hours, some refreshment for hardworking cast, musicians, and stage crew was essential (the rehearsal seems to have included all the intermedi, not just the first as Ferdinando had originally requested). Mess tables for various groups were set up around the Uffizi: Buontalenti and his senior staff at one, the women of the cast separated at another, the Intronati elsewhere, and so on. Rations, too, followed a precise system of rank and gender: apprentice manual workers were each allotted one loaf of bread and one piece of cheese, with a flask of wine for five men; full-fledged carpenters received the same, except one flask for four men, "and the most senior ones [get] some meat." The Intronati and musicians also merited both meat and cheese, while the women shared ten pounds of luxury almonds. During an intermission after intermedio 3, Fabbri and five other men served supplemental bread and wine.[13]

Notes taken down immediately after this preview and confirmed by Cavalieri's signature, plus additional orders issued over the next two days, detail numerous last-minute technical and visual snags and requirements for final supplies. Two clouds of the sixth intermedio did not turn properly; the opening of the heavenly shutters had to be correspondingly adjusted, and the upper edge of the main aperture (*la testata del foro principale*) was seen "trembling and flapping" (*tremando e sventolando*) for a long time, "as if it had been shaken [*scossa*] from behind the canvas." If Cavalieri couldn't see the perpetrator of this sloppiness, elsewhere inadequate camouflage was a problem: the ropes for the flying chariot of intermedio 4 were still too obvious, and crew members could be glimpsed in the overhead catwalk when the clouds opened, which looked "really awful" (*brutissima*). Lighting was still inadequate: "as many as possible" were to be added to the clouds, but taking care that the lamps themselves not be visible, only the light reflected from them onto the gods. The onstage smoke, by contrast, was excessive: Cavalieri begged the technicians to "make it so it doesn't stink." Some refinements were more visual than mechanical: the transverse cloud bearing the sorceress's chariot would have to be painted a different color to stand out better from its heavenly backdrop. A more general problem with set changes was affecting the overall pacing of the performance: "The [crew] men are too slow after the comedians have left the stage in doing what they have to do" (MR 47v–48v, Apr. 16–18).

From April 18 to the 20th, final plans were also made for the Palazzo Vecchio and the Pitti, indicating great urgency. At the Salone dei Cinquecento, canvases were to be gessoed so Alessandro Allori could paint them, "and if the canvas hasn't been sewn yet, have it sewn tonight by any means necessary." The partners Rosselli and Francini, who received a modello from Buontalenti for the sailors' costumes in the Pitti naumachia, were painting samples; the first was patterned in gold, but as this turned out too expensive they were told to make two alternative test pieces, one in silver, the other in tin and grisaille (*stagniuolo biancho aombrato*). On April 20 Seriacopi set a precise timetable for completing one of the chariots for the Pitti parade (probably Don Pietro's, cat. 73–74): its papier-mâché accoutrements were to be nailed onto the frame that evening, and Rosselli and Francini were to gesso it the next morning in preparation for painting. The night-shift overtime fell to the carpenters Orazio Graziadio and Domenico Atticiato, who were provided candles "for staying up tonight." In the event, as so often, the piece was not finished on schedule, and Seriacopi demanded two days later that "it be attended to as soon as possible." His panicky tone was doubtless influenced by the ominous reminders all around him of how little time remained: on the next day, April 23, the wooden barricades between the Loggia de' Lanzi and the church of San Piero Scheraggio, which had closed off the courtyard of the Uffizi during the previous months' busiest construction, came down in antici- pation of the arriving guests.[14]

CHRISTINE IN LIVORNO AND PISA, APRIL 24–27

As Christine's flotilla approached the harbor of Livorno late in the after- noon of April 24, all of its flags and hangings unfurled to the breeze, her first sight would have been the long artificial breakwater jutting out toward her; as the Capitana sailed past its wide opening, before her lay numerous docks overshadowed by high defensive walls. As in Genoa, Livorno had been fully decorated, and the governor came to meet Christine at the dock, surrounded by several hundred dignitaries on horseback and in carriages and boats. Sur- rounded by these serried crowds, as well as by massed cavalry and Ferdi- nando's richly costumed personal delegation, Christine debarked via a wooden drawbridge let out from the massive Fortezza Vecchia, or Old For- tress, at the water's edge.[15] Both setting and actors figured the transformation of the entire grand duchy into a landscape of control, a *theatrum mundi* in which large-scale state administration of geographical and economic re- sources went hand-in-hand with increasingly centralized social order. Be- tween here and Florence, as her route passed from one city to another via reclaimed land, stopping off at the family's country villas, Christine would witness the extensive campaign of technological, military, and economic de- velopment on which rested the well-being and power of the state "in which she is to live and reign" (Gualterotti, *Descrizione*, 4).

Livorno was the centerpiece of a consistent program of urban develop- ment, which Ferdinando carried on after his father and brother (fig. 1). Largely under Buontalenti's supervision, towns throughout the Medici do- mains were fortified and enlarged, from Livorno to Pistoia down to much smaller outposts; the results were praised by Bastiano de' Rossi in his intro- duction to the 1589 *descrizione* (p. 4). What had been a coastal village was rebuilt into an enormous port complex, replacing Pisa, whose harbor had begun to silt up in the fifteenth century. The city center was surrounded by battered walls of unadorned brick with defensive parapets, up to 25 feet high, and a series of fortresses isolated by canals. The goals of this development were both economic and military: to capture a large share of international trade on the Mediterranean circuit, and to serve as a base for the seafaring Order of Santo Stefano, of which Ferdinando had become patron in December. The Order's purpose was to patrol the western Mediterranean against incursions of Turkish pirates, who, despite their setback at the battle of Lepanto (1571), remained a chronic menace.

Such large-scale geographical engineering could not be accomplished without social engineering to provide the necessary work force. Here Ferdinando's policies were pragmatic rather than consistent in principle. On one hand, he declared the port a free city, issuing dispensations to marginal groups to encourage settlement by anyone willing to work, even heretics or criminals (who received amnesty), and various tax abatements to encourage merchants and bankers, Turkish, Armenian, and Jewish. These incentives created a tolerant, cosmopolitan enclave, with one of Italian Jewry's most prominent communities and consulates representing distant maritime cities. On the other hand, less benign methods of labor management were employed: many galleys were staffed by forced labor, sentenced to long terms at the oars for various crimes. Less harsh but more widespread was the *comandata*, the traditional prerogative of the ruler to commandeer peasant labor for the land reclamation, forts, and roads serving the area around the city.[16]

The city's preparations for a protracted entry were, unfortunately, largely nullified by the ever-present vagaries of nature. Because Christine's arrival had been delayed some four days by weather, and because it was late in the day, she spent only two hours in Livorno before setting out in a carriage for Pisa. En route, her party passed through the vast Tuscan marshes, including the Maremma swampland, whose unhealthful miasmas were blamed for the death by malaria of Ferdinando's mother and two of his brothers. For reasons of health and economic exploitation, schemes for draining this area had been advanced sporadically since Roman times and, more recently, by Leonardo da Vinci; but it was only under the grand dukes that significant work was actually carried out, borrowing the unique technical expertise of drainage engineeers from the Netherlands. If this project, like some of Ferdinando's other policy initiatives, was not uniformly successful, it was not for lack of commitment: many acres were made cultivable and travel expedited. The road along which Christine traveled was part of a network of new highways stretched over this reclaimed land; it probably ran parallel to another significant component of geographical restructuring, the canal dug some nine miles in a straight line to connect the new port to Pisa and its great shipbuilding yard, the Arsenale, newly enlarged in 1588 but increasingly marooned by the recession of the Mediter-ranean shoreline.[17]

As Christine approached the outskirts of Pisa, some 3,000 cavalry and infantry were drawn up in continuous lines flanking the road as a "living wall"; firing their weapons, they "honored her with their power." A torchlit citizens' delegation led her along the Arno through triumphal arches, past the shipyard with its flag of the Order of Santo Stefano illuminated by fireworks, to her lodging in the Ducal Palace, overlooking the water. Her enormous entourage had to be billeted in several other state buildings and the homes of obliging prominent citizens.[18]

Pisa, which came under Florentine dominion earlier than Siena, had long since been converted socially and visually into the "second city" of the old Florentine duchy; many buildings were built, remodeled, or decorated by the same artists who were restructuring central Florence in these years. On April 26 Christine attended vespers in the duomo, which featured a crucifix (and later, bronze doors) by Giambologna; and she was undoubtedly shown the church of Santo Stefano and the adjacent palace of its crusading order, whose ships had escorted her to Tuscany: both were redesigned by Vasari as part of a wholesale enlargement of the renamed Piazza dei Cavalieri, which was built in stages from the 1560s until 1602.[19]

Pisa was but the most extensive example of the program to integrate both cities and countryside into a centralized order. As in Livorno, social, eco-nomic, and technological rationalization were everywhere mutually depen-dent: lack of control over nature meant a constant threat from poverty and disaster, which could not be confronted without the social control necessary to mobilize production efficiently and safely. As we have seen, vagabonds, vagrants, and bandits were endemic at the margins of formal authority. As late as 1584, roving brigands virtually laid siege to the town of Arezzo for a month; Ferdinando's arrest in 1590 of the most powerful outlaw, Alfonso Piccolomini, leader of a 300-man army, was greeted with sighs of relief.[20]

The bargain struck between the Medici and their subjects — the trade-off of liberty for security — was generally successful in terms of public safety and economic prosperity. Thanks to increased social order and the regime's ag-gressive development of mining, manufacturing, and trade, Tuscan popula-tion grew from some 586,000 in 1551 to 647,000 in 1622. An important component of technology was scientific research: Ferdinando enticed the renowned astronomer Galileo to the University of Pisa, the most prominent in Tuscany, in 1592, and patronized other institutions of practical learning in the city, such as the botanical garden. If prosperity did not rise as high as was hoped, general economic improvement helped ensure the loyalty of those who profited from expansion.[21]

The most eloquent — though too monochromatically rosy — assessment of Medicean social and economic policy was provided by the Venetian ambassador Francesco Contarini in June 1589, while he was in Florence for the wedding. Observing the citizenry after a half-century of princely domination, he reported that "although they had been accustomed to living under a republic, nonetheless, because the opinions of the people change with the change in government, they have since then become long accustomed to living under the dominion of an absolute prince, and, having accommodated themselves remarkably to his will, enjoy continuous peace and the happiest tranquility." He goes on to specify some of the sources, both civic and fiscal, of that contentment: "The subjects remain universally quite satisfied with the government of this prince, because he has ordained that throughout his state everyone receives swift and fair justice, that plenty is maintained everywhere, and finally he has made many generous loans to communities, guilds, and lands of his domain."[22]

This subjugation, however agreeably profitable, was nonetheless continually reinforced by social ritual. On the occasion of the wedding, local elites were pressured to prepare welcomes. As we have seen, Siena had written to Ferdinando in March "asking" to stage some appropriate tribute. A similar letter of April 8 from the prominent Pisan Ruberto Ridolfi sounds less like a voluntary offer and more like a subordinate's progress report: because "it pleased Your Serene Highness to command us to devise some festivities for the arrival of your bride, and in view of the shortness of time, we have undertaken" a number of plans, among them a naval battle to be staged by "several teams of distinguished gentlemen, who immediately offered their services at their own expense."

The integration of the Pisan patriciate into the larger state network of reciprocal political-economic-cultural favors is manifest in Ridolfi's letter. Not only did the local gentry offer to perform the naval battle at their own expense, but "this community" also undertook the costs of lighting the nocturnal procession, "not wishing to accept the offer made to pay these expenses from Your Highness's funds." All is not altruistic generosity here, however, for Ridolfi goes on to explain that the performers would like to use various military supplies stored in the city's fortress, which the local quartermaster had declined to furnish without Ferdinando's permission. Ridolfi asks for this permission to be communicated, as "it would save all but 150 of the 800 ducats you promised us for these festivities." Here, as with the Florentine nobles who patronized the Pitti events as the cost of doing cloth business with the court, the line between spontaneous gift and carefully orchestrated exchange of ritual tributes is shifting and permeable.[23]

The splendid welcome ceremonies at Pisa were a condensed prelude to the Florentine festivities. Besides the entry, they encompassed continuous balls and banquets, a carriage procession throughout the city of 70 gentlewomen, "all . . . very honorably dressed," and the battle on the Arno, in which a small Christian fleet was beset by two Turkish vessels (*corsari*). The Italian ships, meant to be taken as Christine's escort, took refuge on the quay fronting the Ducal Palace "as a place of safe harbor" (*sicuro porto*) from which the infidels were driven away with noisy firearms and bombs. Turks were the standard villains in nautical entertainments, signifying the Barbary pirates whom the order of Santo Stefano had been founded to repel. More broadly, Tuscan rule, in the person of the grand duke whose consort overlooked the contest from the palace window, was being figured as a safe haven from multiple social and natural perils, the solutions to which were increasingly understood to entail larger political-economic formations than could be mustered by small medieval city-states like Pisa, whose silted-up access to the sea symbolized its geopolitical obsolescence.[24]

THE UFFIZI THEATER, APRIL 25–29

While Christine was being entertained in Pisa, the next full rehearsal in the Uffizi theater took place on April 25. The grand duke had ordered it after the run-through he saw on the 16th, and the lists made on the 18th to prepare for it overlapped with and responded to comments from that rehearsal. (Seriacopi once again complained about the harried Buontalenti's tardiness in providing him with a final list of the entire stage crew.)[25] Immediately after the April 25 rehearsal, noting that "the comedy has to be done a week from now," Buontalenti and the carpenter Orazio Graziadio together compiled a last punch list (MR 50v–51r). They needed ten or twelve painters to remedy further wear and tear on the sets (quickly, so the touch-ups would dry before final rehearsals) and another dozen carpenters to make the final assembly of the large set pieces (boat, inferno, and dragon, whose wings were not ordered until April 25). Seriacopi then commanded that "the usual tailors" be on hand constantly to sew together the remaining canvas backcloths, and Rosselli and Francini to be continuously at the theater from that day onward.

A tense interchange erupted between Buontalenti and Cavalieri on April 27, the day Christine left Pisa. Buontalenti had fired both a painter and the carpenter who was making the granducal palco, along with their crews of assistants. Alarmed at this last-minute delay, Cavalieri ordered Buontalenti himself to find replacements immediately, warning him to complete everything without extra expense, "otherwise he'll make Buontalenti suffer for it." Bernardo replied that he had plenty of carpenters available, but "doesn't know where painters could possibly be found" — not surprisingly, since Seriacopi had already ordered them to work around the clock on existing assignments. Cavalieri countered with permission to transfer some of the painters from the Pitti, except Francini and Rosselli, who were late completing the four large narrative backdrops for the courtyard. With delays everywhere, Cavalieri was forced to make precise distinctions of priority; because the Pitti evening was facing a more distant debut (May 11, nine days after the intermedi's premiere), he declared that, among the Pitti preparations, these four canvases "must come before everything else," but that for the moment "the comedy must be primary, and then the tournament."[26]

CHRISTINE VISITS THE VILLAS, APRIL 27–29

On April 27 Christine set out from Pisa on a two-day trip through the Tuscan countryside toward her rendezvous with Ferdinando at his principal villa, Poggio a Caiano, just outside Florence. Her first day's journey of some 30 miles traversed numerous towns on the south bank of the Arno from Cascina to Ambrogiana, where she stayed the night. The latter villa was only one of several Medici country properties that she passed through along the way; her suite being too large to lodge in any one such estate, many of them stayed behind in nearby Empoli or continued ahead to Montelupo for the night. Departing after lunch the next day, she crossed north over the Arno and reached Poggio, about 9 miles from the capital, by dinnertime (fig. 9).

In this village and farmstead itinerary, she was presented with both living and artistic figurations of the same interlocked efforts toward control of the social and environmental landscape as seen in Livorno and Pisa. Gualterotti enthusiastically records the crowds who lined the roads and the town entries, made up of ordinary citizens, local militia, and rows of infantry who fired welcoming shots; the entire distance "was completely covered with armed men, not only the streets, but almost everywhere the eye could see, a clear indication of the great population, and of the prowess of arms . . . by dint of which have been created a nation, an empire, and riches, and great honor." A literally parallel display bore witness to an equally important, but more peaceful and industrious, source of those riches: along these same thoroughfares,

Christine and her well-wishers were shaded by long rows of mulberry trees, planted on the main roads at Ferdinando's instigation to provide a domestic source of silkworms for the cloth industry.[27]

The total number of villas belonging to the Medici eventually came to seventeen. These country homes, with extensive acreage of orchards, farmland, and vineyards surrounded by hunting and fishing grounds, were spread across the Tuscan heartland from the Pisan coast to Florence and further north and east. Rossi praises the dynasty's program of "building marvelous palaces in the countryside" (*Descrizione*, 4); some, like the reconstructed farmhouses at Careggi and Cafaggiolo, had been in the family since the days of the elder Cosimo de' Medici. Others were added over the ensuing century and a half by purchase or confiscation from other wealthy clans: Ambrogiana, for example, was enlarged by Ferdinando from a small house formerly belonging to the Ardinghelli and Corboli families. He favored several as residences, moving about with the seasons and the hunting, and others were "farmed out" to lesser family members: Francesco's natural son Don Antonio owned La Peggio and Marignolle, and the estate later called Poggio Imperiale had been occupied by Ferdinand's late sister Isabella and her husband Paolo Orsini, parents of Don Virginio.[28]

Although villa life was traditionally extolled, since the Latin rustic poets, as an escape from the physical restrictions and social demands of the city, the relationship between villa and town was less the polar opposition of nature to culture than the reciprocal and complementary one of satellite to center. Beyond providing informal country retreats, villas served equally to urbanize the countryside, laying a grid of orderly and unifying structures over the landscape for political, military, and economic purposes. They provided a network of command and supply posts at short distances from one another, to accommodate the slow pace of overland travel and the large numbers of attendants; some of them were walled for defense and could garrison troops for rural pacification.[29]

Villas were also economic and logistical resources. Benedetto Fedini, the granducal guardaroba, kept notebooks for all phases of Christine's journey; these household accounts, concerned with myriad material necessities, from lumber, oil, and fabric to sugar and wax, refer to many shipments back and forth between city and periphery.[30] The villas sent materials to Florence for quartering guests and themselves housed other guests, an arrangement that required some reverse flow of bedding, linens, and so forth to the villas. At times this outward direction dominated: on a later occasion the Pitti majordomo, Enea Vaini, asked Fedini to transfer plates, silverware, and saltcellars to the palace, "since the butlers [*credenzieri*] from Campagna and Ambrogiana have taken everything away."[31]

If the villas controlled surrounding nature and society, they also figured that control artistically. Ferdinando invested considerable architectural energy in his estates: many were built or remodeled by artists associated with the wedding, among them Buontalenti, Giambologna, Valerio Cioli, and Bartolommeo Ammannati. La Petraia, for example, was enlarged by Bernardo between 1576 and 1589 and its courtyard frescoed by the hyperactive Cigoli — somewhere between his work at the duomo, the theater, and the entry — in time for the bride's arrival.[32] These projects embodied artifice and control at several overlapping levels — siting, geometry, hydraulics, and scenography — often with close connections to contemporary theatrical practices.

Architecturally, the white cubic volumes of the main houses combined with the rectangular patterns of walls, gardens, and fields to impose a geometric order on the irregular contours of the land (fig. 10). These blocks were often sited on hillsides with commanding views, affording a surveillance of the surroundings that combined tactical advantage with a discursive subtext: the reduction of the natural world to a readily comprehensible, and thus manipulable, image seen from above — in short, a map. This specular transformation of the natural environment from something unconsciously surrounding and embedding human life into a spectacle, viewed as a whole from outside — in Ackerman's phrase (*Villa*, 78), "the theater of daily life" — offers an outdoor analogy to the artistic perspective developed for painting and extended into the theater, where the ideal, unobstructed line of sight belonged to the ruler, both enabling and dramatizing his or her effortless, godlike grasp of the totality of the realm (the same pursuit of a distanced, omniscient gaze inspired the contemporaneous telescope and microscope).

The landscape settings of the villas, particularly their gardens, were equally transformed into a "dialectic of nature and artifice," structured in scenographic terms and expressed through "the paradoxical imitation of natural forms by man-made elements." In the country as in the Boboli Gardens at the Pitti, the scale and technology developed for practical engineering were turned to creating such "marvels" as colossal figures spouting water and mechanical automata — amusing reminders of more ponderous environmental machines. The grotesque forms and materials of fountains and sculptures replicated the fascination with the fluid boundary between art and nature that informed the theater designs: Giambologna's 35-foot Apennine statue at Pratolino, with interior waterworks by Buontalenti, was similar in form and piping to the allegorical river gods flanking the Uffizi proscenium or the two giant

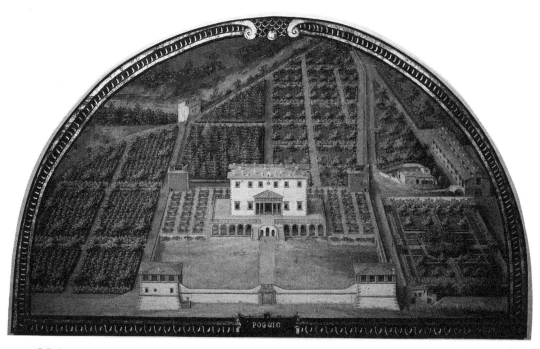

10. *Medici villa at Poggio a Caiano. Justus Utens.*

terra-cotta fountains commisioned from Rosselli and Francini for the Pitti courtyard (Chaps. 3, 4).[33]

The villa landscapes also figure in Medicean arts as subject matter, in a mode that is at once more literally descriptive and more discursively charged. At Ferdinando's personal favorite, Artimino, he commissioned in 1599 a series of paintings that preserve the appearance of the villas only a decade after the wedding: seventeen lunettes for the principal salon constituted a visual inventory of the family villas (fig. 10, the panel of Poggio a Caiano). They functioned not simply as visual records, but more profoundly as a collective document of ownership and control, a catalogue of holdings that asserts possession of the individual pieces while establishing their common identity as parts of a coherent whole. Viewed from an aloof, artificially high vantage point that is perspectively related to the ideal lordly viewpoint of the stage sets, the pictures conflate the conventions of painting and cartography. Mural map programs had an honorable tradition in Italy: the fourteenth-century *mappamundo* in the Sienese city hall charted and illustrated subject towns, visually reinforcing claims to overlordship. With the voyages of discovery from the fifteenth century, this urge to plot the entire surface of the globe intensified: the Artimino series was preceded by the Farnese villa at Caprarola, frescoed in 1573 with large maps of the entire known world, and Ferdinando's commission in 1589 for a *Sala delle carte geografiche* in the Uffizi, with maps of Tuscany (a chamber of the same name was later painted in the Vatican by order of Pope Urban VIII, 1631).[34]

To return to the villas' function as satellite facilities, their role in accommodating wedding guests illustrates the intricate coordination between city and country. The first foreigners began to trickle into Tuscany on April 17; soon an accelerating throng of visitors imposed a logistical burden far beyond housing the performers. The largest delegation, that of Francesco's daughter Eleonora de' Medici and her husband Vincenzo Gonzaga, Duke of Mantua, arrived with 700 people; the grand total was later calculated by Fedini at 2,700 foreign guests, some of whom stayed until mid-June.[35]

Nobility of the highest rank, who were also the most closely related, were lodged in the city center in what were technically, despite their grandeur, private family quarters. Vincenzo and Eleonora stayed at the Pitti, as did Ferdinando's sister Virginia and her husband, Cesare d'Este of Ferrara, who arrived on April 27. But the family palaces could hardly begin to accommodate all the lordly attendees, let alone their enormous retinues. Quarters for less intimate guests, and for everyone's subordinate staffs, had to be spread out across the entire city and well into the surrounding countryside, up to several hours' distance.

At least seven urban palaces were used, both Medici and private. Fedini conducted a survey of available rooms and supplies needed (linens, beds, tables, lamps, saddles); he found 67 beds available in the Palazzo Vecchio (including the family quarters), 53 rooms at the Pitti, and 74 rooms in the Palazzo Medici "to supply for foreigners" (but with only 45 beds). Less ample accommodations were also scouted in attics or upper rooms (*soffitte*), perhaps for accompanying servants; the Mantuan lord and lady stayed at the Pitti, but their suite was put up at the nearby palace of the Bardi (the programmer Giovanni's family), one of several patrician clans who provided such "gift" services to the court.[36] After exhausting these urban sites, Fedini turned to resources out of town, inventorying mattresses available elsewhere. The Guardaroba then proceeded to decorate and furnish the villas, including Ambrogiana and Poggio, and to fill requests for beds, cooking equipment, and lamps for other "lodgings in the country," naming towns as far away as Firenzuola, Scarperia, Poggibonsi, and San Casciano.[37]

In the midst of all this activity, on Friday, April 28, Christine arrived at Poggio a Caiano. Designed a century earlier for Lorenzo de' Medici, decorated by Pontormo and later by Alessandro Allori, this jewel in the necklace of family villas was frequently used as a stopping place for high-ranking visitors. Typically, the villa, surrounded by Buontalenti's defensive perimeter wall and bastions, commanded the summit of an exposed promontory, its sweeping views over the valleys below magnified by a high podium (fig. 10). Gualterotti rather hyperbolically labels it "one of the most delightful and splendid palaces in Europe," attributing its status to the hilltop site, "from which it overlooks [*scopre*] the two lowlands of Florence and Pistoia." His verb *scoprire*, literally "to uncover," emphasizes laying bare the surrounding territory to a gaze of visual and social surveillance: Ferdinando no doubt caught sight of his bride's convoy long before its arrival and watched her progress up the slope before going out on the raised terrace to greet her, at last, in person.[38]

Christine rested at Poggio for two days, touring the grounds and receiving visits from her new relatives. She would also have been busy inspecting the clothes that Ferdinando had had the Guardaroba make for her and her suite over the past several months: one payment in May to Maestro Gottardo the German, the grand duke's personal tailor, was specifically for "outfits for the grand duchess" constructed by six of his staff and sent to Poggio. Farther down the social scale, Ulino Giovacchini, the head coachman who drove Christine through the countryside, and his assistants each received two out-fits, carefully graded as to their rank and the formality of events: a country livery (*livrea da campagna*) of plain red cloth with a velvet collar, then a *livrea grande* for the entry.[39]

On Saturday, April 29, while Christine was at last able to rest, the city was still bustling with last-minute preparations for her reception. Gaddi and Buontalenti, possibly joined by Alessandro Allori, Santi di Tito, or Taddeo Landini as the principal entry designers, were most likely circumnavigating downtown Florence to inspect the next day's arches, which would have been erected and touched up over the past few weeks. And in the Uffizi, notwith-standing the Palm Sunday holiday and festivities, Seriacopi, with two days to go, ordered his various crews to report for work on Sunday until midday (MR 52r). On Saturday evening, Ferdinando left his bride to return to the Pitti Palace, from which he was to ride forth the next morning in his role as official greeter.

THE ENTRY TO FLORENCE, SUNDAY, APRIL 30

On the morning of Palm Sunday, the entire city rose at dawn. Crowds of people from as far off as Genoa, Rome, Naples, and France began lining the streets: lesser folk on foot, the upper classes in decorated carriages or on horseback. Two thousand members of the clergy, dressed in gold brocade, velvet, and damask, left the duomo baptistery about 6 a.m. in procession toward the Porta al Prato, where they were joined by massed troops. While this audience was assembling, Christine awoke early in order to dress and move on to breakfast at the Torre degli Agli, the Spini villa only a mile from the city walls. Ferdinando and other family members rode out to visit briefly there but soon returned to the city walls to await her formal arrival. Christine left the Torre about 9 in a carriage. As they had on her approach to Pisa, the military lined the streets, firing off their guns as she arrived at the western gate at 10, met by Ferdinando himself.[40]

The setting, imagery, and ritual that now confronted Christine established the capital city as a "landscape of control" even more intensive and densely layered than those of town and country. The central Pitti-Uffizi-Vecchio complex, which had remapped the cityscape to reinforce and figure the power of the ruler, was but one of the period's extensive reconstructions of European capitals into "a huge theatrical setting for the display of the court." Reaching outward from that nucleus, the administration headquartered there had now made over the entire city, at least for the time of the wedding, into a scenographically structured extension of that space for a quasi-sacred communal ceremony (map, fig. 9).[41]

The design and iconography of the seven entry arches — two-story constructions of wood, plaster, painted canvas, stucco decorations and sculptures — has been outlined above, as well as the social networks of their production. At this point in our examination of the wedding's patrons, creators, and actors, it is also possible to glimpse the manifold personal meanings that such a diverse mosaic of audiences would have read into the event — beyond, alongside, even instead of its official artistic and historical significance. The responses of spectators are an integral part of the wedding as of all images — a factor that Cinquecento aestheticians were the first to acknowledge implicitly, by addressing their treatises to the viewer of art, not its maker. In more sociological terms, at the heart of the arts of *theatrum mundi* is a notion of performance as ritual, a group action whose intended result is "the small- or large-scale transformation of both the actor and the audience to the transaction." We cannot, therefore, in Richard Trexler's formulation, "analyze a festival or procession and ignore the audience."[42]

Porta al Prato

The large assembly greeting Christine gathered in and around the spacious octagonal forecourt — Gualterotti terms it a theater — of the Porta al Prato, the triumphal arch at the city gate (cat. 1; frontispiece). In addition to musicians and singers, different groups of which performed at each successive arch, the "cast" included the royal family, other rulers, clerics, ambassadors, nobles, and household officials. Gualterotti lists 166 principal attendees, each with a liveried retinue that ranged in number from two or four men up to ten for the

prominent Guicciardini, Francesco and Girolamo, who wore black and turquoise velvet, doubtless from the family mills that had sold velvet to the
Medici for this same occasion. The grand duke's escort was the largest at 110,
while the Duke of Mantua had 40, Don Pietro 30. Ferdinando and these close
family members, also including Cesare d'Este and Virginio Orsini, were all
attired in white and cloth of gold, embroidered with pearls and gems, and
stood under an enormous white and gold canopy; Ferdinando's pages wore
peacock velvet embroidered in red, white, and gold, Vincenzo Gonzaga's red
velvet. Forty to fifty select young Florentine noblemen, including a junior
Guicciardini, in splendid white liveries with gold and silver trim, supported
the canopy under which Christine was to travel throughout the day.[43]

Gualterotti tells us that Christine first "dismounted [from her carriage]
and, while admiring the many lovely pictures, was entertained by two instrumental groups which were in the gallery over the gate." To aid her in grasping
the elaborate program, at this point Christine was probably given a copy of
part 2 of Gualterotti's book, the descriptive catalogue written in advance and
in the present tense: his dedication to her offers it in the hope that "it may
serve you in the capacity of both an interpreter of the new subjects, and a
reminder of the stories of bygone times."[44]

The opening rite was Christine's coronation. Fifteen bishops blessed her
richly worked crown; the Archbishop of Pisa, Carlo Antonio Puteo, handed it
to Ferdinando, who placed it on the head of his kneeling bride. As a consort,
Christine received her crown from her husband, not, as he had, from higher
clerical and secular authority; her status and prerogatives were henceforth
dependent on him. As had already become clear at Poggio, even her physical
appearance was now to be largely managed by the state apparatus of her
husband. Here that transfer of allegiance was made visually manifest: since
leaving her home in mourning for her grandmother, Christine had worn only
black, but on this day she at last exchanged that attire for one of the many new
outfits made for her: a French-style gown in cloth of gold with multicolored
accents in curled rows.[45]

A note in Fedini's planning book offers a suggestive detail of the one sphere
in which married women maintained some degree of economic autonomy.
Francesca Orsini, who sailed on the Capitana as head of Christine's household, had earlier advised him on "what should be put in order [in Florence] for
the arrival of Her Highness the bride," specifying in addition to numerous
items of clothing, hair garlands, and the like "a small empty room, made into a
place to keep and protect the jewels to be worn daily." Special attention is paid
to her jewels because, being a major component of her ample dowry —
possessions she brought into the marriage — they were by tradition the one

form of property, along with clothes and intimate personal effects, that would remain inalienably hers. The display of these objects, then, both asserted her title to them and maintained some vestige of her former identity as she was progressively absorbed into her new position.[46]

Ponte alla Carraia

After the crowning ceremony, Ferdinando returned to the Pitti, and Christine, mounting a white horse covered in gold brocade, set off under the canopy attended by Pietro and Vincenzo; her aunt Brunswick followed with Cesare and Virginio. Their procession retraced nearly the same route as the previous such entry in 1565. Heading inward to the Arno at Ponte Santa Trinita, they then turned left to circle the streets preserving the limits of the Roman *castrum*, spiraling toward the state center, the Palazzo Vecchio. The mile-long entourage moved at a stately pace, due to its sheer size and the press of crowds filling the narrow streets. Accompanying the numerous noble and ecclesiastical marchers already observed — centered on Christine and the Archbishop of Pisa bearing a basin to hold her crown — were a gilded carriage, 17 principal gentlewomen on horseback, civic officials, various orders of knights, and some 500 cavalry. The lead company of household troops were attired in full armor over the grand duke's livery colors of peacock velvet and red silk; their captain of arms, Gianvincenzo Vitelli, Marchese of Cetona, also sported an overvest of cloth of silver.[47]

Starn and Partridge are certainly astute to observe that such a complex procession "defined and exposed social differences . . . [and] sharp distinctions in power and status were delineated by the color, cut, and cost of the costumes, by the order of march," and so on. But it is not enough to discuss the intended meanings of the entry without reference to the audience; as Janet Wolff has phrased it, "a sociology of cultural production must be supplemented with, and integrated with, a sociology of cultural reception." The multiplicity of the entry audience — its patchwork diversity of class, occupation, literacy, and gender — raises the question, How did these various component groups of participants and spectators perceive or "read" the event?[48]

Any attempt to answer this question is necessarily speculative, given the lack of personal records. As an organizing principle, however, I would propose to locate varying responses along two intersecting axes, of depth and surface. These coordinates graph two distinct modes of impact: the intellectual and the pragmatic or, in parallel terms, the binaries of conceptual/perceptual or qualitative/quantitative. Highest on the intellectual scale, the aristocratic audience would have taken some pride in catching whatever was familiar from their store of classics, religion, and contemporary politics; but their own educations varied considerably, especially with respect to gender, and not even the most assiduous among them could possibly have appreciated, or cared about, the plethora of esoteric allusion. (Rossi, in his *Descrizione*, admits that he has gone into too much detail about a costume for Apollo and its literary sources, so "I will keep silent.") At the other end of the social order, the common people who formed the bulk of the street audience would not understand the formal allegories, whether historical or mythical, or their Latin captions. Much of the effect of the procession and décors on the general public was therefore calculated along the perpendicular axis of spectacle, of a conspicuous display of the regime's wealth, skills, and organizational capacity — in a word, by the surface impression of abundance and virtuosity, distinct from any depth of intellectualized content.

To begin with Christine as principal spectator, the theme of the Carraia arch was the most directly relevant to her individually: previous Medici and Lorraine marriages, including highlights of her own marital odyssey (cat. 2). Here she passed under Cosci's painting, discussed in Chapters 1 and 2, that showed her taking leave of her grandmother Catherine de' Medici. This image of an event that never happened could have been read in two ways. On one hand, Christine could not help but be informed by her personal experience: she must have winced at the irony of viewing such a patently fabricated image of what she had lost, on the very day she laid aside her mourning clothes. On the other hand, as with the false breastplates for *La pellegrina*, in this elevated artistic discourse symbolic truth mattered more than underlying fact: for Christine and all the noble women in the procession, the pride of place given (only on this arch) to a woman, in her influential matriarchal role as the "grandmother of Europe," exemplified the highest status and achievement to which women of their class could aspire.

Other noble and patrician viewers may have been able to grasp a fair portion of this iconography, but their personal investment in it varied widely. Judging from his complacent assessment of the Tuscan body politic on this occasion, the Venetian ambassador Contarini, whose suite of 16 were attired in turquoise velvet lined with cloth of silver, appears to have accepted the regime's claims at face value. In contrast, Alfonso Piccolomini — who was to be arrested by Ferdinando the following year for armed brigandage — and his black-clad attendants must have taken a more knowing, even cynical view of the regime's visual pretension to universal authority and its attempt to co-opt him into official circles. Even those aristocrats who, like the grand duke's personal representative Orazio Rucellai, willingly reaped the honors of proximity to his person would also have been aware of the burdens such favor entailed. Not only did the great clans bear the costs of parade floats, lodging guests, and draping their palace façades; after listing the young patricians who carried the canopy, Pavoni notes that "all the abovementioned gentlemen went to a very great and previously unheard of expense for their outfits."[49]

Among the creative team for the wedding, three organizers held sufficiently high rank to be present as actor-spectators in their own show: Niccolò Gaddi (ten staff, in black velvet), Giovanni de' Bardi (five, in red striped with gold velvet and fringed with turquoise and silver), and Emilio de' Cavalieri (six, black velvet with silver trim). Gaddi, who was looking at the very arches for which he had written the program, understood their symbolism better than anyone present; but all three men, with their inside knowledge of the day-to-day planning process, would also have seen the unfolding pageant from some self-conscious distance, as a deliberately constructed cultural artifact. Of the more logistical court functionaries, the majordomo Enea Vaini attended (five escorts, in black velvet), though Fedini did not. As both were in the managerial bureaucracy, we may suppose that Vaini looked on the day's events with something of the same businesslike eye as his co-worker, whose survey for guest housing had referred to Vincenzo Gonzaga's suite as "700 mouths" — an impersonal phraseology indicating that, quite apart from their niceties of rank, all these visitors just looked to him like bodies to be fed.[50]

Most of the entry artists, like Allori and Santi, whose work was long since finished and installed, would have been free to join the crowds in the streets. Their grasp of the official iconography was fragmentary: artisans could not read the Latin inscriptions, though they were told the narratives of single scenes assigned to them. They would have looked upon the arches primarily as objects they had made, tests of their carefully monitored handiwork, and as public works providing a boon to family budgets. Whether a painter like Giovanni Cosci, who depicted Catherine's nonexistent farewell, was troubled by its incongruity or thought of the canvas as simply another made-to-order product, we lack the testimony to say.[51]

Finally, the general public (according to Gualterotti) snatched glimpses of whatever they could from streets, windows, rooftops and bridges, even from nearby hills overlooking the Arno. To them, limited in space to a distant panorama, or in time to what could be seen from a fixed vantage point, the complex sequential iconography can have registered as little more than a particularly grandiose example of the street decorations then common on religious and civic festivals — an occasion for joyous color and sound with little precise meaning. On many such occasions (though not recorded here), rulers were at pains to reinforce the public's sense of physical plenty, of virtually bathing in their lord's largesse, by showering the throngs with less abstract gratifications like coins or fountains of wine.[52]

We may, however, suppose (without too great a risk of anachronism) that at least one aspect of the visual display was scrutinized with knowing interest by a significant segment of the audience: Christine's dress. Marriage, with its attendant ceremonies and decorations, was an experience shared by virtually all women of any class, outside the convents; and both hopeful girls and nostalgic matrons would see reflected and magnified in Christine's costumed procession a focal point of their own lives. (Some, if they worked in weaving and embroidery, might also have seen their own handiwork.) But a characterization of the audience by gender must look at more than fashion: in particular, at the restrictions on woman's participation in public life, as both actor and observer. Among the 166 honored guests Gualterotti lists only one female, Virginia Fiesca, apparently ruler in her own right of Piombino. And because of their high rank, the bride and the Medici princesses rode in the procession, thus seeing it all in proper sequence — a privilege also extended to their 17 female attendants on horseback. For the most part, however, other aristocratic women, if they attended, did so only as spectators, with a stationary view from the newly fashionable enclosed carriages, considered necessary to maintain modesty while their husbands acted the family's public role. Perhaps the festive mood and crowds loosened the customary constraints on females walking the streets unaccompanied, but it seems likely that most women below the aristocracy watched from windows or other enclosed spaces, where the view would be somewhat more limited than that from the pavement below.

Duomo

The procession next turned northward to the Canto de' Carnesecchi; the arch here glorified the bride's house of Lorraine, with whose history she was presumably familiar (cat. 3). Her route then went east toward the duomo, whose exterior décor is the only one of which a few fragments survive (cat. 4). She was welcomed by Archbishop Alessandro de' Medici, her new cousin, before a backdrop that chronicled the history of the Church in Florence — and disguised somewhat the rough façade, still unfinished after yet another inconclusive design competition. The building's interior had been closed for a month for temporary construction; Fedini's Guardaroba was responsible for building a high platform (*residenzia*) with cushioned seating in the nave. But extensive permanent decoration had begun decades earlier; the crowning feature of the duomo, the vast fresco covering the ceiling of Brunelleschi's historic dome, had been recently completed by Cigoli and other artists who were simultaneously employed on the theater and entry. The interior was lit by 38,000 candles (despite broad daylight), and the splendid music and singing were highlighted by a giant white aerial cloud full of performers dressed as angels. While the archbishop delivered an oration, this mechanism descended from the dome and landed in front of the bride's seat, the singing so magnificent that "it seemed like Paradise itself."[53]

Although I know of no records of the churches' preparations for the wedding events, it is possible at least to sketch the outlines of church patronage. On the day of the entry, Ferdinando made a gift of a new black silk hat to Puteo, the Archbishop of Pisa who carried Christine's crown. This was but the latest in a series of pious donations connected to the wedding, which continued an elaborate network of gifts and favors between church and state that paralleled, and intersected with, the reciprocal patronage between state and patriciate. Although all classes craved the spiritual blessings of the church, royalty particularly sought to share in its aura of sacred legitimacy; in return, these religious foundations, often headed by junior members of the great patrician families, were large institutions that depended on the goodwill of the wealthy and powerful.

Two other prominent examples of this triangulated exchange are the churches of the Santissima Annunziata and San Marco, both of which enshrined important relics of special interest to the pious Christine. On April 22, Ferdinando gave a pair of richly chased silver candlesticks — almost six feet high and valued at 5,000 scudi apiece — to the Annunziata, which was scheduled to reveal a relic for Christine in May. Additional endowments were provided by wealthy patricians who, like the grand duke, had blood ties to the church hierarchy: the prior at SS. Annunziata was Domenico Salviati, and it was two Salviati brothers who paid for the new chapel at San Marco, also to be a focus of elaborate ritual involving Christine. These patrons, Antonio and Averardo di Filippo Salviati, witnessed the entry with attendants dressed in black velvet, no doubt (as with the Guicciardini escort) from the family's own cloth mills, which had also purveyed fabrics for the outfits of their customers and cousins, the Medici.[54]

Canto de' Bischeri

After the duomo rituals, the procession headed east to the Canto de' Bischeri, where the Habsburg dynasty was represented by the late Emperor Charles V and his son Philip II of Spain (cat. 5). The honor paid to the imperial family was much reduced here compared to the 1565 entry, because political shifts had led to the selection of Christine, rather than another Austrian archduchess, as Ferdinando's bride. Although he owed the Emperor Rudolf II feudal acknowledgment and needed to remain on civil terms with Philip as Spanish influence in Italian affairs grew, Ferdinando disliked and distrusted them. So it seems hardly accidental that this is the least elaborate set piece, and one of only two that do not form an actual vault; two panels merely frame the street, but lack the "overarching" upper element, passage beneath which would signify submission.

All the same, familial alliances linked both bride and groom to the Empire and Spain, complicating the official line on their states' relations (see Appendix, genealogical table). Through his deceased sister-in-law, Joanna of Austria, Ferdinando had been indirectly related to Philip, her first cousin. Christine's Habsburg connections were closer: her maternal uncle Charles IX of France married Elizabeth, granddaughter of Charles V and sister of Rudolf, and her aunt Elisabeth (sister of Charles IX) had married Philip. No doubt she noticed, while inspecting the painting of Catherine's family at the Carraia arch, that Philip had been pointedly omitted from the painted spouses of the queen's children, a reminder that Christine's new position would require some juggling of personal and political concerns.

Canto degli Antellesi

The next to last arch, at the Canto degli Antellesi, continued the family theme — here the Medici, centered on Cosimo I and his forebears and deeds (cat. 6). Significantly, the main activity chosen was Cosimo's fortification of Tuscan cities, which Christine had just seen at Livorno. Given the slow pace of her procession, at about this point the theater workers would have been leaving their hurried half-day of overtime, encouraged no doubt to attend what was left of the procession, which by then was close to their work site. We may imagine Pagolini and Rosselli, or the carpenters Domenico and Orazio, passing through the remaining barricades around the Uffizi and jostling through the crowds to arrive at the Bischeri or Antellesi arches in time to catch sight of Christine. Like the entry artists and the general populace, these artisans would have known little of interfamily tensions at the upper levels of European society or of distant urbanization. If they were impressed, it was more likely by the thought of the practical benefits this giant local project had brought to their friends, family, or professional associates.

Palazzo Vecchio

Passing through the Antellesi arch, Christine's cortege spilled out into the Piazza della Signoria, curving around the square in a long arc before arriving at the door of the Palazzo Vecchio, the ancient symbol of city power, adorned with a facade whose theme was the apotheosis of Tuscany (cat. 7). In the main scene, Tuscany receives a crown and hands a scepter to Florence: both allegorical figures are female, and in their courtly robes and granducal coronets, must have resembled Christine herself at this moment. Life reflected art as Orazio

Rucellai took the bride's crown and carried it before her as she entered her new home.

As she passed under this image, did she reflect on the disjunction between the ideal allegorical realm, where women reigned supreme, and the actual world she was entering, in which brides merely mediated relations between men and a wife's powers extended only as far as the limits of her own body and dowry? Probably not: she had been schooled to this system since birth, and besides she must have been exhausted from her all-day ceremonial performance (Gualterotti never mentions lunch) and glad to escape from public scrutiny. But the inescapable gender divisions of society also met her inside the palazzo, where the principal ladies of her new family escorted her to her rooms, accompanied by her own female relatives and attendants. While the men of their families carried out duties assigned by the grand duke's establishment, the Medici princesses and such ladies-in-waiting as Camilla Rucellai and Francesca Orsini were already establishing the rituals of Christine's personal household, a court-within-a-court that offered (alongside the convents) one of the few spheres for female administration and artistic patronage.[55]

Christine relaxed in the women's quarters for the late afternoon, then dined quietly, "and having finished supper with great satisfaction, went to rest from the labors of the day." If she was tired, so were the many participants and spectators, like the young noblemen who had carried her canopy all day through the crowded streets. (In compensation for the expense of their own outfits, they were given Christine's horse and its gilded trappings, "as a token of the honor [they had] received" — yet another instance of the complex exchange of gifts and favors.)[56] At least their work was over, as was that of the musicians and soldiers; not so for the theater staff, who had worked half that day, despite the holiday. Though no doubt glad for the afternoon diversion, they, too, probably went to bed early, still tired from their overtime and needing to marshal strength for the following day's final dress rehearsal and Tuesday's premiere performance.

CHAPTER SIX

May 1589

THE WEDDING AS/IN

PERFORMANCE

Throughout the month of May, the multiple interlocking preparations we have been following over most of the past year at last culminated, "playing themselves out" in the actual *theatrum mundi*. As each spectacle in turn reached its opening day, the fundamental quality of theater as a space of controlled artifice spread across the time and space of the entire city. A summary calendar of these events was given in the Introduction; as the most extensive and best documented are those of May 2 (intermedi) and May 11 (Pitti), the following chronological account will focus on them while summarizing the remaining entertainments. (For additional details see relevant Catalogue entries.)

During this period, as already at Christine's entry, the term *production* shifted its principal referent from "making" to "acting," and the most relevant analytical metaphors accordingly shift from those of rehearsal to performance and spectatorship. The play was a performance in the narrowly theatrical sense, but the audiences for all of these events were also performing a large-scale social ritual, costumed and staged throughout the capital city over several weeks: they were "cast" as actors themselves, as well as viewers. Moreover, this audience/cast kept shifting: a number of high-ranking guests arrived too late to participate in Christine's entry and even subsequent events, then staggered their departures through May and June.[1]

Accordingly, we must continue to consider the multiple audiences for the event, and what levels or modes of "reading" predominated along various fault lines of class, sex, age, and occupation. In the analysis of such events as historical texts I seek to excavate how, and in what proportions, audience responses varied along the twin coordinates that were earlier termed depth and surface, ranging from conceptual meaning to perceptual abundance as well as economic and social implications. This attempt, like that of imagining audience interaction with Christine's entry, is unavoidably speculative. Beyond the difficulties inherent in "psychoanalyzing the dead," the available

PLATE I. *Costume design, Siren VIIII (cat. 22).*

PLATE 2. *Costume design, four planetary gods (cat. 23).*

PLATE 3. *Costume design, four planetary gods (cat. 24).*

PLATE 4. *Costume design, Necessity and the Fates (cat. 25).*

PLATE 5. *Costume design, hamadryads (cat. 28).*

PLATE 6. *Costume design, Muses (cat. 30).*

PLATE 7. *Costume design, Apollo (cat. 35).*

PLATE 8. *Costume design, two dancing women (cat. 32).*

PLATE 9. *Stage design, intermedio 3 (cat. 33).*

PLATE 10. *Property design, flying Apollo (cat. 49).*

PLATE 11. *Property design, Python (cat. 50).*

PLATE 12. *Costume design, Delphic couple (cat. 37).*

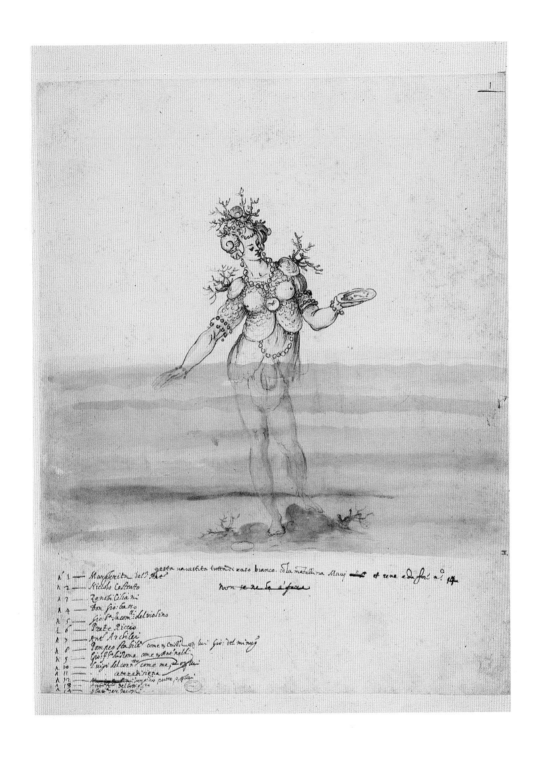

PLATE 13. *Costume design, sea nymph (cat. 56).*

PLATE 14. *Costume design, Arion (cat. 57).*

PLATE 15. Giuoco del calcio, *Piazza Santa Croce (cat. 69).*

PLATE 16. *Allegorical chariot for tournament referees (cat. 73).*

record is fragmentary and biased. Although some indirect access to the activities and thoughts of the theater workers is available through the backstage accounts, all the other written reports are filtered through their authors' identification with the urban elite.

The month began with a typical example of this problem. On Monday, May 1, Christine and the court mainly rested from the rigors of the previous day's entry. The sole ceremonial was provided by the citizens of Peretola, a village then just beyond the city walls, who wheeled two decorated chariots through the gates in tribute to the bridal couple: one bore a working fountain, the other a maypole. May Day, the primitive nature-feast of returning spring and eros, was an appropriate time to present such a ritual fertility charm. Unfortunately, however, about this civic arts project — one of the few contributions to the wedding apparently made and paid for entirely by ordinary citizens — we have only the word of the diarist Giuseppe Pavoni, who remarks patronizingly that the richly garlanded and fruit-bedecked maypole cart "was considered, for something rustic, quite a marvelous invention."[2]

We may never know for certain whether the Peretolan villagers deserved Pavoni's sneering assumption that they did not understand maypole art with the learned depth of a Giovanni Bardi. And we are even further from intuiting how the "rustic" mode of production in a suburban town, based probably on a simpler but widely shared creative tradition rather than on the court's division between self-consciously innovative designer and subordinate executants, might have informed the intentions and perceptions of those anonymous artist-actors. Nor, for that matter, do we know much of Pavoni himself, other than that he must have had some official cooperation in order to join Christine's party at Genoa and follow her for several weeks to record the festivities for publication.

As the following discussion will show, however, in their printed accounts Pavoni and the other chroniclers of these events — Simone Cavallino and, to a lesser extent, Gualterotti and Rossi — unwittingly reveal much about the values and interests of the aristocratic class regarding artistic-political ritual and entertainment. Whether these authors were themselves members of that class or merely its hired scribes, their descriptions and commentaries assume that their readership shares with them three broad concerns of the wealthy elite, in which depth and surface interlock: social rank, titles, and protocol; magnificence of display, especially fabrics and jewelry (fully one quarter of Cavallino's volume details the entry liveries), with an attendant curiosity about such quantitative measures as size and cost, some patently exaggerated; and (largely for men) the physical prowess and competition of the military-chivalric tradition.[3]

TUESDAY, MAY 2

There are no notes in Seriacopi's logbook for the day of the premiere of *La pellegrina* and the intermedi — no doubt because the entire staff and crew were at the Uffizi theater from early morning on and could communicate immediately in person regarding such last-minute preparations as filling lamps, touching up sets, and repairing costumes. The interior of the theater, whose gradual construction and decoration we have followed since the previous summer, was richly hung with rose-pink hangings over the walls and across the proscenium and set about with the great lamps, chiaroscuro paintings, and plaster sculptures and fountains. While certainly grandiose in scale and elaboration, the hall's exact seating capacity is hard to determine. Contemporary estimates range from 3,800 to 5,000, both figures surely exaggerated; the floor area specified by Rossi more likely accommodated between 1,000 and 1,300 persons.[4]

The invited audience began to arrive at the Uffizi late in the afternoon; as they mounted Vasari's heroically scaled entry stair, the laborious climb would have created a figurative as well as architectural elevation, a feeling of heavenward ascent to a transfigured — in Rossi's word, "superhuman" (*sovrumano*) — realm. After filing into the theater, women went up onto the tiered gradi, men to their chairs on the floor. High clerical officials may have watched from above, through the west windows that overlooked the interior of the hall from the gallery level (fig. 5). These openings were hung with red drapes by the grand duke's personal order, and 24 stools were ordered by Cavalieri for "up in the heavens in the rooms of the gallery"; such accommodations, somewhat like box seats in modern theaters, would have allowed the discreet distance from purely secular entertainments that decorum required of churchmen.[5]

Ferdinando and Christine arrived last, probably via Vasari's elevated passageway from the Pitti. (One "Zacharia, guard of the Corridor" received a new livery on this day.) They would thus have avoided any contact with the assembling crowd until the moment of their sudden, quasi-magical arrival into the expectant auditorium. Christine was all in white; whereas her entry gown had been tailored in the French style, Pavoni takes pains to note that she was now dressed in Florentine fashion, completing her transformation into a Tuscan. As the couple approached the foyer outside the theater, she would have seen carved into the landing doors the coats-of-arms of the Medici and Florence, including the lily that the family and city shared heraldically and historically with France. Perhaps she paused to contemplate in this armorial confluence a personal meaning: not only was she now and henceforth a Florentine, but in some dynastically inevitable sense, she had "always already" been one.[6]

The bridal pair entered the room to a musical flourish and seated themselves with their family on the richly draped palco, which had been painted and upholstered with only days to spare. Unlike the rest of the hall, here men and women sat together: at this symbolic level, royal rank somewhat superseded gender divisions. As soon as they were seated, all 16 of the standing candelabra simultaneously burst into light from invisible wicks, while trellises of espaliered greenery rose up to block the waning daylight yet permit air circulation. The audience was left for some minutes to take in the magically transformed atmosphere, an artificial twilight lit by hundreds of candles. A good portion of guests turned their gaze to the living, rather than the architectural, decorations; Rossi's account is worth citing at length, not only because it captures the splendid ambience but because of its blithe assumption — later codified by Sabbattini in his treatise — that the viewers are male, the women around them merely part of the spectacle: "Once the lights were lit, and falling on the ornaments and precious gems that the seated gentlewomen wore on their heads, hands, and clothing, all the gradi seemed loaded with shimmering stars, which drew to themselves the eyes of all those around them, who, with unbelieving pleasure, as if their eyes had never been struck by anything like it, could not get their fill of staring at the splendor of the jewels and the beauties of these young women."[7]

Intermedio 1

The men in the audience were only reluctantly interrupted by the ritual of starting the performance: Rossi goes on, "Nor would they ever have taken their eyes from this most lovely object, had not the Artificer received a sign from the Grand Duke" to begin the performance. In that gesture to Buontalenti, who was ensconced in his windowed control booth beneath the gradi, Ferdinando summoned up all the resources — political, artistic, technological, logistic — at his service, setting in motion the forces he had long been coordinating for the culminating artistic apotheosis of himself, his territory, and his bride.

In an instant, the movable wall hangings dropped behind the gradi and the stage curtain fell, revealing both the auditorium decorations and the first stage set. This architectural colonnade, for which no visual record survives, was apparently planned as part of the view of Rome that Rossi describes at the beginning of intermedio 1 (cat. 8–25). Its Corinthian order exactly matched the wall articulation of the theater, forming a single composition uniting stage with auditorium. Before being removed to make way for subsequent actions, this setting made manifest the subtext of the coming fantasy: that social life and stage life were integral mirror images, that the world was a theater just as the theater was a world.[8]

As the musicians located behind the drops and in the rear balcony struck up their first chords, Vittoria Archilei descended in her green velvet Harmony costume, singing the prologue "From the highest spheres." Her cloud was presumably no longer shaking, as two crew members had been assigned to locations "behind Vittoria."[9] The allegorical themes of the evening were here set out: harmony, both musical and social, descends from a celestial source; control over people, machines, and art were all united at this moment into what Rossi (15–19) called an *anfiteatro perfetto,* the last word carrying overtones of being both innately perfect and actively perfected.

Archilei, joined by the sirens and gods on more clouds in the starry heaven, invoked the twin foci of the evening, addressing them as the "new Minerva, and mighty Hercules." This retrospective, classicizing language was an integral part of Renaissance allegorical discourse. Within the controlling myth of the Golden Age, perfection meant return, the reestablishment of an ideal that once was. The intermedi thus make few overt references to mundane practicality; rather, all contemporary reality is understood to be present by analogy, in traditional tropes that the present aims to replicate. The resultant text is thus overdetermined: multiple meanings could have been discovered, or read into it, by the spectators, probably without the modern historian's frequent sense of the ironic distance between discursive image and earthly actuality. For example, in the chorus "To you, royal lovers," the Fates and Sirens declare, "let us weave garlands for such great rulers," occluding the fact that real people, not demigods, had been mobilized to fabricate the floral decorations onstage — a circumstance probably well known to the audience, whose sisters and daughters filled the convents that contracted so much of this work.

Only one contemporary issue is addressed directly: the next chorus tells of heaven "blazing with amorous zeal" for the newlyweds, making clear the sexual fertility that was Christine's primary function in her new family and that formed a recurrent leitmotif in the ceremonies. Two days before at the duomo, she had been blessed by her cousin the archbishop (now probably present, in the gallery) with a prayer that God "would soon grant her the bearing of children, for the peace and satisfaction of her people," just as one of the hymns by Palla Rucellai had wished her "glorious offspring" (*gloriosa prole*).[10]

Prominently seated in the audience, no doubt — though probably not together — were Giovanni de' Bardi and Emilio de' Cavalieri; Giovanni Battista Strozzi, who invented the theater's decorative program and some intermedi text, was also likely there, as well as Rossi, who had been collaborating with the others for many months. Like Niccolò Gaddi at the triumphal entry, these men had directly conceived the formal iconography of the event and would have understood more of its official significance than anyone present. At the same time, however, as rival leaders of old and new factions in the court artistic hierarchy, Bardi and Cavalieri were well aware of the contingent nature of their creation: they had been jockeying for precedence while forced to work together, and Bardi had seen his planned finale replaced by Cavalieri's, plus other changes made too late to incorporate into Rossi's account. Although all of these creators must have felt considerable satisfaction as members of the intelligentsia with the power to shape culture, they knew that what was finally appearing onstage was no embodiment of transcendent, eternal truth but a hybrid product of conflict and compromise.

La Pellegrina

At the conclusion of the opening intermedio, the heavenly scene rapidly disappeared to expose the fixed houses of Pisa with their smoking chimneys, an imperfect image of which can be gained from the problematic engraving (cat. 68). As we have seen, the play's plot was a compliment to the bride: the dignified matron Drusilla — played by a young Sienese man — enters Pisa, just as Christine had done the week before, and the good citizens of the town are helped out of their overlapping confusions by this devout, wise, and generous *dea ex machina*. The thematic interrelation of play and intermedi, recommended by such theoreticians as Leone de' Sommi and Bernardo Pino, is clear: in the comedy, Juno-like, she brings order and harmony into the sphere of love and domestic relations, just as Ferdinando does, Jove-like, in the wider political realm figured by the interludes. The well-tamed Pisan patricians in the audience were no doubt gratified to see their hometown so flatteringly integrated into the wedding imagery, albeit as the butt of comedy. Though the characters are often foolish or knavish, the aristocratic viewers would have taken no personal offense, because the cast of "locals" is bourgeois and lower-class; the spectators' loyalties on this occasion lay more with the pan-Tuscan elite seated around them than with their local geographic community.[11]

Intermedio 2 and Intermedio 3

At the conclusion of Act 1, the houses of Pisa were covered up by the woodsy springtime backdrop for intermedio 2, the contest of Muses and Pierides (cat. 26–32). By all accounts, the mountain rose from the floor without notable difficulty, and the little boys playing the magpies ran about with suitable comic energy. For the third tableau, the scene returned to the woods, perhaps using some of the same side panels, but now with a charred central area marking the cave of the firebreathing dragon — who must have been dreaded by the mythical Delphians no more than by the stage artisans, who had barely finished the giant, complex creature in time for this performance (cat. 33–50). The cardboard Apollo descended on a wire, to be replaced by a living dancer. The serpent, wheeled about by men hidden inside, bared its fangs and shook its head, spitting flames; once defeated, it died gushing a pool of inky blood. Apollo was meant to figure Ferdinando — a flattering parallel dating back to Cosimo I, who was fond of imaging himself as the sun god and as another dragonslayer, Perseus.[12]

But what of the chief craftworker, Piero Pagolini, who was up on the catwalk to release the cardboard deity? Did he perhaps see this whole back-stage world literally "from another angle" — from above the stage, looking down in a distanced, maplike view at his own handiwork? He had helped make the dragon and probably helped hang the wires for Apollo, and he had crafted some of the coral on the Delphian costumes (before the job was taken away for lateness). Although his position, as subject and spectator, moved from place to place, it was always at the margins, behind the scenes, where the principal focus is on making something physically happen, not on the higher levels of meaning that the frontal face of the illusion might present to the audience's viewpoint.

To see all of this apparatus smoothly operating below him may have given Pagolini some sense of professional satisfaction as a technician. How far such thoughts typified the other hundred stagehands, at whom Pagolini could look across the catwalks and below him — most of them craftworkers, with similar but less specialized tasks of making and moving — is unknown. The symbolic content of the six intermedi, however, must have seemed remote from such pragmatically focused part-time workers, the more so as it made little overt appeal to the working classes, who were not in the audience. Perhaps a generic reference to rustic mortals might have been heard in the Delphians' final chorus, addressing "O fortunate countryside, O fortunate hills," which have been freed from fear by "the eternally glorious gods"; but common people are figured here, if at all, only as grateful supplicants to higher power.

Not that Pagolini or the rest of the crew needed the allegorized landscape of Delos to remind them of their dependency on Ferdinando. Many of the stagehands are identified in Seriacopi's crew list as "our worker" (MR 31r), that is, regularly employed by the palace workshops. No doubt most were grateful for the temporary second income, but Ferdinando was less an Apollo to them than a distant authority who owned this theater where they were employed, dictated their working hours, and disciplined or fired them through bureaucratic intermediaries such as Alfonso Parigi and the dragon-like Seriacopi.

It was at the conclusion of intermedio 3 during the earlier dress rehearsal that a refreshment break was inserted; no such intermission seems to have taken place at the premiere, however, as Rossi always says the sets changed instantaneously to the next, without interruption. Six intermedi and five play acts apparently totaled some seven hours; such a lengthy ritual was physically demanding for all involved, especially for the audience, who seem not to have gotten so much as a short respite to use the crew's toilet buckets. Moreover, in spite of the open windows and the vent holes in the roof, heat and smoke accumulated. Rossi exults that the sweet odors in the theater, combining the gentlewomen's perfumes, the naturalistic Pisa chimneys, and the aroma of the fountain waters, exceeded all but "Arabia itself"; but Cavalieri's request during rehearsal to scent the chimney-smoke "so it doesn't stink" alerts us that perfume in the theater, like that on bodies for whom daily washing was not common, was less a plus than a palliative, at best disguising what was still a pungent atmosphere. In a word, it was crowded, warm, and smelly, and the spectators had to fight off both drowsiness and discomfort.[13]

Backstage, the hardworking personnel of whatever social class — all of whom were, as at rehearsals, provided full meals in shifts — were in this case better treated than the patrician audience. We can imagine typical stagehands such as the mason Francesco Zanobini and the carpenter Giovanni di Domenico — who, like most of the crew, had no assignment for the technically simple intermedio 3 — stopping off during that act to eat their bread and cheese in one of the backstage rooms. They needed the energy: Zanobini was a crew leader (*caporale*) for one of the heavenly clouds (1 and 6) and chief for all of intermedio 4, while Giovanni operated one of the "eels" for cloud-ropes in 1, then moved the stage left houses for 2, and later the winch that raised Lucifer.[14]

Intermedio 4

Invisibly guided by Zanobini and his crew, the sorceress (Lucia Caccini) came across the sky before the Pisa set disappeared, intruding into realistic space and time with another epithalamic vision of the golden age. The limits to the audience's grasp of this recondite iconography can be gauged by their confusion here: the spirits of the air conjured by her on the large central cloud were meant as supernatural but quite "secular" demigods, but as Pavoni frankly recorded, "because they all had artificial wings of fiery red sarcenet [silk], many people took them for angels."[15] The scene for intermedio 4 then changed to hell, whose giant Lucifer, like the dragon, had just barely been completed in time (cat. 51–53). Amid a Dantesque antimasque of tormented souls, the devils lamented that the new era of goodness on earth would deprive them of any future victims. Here Bardi could count on most people spotting his references: Rossi (53–54) cites two iconographically relevant tercets of Dante's *Inferno* which, although not in the sung text, were probably familiar to the literate audience. At the gruesome finale, all the monsters descended back into the trap amid understage smoke and flames that contributed, yet again, to the stuffy atmosphere.

Intermedio 5

Amphitrite, queen of the sea, issued from the wave machines to open intermedio 5, seated on her movable mother-of-pearl shell pulled by dolphins made by Pagolini, and wearing some of his coral pieces (cat. 54–62). The goddess's tribute to Christine, "I who rein in the waves with my power . . . come to bow to you," resonated with Tuscan claims to maritime hegemony, enthusiastically proclaimed elsewhere in the Uffizi by the mother-of-pearl bands and shells with which Buontalenti was then decorating the vault of the Tribuna. But as Christine, Don Pietro, Orazio Rucellai, and the Orsini who had sailed with her all well knew, such docility was a far cry from Christine's actual journey, when the forces of nature often did not cooperate.

Amphitrite's messsage is, once again, fertility: her nymphs and tritons foresee issuing from the royal couple "such a brilliant progeny that it will adorn both poles" of the globe — an allusion to Ferdinando's attempt at world economic and political reach. Beyond the general hope for dynastic continuity, this forecast hid more specific political symbolism: the prophesied demigod will "chase from the world the cruel and evil serpent whose desire to have more constantly increases" — generally understood to refer to Philip II of Spain, then encroaching greedily on Italian soil. If they understood this swipe, it must have been an uncomfortable moment for the Spanish ambassador and for Don Pietro de' Medici, who when not piloting his brother's fleet served Philip as a military commander.[16]

For the second part of this tableau, Arion's giant ship glided onstage, circled about, and dipped its sails to honor the bridal pair; in another late change in the text, Jacopo Peri as Arion sang his own song before jumping overboard. By this time a sense of relief must have been spreading among all backstage, that they had "pulled it off" with no major problems and only one act remaining. At the same time, energy was probably beginning to flag, and they may have enjoyed the comic respite of the finale, as the sailors rejoiced in Arion's supposed death and divided the spoils. This chorus was meant as a macabre burlesque, but the mariners' attitude here was probably not too unlike the actual crews of the Order of Santo Stefano, many of whom were criminals at forced labor; the Order was seen by the Turks, at least, as little more than a pious front for piracy.[17]

Intermedio 6

The culminating and most splendid of the intermedi, requiring 82 stage-hands, filled the entire stage with all seven flower-covered clouds, with golden rays and gold "raining down" from heaven (cat. 63–66). Jupiter sat at the summit, in the open-shuttered heaven, in council with his major deities, while below them on the central cloud Apollo and Bacchus descended to earth with Rhythm and Harmony, Jupiter's consoling gifts to a laboring humankind. Twenty rustic couples came onstage to marvel at the apparition and to receive it joyfully; the gods took these nymphs and shepherds by the hand, and all danced and sang together in the grand epithalamic finale that became known as the "Aria di Firenze."[18]

As before, the text continued to occlude mundane reality: "Let nymphs and shepherds weave a triumphal diadem of the loveliest flowers" again erases the women who made this stage property. The chorus also prays, "May Clio weave the stories of such eternal glories," but that cultural "fabric-ation" was worked, not by the remote and timeless female Muse of history, but by a contemporary team of almost exclusively male propagandists — many of whom, being in the audience, were well aware of this disjunction.[19] In addition to changes already noted, the new text for the finale had been fitted to Cavalieri's music by Laura Guidiccioni Lucchesini; she, too, was probably in the house, but seated to one side on the gradi, and thus made aware of her marginalized status. As she heard her words sung by the trio of female performers (Archilei, Caccini, and Margherita) who also danced and accompanied themselves, perhaps she, and they, were quietly exulting in this breakthrough, however limited and tenuous, in women's access to the creative voice.

Rhythm and Harmony were the basis of the dance, and dance is a continual thread throughout the intermedi; indeed, as implied in the martial ballet of Apollo/Ferdinando, it was the ultimate metaphor of princely authority. Although Rossi is silent on this point, the evening may have ended with a *ballo alla francese* in which Ferdinando and Christine took part.[20] Whether they themselves danced, the scripted finale was already an apotheosis in which the heavenly chorus beckoned the onstage mortals to accept "the sweet sound of celestial harmony." The reference, indirect as always, is to the bargain each Medici prince had struck with the populace, in effect: "Dance to my tune, and I'll provide order and prosperity." And in fact the entire audience for this event was dancing an elaborate ritual pavane of grateful attendance upon their ruler.

Such secular ritual, which already embodies a near-religious willingness of mortals to play their assigned roles in an eternally ordained world theater, dovetails with the parallel role of the dance as the ultimate metaphor and ideal spiritual form of the Neoplatonic cosmology. Both politicians and philosophers envisioned a hierarchical cosmos whose many individual figures and forms revolved around a single center in fixed paths accompanied by that divine "music of the spheres" engendered by the Sirens of the framing intermedi. Cavalieri's choreography for the final *ballo*, which was printed with Malvezzi's score (fig. 11), suggests by its concentric circular patterns this ideal of a harmonically, and harmoniously, stabilized social and physical universe.[21]

Alongside this philosophical conceit, the dance also retained its links to archaic fertility rituals. Guidiccioni's text, invoking Hymen and Venus, declares that "the noble virgin burns with sacred fire and girds herself for the game of love," from which "demigods will be born." The proximate goal of all this sensuously pulsating movement was symbolic orgasm, with its ecstatic promise of renewal and continuity in the birth of an heir. For the space of a few enchanted hours, the cogs of the stage machinery, human as well as mechanical, had meshed as effortlessly and productively as the Sirens' crystal spheres, as pleasurably as two bodies synchronized in lovemaking. The *theatrum mundi* was, for a brief moment, as near to actualization as it could ever come, while Ferdinando and Christine acted both the stars of the divine firmament and the stars of their own earthly show.

Once the stage lights went dark and the music ceased, the hungry audience no doubt moved as fast as decorum permitted across the aerial bridge to the ensuing banquet in the Palazzo Vecchio. Over and above the triumphalist iconography of Vasari's permanent décor for the Sala dei Cinquecento, temporary additions included the raised platform for the bridal table with its sculptured backdrop, this and other ephemera designed and painted by Allori, Buontalenti, and Rosselli. The food served on this occasion represents another intersection of practical production and artistic fantasy. The banquet far exceeded the meal just served backstage not only in quantity (the palazzo kitchens had recently been enlarged) but also in the amount of labor expended to exploit even basic bodily needs as a pretext for decorative artifice. The sole record of artistic involvement in this occasion hints at the splendor of the

BALLO
DELL'VLTIMO INTERMEDIO

Q Vefto difegno ci ha da rappresentare il Palco : & i numeri rappresentano le persone, il qual fegno, ò freggio, come fi chiami, che è dietro a' numeri hanno hauer volte le fpalle; cosi feguirà ftando in Scena, et in ciafcuna attione, che nel prefente Ballo s'interuenga.

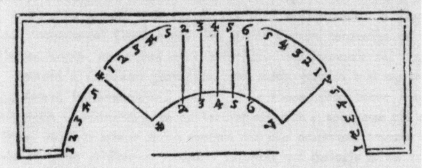

R Itrouandofi tutti in fu la Scena come fi dimoftra fi lafcierà paffar dodici paule e di poi . 1 . 7 . che fon fegnati paffe:áno auanti con due feguiti, & alla fine di quei fi troderanno in Luna come qui fopra fi uede. Auuertendo, che i Vinti che reftano ftaran no fermi, e dipoi i Sette, daranno principio al prefente Ballo.

Q Vefto Ballo farà principiato da Sette Perfone ; ciuè da Quattro Dame, e Tre Huomini, lequali faráno quefte le Dame . 1 . 3 . 5 . 7 . e quefti . 2 . 4 . 6 . gli Huomini, & infieme col pie finiftro faranno la Riuerenza, & à man finiftra le continenze, e una Riuerenza à man finiftra, e . 2 . cangi co'l pie fi.tiftro, & uno feguito trangato auanti, & uno in dietro, e dipoi tutti in ruota à man finiftra col pie finiftro quattro fpezzate, & altre quattro fcorfe ritornando al fuo luogo, e fubito gli Huomini un trabocchetto auanti fu'l pie finiftro, & uno in dietro fu'i deftro, & una fcorta di un feguito barat taudofi i luoghi ; & il fimile faranno le Dame.

XX   Le

11. *Choreography diagram and description, intermedio 6 (Malvezzi 1591).*

food: ten colors of taffeta ribbon were made into some 240 banderoles "for the pastries," on which were painted the coats of arms of various family members and guests. In all likelihood the salone sideboards were also graced with temporary sculptures, up to four feet high, cast from melted sugar. Giovanni Bologna's workshop is known to have created such follies, copied after his own mythological sculptures, for the granducal weddings in 1600 and 1608, and the tradition presumably began earlier. Unfortunately, even though some were painted or gilded, making them inedible, none survives.[22]

WEDNESDAY, MAY 3

The bridal couple attended mass for the feast of the Finding of the Cross, taking communion from Archbishop Puteo of Pisa; later in the day Christine, her aunt, and the Medici princesses went in a carriage procession accompanied by cavalry to the church of the Santissima Annunziata, where the miraculous image of the Virgin was uncovered for the largely female audience, with musical accompaniment. It was in anticipation of this courtesy that Ferdinando had presented the prior, his kinsman Domenico Salviati, with a gift of two large candlesticks.[23]

At the theater, Seriacopi reported to work as usual, only to find a note from Gorini that "S.A.S. definitely wants the comedy to be done again on Friday, and the rest of us [noi altri] will be able to invite friends to it." Faced with the daunting realization that they had to do everything all over again, during the next several days these two men, in a flurry of notes and meetings that also involved Buontalenti, Cavalieri, and Orazio the carpenter, closely coordinated resupply, repairs, inventory of costumes, and cleaning. Inventory was necessary both to track down missing items, such as several pairs of shoes (whose wearers were to be asked for them directly), and to quantify all consumables for strategic planning. Their lists inform us that the lighting for the premiere performance required a total of 490 pounds of white candles and eight barrels of oil, and that ten carpenters and six painters, plus Piero Pagolini, were called in for a day or two of unspecified retouching.

At the same time, Seriacopi's attention was beginning to be diverted elsewhere, as the subsequent events at outlying locations loomed closer: on May 3, for example, he had to deal with a request from the church of San Lorenzo, where Ferdinando was to perform an induction ceremony on the upcoming Easter Sunday, for suitable seating platforms. Accordingly, he issued orders to keep only a skeleton staff at the theater and to transfer surplus workers to the Pitti, "where there is greater need and great urgency": Buontalenti still had to demonstrate to a craftworker how to make certain joust décors on poles, and a group of gentlemen inquired nervously about Allori's progress on their chariot for the parade. Seriacopi also found time for his customary strict discipline: he docked a week's wages from a theater worker called Zanaiuolo for stealing a piece of cheese and other items, presumably after the Tuesday evening performance.[24]

THURSDAY, MAY 4

A painting sometimes attributed to Gualterotti (cat. 69; pl. 15) shows the action and costumes of the *giuoco di calcio*, or Florentine football game, the first of four events staged in the Piazza Santa Croce, the traditional site of outdoor public celebrations. Over the past two weeks, Seriacopi's staff had been responsible for equipping the large and unusually regular piazza with tiers of wooden seating on the north and east sides and a palco for the high officials, visible at the right of the field (MR 50r–51r, Apr. 23–25). Once the princely party and the audience, numbering in the thousands, had assembled on the bleachers as well as at balconies and windows, two teams of 50 young noblemen each made their processional entry — Ferdinando's favorites in pink uniforms, Christine's in light blue — with attendant pages and musicians. After three rounds or innings of the game, similar to soccer but more violent, her team won in a suitably chivalrous outcome.

Pavoni and Cavallino pay the closest attention to such displays of martial and athletic skills, which involved almost exclusively male combatants and were of special interest to male spectators and readers. (The noble academician Bardi had delivered a learned discourse on the rules of the calcio.) This enthusiasm arose from the fact that, at least in theory, the essential role of the male aristocrat remained military, a tradition dating back to the feudal-chivalric code that still loomed large in social relations, educational priorities, and artistic conventions. Both writers devote considerable space to the rules of the game and its "play-by-play" action (unfamiliar and intriguing to their non-Florentine readership), as they do later to the various maneuvers of the naumachia; Cavallino, even more captivated by things martial, counted the cavalry regiments at the entry. It is perhaps indicative of contemporary cultural divisions along gender lines that both men's coverage of literary-artistic events is usually less detailed or precise, and that Cavallino glosses over religious elements like Christine's coronation as "some ceremonies," her dedication in the duomo as "the usual ceremonies."

Like the more serious forms of public ritual already enacted, such games were an effective component of the program to prevent aristocratic males from claiming in life any such military or political role as the chivalric tradition still validated in art. The patricians' young sons staffed the teams, but they were dressed in what amounted to Medici livery and captained by members of the ruling family, Don Pietro and Don Virginio. The wider structures of play also served to defuse individual rivalries and potentially troublesome factions within a competitive and powerful class: many spectators sported pink or blue arm bands or neckwear to signal their harmless team allegiances.

Additionally, after the first round, trays loaded with refreshments were distributed to the crowd, underscoring (like the food and wine given out at entries) the material rewards of "playing by the rules."[25]

FRIDAY–SATURDAY, MAY 5–6

Pavoni claims that there were no activities on May 5, which was Good Friday, but his account from here on does not correspond to the production log, suggesting that the schedule at the Uffizi theater was somewhat different, possibly even more intensive. According to his account, which all subsequent studies have accepted, the second performance of the intermedi took place on Saturday, May 6, with the comedy *La zingara*, and the third on May 13 with *La pazzia*, both presented by the Compagnia dei Gelosi and its rival prima donnas. But, as noted earlier, the logbook speaks of a repeat planned for May 5, and as late as Thursday the 4th the log still refers to such a presentation for "tomorrow"; moreover, it makes no mention of a performance for either May 6 or 13, but does record plans for one on the 15th.[26]

Pavoni's chronology is often inaccurate by a day or more, not only from haste but because the schedule seems to have remained subject to change on short notice — in part, perhaps, to accommodate incoming guests, whose travel times were unpredictable. Immediately after his report about a May 5 performance, Gorini notes that the court also wished a repeat on the following Monday, but he never mentions that date again, and no one records a May 8 presentation. Perhaps the flurry of uncertainty was related to the arrival on Saturday the 6th of the Venetian envoy Michele Contarini, belatedly joining his kinsman Francesco, who had come in time to attend the April 30 entry.[27]

Franco Berti has reasonably suggested that the Good Friday performance was private, primarily for family and friends of performers and staff (as Gorini had said, "the rest of us will be able to invite friends"); the official silence about it would then be explained by both religious and social decorum.[28] If Pavoni's report of a public performance on May 6 is correct, the intermedi would then have been repeated on consecutive days, on one or both of which Vittoria Piissimi starred in *La zingara*; alternatively, the event scheduled for May 5 might have been postponed at the last minute until the 6th and made public, with unknown consequences for the makeup of the audience.

SUNDAY, MAY 7

To celebrate Easter, the granducal family went in the customary carriage and horse procession to mass at the dynastic parish of San Lorenzo, where

Ferdinando invested ten new knights of Santo Stefano. The palchi on which they sat were another instance of Medici cooperation with the church, though Seriacopi carefully specified that they be returned immediately. The new cavaliers included a member of the Salviati clan, Francesco; each received a jeweled collar worth 250 scudi (one to two years' salary for a craftworker). A 32-course banquet and ball followed for 280 prominent gentlewomen and their escorts. Several cardinals attended, but out of decorum they were separated from the other guests behind screens (*gelosie*), where Ferdinando, able to mediate between the two realms as a male and an ex-cleric, spent time dining with his former colleagues.[29]

Meanwhile, Seriacopi and his staff worked yet another holiday weekend, now proccupied with the main event of the following week, at the Pitti. A number of sailors had arrived from Pisa to take part in Thursday's naumachia; the sailors were requisitioned along with their captain from the crews of Ferdinando's galleys, and each was provided a stipend of one ducat for expenses. All of the tailors were ordered to report early Monday morning, for 150 combatants had to be fitted, some with additional new outfits to match those provided from the Guardaroba storerooms.[30]

MONDAY, MAY 8

The second public entertainment in Piazza Santa Croce was a *caccia*, or animal baiting. Ferdinando's ranking male relations and Vitelli, captain of the guard, rode out in heavy protective coats (*giubboni*) of yellow silk and cloth of gold, accompanied by attendants and "hunters" in green wool challis from Pisa, as well as trumpeters, all outfitted by the Guardaroba. In an elaborate succession of episodes, fifteen knights killed several buffaloes and an astounding number and variety of other creatures, and four men hidden in artificial wooden beasts chased live ones around the palisade. Although *caccia* means "hunt," more often the combats were between animals themselves, such as lions dismembering a mule, dogs devouring rabbits, and cats and mice thrown together — the cats fled, to general amusement.

Such spectacles were common and popular entertainment for all classes. The aristocracy were passionately fond of hunting as both chivalric sport and dietary necessity, whereas the enthusiasm of ordinary citizens is shown by the multitude of spectators who skipped a meal to arrive early enough for good seats (the organizers thoughtfully provided free refreshments). Though grimly sadistic to modern eyes, the caccia suggests that Renaissance Tuscans, who lived closer to nature than we do today and for whom it remained a threatening obstacle, viewed wild creatures as "fair game" in a more evenly matched battle and considered animal-animal contests a gory but humorous outlet for the tensions of dependency and lack of control.[31]

TUESDAY, MAY 9

The Medici, nobility, army, clergy, and citizens all participated in the transferral of the relics of Saint Antoninus, first archbishop of Florence and one of the city's patron saints, from his fifteenth-century resting place in San Marco to a new, more sumptuous chapel, by way of a daylong procession through the streets of the city. The line between secular and sacred being highly permeable, the Florentine government required aristocratic attendance at these frequent religious parades, on pain of fines for absence without a doctor's excuse. More active participation was also integral to the ritual exchanges between patriciate, clergy, and court: as noted earlier, the new "great chapel," designed by Giovanni Bologna, was paid for by the Medici relations Averardo and Antonio Salviati, whose kinsman Francesco had been honored by a knighthood two days earlier. The ritual, supervised by the city's current archbishop, Alessandro de' Medici, also involved 500 Dominican friars from throughout Tuscany and 100 troops to clear the way; the previous Saturday, the civic authorities had cooperated via an edict closing all shops on this day to facilitate movement in the streets. With his customary fondness for specifying exorbitant costs and important names, Pavoni notes that the principal guests walked through the streets under a decorated canopy worth 6,000 scudi and borne by the grand duke's pages.[32]

While Christine and Ferdinando were attending the concluding candle-light ceremonies at San Marco, other candles were burning across town for less solemn purposes. In preparation for Thursday's joust, Seriacopi had apparently moved his base of operations to the family palace; he ordered Gorini to "come today to the Pitti to help out." He told the tailors to double their staff for the remaining two days, for "urgency is growing," and he had candles and torches sent to the Pitti so these workers could, as was so often necessary, stay up late.[33]

WEDNESDAY, MAY 10

The third event in the Piazza Santa Croce was a joust *alla quintana* (English "tilt"), in which twenty knights, mounted on rich caparisons and each with a suite of attendants and musicians, rode at a target (cat. 70). The Duke of Mantua, Vincenzo Gonzaga, served as one of the *mantenitori*, or referees, and the usual court and noblemen participated.[34]

While this entertainment was underway, Seriacopi was compiling a lengthy list of items that Gorini was to procure for the next day's Pitti event, from seating to torches and candelabra, costumes and swords, and tailor supplies such as tinsel. In a familiar pattern of thrifty reuse, various clothing, chairs, and flowers were to be transferred from the Uffizi theater. For the painters still hurrying to finish (probably Rosselli and Francini, whose four narrative backdrops were delayed), he requested mattresses or dropcloths; for the tailors, who he foresaw would have to work a second consecutive night, more candles as well as an added incentive. Apparently aware of the best way to keep up morale under the grueling final deadline, he specified "things to eat such as bread, wine, new cheese, and more, so that they'll be as well off as possible." Seriacopi was typically at pains to deflect blame for this last-minute bottleneck onto Buontalenti, who (he reports) had only that day delivered designs for 30 "costumes *alla greca*" and eight for attendants on the grand duke's chariot.[35]

THURSDAY, MAY 11

All was, in the event, ready just in time for the long-awaited trio of Pitti entertainments: the chariot parade (*sfila*), foot joust (*sbarra*), and naval battle or naumachia (cat. 71–87). Those invited had been issued admission tickets in the form of small pieces of porcelain, a novel advertisement for this pioneering Florentine industry; continuing the motif, the Turks' castle reproduced the round tempietto used as a trademark by the Medici pottery factories.[36] Once inside, spectators were again assigned to sex-separated seating: women on gradi under the courtyard arcade, men on the two balconies above. The women's seating rose above a continuous barricade nearly 6 feet high, covered with pitch, to hold in the water for the naumachia. The manifold components of Buontalenti's decorative apparatus, under construction since November 1588, have been discussed in earlier chapters — including the castle with its four barely finished backdrops, the giant pinkish-red awning overhead, lighting, costumes, and wall-coverings of swags, garlands, and painted and gilded papier-mâché cartouches. Many of these constructions are illustrated in the two views of the court that bracket this group of prints: before the opening parade (cat. 71) and during the naumachia (cat. 87).

No sooner had the audience seated themselves than the proceedings were unexpectedly delayed for an hour by a sudden torrential rainstorm which, despite the awning, flooded the sealed arena and drenched the exposed male onlookers. Seriacopi, explicitly foreseeing this threat, had required the awning to be reinforced with ropes "so that it can resist the sudden violence of the winds, which can do incredible damage." Once again, however — as with

Christine's sea journey — the most careful human planning was limited in the face of what Seriacopi called nature's *furia impetuosa*. The universal frustration with a capricious cosmos comes through in Cavallino's complaint that the weather "had no respect for either His Serene Highness or the most noble company."[37]

Although often discussed as if they were discrete events, the first two parts of the program were actually alternating components of an integrated first act; Ferdinando's dislike of his late sister-in-law notwithstanding, both followed the format laid down in the previous such joust at the Pitti, for Francesco's wedding to Bianca Cappello. The chariot parade was a series of some dozen triumphal entries by various individuals and groups of male combatants; each troupe descended from its allegorical vehicle to engage in a period of foot combat (called a *sbarra* from the barrier erected between sides, visible in cat. 71) before quitting the field to make way for the next group's entry. Thanks to the nearly complete sequence of engravings and the two detailed though sometimes conflicting written accounts, it is possible to reassemble much of the sequence and general iconography, though gaps and inconsistencies remain.[38]

First, as prologue, came a bearded necromancer on a chariot drawn by bears (cat. 72), who magically "conjured" up all the following "inventions." Each succeeding float drove into the arena preceded and followed by foot soldiers or other costumed attendants with torches and weapons; some cars were drawn by animals, others by men, at times hidden inside the float to simulate a magic effortlessness. Each suite circled the arena and stopped in front of Christine to pay respects, whereupon the riders dismounted and the chariot drove away, leaving its passengers to perform various feats of arms.

The first of these fictive apparitions (cat. 73–74) bore the two presiding officials (*mantenitori*) of the evening, Duke Vincenzo Gonzaga and Don Pietro de' Medici. Because Ferdinando himself, as host, was already seated, the arrival of his brother and nephew was the closest to an actual monarchical entry in the procession; accordingly, as seen earlier, it was designed by Buontalenti himself and executed by Seriacopi's staff. The four winged demons shown helping to draw the chariot may illustrate part of the suite of eight men in serpentlike green who were "to steer [*governare*] the chariot of S.A.S." (presumably referring to the patron, not the riders) and whose costumes were also provided by the administration to Buontalenti's design: each received "a headdress of a fury, six snakes, a mask, and two devil wings." Some of these items were apparently borrowed from the Uffizi wardrobe: in his orders the day before, Seriacopi had told Gorini to bring over "eight headdresses of infernal furies" (probably from the hell scene of intermedio 4), "eight fury

masks that were used for the comedy" and eight pairs of devil wings.[39] Buontalenti had similarly specified that nine women's outfits, most likely those for
the muses of intermedio 2, were to be reassigned to "the musicians to be
seated on the chariot," probably Don Virginio's, and 16 costumes "from the
ship" (of intermedio 5) would serve for parade attendants on foot, with new
props such as torches and lances (visible in cat. 80, 83).[40]

This reappearance of the identical fantasy equipment across the spatial and
temporal stage of the wedding suggests two inferences about its iconography
and audience responses. First, somewhat generic costumes and attributes
were practicable because the repertory of themes and character types underlying all these chivalric entertainments descended from a few interrelated key-
stones of the Italian literary tradition: from Dante's epic of Christian good and
evil, through Petrarch's descriptions of courtly love and allegorical triumphs,
to the more recent epic poetry of Ariosto and Tasso, whose medievalizing
romances were set in a *meraviglia*-filled world of supernatural enchantments,
chivalric deeds, and natural wonders. (Cat. 81 recalls the animals transformed
by Circe, the enchantress-queen of Ariosto's *Orlando furioso*.)

Second, although the elite audience at the Pitti would certainly have been
weaned on these classics, most were not professional literati, and they varied
greatly in their iconographic sophistication and interest. To judge from a close
reading of our two chroniclers, Pavoni and Cavallino, they (and/or their
intended readers) were familiar with stock types and motifs but not sensitive to
subtleties of detail. As seen earlier in Pavoni's description of the intermedi, the
audience was likely to confuse air-spirits and angels; similarly, although the
learned Rossi had specifically noted that the rustic opening of intermedio 1
featured Doric Harmony descending into a Doric temple, Pavoni refers to
Vittoria Archilei simply as "a lady" who hides behind "certain rocks." Cavallino is even more vague and confused, getting the intermedi out of order and
conflating several into one; for the joust and chariots, however, he is the more
systematic and detailed guide, perhaps betraying a particular military bent or
background.[41]

The conclusion suggested by these readings is that the audience was interested in these various familiar narratives less for their depth of exact meaning
than as standardized pretexts for surface display, astonishment, humor, and
the celebration of a generic valor. To be sure, there are nuances as to which
aspects of such spectacle attract individual eyes: only Pavoni, more alert to
mannerist artifice, describes the moving topiary of the finale, whereas Cavallino concentrates on swordplay. In both accounts, however, it is clear that the
succession of complex retinues and actions moved too quickly to be analyzed
at length. The disparities between the descriptions, the different details they

select out of an overwhelming richness, suggest that it was simply impossible for even the best-intentioned observer to take it all in.

Other floats included one sponsored by the prominent Guicciardini family (cat. 76), whom we met in Chapter 2 as suppliers of fabric to the court and in Chapter 5 with a large escort at Christine's entry, where one young son of the clan helped transport her canopy. Their knights rode a smoking volcano, drawn by more winged devils generically similar to those described for the Medici chariot. Further prints show floats of a ship, Death, an unidentified single knight, and various attendants on foot (cat. 77–80). Both Pavoni and Cavallino also mention one or two floats filled with nymphs in a green and pastoral spring setting, of which no visual record survives.[42]

The grand finale comprised a series of interrelated floats organized by Don Virginio Orsini that transcended all others in scale and mechanical wonderment (cat. 81–86). A magician rode in on one chariot filled with animal prisoners (cat. 81), followed by a giant fountain pulled by satyrs, which sprayed considerable water over the women in the lower seats (cat. 82). Then came Virginio himself dressed as Mars and accompanied by the eight female singers in borrowed costumes (cat. 83), who distributed flower-filled baskets (perhaps the nuns' handiwork, borrowed from the theater) full of his own poetry to the ladies. Only the somewhat more literarily inclined Pavoni noted this homage to aristocratic creativity; in contrast, Cavallino singled out the marchers behind Virginio's car, "eight soldiers dressed oafishly as women, quite ridiculous with their ugly faces." It is not surprising that Cavallino, with his predilection for things military, finds these figures comic: once again, however, his lack of interest in their precise identity suggests that the audience appreciated the stock grotesque humor of antimasque types more than allegorical specifics.

Virginio's own chariot was followed by another bearing six armed noblemen (cat. 84). After he dismounted a boxlike garden float appeared (cat. 85), from which slowly unfolded a series of trellised fence units that encircled the entire courtyard, engulfing the sorcerer's float, which had remained on the field (cat. 86). The final combat, featuring Virginio and his companions, took place within this enchanted enclosure. Casting the grand duke's popular young nephew as both a surrogate crown prince and a valiant hero in some episode from *Orlando*, the combat climaxed with a burst of fireworks from the central barrier.[43]

While the audience went inside to dinner, the courtyard was flooded from the grotto piping for the naumachia that followed the intermission (cat. 87). The numerous boats scavenged from the countryside since December were launched from within the grotto arches (visible in the background of the print). A costume sign-out sheet details the combatants: for the Christian forces, 120 assailants in 17 boats, outfitted with jackets, breastplates, and weapons, some in Ferdinando's livery colors of pink and turquoise; and for the Turks, dressed in trousers *alla greca*, one flagship and 14 defenders "on land," that is, in the castle. Many of these men are identified by place of origin; besides the professional sailors from Pisa noted earlier and a contingent from the villa at Poggio a Caiano, listed locales are widely dispersed around the Mediterranean: Corfu, Genoa, Naples, Crete, Marseilles, and Cyprus. The overlap between this list, the provenance of the vessels accompanying Christine, and her itinerary suggests that many participants were actual foreign seamen, hired briefly while on shore leave following their recent arrival in Livorno.[44]

The prolonged, multistage attack on the fortress is described with tedious relish by both chroniclers: Cavallino, sounding increasingly like an experienced military man, takes even more boyish delight than Pavoni in the noise, smoke, and commotion. Fireworks and artillery bombardments resulted in much splashing about of wounded or panicked fighters in what must have been a very crowded courtyard; the defenders realistically cried out in Turkish, no doubt familiar to sailors. As always in this conventionalized combat, the Christian assailants were victorious, storming the citadel and raising their ensign: the ever-chivalric Cavallino observed that the soldiers then brought the enemy standard as a final tribute to Christine, and the evening ended about 2 a.m. in celebratory music and singing.[45]

The Pitti spectacular was the last large-scale, state-sponsored cultural debut; all that remained were several simpler productions and repeat performances. From May 11 on, as the festivities began to wind down, the names of various foreign guests appear in scattered documents as taking their leave. In Settimani's survey of these records, the pace of departures increased through the end of the month, then continued at an ebbing pace into June.

SATURDAY–MONDAY, MAY 13–15

According to Pavoni, the third public performance of the intermedi — this time accompanied by the Compagnia dei Gelosi in their second comedy, *La pazzia* — took place in the Uffizi on Saturday, May 13. As with some of his other dates, this one is problematic. Seriacopi's log makes no mention of preparations for a spectacle on that day; rather, on Saturday Gorini was still replenishing the necessary consumable materials for a performance ordered by Ferdinando for two days later. It would seem more likely, then, to reassign this public evening to Monday, May 15. Given the fluidity of scheduling, however, it is also possible that the event was initially planned for the 15th but suddenly moved up due to unknown circumstances, or that performances were staged on both days.[46]

Whichever the date, it was now Isabella Andreini's turn in the spotlight, in a play of her own invention. Pavoni's personal attitudes are again responsible for specific information about the event. As we have seen, he identified with the elite, going so far as to idealize the bejeweled noblewomen attending the Easter investiture as "goddesses, not women." As his earlier condescending comment on the rustic maypole demonstrated, however, he was not so respectful of social inferiors, and it is to him that we owe the gossipy report of the rival actresses' backstage battle.

Andreini's script featured another convoluted plot of frustrated lovers and confusing disguises, centering on the eponymous Isabella, her *innamorato*, and their respective servants, who are also in love and serve as conduits between master and mistress. When Isabella's plan to elope with Fileno is derailed by a jealous rival, she goes insane from grief and rage; it was here that she trumped her predecessor Piissimi with the mad scene, chattering nonsensically in a mix of fractured Spanish, Greek, and other languages. She ended in French, even bursting into French song, from which Pavoni (always the courtier attentive to the moods of his superior) noticed that Christine derived "so much delight that she could not express it." Whether out of tact or ignorance, he does not speculate whether the new bride, so recently separated from her childhood home and language, also felt homesick, or acutely aware that she was henceforth to live among foreigners who found her native tongue a source of laughter.[47]

Pavoni tells us that he left Florence on May 15 for Bologna, rushing home to put out his account of events up to that date. It seems likely, given the overlap between his detailed intermedi description and that of Rossi, that Pavoni took with him for reference a copy of Rossi's *descrizione*, published (according to its dedication) the day before. Among the increasing departures was Michele Contarini's on May 17; on the same day the luckless ambassador of the Duke of Savoy was just arriving, having missed almost all of the major events. With no further attendance anticipated at the Uffizi theater, the only note in Seriacopi's log for the week after this performance was a money-saving suggestion from the custodian Cialle Fabbri to raise the curtain separating backstage area from auditorium so the entire interior could be visually surveyed (*si scopri*) by a single watchman rather than the two who were needed as long as the stage curtain hung fully in place.[48]

MAY 23–28

The final event in the Piazza Santa Croce took place on May 23: another form of the joust, a *corso al saracino*, especially favored by the Duke of Mantua. The entire court attended, the combatants again in splendid costumes; on this occasion, or perhaps at a second performance the next day, there were also allegorical marchers costumed as goddesses and times of day. In a repeat of the bad luck of the Pitti evening, here exacerbated by the lack of covering, "the weather, with unexpected rain, ruined such a fine festival."[49]

On Sunday, May 28, the last festival procession was staged by 24 young noblemen (*giovani nobili*) who paraded through the streets dressed as river gods, each with a liveried escort, accompanying the sea god Neptune on a whale-drawn chariot (cat. 88). The equestrian train stopped at various ladies' houses to sing songs explaining their conceit: that the waters of the earth had come to Florence to pay tribute to the new grand duchess.[50] This event was part of a gradual and deliberate absorption into the public ceremonial arena of the *giovani*, a specific legal category of men age 18 to 24. Traditionally distrusted in age-conscious Florentine society as potentially disruptive or rebellious, they were grudgingly allowed to participate in ritual life, usually under adult supervision, in an attempt to both co-opt and distract them. We have already encountered the young men on the calcio teams, who were captained by men who outranked them in age as well as class; Settimani's comment that the young river gods' procession "issued from the stables of the Grand Duke" reveals once again the presiding authority and resource behind the young nobles' artistic display.[51]

In fact, a considerable number of the events already discussed here were largely entrusted to, or performed by, giovani: the Intronati were young Sienese of this age, as were the scores of canopy holders at Christine's entry, and the finale to the Pitti parade was organized by Don Virginio Orsini, then about age 17 and a favorite champion of the ladies. One further wedding pageant, whose precise date remains unknown, was an elaborate religious drama (*sacra rappresentazione*) performed by young members of the Compagnia di San Giovanni Evangelista: *L'esaltazione della croce* by Giovan Maria Cecchi (1511–87), along with intermedi, took place on a large outdoor stage erected in an open field.[52]

On a symbolic level, the community looked to these splendidly dressed young bucks, then at the peak of their vigor and sexual energy, to embody and invoke sexual virility. In their close attendance on the physical membrane surrounding the bride as she penetrated the city walls and, in the climactic Oceanic procession, showering her with lifegiving liquid, we can espy a decorous displacement of the hoped-for potency of Ferdinando himself in the conception of a dynastic heir. This ritual function cast the giovani in a conflicted and potentially frustrating role: although they figured and fertilized a union, they were not themselves considered mature enough for marriage. Ironically, it was precisely this forced deferral of licit sexual satisfactions, an extended hiatus between adolescence and adult responsibility, that made their elders fear the unfocused high spirits of the young and bred concern over their spending time under the immoral influence of female prostitutes and/or the roving males who might solicit, or be solicited, among the city's homosexual networks. Also ironically, and perhaps not without connection, one widely encouraged outlet for youthful energy was the theater: a world whose reliance on transvestism, with its fluid ambiguities of gender and sexual identity, made it a suspected hotbed of loose morals, especially sodomy (at least in the better-documented English theater); further, the theatrical milieu intersected with such equally sexually suspect Italian institutions as music schools, like Bartolommeo Franciosino's, which provided many freelance performers for the wedding festivities.[53]

Although all of this evidence indicates that youth had their own social networks, cultural institutions, and spectator positions, we know little of their reactions to the roles that society assigned them. The anonymous young Sienese gentleman who impersonated Drusilla, disguised under 44 yards of heavy fabric, was charged with embodying just the sort of "solid" matron he could not himself yet aspire to possess; unfortunately, what he made of this incongruity is lost to us. No doubt most upper-class men eventually made the transition to exclusively heterosexual patriarch, but they were first exposed to other, very different worlds, with consequences for their reading of cultural and especially theatrical texts that await further study.

Among the working classes, officially denied any role in political life and ceremonial, young male participation in the wedding was largely subsumed under the workplace. Besides the youthful musicians and actors (a few of them female), young craftworkers participated in the construction and decorations, and some of the stagehands are explicitly called apprentices (garzoni) in the crew lists; of these, the most notable were Francesco Buontalenti and Giulio Parigi, both then young men training under their fathers Bernardo and Alfonso. One formalized conduit then available to commoners for artistic patronage and creativity is surprisingly absent from the wedding records: the companies of neighborhood revel-masters known as potenze, or "powers," mock courts of working- and middle-class giovani who provided public entertainment — floats, armed combats, and street processions — for carnival and holidays. These clubs, supported by the earlier Medici to curry popularity with working classes, were sufficiently influential by 1573 to mark their geographic boundaries on prominent buildings. It seems all but inconceivable that such populist institutions, then near their apogee, would not have contributed in some way to the festivities. If they did, then the silence of the elite chroniclers perhaps represents a hardening absolutism, less concerned than in immediately postrepublic times to trumpet its support from common urbanites.[54]

By the date of the concluding Neptune procession, its audience would have been principally local citizens: as May turned to June, many of the guests and reporters who had converged so brilliantly over a period of three to six weeks had already gone home. For the new grand duchess, it was time to develop the routines of a daily life; for her many subjects, employees, and other contributors to the wedding festivities, to settle slowly back to normal. Seriacopi made only a few more entries in his log, and closed it on June 10, after a last performance of the intermedi on June 8. The final curtain had rung down on the wedding; all that remained was to clean up, settle the accounts, and complete the propagandistic work of commemorative texts and images.

CHAPTER SEVEN

June 1589 and Beyond

AFTERMATH AND LATER

INFLUENCE

The repeat performance in early June was the last event of the wedding, and the remaining guests continued to leave the city through the middle of the month. The many aristocrats, administrators, and artisans, their collective sigh of relief as the curtain closed on the hectic May season notwithstanding, must also have experienced the summer of 1589 as an extended anticlimax. But in its long twilight, stretching well into the next century, this brilliant festival cast an influential shadow over artistic, social, and economic terrain. The household documents continue for several years after the wedding itself, concerned with dismantling and storage of equipment, payment of outstanding bills, and final accounting. From other evidence, we can follow something of the protracted creation and dissemination of the commemorative prints and texts over the following three years; the subsequent reuse of machinery, settings, and props; and, finally, the later careers of at least those wedding protagonists from the aristocratic and upper-artisan classes.

The concluding entries in Seriacopi's log concern a final performance of the intermedi and an unspecified comedy, which took place on June 8. His orders to Francesco Gorini and Cialle Fabbri say little about the usual technical-stagecraft matters, which must have become a smooth routine after a month of repetitions. Besides normal cleaning and touch-ups, the numerous buckets used as urinals were to be refilled and put back in their places, and the musicians were to be fed in shifts in the workroom where the headdresses had been made, now cleaned out. The evening before the show, Bernardo Buontalenti's son Francesco went to receive detailed instructions from Seriacopi, suggesting that his otherwise obscure role in the production was somewhat more extensive than that of the average young apprentice.

On the morning of the performance, Jacopi Peri came to the Uffizi theater to help out, tailors once again made last-minute repairs, and four security officers (*birri*) were stationed at the door. Ever ready to threaten his apparently feckless workers, Seriacopi had informed the stage crew that this time "anyone who is missing will be dealt with by the police, and severely." Regarding the boys who played magpies and damned souls, he ordered cryptically, "Pay close attention" (*si faccia diligentia*) — had they, too, misbehaved earlier, as oversupervised children might, taxing the patience of this strict disciplinarian?[1]

Once this show was finished, nothing remained but the dismantling and storage of sets, equipment, and costumes and the inventory and return of unused materials. Plans for cleaning, repair, and storage had been noted as early as May 1 (MR 52r), and on the day before the Thursday performance, Seriacopi ordered a cart to take supplies back to other buildings on Friday. On Saturday, June 10, Emilio de' Cavalieri gave orders to take down and store seats, curtains, and the granducal palco, and to put away the dragon from intermedio 3 "in the rooms of the Guardaroba" adjacent to the stage area. The cloud machines were hoisted into the loft and lashed securely to prevent falling, and all the flyropes were labeled for ease of reinstallation with numbers or letters corresponding to their labeled locations on the grid, then stored in chests. Alfonso Parigi supervised these arrangements, which employed nine stagehands; typically distrustful, Seriacopi ordered these men to bring their lunch, as Gorini was to lock them in until the job was completed. Once shut down, the hall was to be cleaned once a month, with some thought given to exterminating the resident mice.[2]

Fabrics and other costume supplies were carefully inventoried: unused amounts reconsigned to the Guardaroba constitute the terminal entries on the debit side of most double-entry pages in Cavalieri's account book. Many are dated September 1, apparently the point at which the theater accounts were closed out. Among the diverse items returned, several will be familiar: 67 braccia of the prestigious green velvet, out of a total of 233 ordered, and 4,081 braccia of the ethereal velo di bologna, representing the only significant overestimate by the costume staff.[3]

As physical materials returned from their temporary sojourn at the theater to their original homes, so did the remaining guests. On June 15 the last of the French delegation left, among them Christine's aunt, the Duchess of Brunswick. A pious woman like her niece, she was accompanied by the majordomo Enea Vaini as far as Cortona, whence she was extending her journey into a pilgrimage to Loreto. Since her party had landed in Tuscany in late April and had been aboard Tuscan vessels since April 11 Ferdinando had extended fully two months' hospitality to his in-laws.[4]

On August 20 news reached Florence of the assassination of Christine's uncle and brother-in-law, King Henri III, on August 1 — yet another in the tragic series of family deaths since December 1588. This political stroke intensified the ongoing civil war, in which the Valois dynasty was ultimately supplanted by its distant Bourbon cousin, Henri IV. The outcome did not, however, undo Ferdinando's attempt to ally himself with the French crown: the founder of the new line was married to Marguerite de Valois, sister of Henri III and of Christine's mother, so the king of France was once again the grand duchess's uncle.

In late September, Don Pietro de' Medici sailed again from Livorno aboard the Capitana, this time to return to Spain, where he had been before the wedding as an officer of King Philip's Italian troops. The musicians, too, gradually dispersed or found other employment as court opportunities declined. The composer Luca Marenzio, who had come to Florence with Ferdinando in 1588, was let go from the granducal payroll on November 30, 1589, when he returned to Rome; earlier that month, Antonio Archilei's salary was reduced from 18 to 11 scudi per month.[5]

THE ECONOMIC AFTERMATH

Many bills remained outstanding at the time of performance, and it took most of the rest of the year to close them out. Once Seriacopi's temporary administration for the theatricals had been disbanded, later dealings with tailors and suppliers were handled by the permanent Guardaroba and household staff: Cavalieri's *Libro di conti* records transfers of various sums to Vaini, the *guardaroba maggiore* Orazio Rucellai, and the *maestro di casa* Giovanni del Maestro, with which they were authorized to pay contractors.[6]

The cumbersome procedures and delays of this fledgling bureaucracy must have been as frustrating to state employees as the proverbial "red tape" is to their modern descendants. A request for reimbursement came in on May 11, for example, from one Teofilo Rettori, who was temporarily transferred from the naval staff to the service of the comedy and had incurred expenses for various trips between Livorno, Siena, and Florence. On May 23 Cavalieri approved repayment but stipulated that Rettori "should submit a new invoice in proper form, since the other one was no good, lacking the date, name, and signature, and it should include details."[7]

The Guardaroba records of payments to Oreto Berardi and Niccolò Serlori, the principal tailors, reveal that after the weekly salaries of fall 1588 were discontinued in favor of block payment to the subcontracting master tailors, there seems to have been a consistent lag of nearly two months between work and payment. Although Oreto and Niccolò had received in advance roughly 130 scudi, a considerable amount of their total fee for the intermedi, their outstanding bills were still being settled through summer 1589, and Oreto received the final 30 scudi due him only on September 16.[8]

Some estimates are available for the overall quantities and costs of principal elements of the preparations. As to hospitality, the court footed the bill for 2,700 foreign "mouths," as well as for various local pages and servants hired for the duration; the total expense of room and board from April 1 to June 30 amounted to 85,959 scudi, including 9,000 barrels of wine, 7,286 *staia* (about 4,800 bushels) of grain, and 16,500 *staia* of fodder. Additional amounts were disbursed for coaches (*vetture*, 1,884 scudi) and saddlery (*vetture di sella*, 2,160). In July, the state treasury reimbursed Orazio Rucellai for the balance of expenses incurred on his voyage to France "to conduct the bride": the payment of 40,161 scudi indicates that the scale of outlay expected of high officials made court service a privilege affordable only by the very rich. Lastly, Pavoni, always fond of numbers, reports that the total cost for the liveries of 180 nobles at the entry (not including the Medici family) came to more than 30,000 scudi.[9]

A final accounting for the principal wedding theatricals was submitted by the Ufficiali di Monte, officers of the quasi-independent public bank, on May 26, 1593. The auditors precisely calculated the total cost of the intermedi and comedies at 30,255 scudi, 4 lire, 2 soldi, and 11 denari; the Pitti parade and joust cost an additional 14,457 scudi. Seriacopi's continual insistence on inventory control and written procedures notwithstanding, the investigators noted self-protectively that because the materials he returned to the Guardaroba and the Fortezza da Basso were "a confusion of so many different things, it was not possible for us to review everything properly and exactly." Their observation that the entertainments "seem to us to have been carried out with little concern for economy" (*con poca diligentia di rispiarmo*) is somewhat less surprising, as the total expenditures for these events alone would equal, in modern terms, on the order of five to seven million dollars. All the same, in light of all we have witnessed of the harried quartermaster's constant attention to cost-cutting, jawboning prices, and reusing equipment, this judgment seems unduly harsh.[10]

As always, Florentine attitudes oscillated between pomp and parsimony. On one hand, as the chronicler Pavoni put it in his summation of the wedding spectacles (*Diario*, 47), "the great expenditures, and the magnificence and splendor deployed by the Grand Duke in these nuptials of his . . . have certainly shown the world the power and grandeur of the House of Medici." (Actually, of course, royal marriages were income-producers for the groom's family: Christine brought a dowry of 600,000 scudi, although, with the known expenses alone running to some 200,000 scudi, the net profit was considerably reduced.) On the other hand, only a year later, in August 1590 — perhaps prodded by the birth of their first child, the future Cosimo II — Ferdinando and Christine, after consultation with del Maestro and Vaini, saw fit to decree a cutback of some ten percent in their ordinary household expenses, which over the past year had totaled 59,894 ducats.[11]

At a broader macroeconomic level, this prudent retrenchment may also have been motivated by the early signs of incipient economic shrinkage, from the exhaustion of mineral deposits at the renowned Pietrasanta quarry in late 1587 to the onset of decline in the wool industry about the same time. The full impact of Tuscany's gradual but inexorable economic and geopolitical marginalization was not to become widely apparent for another decade, but it may have been felt enough by 1593 to render public officials more sensitive to extravagance than the court had been four years earlier — and even more so by 1596, when the English traveler Robert Dallington observed tartly that, for the grand duke, "great sparing is a great revenue."[12]

COMMEMORATIVE PRINTS AND BOOKS

In the end, the Medici never tightened their belts enough and, like other smaller Italian courts, all but bankrupted themselves in continuing artistic assertions of a power no longer backed by dwindling resources. At the time of the wedding, however, they could also afford to create an unparalleled propaganda record of their magnificence, and they still played a large enough role on the world stage that audiences outside their realm were eager for such accounts. It is in large part thanks to these detailed and widely disseminated texts and images that the 1589 production exercised so much influence over succeeding generations and is recoverable today. Unfortunately, however, the reliability of all of these documents is compromised to varying degrees: the pictures by their temporal distance from an ephemeral original, the texts by the pressures of timely publication and/or the second-hand reliance of more remote writers on local authors or informants whom they sometimes misunderstood.

The two major Florentine books are the earliest, most ample, and generally trustworthy; though not without errors themselves, they served as the parent texts for a complicated genealogy of subsequent publications. Raffaello Gualterotti's *descrizione* of Christine's entry is the only such souvenir that combines word and image. As we saw earlier, its long illustrated guidebook, dedicated to Christine and probably in her hands during the April 30 procession, was prepared well in advance, with direct access to the arch designs; but its briefer narrative part, hastily written after the fact, was dedicated to Ferdinando on June 4, barely a month later, and begs indulgence for the "many imperfections" in this section, "since it was necessary for me to set down and illustrate in a few days all this, which could well have taken many years."[13] Bastiano de' Rossi's souvenir of the comedy and intermedi, released on May 14, was also written largely ahead of time, in order to be available before the guests' departure. As seen earlier, although his encyclopedic record of Bardi's original programmatic intentions is invaluable, his early press deadline (to say nothing of personal rivalries) resulted in Rossi's failure to include various late changes in text, music, cast, and perhaps scenography.

Before the end of the calendar year more than a dozen further accounts were issued throughout Italy and beyond. Both Giuseppe Pavoni and Simone Cavallino published their "diaries" in the neighboring Papal States — close to Tuscany not only geographically but historically, from the Medici popes through Ferdinando's long residence in Rome — where a considerable readership might be expected for the activities of a well-known neighbor. Probably for similar reasons, the only non-Italian souvenir account was published in Lyons, the French city with closest ties to Tuscan banking, a large Florentine community, and the publishing center for Christine's former homeland.

Pavoni's publication was produced by June 10, less than a month after he returned to Bologna, and haste partly explains his errors in dating various events (the Pitti evening is listed as both May 11 and 15, *Diario*, 4, 35). Though he clearly attended the major events in person, Pavoni must also have taken home with him copies of both Gualterotti and Rossi to supplement or refresh his own memories. He quotes from Gualterotti in some aspects of his entry description (p. 11, for example), and his account of the intermedi follows Rossi in compressed form. The Roman Cavallino seems to have been further removed from some events: although he describes the Pitti parade and naumachia in sharply observed detail, his account of the intermedi is so garbled that he probably relied on personal informants rather than Rossi's authoritative text. His description of the entry depends heavily on Gualterotti, to the point of repeating the latter's use of the present tense, uniquely intended for guiding Christine's experience on the entry day but inappropriate to a chronicle. (Their livery lists, however, differ greatly.) Both Cavallino and Pavoni, being foreigners, are unfamiliar with the streets and public spaces of Florence and hence confuse the sequence of arches and the route of the entry procession.

A "third generation" is represented by the seven-page anonymous booklet titled *Li sontuosissimi apparecchi . . .*, published in both Florence and Ferrara, with summaries of the entry and intermedi. Although its entry account contains some freshly observed details, the description of the ensuing banquet is compressed from Pavoni almost verbatim, and the few details given about the intermedi are often wrong. The author seems to have been Ferrarese, or at least to have been aiming at that readership: he devotes exceptional attention to participants from that state, always noting the presence, role, and costume of Cesare d'Este and uniquely reporting an audience on May 3 at which the Ferrarese ambassador presented Christine with a gift of jewelry from Duke Alfonso (p. 7). The auspices of this text are unknown, but it may have been instigated by the Florentines to impress their nearby cousins and friendly cultural rivals (Rossi's opus is dedicated to Alfonso).

Apart from the 65 plates in Gualterotti, known visual remains include a total of 32 independent engravings or etchings, illustrating events from Christine's entry through the final river god procession. A few prints are the work of Agostino Carracci and Cherubino Alberti, both well known as reproductive engravers; the bulk are by two other artists, Orazio Scarabelli and the monk Epifanio d'Alfiano, about whose activities beyond this occasion little is known. Various series of these prints continued to be issued as late as 1592, the date inscribed by d'Alfiano on cat. 27. The existence of three states of the print showing intermedio 5 (cat. 55), each with a different coat of arms on the cartouche held by Amphitrite, suggests that some editions were tailored for presentation to individual aristocratic recipients.[14]

Although, as with the written commemoratives, details of the genealogy of these prints remain uncertain, at least two distinct series, in different sizes, were originally produced separately: a set of 12 small prints (approximately 5 by 8 inches) of the Pitti chariot parade, by Scarabelli and Alberti (cat. 72–73, 75–81, 83–85), and a more comprehensive group in a larger format (approximately 9 by 13 inches) engraved by Scarabelli, Carracci, and d'Alfiano, of which 31 images survive, illustrating as well the other Pitti events, intermedi, comedy, joust, and river god parade. In order to integrate the 12 smaller prints into this larger set, 11 of the former were at some point reprinted with the addition of a decorative border to bring them up to the size of the 20 larger ones, which might also have been printed previously as a separate group (or groups).[15]

The relation of these visual documents to the original events and images is also as clouded and intertwined as that of the written texts. Even the prints credited to Gualterotti, who had prior access to the ateliers of the entry artists, can be unreliable; the others were made at some distance in time from vanished originals, often via intermediary images, and are sometimes inconsistent with the written accounts or other visual evidence. Some Pitti elements mentioned by both diarists, for example — notably the float or floats containing only women — are omitted from the surviving prints. In his series recording the arches for Christine's entry, Scarabelli depended closely on the corresponding images in Gualterotti, incorporating into his detailed composite of each arch miniature copies of several reproductions that were printed separately by his predecessor: his view of the Carraia arch (cat. 2) reproduces, among other scenes, Christine taking leave of her family (fig. 3) and embarking at Marseilles (fig. 8), the latter accepting Gualterotti's alteration of the original painting's proportions.[16]

In other cases the reproductive teams had to work from the original artists' preliminary sketches or cartoons, some of which are still extant (see cat. 1–7), and perhaps from written descriptions. For the Uffizi and Pitti performances, the engravers had access to Buontalenti's own designs, or at least to reductions of them made largely by Andrea Boscoli to match the chosen formats of the two print series (cat. 9, 54, 74). As the scenery sketches were rough and conceptual, Boscoli amplified his intermediate versions with more precise details of dress which, though loosely consistent with the textual record, do not exactly match the known costume designs for these scenes. In at least two cases the engravers must have had some additional guides, for their prints differ from the known scene designs, showing another moment in the action (cat. 27, 52): the Lucifer in d'Alfiano's hell scene, for example, which is not in the surviving scenery sketch, could have been adapted from Cigoli's detail drawing of the monster (cat. 53) or from the actual construction by Piero Pagolini and Francesco Rosselli, still in storage backstage.

Inevitably, the printmakers invented or embellished certain details. Boscoli and Carracci in particular exhibit a stylistic tendency to regularize what was in reality less geometrically smooth or complete. In Carracci's print showing intermedio 1, engraved after Boscoli's similar reduction drawing (cat. 9, 10), the precise semicircle of heavenly clouds with seated gods looks suspiciously like Raphael's Vatican fresco of the *Disputa*, a canonical ideal for late Cinquecento neoclassicists. The actual stage clouds were, however, seven distinct units arranged in discontinuous receding planes, all necessarily parallel to the proscenium and to the grid of beams behind it (fig. 7) — a jagged disposition that comes through more clearly in the cruder, less idealizing print by d'Alfiano of the similar configuration for intermedio 6 (cat. 64).

LATER INFLUENCE IN ITALY

Besides the impact of written and visual records of their work, the creators of the 1589 theatricals themselves exerted a powerful influence on the development of musical theater in Florence, Italy, and beyond, in three ways. Most directly, the individual authors, composers, performers, and scenic artists, whose careers extended into the seventeenth century, continued to refine and work variations on the same themes and images; later, as these pioneers began to retire from creative activity, they were gradually replaced by descendants and pupils who continued their ideas down to the 1650s. Second, the physical pattern of the stage machinery that they had put in place for the theater's premiere created a limited repertory of stage components and actions within which all future performances had to operate. And finally, the actual set pieces and costumes that they had designed for 1589 were reused from one production to the next.

Nine years later, the intermedi veterans Jacopo Peri and Ottavio Rinuccini collaborated as composer and librettist on *La Dafne*, generally considered the first true opera, which was performed on several occasions. Rinuccini's scenario for 1598, which centered on the god Apollo and included the same combat with the Python as the third intermedio from 1589, adapted his own earlier text and its classical sources. The lost stage sets were probably again designed by Buontalenti, who may have used some of the set pieces in storage since 1589, such as the movable fire-breathing dragon.[17]

For subsequent Medici occasions, notably further dynastic weddings in 1600 and 1608, members of the same team also created a series of court entertainments that were heavily dependent on the themes, forms, and physical machinery that they had laid down in 1589. Buontalenti was again the chief designer in 1600 for the wedding of Maria de' Medici, Ferdinando's niece, to Henri IV, a continuation of the French alliance. (Henri's marriage to Christine's aunt, Marguerite de Valois, had been annulled in 1599.) The major performance on this occasion was another early opera, *The Abduction of Cephalus* (*Il rapimento di Cefalo*), largely composed by the 1589 veteran Giulio Caccini, who took the post of court musical director after Cavalieri returned to Rome. Unfortunately, no visual records survive for this production, which was the climax of the aging Buontalenti's theatrical career, and for which he utilized several assistants, notably Giulio Parigi and Alessandro Pieroni — who had served in 1589 as, respectively, an 18-year-old trainee and an architectural painter.

The themes and locales here were so similar to 1589 that Roy Strong could understandably misidentify one scene design for the earlier event as belonging to 1600 (cat. 26). Although this drawing for the Apollonian contest of intermedio 2 is securely datable to 1589, it may in fact quite accurately represent the (re)appearance of Apollo's mountain a decade later, for the inventory of Buontalenti's possessions drawn up shortly before his death reveals that he kept many of his drawings, presumably for reference and adaptation. Moreover, the basic configuration of machines that he constructed in 1589 had fixed the repertory of possibilities for scenic pattern and movement: although they would be used in different combinations, these flies, traps, and shutters had established all the potentials that would be available throughout the life of the Uffizi Theater.[18]

Buontalenti was still the inspiration behind the 1608 performance of *The Judgment of Paris*, a drama by Michelangelo Buonarroti the Younger with intermedi by Giovanni de' Bardi, Giovanni Battista Strozzi, and others, staged for the marriage of Cosimo de' Medici, son of Ferdinando and Christine, to Maria Maddalena of Austria. But by this time he was old and frail; he died on June 6, some months before the event, bequeathing his modelli to the Medici archives. Giulio Parigi, who succeeded him as court architect-engineer, essentially continued his teacher's traditions. In fact, the entire calendar of public ceremonies and entertainments was consciously conservative, reinforcing the official hunger for precedent and continuity stretching back to Buontalenti's predecessors: the route of the bride's entry (decorated by Cigoli, who temporarily returned from Rome for the commission) repeated that of Joanna of Austria and Christine, and Giulio's costumes were partly inspired by those of Vasari for Joanna.

Giulio's stage designs also reveal the extent of his inevitable debt to the infrastructure provided by Buontalenti. His fourth intermedio, in which a ship bearing the Florentine explorer Amerigo Vespucci sailed over the Indian Ocean (fig. 12), combined several stock elements of the 1589 machinery previously used only independently: to the side shutters, ship, and wave machine from Buontalenti's nautical intermedio 5, he added the rising central mountain (from the original intermedio 2) and the upper semicircular choir of seated deities (intermedi 1 and 6). Other artists remained constrained by prior performances in more mundane ways: a letter concerning Cigoli's repeat assignment designing entry arches mentions that "there have remained some remnants of the décor of 1589," pilasters and other architectural units, which it was proposed to refurbish for this occasion; and Ferdinando himself ordered Giulio to look at an existing chariot to see if it, too, could be reused.

Among numerous later festivals designed by Giulio, the most significant was the 1617 Uffizi performance of *La liberazione di Tirreno e Arnea*, known from the engraving of the theater interior by his pupil Jacques Callot (fig. 6). Except that it takes place on land, the scene shown by Callot once again recombines the same stage elements as the 1608 ship scene: a central upper group in a heavenly "cloud hole," plus a lower apsidal tier of cloudborne figures, then a rock below (probably ascended from the trap), and side shutters with trees.[19]

12. *Fourth intermedio, Florence, 1608: Amerigo Vespucci.*
Remigio Cantagallina, after Giulio Parigi.

TUSCANY AND THE ENGLISH COURT THEATER

Broadening out beyond Florence, the next generation of descendants of the 1589 theatricals were the European tradition of Baroque courtly scenography — the Farnese theater, built at Parma between 1618 and 1628, was only the first of many to follow the prototype laid down by the Uffizi — and particularly the Stuart court masques created by Inigo Jones.[20] The architect-designer Jones, Britain's counterpart to Buontalenti, traveled in Italy in 1597–1603 and 1613–14 to study recent architecture and theater (particularly the work of Palladio, which he was instrumental in popularizing in England). During his first trip, he attended the Florentine academy operated by Giulio Parigi; once back in England he often adapted Florentine theatrical models through the intermediary of prints after Parigi's productions. For *The Temple of Love*, for example, staged for King Charles I in 1635, he took his design for an Indian shore from the engraving after the similar Vespucci scene in the 1608 intermedi — making his image something of an artistic grandchild of the 1589 designs.[21]

The granducal payment records reveal another link between the Stuarts and Florence, more directly involving the personnel and perhaps images of 1589. About 1610 the Florentine Costantino de' Servi, who had painted a portrait of Christine at the time of her wedding while employed at the granducal workshops, joined the crowd of foreign artists and craftworkers lured to England in the Italophile building boom that began in the late sixteenth century. In 1612, while working under Jones as a court theatrical designer, Servi wrote back to his native city asking a Medici secretary to arrange for the Guardaroba to send him "two or three books of inventions" for various intermedi or other entertainments, for use in his current commissions. If Servi's request was granted, perhaps the drawings sent to him included the separate "books" or costume folders for intermedi 4 or 6 from 1589, and perhaps the original large schematic stage designs as well. These were presumably held by the Medici archives, at least after Buontalenti's will of 1608, and their disappearance from that otherwise carefully retentive agency is hard to explain except by such deliberate action. Possibly the arts administrators felt they could spare these sketches because the costumes for intermedio 6 were generally similar to intermedio 1 and the sets, now superseded by two decades of further development, were in any case well recorded in prints.[22]

EPILOGUE

The later lives of the numerous protagonists at the 1589 wedding offer some concluding glimpses of the continuing influence of that grand occasion despite the parallel ebbing of Tuscany's artistic and political importance. Ferdinando died in 1609 and was buried in the Cappella dei Principi, which he had had built by Buontalenti at San Lorenzo. His energetic and responsible reign was, in retrospect, the high-water mark of Florence's fortune and cultural prestige. As Ferdinando had foreseen in allying himself with the French, the European center of gravity had already begun to shift northward, particularly to England and France, where Maria de' Medici's grandson Louis XIV staged the sumptuous theatricals of Versailles.

Of the artists, Buontalenti and the Parigi family stayed on, as did others with strong local roots such as Alessandro Pieroni, the painter of architecture who later assisted at the performance of 1600 and the Cappella dei Principi. Even within Italy, however, Florence became increasingly provincial: the local Baroque school, while not without accomplished practitioners, exerted nothing like the centrality of Tuscan art during the previous two centuries. Cigoli, among others, left for Rome, and shortly after the wedding the arch designer Giovannantonio Dosio was lured by greater architectural opportunity in Naples, where he enjoyed an influential career. Similarly, as noted earlier, several musicians left for Rome by the end of 1589; a few years later the composer-impresario Cavalieri, after staging musical works in Florence written in collaboration with the intermedi poet Laura Guidiccioni Lucchesini, also returned to his native city, where he turned to *sacre rappresentazioni*, the religious equivalent of music drama.[23]

As for Ferdinando's many household and public administrators, the later careers of the principal Guardaroba officials, though traceable in the archives, remain largely unknown or unstudied. Those employees of lower social status like Seriacopi and Gorini, plus the myriad local performers and craftworkers — from Piero Pagolini to the painter-partners Rosselli and Francini and the carpenter Domenico del Atticiato, as well as the anonymous nuns, tailors, and sailors — are, at least in the present state of research, even less accessible after their brief documented appearance on the "stage" of theater history.

In 1600, Christine escorted her niece Maria de' Medici to France to marry Henri IV, reversing her own journey a decade before in order to reciprocate Catherine de' Medici's desire to "send back to her homeland . . . someone of her own blood" (Gualterotti, *Descrizione*, 1: 4). The women's landing at Marseilles was portrayed, with considerable license, in the biographical series painted for Maria in 1622–23 by Peter Paul Rubens (fig. 13). Here Christine makes her farewell appearance on the artistic stage, now represented as the older, black-clad chaperone, the role once played for her by her own paternal aunt Brunswick. Although it represents a debarkation rather than Christine's embarkation from the same port a decade before, Rubens's composition, despite being more panoramic and enlivened by his characteristic Baroque diagonals and proliferation of allegories, is typologically and — in such details as the gangplank, mast, and furled sails and the energetic nautical denizens in the foreground — even compositionally similar to Cosci's portrayal of Christine at the dock for her second entry arch (cat. 2; fig. 8). Maria, 16 years old when she rode through the streets accompanying Christine in 1589, must have realized then that she was next in line for such an apotheosis, and would seem to have paid close attention to potentially useful precedents.[24]

After Ferdinando died, Christine served twice as head of government, first as regent for their son Cosimo II and then, following his early death in 1621, as coregent with Cosimo's widow Maria Maddalena for the eleven-year-old Ferdinando II. Her administration was increasingly unpopular due to her continued spending on courtly pomp amid the downward economic spiral, as well as her rigidifying religious orthodoxy and partiality to ecclesiastical policies. Upon the death of Giulio Parigi in 1635, Christine became the sole survivor among the principals involved in the 1589 celebration, a last remnant

13. *Debarkation of Maria de' Medici at Marseilles. Peter Paul Rubens.*

of the artistic world of a half-century ago. When she died at the family villa of Castello the following year and was buried alongside her husband in the Cappella dei Principi, her wedding passed from living memory into the realm of legend. Yet even after her demise, the court artistic staff continued unbroken into its third generation of related artists: her catafalque and funeral décors were designed by Giulio's son and successor Alfonso Parigi the Younger (1606–56).[25]

The Uffizi theater itself ceased operating as a performance space in the later seventeenth century, around the end of Alfonso the Younger's career. The vast assembly hall found a second function as the seat of the national parliament when Florence was briefly the capital of a newly unified Italy from 1865–71, but was subsequently partitioned for its present use by the Drawings and Prints Department and other components of the Uffizi Museum. All that remains of the original fittings are Buontalenti's entrance door, which now leads into the departmental exhibition gallery, and some wall moldings visible in the museum's Botticelli areas.[26]

The vanished festival of 1589 may now seem at best little more than a faded memory or half-forgotten dream, at worst a quaint or propagandistic self-delusion. But the prophecy of Amphitrite's nymphs in intermedio 5 did come true, albeit not in the sense that the librettist Rinuccini intended. When they foretold "issuing from you a progeny of such luster that it will adorn the earth from one pole to the other," the nereids meant Cosimo II; but henceforth Florence was to enjoy fame for its past more than its future, its legacy more than its leaders. And within that half-remembered, fragmentarily documented history, we are still able to make out, however dimly, Ferdinando and Christine's first and most lasting offspring: not only the dazzling surface appearance and elaborate iconography of their wedding, but tantalizing glimpses of who made it, and how, and what it meant to the many people who worked on, acted in, and viewed this memorable *theatrum mundi*. The record of their stage productions offers valuable insight into the entire production of culture in this most storied of Renaissance courts.

Catalogue

Dimensions for prints are those of the image, not the entire sheet. Where more than one location is given for a print, the first exemplum listed is the one illustrated and measured.

ENTRY TO FLORENCE, APRIL 30
(Catalogue 1–7)

For the route and sequence of arches, see fig. 9. For general description of arches, including 65 reproductions, see Gualterotti 1589, book 2; for participants and narrative of activities, see his book 1; Pavoni 1589 is less reliable. According to Baldinucci 1681 (life of Pagani, 3: 40), the paintings for the arches were taken down and stored in the Pitti Palace but later destroyed by fire; one lone survivor has recently been published (see cat. 2). Each arch is illustrated here with one of the composite prints by Scarabelli, which, although made later than Gualterotti's, are more detailed and comprehensive; individual paintings and sculptures attached to that arch are identified in the order of the page numbers in Gualterotti at which he reproduces these components. Surviving sketches for the paintings and later copies are cited after the relevant titles.

[1]
First entry arch, Porta al Prato. Orazio Scarabelli (signed lower right).
New York, Metropolitan Museum of Art (Harris Brisbane Dick Fund, 1931), no. 31.72.5(5).
24.0 × 34.7 cm (9⅜ × 13½ in.). Engraving.
Daddi Giovannozzi 1940, 89–91; Gaeta Bertelà and Petrioli Tofani 1969, 67–69; Strong 1973, 174–75; Borsi 1980, 351, no. 4.34; Strong 1984, fig. 84.

Located at the city gate, this "arch," designed by Alessandro Allori, was actually an octagonal structure that enclosed an open-air "theater" some 30 × 35 braccia (57 × 67 ft.) in which Christine's coronation took place; its height rose from 23 braccia at the sides to 37 in the central zone. In addition to the narrative paintings described below, whose theme was the military history of Florence from its founding into the fourteenth century, the arch was also decorated with allegorical images of the administrative quarters within the capital city, its nearby suburbs, and subject cities in Tuscany.

Gualterotti, p. 11: Architectural plan of arch.
    Drawing by Cigoli showing octagonal plan: Florence, Uffizi, no. 2585A; Matteoli 1980, 274–77.
12: Perspective view of arch.
14: The founding of Florence, by Giovanni Bizzelli.
16: Charlemagne restores Florence, Giovanmaria Butteri.
19: Defeat of Radagasius, Francesco Mati.
22: Charlemagne building the church of Santi Apostoli, Pier Vieri.
25: Florence united with Fiesole, Lorenzo Sciorini.
28: Charles of Anjou at the battle of Benevento, Ludovico Cigoli.
    Preparatory compositional sketch, Oxford, Ashmolean Museum: Parker 1956, 2: 92, no. 196; Chappell 1992, 6.
    Preparatory study for soldier, Florence, Uffizi, no. 9036F: Chappell 1992, 5, no. 3.

I

30: Relief of the siege of 1312, Andrea
Commodi.

33: Defeat of Gian Galeazzo Visconti at Mantua, Alessandro Pieroni.

38: Good Government in Florence, Alessandro Allori.

42: Certaldo and San Giovanni, Lorenzo di
Berlincione.

44: San Miniato and Scarperia, Gabriello
Ughi.

[2]
Second entry arch, Ponte alla Carraia. Orazio
Scarabelli (signed lower right).
New York, Metropolitan Museum of Art
(Harris Brisbane Dick Fund, 1931), no.
31.72.5(3). London, British Museum, no.
1897-1-13-47.
25.0 × 34.2 cm (9⅞ × 13½ in.). Engraving.
Daddi Giovannozzi 1940, 92–93; Gaeta
Bertelà and Petrioli Tofani 1969, 69–70;

Strong 1973, 175–76; Borsi 1980, 351, no.
4.35.
Designed by Giovannantonio Dosio, this arch
was placed near the Arno River (visible at
right) and was backed against the Palazzo
Ricasoli; the print omits the building,
whose façade would have risen behind the
main central unit. Theme: previous marriages of the Medici and Lorraine dynasties,
and preceding episodes in the wedding of
Ferdinando and Christine.
Gualterotti, 51: Architectural plan.
54: Perspective elevation.
58: Catherine de' Medici enthroned with her
family, by Cosimo Gamberucci (center).
60: Wedding of Catherine and Henri II, Cosimo Dati.
62: Wedding of Duke Lorenzo de' Medici
(Catherine's father), Battista Naldini and
Giovanni Cosci (Balducci).
64: Wedding of Duke Charles III of Lorraine

and Claude de France (Christine's parents), Valerio Marucelli.

66: Christine taking leave of her family, Giovanni Cosci (Balducci; illustration above, fig. 3).

Preparatory drawing: London, British Museum, no. 1895-9-15-572; Langedijk 1981, 1: 674, no. 44; Turner 1986, 229, no. 181.

68: Allegories of Lorraine and the river Moselle, Passignano (Domenico Cresti).

70: Allegories of Florence and the river Arno, Passignano.

72: Don Pietro de' Medici welcomes Christine aboard the Capitana in Marseilles, Giovanni Cosci (illustration above, fig. 8).

Painting: Florence, Pitti Palace, inv. 1890 no. 7760; Langedijk 1981, 1: 674 no. 45, 1: 1351 no. 14 (illustrated). This enormous painting, ht. 4.60 m, is the only original arch decoration to survive; its tall proportions relative to the engraved reproduction indicate that Gualterotti took liberties with the original compositions to make them fit the uniform format of his pages.

In addition, four statues, each some 6 braccia high, were erected on the nearby Ponte Santa Trinita, without an architectural backdrop, and were described and illustrated by Gualterotti along with the Carraia arch:

74: Octavian Augustus, Giovanni Bologna.

76: Charlemagne, Giovanni Bologna.

78: Grand Duke Cosimo I, Giovanni Caccini.

80: Cosimo de' Medici *Pater Patriae*, Giovanni Caccini.

[3]

Third entry arch, Canto dei Carnesecchi. Orazio Scarabelli.

New York, Metropolitan Museum of Art

3

(Harris Brisbane Dick Fund, 1931), no.
31.72.5(7).
24.5 × 34.6 cm (9⅝ × 13⅝ in.). Engraving.
Daddi Giovannozzi 1940, 98–100; Gaeta
Bertelà and Petrioli Tofani 1969, 70; Borsi
1980, 352, no. 4.36.
Designed by Santi di Tito, overall height 14
braccia. Theme: military history since the
First Crusade of the house of Lorraine-
Guise, whose arms top the central pedi-
ment. Daddi Giovannozzi illustrates two
architectural drawings in the Uffizi (nos.
3053A, 2994A, her figs. 7, 8) and suggests
that they could be Santi's preparatory
sketches for this arch, but Gaetà Bertela
and Petrioli Tofani attribute them to Cigoli.
Gualterotti, 82: Plan of arch.
83: Perspective elevation of arch.
86: Godefroy, Duke of Lorraine, at Constant-
inople, by Santi di Tito.
88: Siege of Nicea, Antonio Boschi.
90: Corbana, general of the Persians, defeated

by Godefroy of Bouillon at Antioch, Gregorio Pagani.
Study: Florence, Uffizi, no. 10500F; Gaeta
Bertelà and Petrioli Tofani 1969, 75,
no. 33, fig. 13.
Studies: Paris, Louvre, Cabinet des Dessins, inv. nos. 1390, 21195; Bacou and
Bean 1959, 91, nos. 216, 217; Viatte
1988, 160, nos. 287, 288.
92: Godefroy of Bouillon leading Crusaders
in battle at Jerusalem, Santi di Tito.
Study: Florence, Uffizi, no. 7667F; Gaeta
Bertelà and Petrioli Tofani 1969, 75,
no. 34, fig. 11.
94: Godefroy of Bouillon refuses the crown of
Jerusalem, Valerio di Santi (Valerio Titi,
son of Santi di Tito).
Study: Florence, Uffizi, no. 761F; Gaeta
Bertelà and Petrioli Tofani 1969, 76,
no. 35, fig. 12.
96: François de Guise at the battle of Dreux
(Normandy), Andrea Boscoli.

98: The Duke of Guise attacks Calais in 1558, Agostino Ciampelli.

100: René of Lorraine defeats the Duke of Burgundy at Morat, Camillo Pagni.

[4]

Fourth entry arch, duomo façade. Orazio Scarabelli (signed lower right).

New York, Metropolitan Museum of Art (Harris Brisbane Dick Fund, 1931), no. 31.72.5(6).

24.2 × 34.7 cm (9⅝ × 13¾ in.). Engraving.

Daddi Giovannozzi 1940, 94–98; Gaeta Bertelà and Petrioli Tofani 1969, 70–71; Borsi 1980, 340, 352, no. 4.37; Blumenthal 1990, 98–99.

Designed by Giovannantonio Dosio; although Gualterotti does not name him, his role is clear in the payment records (see Chap. 4). The cathedral still lacked a finished façade, and Dosio proposed his temporary decora-tion as a model for a permanent one.

Theme: history of the Church in Florence. The six large, gessoed-staff statues of Tus-can saints from the lower level niches, dis-played in the north semidome of the cathedral, were first identified by James Holderbaum in a lecture, "Surviving Colos-sal Sculpture for the Florentine Wedding Festivities of 1589," St. Louis, College Art Association, 1968, summarized in *Journal of the Society of Architectural Historians* 27 (1968): 210–11; clockwise from front left, they are Poggio, Zenobio, Antonino (miter missing), Andrea, Miniato, Giovanni. Gual-terotti also describes the rich decorations of the cathedral interior, 127.

Gualterotti, 104: Elevation drawing.

Upper level, L–R:

107: Pope Martin V raising the bishopric of Florence to an archbishopric in 1420, by Andrea Verrocchi.

109: St. Ambrose consecrates the basilica of San Lorenzo, Francesco Terzo.

111: Pope Clement honoring the Guelphs, Simone da Poggibonsi.

112: Pope Eugenius IV consecrating the duomo in 1436, Stefano Pieri.

Lower level, L–R:

114: San Miniato, statue by Battista Lorenzi.

116: San Zenobio, statue by Pietro Francavilla.

118: Election of Pope Stephen IX in 1059, Passignano.

120: San Giovanni Gualberto, statue by Giovanni Caccini.

122: San Poggio, statue by Francavilla.

124: Council of Florence in 1439, Giovanbattista Paggi.

126: San Andrea, bishop of Florence, anonymous statue.

128: Sant'Antonino, archbishop of Florence, statue by Battista Lorenzi.

[5]

Fifth entry arch, Canto de' Bischeri. Orazio Scarabelli.

New York, Metropolitan Museum of Art (Harris Brisbane Dick Fund, 1931), no. 31.72.5(1).

24.2 × 34.5 cm (9½ × 13⅝ in.). Engraving.

Daddi Giovannozzi 1940, 98–100; Gaeta Bertelà and Petrioli Tofani 1969, 71; Zorzi 1977, 103, 209–10n125, fig. 65; Blumenthal 1980, 5–7, no. 2; Borsi 1980, 352, no. 4.38; Blumenthal 1990, 99.

Designed by Taddeo Landini; the street shown is alternatively called Via del Proconsolo, in which can be seen the Badia and the Bargello (also confusing, Gualterotti includes this arch in the same chapter devoted to cat. 4). The theme is the House of Habsburg; the honor paid to Tuscany's nominal imperial overlords is here much reduced in scale from the previous Medici

5

wedding, when Francesco I married a Habsburg archduchess. Upper zone: allegories of America, Europe, Africa, Asia, in reference to the Habsburg world empire.

Gualterotti, 130: Elevation drawing.

133: Charles V, statue by Landini (left niche). Illn. in Steven Ostrow, "Gianlorenzo Bernini, Girolamo Lucenti, and the Statue of Philip IV," *Art Bulletin* 73 (1991), 106, fig. 12.

136: Charles V defeating Turks near Vienna, Giovanni Strada (Stradano?).

139: Philip II, statue by Landini (right niche). Reproduced in Ostrow, 106, fig. 13.

142: Battle of Lepanto, Girolamo Macchietti and Bernardino Monaldi.

[6]

Sixth entry arch, Canto degli Antellesi.
  Orazio Scarabelli.

New York, Metropolitan Museum of Art (Harris Brisbane Dick Fund, 1931), no. 31.72.5(4).

24.1 × 33.2 cm (9½ × 13⅛ in.). Engraving.

Daddi Giovannozzi 1940, 100; Gaeta Bertelà and Petrioli Tofani 1969, 71–72; Strong 1973, 177; Borsi 1980, 352–53, no. 4.39; Strong 1984, fig. 85.

Designed by Taddeo Landini; theme, history of the Medici since the grandfather of Duke Cosimo I. Additional sculptures depicted the arms of the Salviati (the family of Cosimo I's mother), his wife Eleonora of Toledo, and their children, including Cosimo's natural son Giovanni. Gualterotti calls this section both "chapter 5" and "chapter 6."

Gualterotti, 145: Plan of arch.

146: Elevation drawing.

150: Pope Pius IV approves the Order of Santo Stefano, Alessandro del Barbieri.

152: Cosimo I fortifies Tuscan cities, Benedetto Velli.

154: Giovanni delle Bande Nere (father of Cosimo I), statue by Valerio Cioli.

156: Giovanni (father of Giovanni delle Bande Nere), statue by Cristofano da Bracciano.

159: Cosimo I acclaimed as Duke, Jacopo da Empoli.

Study: Florence, Uffizi, GDS no. 7731F; *Firenze e la Toscana* 1983, figs. 12, 13.

162: Cosimo I enthroned, reorganizing the Tuscan military, Ludovico Buti.

[7]

Seventh entry arch, Palazzo Vecchio façade. Orazio Scarabelli.

New York, Metropolitan Museum of Art (Harris Brisbane Dick Fund, 1931), no. 31.72.5(2).

26.0 × 35.2 cm (10¼ × 13⅞ in.). Engraving.

Daddi Giovannozzi 1940, 91–94; Gaeta Bertelà and Petrioli Tofani 1969, 72; Strong 1973, 177–78; Borsi 1980, 352–53, no. 4.40.

Designed by Giovannantonio Dosio; theme, apotheosis of Florence and of the three grand dukes, centered on the allegorical crowning of modern Tuscany by Cosimo I as successor to the ancient Etruscans.

Gualterotti, 166: Elevation drawing.

170: Apotheosis and crowning of Tuscany, Jacopo Ligozzi.

Reproduced: Strong 1973, fig. 131; Strong 1984, fig. 86.

Preparatory drawing: London, British Museum, no. 1874-8-8-35; Turner 1986, 224, no. 173.

Copy: New York, Metropolitan Museum, no. 53.601.179. Engraved by Cherubino Alberti, dedicated to Don Virginio Orsini, 1589. Bartsch 17.108.157; Blumenthal 1973, 82, no. 33.

7

173: Pope Pius V crowns Cosimo I, Bernardino Poccetti.

175: Emperor Maximilian I affirms the rule of Francesco I, Michelangelo Ciampanelli.

UFFIZI THEATER, MAY 2
(Catalogue 8–68)

For general description of the settings, costumes, characters and action of the intermedi and comedies, see Rossi 1589, Pavoni 1589; for text of the intermedi and music see Malvezzi 1591, Walker 1963. Within each intermedio, drawings precede prints made after them, and the costume drawings are arranged as far as possible in the sequence in which they were originally kept (indicated by the numbers in the upper right corner).

INTERMEDIO I

[8]

Stage design, Intermedio 1. Bernardo Buontalenti.

London, Victoria and Albert Museum, no. E.1186-1931.

37.9 × 55.7 cm (15 × 21⅞ in.). Pen and watercolor, brown ink, red color in costumes. Vertical fold, center; cropped at left.

Warburg 1895, 109, 269–71, 276, 415n; Laver 1932, 294–300; Jacquot 1964, 81; Fabbri 1975, 111, no. 8.10; Borsi 1980, 358, no. 5.13A; Strong 1984, fig. 88; Blumenthal 1986, 91–93.

Buontalenti's conceptual sketch for the second part of this intermedio, showing the heavenly harmony of the spheres. Necessity and the Fates are enthroned upper center, with the seven planets and Astraea on flanking clouds; a circle of twelve virtuous heroes in the starry opening above (identified by Rossi, 28–32; either painted figures, or costumed musicians, for whose names see LC N423–24); and twelve Sirens on the stage floor. After the prologue, which featured Doric Harmony (cat. 11) singing above a

8

Doric temple, the scenery was composed, as here, entirely of seven clouds, which rose and fell bearing the Sirens and Planets as they sang a dialogue with each other. The number and appearance of these various figures do not correspond exactly to the text and other (probably later) costume drawings. The iconography is based on Plato's *Republic*, book 10.

[9]

Stage design, Intermedio 1. Andrea Boscoli.
Florence, Uffizi, GDS no. 15115F.
26.6 × 37.6 cm (10½ × 14¾ in.). Pen and wash on pale yellow paper, traces of pencil.
Gaeta Bertelà and Petrioli Tofani 1969, 80, no. 38; Mancini 1975, 42–43; Blumenthal 1986, 91n115.
Copy after cat. 8 by Buontalenti's assistant, at a reduced scale. Its size, increased detail and precise style, and incised stylus marks indicate that it was prepared for use by the engraver Carracci (see cat. 10; compare cat.

54), but the costumes shown do not correspond to Buontalenti's costume drawings (cat. 11–25).

[10]

Stage design, Intermedio 1. Agostino Carracci (signed lower right).
New York, Metropolitan Museum of Art (Harris Brisbane Dick Fund, 1926), no. 26.70.4(32). London, Victoria and Albert Museum, no. E.217–1942 (inscribed bottom center, "Filippo Suchielli"); London, British Museum; Florence, Uffizi, GDS no. 92294.
23.7 × 34.5 cm (9⅜ × 13⅝ in.). Etching and engraving.
Bartsch 18.106.121; Warburg 1895, 109, 120, 266; Laver, 1932, 294–300; Bacou and Bean 1959, 45; Nagler 1964, 74–78; Botto 1968, 46; Molinari 1968, 27; Gaeta Bertelà and Petrioli Tofani 1969, 78–80, no. 37; Blumenthal 1973, 88, no. 37; Strong 1973, 185; Fabbri 1975, 113, no. 8.11; Mancini 1975, 43–46; Bohlin 1979, 266–71, nos.

9

10

153–54; Blumenthal 1980, 9–11, no. 4;
Borsi 1980, 358, no. 5.13B; Blumenthal
1990, 101–2.
Engraving after the drawing by Boscoli, cat.
9, with some variations. The similarity of
the composition to Raphael's Vatican *Disputa* (1509–10) has been noted by Molinari
and others.

[11]
Costume design, Doric Harmony. Bernardo
Buontalenti.
Florence, Biblioteca Nazionale Centrale,
Palatina C.B.3.53, vol. 2, c. 11r.
47.3 × 36.9 cm (18⅝ × 14½ in.), cropped
right, thin strip added left. Pen and brown
ink, watercolor, pencil.
Warburg 1895, fig. 80; Nagler 1964, fig. 47;
Strong 1973, 180; Borsi 1980, 364, no.
5.14A.
Above the figure, roman numeral I (see cat.
12). Like most of the costume drawings,
this sheet bears a separate, boxed arabic
number in the upper right corner, which
indicates its sequence in the portfolio of
costume drawings for each respective intermedio: here, number 1 (in ink, altered to 13
in pencil). Doric Harmony appeared at the
beginning of intermedio 1, accompanied by
the other ancient musical modes, and sang
the prologue. Costume beige to ocher and
blue, with pink trim, though the fabric orders specify green velvet (Rossi, 22, for description and sources). Seated on a pink
cloud, with rays in pencil. Caption upper
right: *In capo sette gioie sopra le treccie e acon-
ciatur / vestita tutta di lionato e adorna di
vel[luto?] / daltri colori che canpeggino co[n] lionato. / in mano larpe / sopra una nugola as-
edere.* Cast note, lower left: *S.a Vitoria*
[Archilei].

[12]
Costume design, Siren II (Moon). Assistant,
after Bernardo Buontalenti.

Florence, Biblioteca Nazionale Centrale,
   Palatina C.B.3.53, vol. 2, c. 32v.
41.2 × 28.8 cm (16¼ × 11⅜ in.), cropped
   top and right. Pen and brown ink,
   watercolor, pencil.
Warburg 1895, 1: 267.

Cat. 12 through 22 illustrate the Sirens of intermedio 1, each of whom has a distinctive
costume, and most of whom are identified
by a roman numeral above the head and,
below the figure, an arabic number. (Each
arabic number is one digit less than the cor-

12

[13]

Costume design, Siren III (Mercury).
  Assistant, after Bernardo Buontalenti.
Florence, Biblioteca Nazionale Centrale,
  Palatina C.B.3.53, vol. 2, c. 32r.
41.2 × 28.8 cm (16¼ × 11⅜ in.), cropped.
  Pen and brown ink, watercolor, pencil.
Warburg 1895, 1: 267.
Roman numeral cropped; arabic numeral 2.
  Color notes on the fabrics, or next to them,
  correspond to paint colors: *cenerognio, doro,
  rosso, incarnato, turchino, bianco;* blue buskins.
  Played by Lucia Caccini.

[14]

Costume design, Siren IIII (Venus). Assistant,
  after Bernardo Buontalenti.
Florence, Biblioteca Nazionale Centrale,
  Palatina C.B.3.53, vol. 2, c. 33r.
47.4 × 36.6 cm (18⅝ × 14⅜ in.). Pen and
  brown ink, watercolor, pencil.
Arabic numeral 3 below figure; number 3 up-

responding roman because Doric Harmony,
who appeared before the Sirens, was labeled as roman I — see cat. 11.) The roman
number has been cropped from this drawing, but it bears an arabic 1. The Sirens are
all traced, by an unknown hand (Boscoli's?),
from the same original drawing of Buontalenti (cat. 22), then reworked slightly in
different colors (all costumes have gold
edging, except Buontalenti's original) and
with appropriate planetary symbols and
costume details. Text on drawing: color
notes, *rosso* and *bianco tutto l'abito;* upper
right (cropped), *vestita co / di penne / dal
mezo / e cosi que / le penne* (for the complete
text of this repeated prescription for feathered costumes, see cat. 14). This Siren, pertaining to the sphere of the Moon, as
indicated by her headdress, was sung by
Antonio Archilei (for cast lists encompassing cat. 12–22 see LC Q291–96).

14

15

per right. Mustard hair, blue buskins, blue feathered tunic. Note at shoulder: *vestita come si vede di penne.* Color notes: *rosso, incarnatino tutto labito* (canceled, though the paint actually is pink), revised *da qui in giù bianco.* Cast note, lower left: *Jac[op]o Peri detto il zazerino.*

[15]
Costume design, Siren V (Sun). Assistant, after Bernardo Buontalenti.
Florence, Biblioteca Nazionale Centrale, Palatina C.B.3.53, vol. 2, c. 33v.
47.4 × 36.6 cm (18⅝ × 14⅜ in.). Pen and brown ink, watercolor, pencil.
Borsi 1980, 364, no. 5.14B.
Arabic numeral 4 below figure. Blue feathered tunic. Casting note, lower left: *Bardella* (Antonio Naldi).

[16]
Costume design, Siren VI (Mars). Assistant, after Bernardo Buontalenti.
Florence, Biblioteca Nazionale Centrale, Palatina C.B.3.53, vol. 2, c. 34r.
47.1 × 36.9 cm (18½ × 14½ in.). Pen and brown ink, watercolor, pencil.
Borsi 1980, 364, no. 5.14B.
Arabic numeral 5; upper right number, illegible (4?). Red skirt, blue feathered tunic, labeled *vestita come si vede di penne;* gold trim, blue buskins. Color notes: *rosso, tutto rosso labito.* Cast note lower left, *Baccio Palibotria,* canceled and replaced by *Giovanni Lapi* (on whom see cat. 22).

[17]
Costume design, Siren VII (Jupiter). Assistant, after Bernardo Buontalenti.

16

17

Florence, Biblioteca Nazionale Centrale,
  Palatina C.B.3.53, vol. 2, c. 34v.
47.1 × 36.9 cm (18½ × 14½ in.). Pen and
  brown ink, watercolor, pencil.
Arabic numeral 6. Blue and brown tunic, blue
  skirt, pink buskins. Color notes: *come si vede
  di penne, rosso, turchino tutto labito* (canceled),
  da qui in giu bianco. Cast note, lower left:
  Bacio Palibotria.

[18]
Costume design, Siren VIII (Saturn).
  Assistant, after Bernardo Buontalenti.
Florence, Biblioteca Nazionale Centrale,
  Palatina C.B.3.53, vol. 2, c. 35r.
47.2 × 36.8 cm (18½ × 14½ in.). Pen and
  brown ink, watercolor, pencil.
Arabic numeral 7; upper right, number 5.
  Blue and brown tunic, skirt white with

brown wash, violet buskins. Color notes:
*come si vede di penne, cenerogniolo tutto l'abito,
rosso.* Cast note, lower left: *Nicholo Castrato.*

[19]
Costume design, Siren X (Ninth Sphere).
  Assistant, after Bernardo Buontalenti.
Florence, Biblioteca Nazionale Centrale,
  Palatina C.B.3.53, vol. 2, c. 35v.
47.2 × 36.8 cm (18½ × 14½ in.). Pen and
  brown ink, watercolor, pencil.
Testaverde 1988, fig. VII.
Cat. 19–22 represent the Sirens of the outermost heavenly spheres (Eighth to Tenth,
  plus the Empyrean) rather than those associated with the seven planets (cat. 12–18);
  except for Buontalenti's modello (cat. 22)
  they are nearly identical. While their
  dresses are of the same design as the plane-

18

19

tary Sirens, in place of the former's zodiacal headdresses they wear a halo of flames and stars. Moreover, while the tunics continue to be labeled *come si vede di penne*, the material notes on cat. 20–22 specify that the skirts (although colored blue) should be *trasparente siccome la foglia del diamante tutto l'abito*. Pink buskins. Color note: *verde* (though the mantle indicated is actually sepia). Cast note, lower left: *Gio. batista d[e]l violino Jacomelli.*

The three identical drawings (cat. 19–21) were to serve as models for a total of five such Siren costumes, later increased to six, which with cat. 22 would then match the number of the seven planetary ones; a note at lower left reads, *di questa sorte dove cenesono diseg.to tre anno aessere [cinque*, canceled] *7 i 7.* These changes may explain the discrepancies in various accounts regarding the total number of Sirens (eventually 14)

and their performers: some shifting of roles and temporary confusion seems to have accompanied the increases, indicated by changes in captions and by inconsistencies between drawings and account records. Beneath the roman numeral X here can be faintly seen an earlier number VIIII, probably scratched out when the copyist realized that this number had been assigned to the costume for Giovanni Lapi that had earlier been designated as VI (see cat. 22). The present costume X is alternatively assigned to Raffaello Gucci in the written records, LC Q291 (but see cat. 20).

[20]

Costume design, Siren XI (Tenth Sphere). Assistant, after Bernardo Buontalenti. Florence, Biblioteca Nazionale Centrale, Palatina C.B.3.53, vol. 2, c. 36r.

20

21

47.4 × 37.5 cm (18½ × 14¾ in.). Pen and brown ink, watercolor, pencil.

Arabic numeral below figure, 10; upper right number, partially cropped, 6 [?]. Colors and captions: same as cat. 19. Cast note, lower left, *Raffaello Gucci* (but see cat. 19 for his change of role; the same cast and costume list, LC Q291, assigns the present costume to Giulio Caccini).

[21]

Costume design, Siren XII (Empyrean). Assistant, after Bernardo Buontalenti.
Florence, Biblioteca Nazionale Centrale, Palatina C.B.3.53, vol. 2, c. 36v.
47.4 × 37.5 cm (18½ × 14¾ in.). Pen and brown ink, watercolor, pencil.
Nagler 1964, fig. 46.
Arabic numeral below figure, 11. Colors and captions: same as cat. 19. Cast notes, lower left, indicate the performer of this role and

four added Sirens (arabic numerals 13–16): *12 p.mo Giulio romano / 13 s.do Uno contralto / 14 t.zo Batista S[er] Jacopi / 15 q.to Durizio / 16 Zanobi Ciliani.* However, LC Q291–96 assigns these same costumes and roles using different numbers. In a first note, Q291, the arabic equivalent of the costume's proper roman numeral XII is followed by the actual arabic number below each costume, as follows: "12a Giulio Caccini (10), 12b Gio. ba. Seriacopi (11), 12c Duritio (12), 12d Zanobi ciliani (13)"; later (Q296), however, the register refers to the same group as "costumes 10–16," adding as the final no. 16 "un contralto che vien da Roma." Apparently the costumes were repeatedly reassigned as their total numbers changed (no drawings with arabic 12 or 13 survive, as those costumes were simply copied from the existing drawings). Moreover, the total of 16 such costume numbers (actually 15, because Doric Harmony was numbered 1 in this series) would make 15 Sirens, one more than the projected total of 14; perhaps one of these later cast members was added for musical reasons but kept somehow apart from the otherwise symmetrical stage picture.

[22] (plate 1)
Costume design, Siren VIIII (Eighth Sphere). Bernardo Buontalenti.
Florence, Biblioteca Nazionale Centrale, Palatina C.B.3.53, vol. 2, c. 37r.
47.2 × 34.4 cm (18½ × 13½ in.), cropped left. Pen and brown ink, watercolor, pencil.
Warburg 1895, 266–69, fig. 79; Borsi 1980, 361–64, no. 5.14B.
The roman numeral was originally a VI, to which three dissimilar strokes were added;

22

upper right number 7. Although placed last in the series in the costume portfolio, this drawing, by Buontalenti himself, was the modello from which cat. 12–21 were copied; it contains subtle patterns in brown wash on the skirt, a coral necklace, and other details lacking in the copies. It was used for the construction of a sample costume for Siren VI, originally intended for Giovanni Lapi, but when this drawing was reassigned to Siren VIIII the performer was also changed (see Chap. 3 and cat. 16). Headdress of a bear and stars. Pink shoes, white trim, pink headdress. Material note: *come si vede di penne.* Color notes: *rosso, apparire di colore turchino tutta.* Cast note, lower left: *[Ce]serone Basso.* For written notations on the verso of this sheet, see cat. 23.

[23] (plate 2)
Costume design, four planetary gods. Bernardo Buontalenti.
Florence, Biblioteca Nazionale Centrale, Palatina C.B.3.53, vol. 2, c. 28r.
36.5 × 45.7 cm (14⅜ × 18 in.), cropped at top, bottom, left. Pen and brown ink, watercolor.
Borsi 1980, 364–65, no. 5.14C.
Upper right number, partly illegible (8?). Four of the gods enthroned on their cloud platforms; the caption at top, *Manritta*, indicates they are for the right side of the stage (from audience viewpoint). Each figure has above it an identifying letter and number (following continuously after the costume numbers 1–16 for Doric Harmony and the Sirens), an associated zodiac sign, and a descriptive label below the seat. L–R: Moon/Diana, A 17, crab/Cancer, *[se]ggio di q.a a essere [d'a]rgento;* Venus, B 18, bull/Taurus, *segg. di ariento;* Mars, C 19, Scorpio, *seggo doro, e di Rosso;* Saturn, D 20, ram/Aries, *s. cēnerognolo.* Further written captions referring to these four costumes are on the blank verso of cat. 22 (which must therefore have preceded cat. 23 in the

23

costume folder). Those captions are written vertically, so as to read horizontally when the portfolio was turned to look at this drawing, one of a pair (see cat. 24) whose format is horizontal (at the same time, both sheets are folded vertically in four parts, corresponding to the four figures in each, apparently in an alternative attempt to insert them into the folder with the figures reading vertically, which necessitated folding the protruding outside quarter of each sheet inward): *A. aessere tutta bianca / B. aessere coperta di velo turchino ch[e] traspara la carne / C. tutto armato co[n] sopravesta rossa accesa / D. tutto bigio cenerogniolo.* For complete descriptions of all eight gods and their attributes, see Rossi 1589, 25–28. Cast members assigned to these roles (left to right): Mario Luchini, Alberigo [Malvezzi?], Gio. del Minugiaio, Luca Marenzio (LC N431 ff.).

[24] (plate 3)
Costume design, four planetary gods.
  Bernardo Buontalenti.
Florence, Biblioteca Nazionale Centrale,
  Palatina C.B.3.53, vol. 2, c. 29r.
36.1 × 45.1 cm (14¼ × 17¾ in.), cropped
  right and top.
Warburg 1895, fig. 81; Strong 1973, 184;
  Borsi 1980, 364, no. 5.14c.
Upper right (when sheet is held vertically),
  number 9. The pendant to cat. 23, showing
  four gods for the audience-left side of the
  stage (the cropped caption at upper left
  probably read *Mano Sinistra*). Like cat. 23,
  each figure has a set of identifying labels
  above and notes below the throne. L–R:
  Mercury, F 25, goat/Capricorn, *o di q.o a
  daessere chome / to, cioe di 6* [over canceled 7]
  colori; Sun/Apollo, G 26, lion/Leo, *il seggo
  doro* (for similar depictions of Apollo, see
  cat. 35, 65); Jupiter, H 27, fish/Pisces, *seggo*

24

di oro, et avori co[n] gioie; Astraea (goddess of the Golden Age: see Ovid, *Metamorphoses* 1: 150; Virgil, Eclogue 4), I 28, scales of justice/Libra, *seggo turchino pieno di stelle.* Costume descriptions written on the verso of cat. 23 refer to this drawing, which followed it in the portfolio: *F. mercurio ignudo con un manto di sei colori G. di drappo doro col fondo rosso co[n] un ma[n]to simile H. sino amezo nudo. dal mezo in giu con un ma[n]to turchino fregiato doro. I. vestita tutta turchina maniche daltra sorte.* Cast: 25 Mercury, Pierino; 26 Jupiter, Mongalbo; 27 Apollo, Ser Bono; 28 Astraea, Cristofano [Malvezzi?] (LC N441).

[25] (plate 4)
Costume design, Necessity and the Fates.
    Bernardo Buontalenti.
Florence, Biblioteca Nazionale Centrale,
    Palatina C.B.3.53, vol. 2, c. 27r.

48.1 × 34.9 cm (19 × 13¾ in.), cropped left (and right?). Pen and brown ink, watercolor.
Warburg 1895, fig. 95; Strong 1973, 181; Borsi 1980, 364, no. 5.14C.
The central cloudborne group, between the flanking gods (cat. 23, 24): the goddess Necessity (wearing a headdress of cypress and holding two large nails and a mass of entrails, symbols of torment), enthroned with her diamond spindle, which is supported by her three daughters, the Fates, or Parcae (Rossi, 25). The composition is derived from an illustration in Vincenzo Cartari's iconographic handbook, *Le imagini de i dei antichi,* 1571 (Donington 1981, pl. IV). Caption above: *figure del c[i]elo,* and the R-like symbol of Necessity with a line to her. Light brown geometric patterns on all four dresses. A note on the verso of cat. 24, referring to this drawing, which followed it

25

in the sketch folder, gives costume colors: *tutte le dicontro tre figure dappie vanno vestite tutto biancho / R* [Necessity] *va vestita di ceneragniolo tutta.* Cast: 23 Necessity, Onofrio Gualfreducci; Fates, 21, Don Gio. Basso; 22, Ludovico Belevanti; 24, Piero Masselli (LC N432, 441).

INTERMEDIO 2

[26]
Stage design for Intermedio 2. Bernardo Buontalenti.
London, Victoria and Albert Museum, no. E.1187-1931.
38.1 × 56.2 cm (15 × 22⅛ in.), irregularly cropped, central vertical fold. Pen and brown ink, wash, some red color on costumes.
Laver 1932, 294–300; Nagler 1964, 81; Reade 1967, no. 3; Strong 1973, 202; Fabbri 1975, 113, no. 8.12; Blumenthal 1980, 27n2; Borsi 1980, 358, no. 5.13c;

26

Strong 1984, fig. 98; Blumenthal 1986, fig. 199.

Erroneously identified by Strong (followed by Blumenthal) as a design for Caccini's *Il rapimento di Cefalo* of 1600, this drawing is Buontalenti's initial conception for the 1589 singing contest between the nine Muses and the nine Pierides, daughters of King Pierus of Nemathia (Ovid, *Metamorphoses* 5: 300). The setting, a wooded clearing, subsequently underwent considerable changes: cat. 27, engraved after the event, does not show the winged horse Pegasus here depicted atop Apollo's central Mount Parnassus (or Helicon) but does include the trellised grottoes that were wheeled or slid onstage bearing the competing choirs, who in the earlier drawing simply stand to either side of the mountain. The six hamadryads (wood nymphs) seated on the mountain, which rose some 12 braccia (23 ft.) in telescoping sections from beneath the stage floor, were later increased to 16; they acted as judges of the competition. At the base of the mountain, a male river god represents the Castalian spring, generated by Pegasus' hoofkick; perfumed water flowed from his vase and additional onstage fountains. Buontalenti had earlier designed a similar hill, Apollo, and Pegasus for the villa at Pratolino (Lazzaro 1990, 132–33, fig. 122).

[27]

Stage design, Intermedio 2. Epifanio d'Alfiano (signed and dated 1592, lower right).

New York, Metropolitan Museum of Art (Harris Brisbane Dick Fund, 1931), no. 31.72.5(14). Florence, Biblioteca Marucelliana, 1, 400; London, British Museum.

23.8 × 34.4 cm (9⅜ × 13½ in.). Engraving.

Warburg 1895, 298–99, 411; Laver 1932, 294–300; Bacou and Bean 1959, 45; Nagler 1964, 80–82; Gaeta Bertelà and Petrioli Tofani 1969, 80, no. 39; Strong 1973, 187; Fabbri 1975, 113, no. 8.13; Mancini 1975,

27

44–46; Borsi 1980, 358, no. 5.13D; Strong 1984, fig. 89; Blumenthal 1986, 93–94.

As noted in cat. 26, this print represents a later conception of the stage picture, closer to what was actually built. It also conflates two successive moments of the action, showing the singers in human form in the rear grottoes (only five of each nine, the Muses on audience left, Pierides audience right) as well as, across the foreground, the chattering magpies into which the humiliated Pierides were transformed at the finale. The central mountain is here topped by Apollo, leader of the Muses, rather than his horse Pegasus, and the number of seated hamadryads is increased to nine (actually 16), whose costumes and attributes (books and trumpets) do not correspond to the costume drawing for these figures (cat. 28). The grottoes, trellised arbors, and woodland backdrop were full of fragrant orange and lemon trees simultaneously bearing flowers and fruit. A drawing of a garden scene with trellises (Florence, Uffizi, 5113A) has been suggested as a study for this scene (Pirrotta and Povoledo 1982, 368n59). Warburg describes two paintings that may have been derived in part from d'Alfiano's print, one by Pellegrino Tebaldi (Bologna, Pinacoteca, no. 575) and the other anonymous (Parma, Galleria, no. 191).

[28] (plate 5)
Costume design, Hamadryads. Bernardo Buontalenti.
Florence, Biblioteca Nazionale Centrale, Palatina C.B.3.53, vol. 2, cc. 30v–31r.
74.0 × 48.1 cm (19 × 29½ in.). Pen and brown ink, watercolor.
Nagler 1964, fig. 49; Borsi 1980, 360–64, no. 5.14D; Blumenthal 1986, 94; Testaverde 1988, fig. VI.
The only costume drawing with a detailed background (brown wash, some olive and pink), this is also the only double-page de-

28

sign that is actually pasted together to form one sheet, which would then have been folded to fit into the portfolio of costume drawings for this intermedio (compare cat. 49, 50). Twelve of the 16 hamadryads are shown, seated on Apollo's mountain above the Castalian spring. Above each costume are identifying numbers 1–12; below the bottom left figure (no. 8) are written the additional numbers 13–16, indicating that the four further figures (probably a late addition, since the following numbers had to be adjusted — see cat. 29–30) were to be produced from this model (compare cat. 21); following the color notes is the indication, *nota ch[e] le sud.e figure anno aessere 16*. Color notes, upper left: *1 vestita turchino sino meza resta rossa / 2 rosso turchino e incarnato / 3 pagonazo biancho e verde / 4 lionato azurro e incarnato / 5 azurro biancho e incarnato / 6 lionato pagonazo e incarnato / 7 verde pagonazo e bianco / 8 giallo turchino e incar-*

nato / 9 giallo bianco e rosso / 10 giallo verde e turchino / 11 pagonaza bianca e verde / 12 incarnata turchina e bianco. The colors as written do not match those painted on the figures, indicating that final specifications came only after the drawing was already finished. Headdresses vary (laurel, Phrygian cap), as do the attributes that some figures hold or wear (quiver and bow); for detailed description of the costumes, see Rossi, 40.

[29]
Costume design, Pierides. Bernardo
   Buontalenti.
Florence, Biblioteca Nazionale Centrale,
   Palatina C.B.3.53, vol. 2, c. 9.
46.8 × 37.1 cm (18½ × 14⅝ in.), diagonal
   fold upper right. Pen and brown ink,
   watercolor, pencil.
Borsi 1980, 364, no. 5.14E.

Upper right, number 2. Tunic blue, sleeves gadrooned with salmon dots, lion's-head epaulets; skirts coral, gold. Note below figure: *la disopra figura va vestita disopra azurro giallo incarnato e verde / e di questo abito ne assere fatti n.o* [9, canceled] *1.* Costume number below, *n.o* [13, canceled] *17.* Originally, at least, the costume for all nine Pierides, though the canceled number is unexplained. Rossi, 41, notes that the Pierides' dresses are more elaborate than those for the Muses (cat. 30) "to show their vanity and haughtiness."

[30] (plate 6)
Costume design, Muses. Bernardo
   Buontalenti.
Florence, Biblioteca Nazionale Centrale,
   Palatina C.B.3.53, vol. 2, c. 8.
46.9 × 37.1 cm (18⅝ × 14⅝ in.). Pen and
   brown ink, watercolor, pencil.
Borsi 1980, 358, no. 5.14E.

29

30

Upper right number 3. For nine Muses: leaves in hair, olive green (Rossi calls them feathers); tunic coral, skirts gold, pink. Note below figure: *la disopra vavestita sopra incarnato bianco verde e pagonazo / di questo abito ne assere n.o 9*. These colors are closer than the painted ones to de' Rossi's description. Costume numbers below: [14, canceled] 18–26.

[31]

Costume design, Magpies. Bernardo Buontalenti.

Florence, Biblioteca Nazionale Centrale, Palatina C.B.3.53, vol. 2, c. 7.

47.1 × 37.3 cm (18⅝ × 14¾ in.). Pen and brown ink, brown wash.

Nagler 1964, fig. 50; Strong 1973, 188; Borsi 1980, 361–64, no. 5.14F.

Upper right, number 4. For the nine birds, played by young boys, into which the Pierides are transformed. The drawing is clearly a conceptual sketch that would have to be modified for the tailors, as the boys

31

would have different proportions and human legs rather than the spindly avian ones shown here. Note below figure: *nove maschere di questa sorte*. Costume numbers below, 27–35.

[32] (plate 8)

Costume design, two dancing women. Andrea Boscoli.

London, Victoria and Albert Museum, Theater Museum, no. E.614-1936.

26.4 × 28.1 cm (10⅜ × 11⅛ in.), cropped on all sides, central vertical fold. Pen and brown ink, watercolor.

A. E. Popham, *Italian Drawings Exhibited at Burlington House* (London, 1931), pl. CCIIa; *Catalogue of the Famous Collection of Old Master Drawings Formed by the Late Henry Oppenheimer* (London: Christie's, July 1936), 103, no. 204; Reade 1967, no. 5; Newton 1975, 202–3.

Although erroneously inscribed in the seventeenth century with an attribution to Vasari and more recently ascribed to Buontalenti himself, this drawing is closest in style to his assistant Boscoli: compare similar fluttering drapery and hems, body proportions, facial type, hands, feet, and decorative vocabulary in cat. 9 (sixth figure from left, fourth from right), 54, and many drawings for other projects. Although no caption or documentation provides firm proof, the similarity of this costume to others for 1589 by Boscoli and by Buontalenti himself (cat. 8 [esp. second from left], 28, 29, 30, 34 [fourth from left]) suggests that it might be a lone survivor of the many detail drawings that must have been made as intermediaries between Buontalenti and the tailors. The figures, whose dresses in red, mauve, blue, and brown are richly decorated with animal heads (compare cat. 73), fringes, tassels, and ribbons, are wearing backless sandals (*pianelle*) that must have limited dance movement.

32

INTERMEDIO 3

[33] (plate 9)
Stage design for Intermedio 3. Bernardo
  Buontalenti.
London, Victoria and Albert Museum, no.
  E.1188-1931.
37.8 × 56.6 cm (14¾ × 22⅜ in.), cropped for
  water damage, central vertical fold. Pen and
  brown wash, red watercolor on dragon and
  figures, green in trees.
Laver 1932, 294–300; Fabbri 1975, 113, no.
  8.14; Borsi 1980, 360, no. 5.13E;
  Blumenthal 1986, 94–95.
The conceptual study for the setting of the
  combat between Apollo and the Python, a

woodland clearing on the island of Delos,
with faint markings of a perspective grid on
the floor. It depicts an early moment in the
intermedio: Apollo has not yet appeared,
and the giant fire-breathing dragon stands
in the center before his charred cave,
threatening lines of standing Delphians,
who include children and an old man in
contrast to the 18 exclusively adult couples
in the actual costume sketches (cat. 36–48).
Above right, in the trees, sit three goddesses not mentioned by Rossi. Subsequently, a cardboard Apollo descended
from heaven on a wire (cat. 49) and was replaced by an identically costumed living
dancer (cat. 35) who challenged the serpent

33

to a battle, killed it, and performed a vic-
tory dance with the Delphic couples. At the
finale, all exited singing a hymn of praise.
The plot is derived from Ovid, *Metamorphoses* 1: 438 ff.; Julius Pollux, *Onomasti-
con* 4: 10: 84; Lucian, *De saltatione* 16
(Rossi, 42–48, including a detailed description of Apollo's dance).

[34]
Stage setting of Intermedio 3. Agostino
Carracci (signed lower right).
New York, Metropolitan Museum of Art
(Harris Brisbane Dick Fund, 1931), no.
26.70.4(33). Florence, Uffizi, no. 100838;
London, Victoria and Albert Museum, no.
23088.8 (inscribed *filippo suchielli for Siena*);
London, British Museum.
24.1 × 34.0 cm (9⅞ × 13¾ in.). Engraving
and etching.
Bartsch 18.106.122; Warburg 1895, 109, 266;
Laver 1932, 299; Bacou and Bean 1959, 45;
Nagler 1964, 83–84; Reade 1967, 3, no. 6;

Gaeta Bertelà and Petrioli Tofani 1969, 81,
no. 40; Blumenthal 1973, 92, no. 39; Strong
1973, 189; Fabbri 1975, 113, no. 8.15;
Mancini 1975, 44–46; Bohlin 1979, 154;
Blumenthal 1980, 11–13, no. 5; Borsi 1980,
360, no. 5.13F; Strong 1984, fig. 90;
Blumenthal 1990, 102.
Shows a later moment in the action than the
scenic design on which it is based (cat. 33),
with Apollo descending forward in fore-
shortening. The dragon is smaller than in
the drawing, and the trees higher. Although
produced after the event, perhaps from an
intermediary reduction by Boscoli, the
print still includes the children and single
figures not attested by the texts; the three
goddesses, however, are eliminated. A
drawing of the dragon in the print, attributed to Buontalenti but perhaps a later
copy, is in New York, Pierpont Morgan Library, no. 1960.20 (Blumenthal 1973, 90,
no. 38, illd.; Blumenthal 1986, 117n70, fig.
189).

34

[35] (plate 7)

Costume design, Apollo. Bernardo
Buontalenti.

Florence, Biblioteca Nazionale Centrale,
Palatina C.B.3.53, vol. 2, c. 1r.

47.1 × 37.3 cm (18½ × 14¾ in.). Pen and
brown ink, watercolor, pencil.

Warburg 1895, 283–86; Borsi 1980, 364, no.
5.14G.

Upper right, number 1, beginning the numer-
ical sequence for the costume folder for intermedio 2 (cat. 35–50). Apollo in classical
armor, holding bow and arrow; tan and
blue tunic with pink trim, blue and green
skirt, pink and tan buskins. Note below figure: *la disopra figura va vestito di tela doro
sopra turchino e rosso il resto*, loosely corresponding to the paint colors. Following, in
another hand: *e la spallatura d'oro*. Another
note in the same hand, at top: *vestita come
l'ultima maschera di n.o 37*, an indication

that the dancer taking this part should be
identical to the cardboard flying Apollo
whose drawing bears that sequence number
(cat. 49). Rossi, 44, recorded that Apollo in
intermedio 2 was dressed "in the same fashion as in the first intermedio"; compare the
similar outfits for the same god in cat. 24
and 65.

[36]

Costume design, Delphic couple. Bernardo
Buontalenti.

Florence, Biblioteca Nazionale Centrale,
Palatina C.B.3.53, vol. 2, c. 26r.

46.5 × 37.3 cm (18⅝ × 14¾ in.). Pen and
brown ink, watercolor.

Warburg 1895, 288–89, fig. 84a; Nagler
1964, fig. 55; Borsi 1980, 364, no. 5.14H.

Upper right, number 2. The first of 13
sketches for the 18 couples who form the
chorus of frightened and then grateful resi-

35

pink tunic, gold and violet robe, pink buskins; note below, *questo va vestito di sopra rosso / verde e azzurro*; notes above, *n.o 1 [Ruberto*, canceled] *Onofrio chome la maschera qui sotto / n.o 3 franc.o di bruno vestito come n.o 15 / ma variato di colore*. Female figure, right: pink and blue bodice, beige and pink skirts with embroidery pattern, coral in hair; note below, *questa va vestita turchino il busto / le maniche rosse e p[er]el ch[e] va nelle falde / incarnato / biancho*; notes above, *n.o 2 oratio chome la maschera qui sotto / n.o 4 oratio benvenuti vestito come / n.o 15 ma variato di colore*.

[37] (plate 12)
Costume design, Delphic couple. Bernardo
  Buontalenti.
Florence, Biblioteca Nazionale Centrale,
  Palatina C.B.3.53, vol. 2, c. 13r.
46.8 × 37.3 cm (18½ × 14¾ in.). Pen and
  brown ink, watercolor.
Warburg 1895, 288–89, fig. 84b; Borsi 1980,
  362–64, no. 5.14H.
Upper right, number 3; see cat. 36. Male figure left: gold and pink tunic, pink spiral
  turban, pink and violet robe, pink buskins,
  holding a shell; notes below: *questa va vestito disopra azzurro / rosso / e verde*; cast notes above: *n.o 5 [Gio. batista violino*, canceled] *Lapi / n.o 7 [m.o Jac.o zazzerino*, canceled] *Cornetto d[e]l franzosino*. Female figure right: pink and beige bodice, blue and green skirts, pink buskins, coral in hair; notes below: *questa va disopra vestita di rosso / maniche gialle / biancho et mavi*; cast notes above: *n.o 6 [Nicholo Castrato*, canceled] *Alberigho / n.o 8 [Plauto*, canceled; *Ant.o franc.o* (?), canceled] *Gio. batt.a del franc.no*. Rossi, 47, adds that the woman's skirt had stripes made of yellow and turquoise ribbon; her girdle was cloth of gold, its clasp a lion's head, the veils hanging from it silk and cloth of gold; and she wore a pearl necklace.

dents of the island of Delos (cat. 36–48; the surviving drawings, some intended for more than two costumes, lack one couple). Color notes are written below most figures (not always corresponding to the paint colors), and cast names (often changed) are written above them, each with an identifying costume number. Rossi, 46–48, describes the costumes of cat. 36 and 37 in greater detail than is shown in the drawings, suggesting that these two pairs were completed earlier than the rest of this series and seen by him while he was writing. To suit the marine locale, many costumes are decorated with shells, coral, snails, and other sea motifs. Some features of the costumes are Turkish or Levantine (Rossi, "quasi alla greca"), an anachronistic nod to the eastern Mediterranean site of the island. Male figure, left:

36

[38]
Costume design, Delphic couple. Bernardo
  Buontalenti.
Florence, Biblioteca Nazionale Centrale,
  Palatina C.B.3.53, vol. 2, c. 14r.
46.3 × 37.2 cm (18¼ × 14⅝ in.). Pen and
  brown ink, watercolor.
Borsi 1980, 364, no. 5.14H.

Upper right, number 4; see cat. 36. Male figure left: gold and mauve robe with pattern,
  pink skirt, blue buskins, holding coral;
  notes below: *questo va disopra di*
  pagonazo / verde / rosso; cast notes above:
  n.o 9 Cieserone basso. Female figure right:
  blue and tan bodice, orange and pink skirts,
  coral headdress, shell in hand; notes below:

37

questo va disopra il busto turchino / maniche gialle e la sotto vesta / incarnato piu abasso; cast notes above: *n.o 10 Zanobi Ciliani.*

[39]
Costume design, Delphic couple. Bernardo Buontalenti.

Florence, Biblioteca Nazionale Centrale, Palatina C.B.3.53, vol. 2, c. 15r.
46.2 × 37.2 cm (18⅜ × 14⅝ in.). Pen and brown ink, watercolor.
Borsi 1980, 364, no. 5.14H.
Upper right, number 5; see cat. 36. Male figure left: gold, violet, and coral robe, blue

38

leggings, gold buskins, holding coral; notes
below: *questa va di sopra vestito
pagonazo / incarnato e turchino*; cast notes
above: *n.o 11* [*Gucci*, canceled] *Mario Luchini*. Female figure right: gold and mauve
bodice, blue and mauve skirts, dolphin
headdress, holding shell; notes below: *questa

va vestita di rosso biancho e mavi*; cast notes
above: *n.o 12* [*Biondino del franzosino*, canceled; *Gio. f.co di roma*, canceled].

[40]

Costume design, Delphic couple. Bernardo
Buontalenti.

Florence, Biblioteca Nazionale Centrale, Palatina C.B.3.53, vol. 2, c. 16r.

46.8 × 37.0 cm (18⅜ × 14⅝ in.). Pen and brown ink, watercolor.

Borsi 1980, 364, no. 5.14H.

Upper right, number 6; see cat. 36. Male figure left: blue and gray jerkin, gold sleeves and leggings, coral hat; notes below: *questo va di sopra vestito turchino / incarnato / e verde;* cast notes above: *n.o 13 Gio. franc.o vene da roma.* Female figure right: mauve and gray bodice, coral and gray skirt, gold buskins and veils; notes below: *questa va di-sopra il busto incarnato / turchino / e verde e*

40

rosso; cast notes above: *n.o 14 Bardella* (Antonio Naldi).

[41]
Costume design, Delphic couple. Bernardo
   Buontalenti.
Florence, Biblioteca Nazionale Centrale,
   Palatina C.B.3.53, vol. 2, c. 17r.

46.8 × 37.2 cm (18½ × 14⅝ in.). Pen and
   brown ink, watercolor.
Warburg 1895, 288, fig. 84c; Borsi 1980, 364,
   no. 5.14H.
Upper right, number 7; see cat. 36. Male figure left, notes below: *questa va col ma[n]to
   turchino / sotto verde bianco incarnato;* cast
   note above: *n.o 15 Ruberto ronai* [or *rovai?*].

y 15 Ruberto come

y 16 Benedetto Guardi
Veste Come n.o 15

7

porta ua [s]mato turchino
sottoueste biancho . e pisarnato.

porta ua [s]mato rosso
il busto turchino e fino 'a piedi
insarnato

41

Female figure right, notes below: *questa va col ma[n]to rosso / il busto turchino e fino a piedi / incarnato;* notes above: *n.o 16 Benedetto Guardi / vestito come n.o 15.* Like costume nos. 3 and 4 in the Delphian series (cat. 36), no. 16 is marked to be dressed similarly to no. 15, perhaps indicating that no. 15 was constructed early as a modello for others in the series (compare cat. 22).

[42]

Costume design, Delphic couple. Bernardo Buontalenti.

Florence, Biblioteca Nazionale Centrale, Palatina C.B.3.53, vol. 2, c. 18r.

46.9 × 37.0 cm (18½ × 14⅝ in.). Pen and brown ink, watercolor.

Borsi 1980, 364, no. 5.14H.

Upper right, number 8; see cat. 36. Male fig-

42

ure left: purple robe, gold and coral trim, holding coral; cast notes above: *n.o 17* [*Gio. Lapi*, canceled] *Gio. batt.a violino*. Female figure right: coral tunic and skirt, blue underskirt, holding shell (alternative head in pencil); cast notes above: [*Alberigho*, canceled] *Nicholo Castrato*. From here to the end of the series (cat. 48), no color notes are written below the figures.

[43]

Costume design, Delphic couple. Bernardo Buontalenti.

43

Florence, Biblioteca Nazionale Centrale,
  Palatina C.B.3.53, vol. 2, c. 19r.
46.8 × 36.9 cm (18⅜ × 14½ in.). Pen and
  brown ink, watercolor.
Borsi 1980, 364, no. 5.14H; Testaverde 1988,
  figs. 25–26.
Upper right, number 9; see cat. 36. Male fig-

ure left: pink robe with gold lining and
sleeves, blue-gray hat with coral trim, holding coral; cast note above: *n.o 19 lessandro
del franzosino.* Female figure right: white
and gold dress, blue cloak, pink hat; cast
note above: *n.o 20 . . . . ch[e] suona
di / trombone d[e]ll franzosino.* The female

costume is closely derived from a woodcut series illustrating current fashions in the Islamic-Levantine world, in this case Syria (compare cat. 46, 48).

[44]
Costume design, Delphic couple. Bernardo Buontalenti.

Florence, Biblioteca Nazionale Centrale, Palatina C.B.3.53, vol. 2, c. 20r.
46.9 × 37.4 cm (18⅝ × 14¾ in.). Pen and brown ink, watercolor.
Upper right, number 10; see cat. 36. Female figure left: coral robe with gold lining, white skirt, blue-gray hat; cast note above: *n.o 21 s.ra Margherita* (Archilei). Male fig-

ure right: gray-blue and white robe with pink trim, pink pantaloons, leafy headdress; cast note above: *n.0 22 s. lucia* [or *lucca*?]. The subsequent drawing from the series, numbered 11 and illustrating costume nos. 23 and 24, is lost.

[45]
Costume design, Delphic couple. Bernardo Buontalenti.
Florence, Biblioteca Nazionale Centrale, Palatina C.B.3.53, vol. 2, c. 21r.
46.6 × 36.9 cm (18⅜ × 14½ in.). Pen and brown ink, watercolor.

Upper right, number 12; see cat. 36. Male figure left: blue mantle with gold lining, white
robe, blue-gray boots, holding coral; cast
note above: *n.o 25 stabile.* Female figure
right: gold mantle, coral dress with blue
sleeves, blue hat with white drape; cast note
above: *n.o 26* [(illegible) *putto,* canceled] *cen-
cio* [?].

[46]
Costume design, Delphic couple. Bernardo
   Buontalenti.
Florence, Biblioteca Nazionale Centrale,
   Palatina C.B.3.53, vol. 2, c. 22r.
46.7 × 36.6 cm (18⅜ × 14⅜ in.). Pen and
   brown ink, watercolor.
Testaverde 1988, figs. 27–28.

Upper right, number 13; see cat. 36. Female figure left: blue and mauve skirts, gold mantle, pink and gray plumed hat; cast note above: *n.o 27 Lucha* [or *Lucia?*]. Male figure right: gold tunic, violet skirt, blue mantle; cast note above: *n.o 28 Tommaso*. The female costume is closely derived from a woodcut series illustrating current fashions in the Islamic-Levantine world, in this case again Syria (compare cat. 43, 48).

[47]
Costume design, Delphic couple. Bernardo Buontalenti.
Florence, Biblioteca Nazionale Centrale, Palatina C.B.3.53, vol. 2, c. 23r.

46.9 × 36.7 cm (18½ × 14½ in.). Pen and brown ink, watercolor.

Borsi 1980, 364, no. 5.14H.

Upper right, number 14; see cat. 36. Male figure left: tan tunic, blue tights, coral boots, pink cape with gold trim; cast notes above: *n.o 29 frate basso / n.o 31 monghallo.* Female figure right: violet dress and sleeves, white overdress, violet hat with pink ribbons; cast notes above: *n.o 30 Ant.o franc.o del botiliere / n.o 32 frate d[e]lla nuntiata / tenore.*

[48]

Costume design, Delphic couple. Bernardo Buontalenti.

Florence, Biblioteca Nazionale Centrale, Palatina C.B.3.53, vol. 2, c. 24r.

47.1 × 36.6 cm (18⅝ × 14½ in.). Pen and brown ink, watercolor.

Warburg 1895, 288, fig. 84d; Testaverde 1988, figs. 23–24.

Upper right, number 15; see cat. 36. Female figure left: green dress with coral lining, red headdress; cast notes above: *n.o 33 Baccio palibotria / n.o 35 [cornetto del franzosino,* canceled] *Jac.o zazerino.* Male figure right: gold cloak, gray boots, green headdress; cast notes above: *n.o 34 Duritio / n.o 36 [Gio. franc.o sanese / Placito s(er) batt.,* both canceled] *Placito.* The female costume is derived from a woodcut series illustrating fashions in the Islamic-Levantine world, here Persia (compare cat. 43, 46).

[49] (plate 10)
Property design, flying Apollo. Bernardo Buontalenti.
Florence, Biblioteca Nazionale Centrale, Palatina C.B.3.53, vol. 2, c. 24v.
47.1 × 36.6 cm (18⅝ × 14½ in.). Pen and brown ink, watercolor.
Warburg 1895, fig. 83a; Strong 1973, 184; Borsi 1980, 364, no. 5.141.

One of a pair with cat. 50, showing the air-borne cardboard Apollo shooting an arrow at the artificial Python; though the two drawings are on separate sheets and mounted independently, they faced each other in the costume folder, and have often been reproduced as if the sheets were joined. Above Apollo is written *n.o 37 Aghostino. come la prima maschera senza numero;* below, *la presente figura va vestita di abito e cholori simili alla prima di q.o 3.o intermedio,* that is, the puppet figure should match the costume of the living Apollo (cat. 35), played by the dancer Agostino. As this figure is assigned a costume number, the cardboard cutout was apparently dressed in actual clothing made by the tailors.

[50] (plate 11)
Property design, Python. Bernardo Buontalenti.
Florence, Biblioteca Nazionale Centrale, Palatina C.B.3.53, vol. 2, c. 25r.
46.8 × 36.7 cm (18⅝ × 14⅝ in.), diagonal fold lower right. Pen and brown ink, watercolor.

49

50

Warburg 1895, fig. 83b; Strong 1973, 184; Borsi 1980, 364, no. 5.141; Blumenthal 1986, 94–95.

Upper right, number 16. See cat. 49, with which it forms a unified composition. The creature's scales are salmon, ocher, blue, and green; salmon flames shoot from the mouth (Rossi, 43, describes it as greenish-black and covered with sparkling mirrors). The curling tail, sketched in pencil, is not entirely inked. The movable creature, with a stagehand inside, was constructed in separate units of papier-mâché modeled over clay forms and assembled on a wooden framework.

INTERMEDIO 4

[51]

Stage design, Intermedio 4. Bernardo Buontalenti (?).
Paris, Louvre, Cabinet des Dessins no. 867.
46.7 × 72.6 cm (18⅜ × 28½ in.), central vertical fold, central horizontal fold. Pen and brown ink and wash, watercolor.

Bacou and Bean 1958, 21, no. 16; Bacou and Bean 1959, no. 19; Jacquot 1961, fig. IV; Nagler 1964, 86; Bacou 1965, 90, no. 214; Fabbri 1975, 38, 113 no. 8.16; Borsi 1980, 360, no. 5.13g; Blumenthal 1986, 95–96; Viatte 1988, 61, no. 92.

The only surviving design for the entire stage picture of this intermedio (at top center of the sheet is written the number 4). In this act, a sorceress on an airborne cloud drawn by dragons summoned the spirits of the air to sing a prophecy of the golden age, after which a hell scene appeared in which devils, while tormenting the dead, lamented that the return of earthly paradise would deprive them of any future sinful souls. The drawing shows an early conception of the scene, in which the devils cavort in a cavern set on the stage floor, before the idea was developed of opening the trapdoor to reveal the giant Lucifer and his infernal companions rising from below (compare cat. 52, 53). Twenty figures representing the demons of the air (but lacking the wings described by Rossi) sit on the upper apselike cloud; the

51

iconography is derived from Plato; Iamblichus, *De mysteriis;* and Dante, *Inferno* 3 (Rossi, 49–54).

Although this drawing is often ascribed to Buontalenti himself, Nagler and others have reasonably questioned that attribution. The drawing, smaller than the uniform group of initial sketches by Buontalenti that has survived, was probably copied at a re- duced scale from his lost original, a task usually delegated to an assistant. When folded in half vertically, each side of this sheet is the same size as the individual cos- tume drawings, suggesting that a copy was needed that would fit, when folded, into the existing portfolio of drawings for inter- medio 4 (there may well have been one such reference reduction for each act, the others now lost). This sheet is more color- ful than Buontalenti's surviving stage de- signs: sky pink above, blue below; rocks brown, with red flame reflections; figures in

the flames colored olive, pink, and blue; prophetess, wearing a blue dress and green overmantle, in a yellow chariot drawn by yellow, turquoise, and green dragons. The similarity of these monsters to the Python of intermedio 3 (cat. 50) underscores the related theme in both acts of chthonic, frightening forces controlled by benign heavenly figures.

[52]

Stage setting, Intermedio 4. Epifanio d'Alfiano (signed and dated 1592 on chariot wheel).

New York, Metropolitan Museum of Art (Harris Brisbane Dick Fund, 1931), no. 31.72.5(13). Florence, Biblioteca Marucelliana, 1, 399; London, British Museum.

25.3 × 36.2 cm (10 × 14¼ in.). Engraving.

Warburg 1895, 109, 144–45; Laver 1932, 294–300; Bacou and Bean 1959, 44–45;

52

Nagler 1964, fig. 56; Gaeta Bertelà and Petrioli Tofani 1969, 83–84, no. 41; Strong 1973, 190; Fabbri 1975, 114, no. 8.17; Mancini 1975, 44–46; Borsi 1980, 360, no. 5.13H; Pirrotta and Povoledo 1982, 370–72; Strong 1984, fig. 91; Blumenthal 1986, 95–96.

This print, made after the event, may conflate two sequential episodes from the action but still corresponds more closely than the initial conception (cat. 51) to the action as Rossi describes it. In the first part of the act, the sorceress made her initial appearance above the backdrop of the city of Pisa, which stayed in view from the set of *La pellegrina;* Pirrotta and Povoledo read parts of the cityscape visible in the print as recognizable Pisan monuments, though these generalized structures may also represent the later view of a burning infernal city that replaced the earthly town. The upper zone of the print, close to cat. 51 but reversed, shows only 18 heavenly figures, still lacking their wings and looking more like classical gods than spirits of the air. Below, the second part of the action is condensed to the giant Lucifer who rose from the ground, devouring human souls played by boys (see cat. 53); the other underworld figures specified by Rossi are not shown. This image served as a model for Callot's engraving of *The Temptation of St. Anthony,* 1617.

[53]

Property design, Lucifer. Ludovico Cigoli.

Florence, Uffizi, GDS no. 8951F.

26.4 × 19.7 cm (10⅜ × 7¾ in.). Pen and ink, blue watercolor, over red chalk.

Fabbri 1975, 114, no. 8.18; Matteoli 1980, 279; Blumenthal 1986, 118n78; Viatte 1988, 62; Chappell 1992, no. 4.

Preparatory sketch for the freestanding puppet of three-headed Lucifer, eight braccia in height from chest to head; the Lucifer rose from the open trapdoor, which was decorated to simulate a lake of ice (its

53

stage-level and lower circumferences suggested by the elliptical outlines at his chest and knees). According to Rossi (53–54), Lucifer was surrounded by other personages of the classical-Christian underworld not depicted here: Charon, Minos, Geryon, Cerberus, the Minotaur, centaurs and harpies. Cigoli's figure is derived from Federico Zuccari's similar hell scene in the cupola frescoes painted from 1576–79 in the Florence Duomo (see drawing, British Museum no. 1862-10-11-188; Turner 1986, 218, no. 165).

INTERMEDIO 5

[54]

Stage design for Intermedio 5. Andrea Boscoli.

Paris, Louvre, Cabinet des Dessins no. 866.

23.3 × 34.5 cm (9⅛ × 13½ in.), cropped on all sides. Pen and brown ink, brown wash.

Bacou and Bean 1958, no. 16; Bacou and Bean 1959, 45, no. 19; Bacou 1965, 90;

54

Blumenthal 1986, 96–97; Viatte 1988, 54, no. 69.

This drawing, heavily marked by the stylus, is doubtless a copy after Buontalenti's lost scene sketch made by Boscoli at a reduced scale for the engravers (compare cat. 9, 55). The ocean setting flanked by rows of overhanging cliffs is shown at the opening of the intermedio: Amphitrite, queen of the sea (Vittoria Archilei), arrives on a mother-of-pearl shell accompanied by 14 tritons and 14 sea nymphs, splashing real water and leaping between the mechanically undulating waves, to sing a marital blessing. At right appears the ship that bears the musician Arion; it sailed onstage for the second part of the action. Arion himself is shown proleptically at lower left, riding the dolphin that finally saves him from the ship's greedy crew. The principal literary source is Plutarch, *Moralia* (Rossi, 55–59). As with Boscoli's other surviving modello, the influence of Raphael's classicism is apparent, here his fresco of Galatea (Villa Farnesina).

[55]

Stage scene, Intermedio 5. Epifanio d'Alfiano (signed lower right).

New York, Metropolitan Museum of Art (Harris Brisbane Dick Fund, 1931), no. 31.72.5(15).

24.4 × 35.7 cm (9⅝ × 14 in.). Engraving.

Nagler 1964, 65–66, fig. 57; Strong 1973, 190; Fabbri 1975, 109 no. 8.4, 115 no. 8.19; Mancini 1975, 45–46; Borsi 1980, 360, no. 5.131; Strong 1984, fig. 92; Blumenthal 1986, 96–97.

A print, in reverse, after cat. 54. In variant versions, the cartouche held by Amphitrite bears at least three different symbols or coats of arms, suggesting that this plate was reworked on several occasions when editions were prepared as gifts for specific noble recipients. In the Metropolitan impression shown here the insignia is a peacock, perhaps alluding to Juno and marriage; Strong 1973 illustrates arms consisting of a horizontal center band with a tree above, two facing birds below; in Mancini's example the arms are two semicircular

55

mounds surmounted by a single similar mound, resembling a stylized hill, with a bushy tree above, and the ensemble is topped by a cardinal's hat.

[56] (plate 13)
Costume design, sea nymph. Bernardo
  Buontalenti.
Florence, Biblioteca Nazionale Centrale,
  Palatina C.B.3.53, vol. 2, c. 10r.
47.9 × 37.9 cm (18⅞ × 14⅞ in.). Pen and
  brown ink, watercolor.
Nagler 1964, fig. 59; Fabbri 1975, 362–64,
  no. 5.14L.
First in the sequence of costume sketches for
  intermedio 5 (cat. 56–61, incomplete); upper right, number 1. Model for the sea
  nymphs, twice increased in number, from
  six to 12 and finally 14, with attendant cast
  changes. The lower body, which would be
  obscured onstage by the vertical panels of
  the wave machine (as it is by water in the
  drawing), is barely clothed; the upper body

is covered in coral and pale blue shells. At lower right of the painted area is a monogram combining the letters B and T (for BuonTalenti?). Notes below the image: *questa va vestita tutta di raso bianco co[n] la ma[n]tellina mavi n.o [6, canceled] et se ne a da fare [12, overwritten] 14/ [non se ne ha à fare, canceled]*. Cast notes, lower left: *n.o 1 Margherita del S.r Ant.o / n.o 2 Niccolo castrato / n.o 3 zanobi ciliani / n.o 4 don gio. basso / n.o 5 Gio. b.a Jacom.li del violino / n.o 6 Prete Riccio / n.o 7 Ant.o Archilei / n.o 8 Pompeo Stabile come m.o crist.o o p[er] lui Gio. del minug.o / n.o 9 Gio. f.co di Roma come m.o Ant.o Naldi / n.o 10 Luigi del corn.tto come mes.o o p[er] lui / n.o 11 . . . cetera di siena / n.o 12 [Mario Luchini (?), canceled] vergilio putto, o, p[er] lui / n.o 13 Ant.o fr.co del bottigl.re / n.o 14 G batt.a ser Jacopi.*

[57] (plate 14)
Costume design, Arion. Bernardo
  Buontalenti.

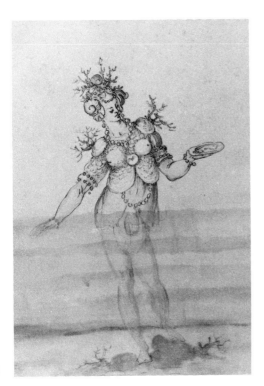

57

56

Florence, Biblioteca Nazionale Centrale,
Palatina C.B.3.53, vol. 2, c. 6r.
47.5 × 37.5 cm (18¾ × 14¾ in.). Pen and
brown ink, watercolor.
Warburg 1895, 409, fig. 92; Borsi 1980, 364,
no. 5.14M.
Upper right, number 4. The wealthy musician
and poet, shown holding his harp, was
played by Jacopo Peri, who accompanied
himself in a song of his own composition.
He escaped from the sailors, who hoped to
seize his treasure, by jumping overboard
(whereupon real water splashed upward),
and was saved by a movable dolphin who
took him to shore. Pink tunic and skirt,
blue sash, green wreath in hair, tan harp;
pencil underdrawing indicates a long staff
in his right hand. Notes below (in three different hands): *questa figura va vestita tutta di
rosso co[n] fondo doro sotto e sopra; La vesta di
questa figura intera, e grande / Arione, n.o 16
– Jacopo Peri zazzerino.*

[58]
Costume design, sailor. Bernardo Buontalenti.
Florence, Biblioteca Nazionale Centrale,
Palatina C.B.3.53, vol. 2, c. 5r.
47.4 × 37.4 cm (18⅝ × 14¾ in.). Pen and
brown ink, watercolor.
Borsi 1980, 363–67, no. 5.14N.
Upper right, number 5. Accounts differ about
the size of the crew on board the ship that
was pulled onstage bearing Arion; Rossi
claims 40 men, but the surviving drawings,
cat. 58–61, account for only 21. The
sketches represent several different types of
sailors: here, oarsmen, increased from an
initial four to six, with cast changes. Tan
and brown pants, scarlet shirt and hat; pencil underdrawing of swirling cloak behind
figure to right. Notes below figure: *di questa
figura vanne vestito n.o 4 / hanno aessere ma-
rinari di [diversi, canceled] colori bianchi e
rossi / diversi luno dall'altro.* Cast notes, upper left: *n.o 17 [Honofrio Gualfreducci / horat.no del S.r emilio,* both

5

58

canceled] *Placito / 18 alex.o del francios.no del cornetto / 19 [m.o crist.o, canceled] il biondino tonino del francios.no / 20 oratio del francios.no / 21 gio. del francios.no / 22 [gio. del minugiaio, canceled] o p[er] lui dom.co rossino / [23, canceled].*

[59]

Costume design, sailor. Bernardo Buontalenti.
Florence, Biblioteca Nazionale Centrale,
  Palatina C.B.3.53, vol. 2, c. 4r.
47.5 × 37.4 cm (18⅝ × 14¾ in.). Pen and
  brown ink, watercolor.

59

60

Borsi 1980, 367, no. 5.14N.

Upper right, number 6. Costume for two older steersmen or pilots, which matches Rossi's description of the chief sailor: white pantaloons, blue midthigh tunic, red hat, whistle around neck, holding a staff. Notes below: *questa figura ch[e] e un nochiere va vestito di drappo [di, canceled] turchino / e calzoni bianchi.* Cast notes, upper left: *n.o 23 Paolino del franc.no / n.o 24 [oratio del S.r emilio, canceled] oratino del franc.no.*

[60]

Costume design, sailor. Bernardo Buontalenti.

Florence, Biblioteca Nazionale Centrale, Palatina C.B.3.53, vol. 2, c. 3r.

47.4 × 37.4 cm (18⅝ × 14¾ in.). Pen and brown ink, watercolor.

Nagler 1964, fig. 60; Borsi 1980, 367, no. 5.14N.

Upper right, number 7. Design for young sailorboys, increased from four to six. Blue-green pants, ocher jacket, salmon hat, holding a rope in his right hand; pencil under-drawing of a tall shaft or oar in his left hand. Notes below: *questo e un mozo vestito di verde et azurro n.o 4*, and below that, in faint pencil, *un mozzo di nave.* Cast notes, upper left: *25 gio. b.a del franc.no / 26 [Tom.so di Roma come me., canceled] s[er] Piero masselli / 27 Mario luchini / 28 Rafl.o Gucci / 29 fra lazzero / 30 [Gio. f.o tromb.ne san.se, canceled] Zanobi ciliani.*

[61]

Costume design, sailor. Bernardo Buontalenti.

Florence, Biblioteca Nazionale Centrale, Palatina C.B.3.53, vol. 2, c. 2r.

47.6 × 37.0 cm (18⅝ × 14⅝ in.). Pen and brown ink, watercolor.

61

Florence, Uffizi, GDS, Museo Horne no. 5812.

28.1 × 23.2 cm (11 × 9⅛ in.), cropped all sides. Pen and brown ink, watercolor.

Warburg 1895, 411, fig. 93.

Although attributed to Giulio Parigi by Horne, stylistically and even in dimensions this male figure supporting a viol resembles Buontalenti's other costume sketches. Tunic and sleeves mauve, outer jacket pale mauve with pale turquoise lining (both with painted patterns; compare cat. 25), turquoise boots. The identification of this figure and the relation of the drawing to 1589 are, however, problematic. Identifying notes, if any, were lost in cropping. While the pose and costume mirror those of Arion in cat. 57, the stance and gestures are even closer (in reverse) to those of Apollo in cat. 35 and 65; in the latter Apollo holds a lyre, another string instrument associated, like the viol, with his stewardship of the arts. As with cat. 32, whose figures are of similar di-

Borsi 1980, 367, no. 5.14N.

Upper right, number 8. Design for a mustachioed sailor, probably a galley slave: in his left hand he holds a chain attached to one of his leg-irons, and he wears a metallic blue collar with a long handle. Four of this type were first specified, then six, and finally one additional one. Blue robe, beige mantle, blue cap, brown shoes. Note below figure: *questo marinaro aessere vestito di biancho e turchino n.o 4.* Cast notes, above left: *31 m.o crist.o / 32 m.o Ant.o Naldi / 33 Ceserone basso / 34 [Alberigho, canceled] s[er] lod.co belevanti / 35 Gio. Lapi / 36 Tonino del franc.no / n.o 37 un putto che alza e mant.ei / vestito a med.o modo / che si chiama Piero castrato / detto Aquatrice.*

[62]

Costume design, Arion (?). Bernardo Buontalenti.

62

mensions, this drawing seems to be a rare survivor of the many working sketches, though we cannot ascertain whether it was a preliminary study or a later copy.

INTERMEDIO 6

[63]
Stage design, Intermedio 6. Bernardo Buontalenti.
London, Victoria and Albert Museum, no. E.1189-1931.
42.0 × 54.7 cm (16½ × 21⅝ in.), cropped sides and top. Pen and brown ink, brown wash, red and green watercolor in costumes.
Laver 1932, 294–300; Reade 1967, no. 4; Strong 1973, 182; Fabbri 1975, 115, no. 8.20; Borsi 1980, 360, no. 5.13L; Strong 1984, fig. 93; Blumenthal 1986, 97–98.
The last of the surviving large original scene studies, this drawing is similar in composi-

tion and characters to that for the first intermedio (cat. 8), the two deliberately mirroring one another to bracket the evening with a symmetrical visual structure. Twelve Olympian gods sit in the uppermost of the flowered cloud banks, flanked slightly lower by eight of the Muses, as Jupiter sends the central cloud downward bearing Rhythm and Harmony, accompanied by Apollo and Bacchus, to ease the toil of humankind. Wavy vertical lines in the background indicate the "rods of gold" (Pavoni) that expressed this largesse flowing from heaven. On the stage floor, ten mortal shepherds and nymphs gather to receive these gifts, after which all danced and sang the final apotheosis of the bridal couple. The narrative is derived from Plato, *Laws* 2: 653 ff. (Rossi, 60–72). The identities of those in the central cloudborne group, however, are ambiguous in the drawing, and any inconsistency may reflect late

63

changes in the text and action of this act
(see Chap. 2).

[64]

Stage setting, Intermedio 6. Epifanio
    d'Alfiano (signed lower left).
New York, Metropolitan Museum of Art
    (Harris Brisbane Dick Fund, 1931), no.
    31.72.5(6).
25.9 × 35.6 cm (10⅛ × 14 in.). Etching and
    engraving.
Nagler 1964, fig. 62; Strong 1973, 190;
    Fabbri 1975, 116, no. 8.20; Mancini 1975,
    45–46; Blumenthal 1986, 97–98.
This print version of cat. 63 adds many fig-
    ures and details that generally correspond
    more closely to Rossi's description of the
    scene. Present are 16 of the 21 upper gods
    and allegories he mentions, and nearly all of
    the 20 earthly couples. The Muses and cen-
    tral descending group now occupy all five
    movable clouds, and the golden shower

from heaven is more precisely indicated as
droplets of liquid. The gilded heavenly sunburst at top is here clearly delineated; its
brilliance was softened somewhat by atmo-
spheric vapors released onstage. The figures
on the central descending cloud have been
altered, however, perhaps indicating the
three Graces who were added to the performance (played by Vittoria and Margherita
Archilei and Lucia Caccini). Like his fellow
print maker Carracci (cat. 10, 34), d'Alfiano
approximates his figure style to Raphaeles-
que models: the seated gods loosely echo
the Farnesina banquet frescoes, and the
central deity, more Apollonian than Jovian,
resembles the Apollo in Raphael's Vatican
Parnassus.

[65]

Costume design, Apollo. Bernardo
    Buontalenti.

64

65

Florence, Biblioteca Nazionale Centrale,
Palatina C.B.3.53, vol. 2, c. 12r.
46.9 × 36.9 cm (18½ × 14½ in.). Pen and
brown ink, watercolor.
Nagler 1964, fig. 63; Borsi 1980, 367, no.
5.140.
Although almost all the drawings for the 90
costumes of this act have been lost, many of
them represented the same classical characters as intermedio 1, and were deliberately
similar to their predecessors. This sketch
lacks any identifying text except the sequence number 23 at upper right; but it
corresponds to Rossi's description (61, 66)
of Apollo's costume for intermedio 6, which
he notes was identical to that god's earlier
outfits (cat. 24, 35) with minor variations,
such as the musical or martial attributes
(here a lyre, as in intermedio 1) and the
crown reminiscent of the Tuscan granducal
diadem (compare also the mirror-image
pose of cat. 62). The drawing depicts a pink
tunic with blue trim; coral sleeves; pink,

blue, and green skirt; pink, blue, and tan
boots; oval aureole behind, in pencil. Rossi
differs somewhat in describing this costume
as made of cloth of gold and a flame-
colored fabric.

[66]
Costume design, Fortune. Bernardo
Buontalenti.
Location unknown; London, collection
Henry Oppenheimer, to 1936.
Pen and ink, watercolor.
Warburg 1895, 410–11, fig. 94.
This drawing, untraceable since the dispersal
of the collection in which Warburg studied
and reproduced it, corresponds exactly to
one of the enthroned heavenly allegories
described by Rossi (71). The spirit whom
he calls *Fortuna Giovevole ad Amore* holds a
cornucopia in her right hand and a winged
putto in her left, and is dressed in peacock-
blue velvet; although the sheet has been se-

66

verely cropped, the remaining color note below the figure, in the same hand as the other costume sketches, specifies *tutta di pagonazo*.

STAGE COMEDIES

[67]

Costume design, *La pellegrina* (?). Bernardo Buontalenti.

Florence, Biblioteca Nazionale Centrale, Palatina C.B.3.53, vol. 2, c. 74r.

40.9 × 30.5 cm (16⅛ × 12 in.), cropped. Pen and brown ink, slight green watercolor on ground.

Warburg 1895, 226–27, 412; Newman 1986, 100–111.

Female figure cloaked in a voluminous white hooded mantle; note below, *tutta vestita di bianco*. Very close in style, size, and labeling to those on the intermedi costume sheets, this figure was identified by Warburg as a Vestal Virgin from intermedio 1. The Vestals do wear white, but the rest of Rossi's elaborate description does not correspond to this simple outfit. More plausibly, New-

67

man has suggested that the costume is for Drusilla, the heroine of *La pellegrina*, the first play performed with the intermedi. A long cloak covering the head was typical dress for women travelers and religious figures, and white symbolizes faith, appropriate to Drusilla's actions and role. (The costume records of the *Libro de' conti*, however, do not mention such a cloak.) Newman describes and illustrates another costume drawing, attributed to Buontalenti, that may pertain to the 1589 comedy costumes, whose appearance is otherwise undocumented visually.

[68]

Stage perspective. Orazio Scarabelli (signed lower right).

New York, Metropolitan Museum of Art (Harris Brisbane Dick Fund, 1931), no. 31.72.5(8). Florence, Uffizi, GDS no. 13292 *stampe sciolte*.

24.0 × 34.7 cm (9½ × 13⅝ in.). Engraving.

Gaeta Bertelà and Petrioli Tofani 1969, 77, no. 36; Strong 1973, 180; Fabbri 1975, 111, no. 8.9; Borsi 1980, 340, no. 3.19; Blumenthal 1986, 99, 120n92, fig. 27.

The only surviving view of the stage sets for any of the three comedies performed with the intermedi. Receding pairs of three-dimensional side houses (*case*) flank the open central area, from the rear of which run three long narrow streets, visually extended into the painted backdrop of a distant generalized cityscape. These elements correspond to the probable disposition of stage units at the Uffizi and to Rossi's account (33) of a novel feature introduced by Buontalenti in *La pellegrina*, namely the two side streets that recede on a perspectively ingenious curve. The print does not, however, represent that specific play, whose backdrop featured a topographically precise view of Pisa, the locale of the action. Pavoni (44) records that all three comedies were performed in the same set; he proba-

68

bly means that the side houses were used repeatedly, while a different painted backdrop could easily have been hung for each production. The particular configuration shown here, copied from unknown sources or perhaps observed in place, could have served *La zingara*, *La pazzia*, or both. Elements of this stage set may have been re-used for several decades, as in a production of *Solimano* designed by Giulio Parigi in 1619 and recorded in an engraving by Callot (Gaeta Bertelà and Petrioli Tofani 1969, nos. 136, 138, figs. 63, 64; Blumenthal, fig. 27).

OUTDOOR ENTERTAINMENTS,
MAY 4–10
(Catalogue 69–70)

[69] (plate 15)
Giuoco del calcio, Piazza Santa Croce.
   Florentine school, ca. 1589.

Sarasota, Ringling Museum, no. SN 36.
87.6 × 116.2 cm (34½ × 45¾ in.). Oil on canvas.
Gaeta Bertelà and Petrioli Tofani 1969, 73; Strong 1973, 195; Peter Tomory, *Catalogue of the Italian Paintings Before 1800* (Sarasota: Ringling Museum, 1976), 26–27, no. 20; Arthur Blumenthal, *Italian Renaissance and Baroque Paintings in Florida Museums* (exh. cat., Winter Park, Fla.: Cornell Fine Arts Museum, 1991), 22, no. 11.
The first of three public events held in the large piazza, traditional site for such mass entertainments, was this match of Florentine-style football on May 4. The unfinished façade of Santa Croce is visible behind the temporary tiered stands lining two sides of the square (compare cat. 70). Noble guests and referees are at the right side of the piazza, on the field and a balcony above; at center left, one male spectator sits in a carriage. The two large teams

69

seen within the palisade, just beginning
play, were dressed in pink for the grand
duke's side and blue for the grand duchess
(on the game see Chap. 6). In the foreground are three clowns or jesters and two
large mounted knights. The circumstances
of this commission, apparently a unique
one to paint a wedding event, are unknown;
the picture has been variously attributed to
Gualterotti, otherwise known only as a possible designer for prints, or to other Florentine artists in the circles of Alessandro
Allori and Giovanni Stradano. According to
Blumenthal 1991, a pendant to this picture
(not described) was on sale in 1988.

[70]
Joust in Piazza Santa Croce. Orazio Scarabelli
   (signed lower right).
New York, Metropolitan Museum of Art

(Harris Brisbane Dick Fund, 1931), no.
31.72.5(10).
22.8 × 34.3 cm (9 × 13½ in.). Engraving.
Borsi 1980, 397, no. 9.33; Blumenthal 1980,
   13–15, no. 6; Blumenthal 1990, 103–4.
This tournament, a tilt at the quintain (target), took place on May 10, in the same
temporary arena already in place (compare
cat. 69); the print gives more details of the
enclosure, such as its painted imitation of
brick and stone, and repeats the canopied
balcony at right for the granducal party. An
opening procession of mounted knights,
trumpeters, and pages circles the field, passing behind a barrier at right, where one
combatant rides a camel. The page costumes, with conical hat and skirted jacket,
are similar to a sketch by Buontalenti in the
Libro di conti (LC N430, illd. Fabbri 1975,
136–37, no. 9.21, who suggests that it was

70

for the Pitti). This scene was modeled on
an earlier print recording a similar joust for
the wedding of Francesco I and Bianca
Cappello in 1579 (Borsi 1980, 397, no.
9.30, illd.).

PITTI PALACE ENTERTAINMENTS,
MAY 11
(Catalogue 71–87)

[71]
Pitti Palace courtyard equipped for foot-
   combat. Anonymous.
New York, Metropolitan Museum of Art
   (Harris Brisbane Dick Fund, 1931), no.
   31.72.5(9).
23.0 × 33.3 cm (9 × 13⅛ in.). Etching.
Fabbri 1975, 137, no. 9.22.
The first in a series of prints documenting the
   chariot parade, military contest, and naumachia staged in the richly decorated Pitti
   courtyard, here presented as closely as pos-

sible in chronological order (basic sources
are Pavoni 1589 and Cavallino 1589; see
Chap. 6). The huge court, some 100 × 140
feet, is already decorated with the castled
backdrop, whose central upper pavilion recalls the domed trademark of the granducal
porcelain factory. The same backdrop was
used later for the naumachia; compare the
more detailed view of the same court, cat.
87, from which this print seems to have
been rather crudely adapted. No audience
is yet present, however, the yard is not yet
flooded, and the barrier to separate the foot
combatants (*sbarra*, from which the tournament takes its name) is placed in the center.
The great red canvas awning is visible with
its rope supports, as are the three levels of
lamps noted by Seriacopi. Written accounts
also record a palco, or raised platform, for
the granducal party; inasmuch as this is not
shown in the print, it was probably centered on the side of the courtyard from

71

which the view is taken, facing the open side and the backdrop. The viewer of the print is thus placed in the same spectator position as the most elevated actual attendees. This print is similar to the etching by Gualterotti of the previous sbarra on this site, for Francesco's wedding in 1579 (illd. Fabbri 1975, 132, no. 9.5, and Blumenthal 1980, no. 27).

[72]
Allegorical chariot, necromancer. Cherubino Alberti.
New York, Metropolitan Museum of Art (Harris Brisbane Dick Fund, 1931), no. 31.72.5(26). London, Victoria and Albert Museum, no. E.5225-1907.
Inner image 14.8 × 22.0 cm (5¾ × 8⅝ in.), engraving; outer border (New York only) 24.3 × 34.5 cm (9½ × 13½ in.), engraving.
Fabbri 1975, 137, no. 9.23; Massar 1975, no. 1; Blumenthal 1980, 16, no. 8.

Twelve images recording the Pitti floats and marchers were originally printed at a uniform small size of some 5 × 8 inches, in varying combinations of etching and engraving. Eleven of these were subsequently reissued with an engraved border of military motifs (signed by Orazio Scarabelli) to harmonize them with the other larger commemorative prints, roughly 10 × 14 inches. The small series are mainly preserved in London, the larger ones in New York; see cat. 74–86 and discussion of the various series in Chap. 7. (The repeated outer frame of most New York examples is omitted from the remaining illustrations.) The imagery and characters are loosely based on such chivalric epics as Ariosto's *Orlando furioso* (1516) and Tasso's *Gerusalemme liberata* (1575). Alberti's engraving shows the prologue to the festivities provided by the first chariot, on which sat an aged male magician who conjured up the fantasy to follow,

72

and two females, possibly sirens; two more such women walk ahead of the float, which is drawn by two bears (for detailed iconography see Pavoni, 37; Cavallino, 41). Construction of this chariot by the granducal workshops was begun on December 25 (MR 21v).

[73] (plate 16)
Allegorical chariot for tournament referees.
    Bernardo Buontalenti and Andrea Boscoli.
London, Victoria and Albert Museum, no.
    E.1731-1938.
11.2 × 21.9 cm (4⅜ × 8⅝ in.), cropped at top. Pen and brown ink and pale brown wash.
Massar 1975, 21, pl. 4.
This drawing, showing the second float in the series, was prepared for the guidance of the engravers at the same size as the small series of prints (see cat. 72). The chariot itself, covered with papier-mâché

attachments of swags, winged dragons, and a snaky hellmouth, is by Boscoli; the walking winged furies and the dragon pulling the float are by Buontalenti. The two armored knights seated at the summit in plumed helmets (partly cropped) are the *mantenitori*, referees or chief combatants of the foot tourney: Duke Vincenzo Gonzaga of Mantua and Don Pietro de' Medici (Pavoni, 37; Cavallino, 41–42). As with cat. 72, construction of this car, sometimes referred to as "the chariot of S.A.S." (Ferdinando, i.e., the official "state" vehicle) was begun on December 25 (MR 21v).

[74]
Allegorical chariot for tournament referees.
    Orazio Scarabelli.
New York, Metropolitan Museum of Art (Harris Brisbane Dick Fund, 1931), no. 31.72.5(24) (with border). London, Victoria

73

and Albert Museum, no. E.5222-1907
(without border).

Fabbri 1975, 137, no. 9.24; Massar 1975, no.
2; Blumenthal 1980, 18, no. 9; Strong 1984,
fig. 94; Blumenthal 1990, 104–5.

Small etching-engraving after cat. 73, also
published with outer border (see cat. 72).
The scrolled or wrapped stair was a favorite
motif of Buontalenti's; other details of this
chariot inspired Giulio Parigi's design for a
ship in the Arno River fête for Cosimo II's
wedding in 1608 (Gaeta Bertelà and Petrioli Tofani 1969, 122 no. 70, 126 no. 78,
illd.).

[75]
Foot procession of musicians, knights, and
pages. Orazio Scarabelli.

New York, Metropolitan Museum of Art
(Harris Brisbane Dick Fund, 1931), no.
31.72.5(19). London, Victoria and Albert
Museum, no. E.5230-1907 (without border).

Fabbri 1975, 137, no. 9.25; Massar 1975,
no. 3.

Small etching-engraving, also published with
outer border (see cat. 72). Although this
group might belong to the entourage of
several floats, the two plumed knights are
similar to the seated figures of Don Pietro

de' Medici and Vincenzo Gonzaga (cat. 73–
74), who dismounted from their chariot to
take the field accompanied by foot soldiers
and musicians (Cavallino, 41–42).

[76]
Allegorical float, smoking mountain. Orazio
Scarabelli.

New York, Metropolitan Museum of Art
(Harris Brisbane Dick Fund, 1931), no.
31.72.5(21). London, Victoria and Albert
Museum, no. E.5224-1907 (without border).

Fabbri 1975, 137, no. 9.26; Massar 1975,
no. 4.

Small etching-engraving, also published with
outer border (see cat. 72). This float, pulled
by winged furies similar to those of cat. 74,
represented the infernal Mount Mongibello
covered in flames and emitting smoke, and
with a cavelike opening in which rode two
knights; it was paid for by the Guicciardini
family (Pavoni, 37; Cavallino, 42).

[77]
Allegorical float, ship. Orazio Scarabelli.

New York, Metropolitan Museum of Art
(Harris Brisbane Dick Fund, 1931), no.
31.72.5(27). London, Victoria and Albert

74

75

76

Museum, no. E.5223-1907 (without border).

Fabbri 1975, 138, no. 9.27; Massar 1975, no. 7.

Small etching-engraving, also published with outer border (see cat. 72). This float represented an elaborate oared ship with firing cannons, on which rode musicians and knights (Pavoni, 38; Cavallino, 42).

[78]

Allegorical chariot, Death. Orazio Scarabelli.

New York, Metropolitan Museum of Art (Harris Brisbane Dick Fund, 1931), no. 31.72.5(22). London, Victoria and Albert Museum, no. E.5228-1907 (without border).

Fabbri 1975, 138, no. 9.28; Massar 1975, no. 6.

Small etching-engraving, also published with outer border (see cat. 72). This chariot drawn by two skeletal horses represents the triumph of death, a Petrarchan staple for carnival floats; on it ride two knights dressed as dead men, a female figure hold-

ing a wand, and two musicians (Pavoni, 38; Cavallino, 42).

[79]

Allegorical chariot, single knight. Orazio Scarabelli.

New York, Metropolitan Museum of Art (Harris Brisbane Dick Fund, 1931), no. 31.72.5(20). London, Victoria and Albert Museum, no. E.5226-1907 (without border).

Fabbri 1975, 138, no. 9.29; Massar 1975, no. 9.

Small engraving, also published with outer border (see cat. 72). This float, not described by either Pavoni or Cavallino, carries a single armed knight on a high throne and several crouching satyrs and is drawn by a swan. Attendants include satyrs holding flaming torches and playing panpipes, and a rider mounted on a rhinoceros. The text cited by Fabbri as pertaining to this chariot more consistently describes cat. 82, below.

77

78

79

[80]

Foot procession and riders on giant birds.
   Orazio Scarabelli.
New York, Metropolitan Museum of Art
   (Harris Brisbane Dick Fund, 1931), no.
   31.72.5(29). London, Victoria and Albert
   Museum, no. E.5227-1907 (without border).
Fabbri 1975, 139, no. 9.35; Massar 1975, no.
   8; Blumenthal 1980, 21, no. 11.
Small etching-engraving, also published with
   outer border (see cat. 72). This entourage,
   probably attendants for one of the floats,
   includes trumpeters, pages bearing
   weapons, torchbearers, and men in plumed
   helmets riding large birds, variously identified as geese or swans. Not described by
   Cavallino, and mentioned by Pavoni only
   vaguely as "very large birds" (37), the group
   is conjecturally placed here in proximity to
   the chariot in cat. 79, which is drawn by a
   similar swan.

[81]

Allegorical float, magician atop a crocodile.
   Cherubino Alberti.
New York, Metropolitan Museum of Art
   (Harris Brisbane Dick Fund, 1931), no.
   31.72.5(28). London, Victoria and Albert
   Museum, no. E.5231-1907 (without border).
Fabbri 1975, 139, no. 9.33; Massar 1975,
   no. 10.
Small engraving, also published with outer
   border (see cat. 72). Cat. 81–86 record sequential elements of the culminating, five-
   part spectacle staged by Don Virginio Orsini (Pavoni, 38–39; Cavallino, 42–44). As
   reconstructed here, the group was led off
   by this float, followed by cat. 82; while cat.
   81 remained in the court, cat. 82 left to
   make way for the entries of Virginio and his
   knights in cat. 83 and 84. After they dismounted and their chariots drove off, cat.
   85 came onto the field and expanded to sur-

80

81

round the remaining initial float (as shown in cat. 86); the ensuing combats took place within the enclosure, which symbolized a garden of love. The amorous theme is announced by this first float, with its harpist seated on a winged crocodile atop a mountain whose arched caves enfold various animals and birds, recalling the humans transformed by the enchantress Circe and probably representing base (animal) lust. The suggestion (see cat. 79) that Cavallino's *di Salviati e di botti* refers to patronage by the Medici's cousins the Salviati family is appealing, but the word here is more likely a variant term for wild beasts.

[82]
Allegorical float, fountain. Orazio Scarabelli.
New York, Metropolitan Museum of Art
    (Harris Brisbane Dick Fund, 1931), no.
    31.72.5(17).
22.7 × 34.7 cm (9 × 13⅝ in.). Engraving
    (large format only).
Fabbri 1975, 139, no. 9.31.

The second element in Don Virginio's finale, described by Cavallino immediately after cat. 81 as "the form of a fountain with an entourage of satyrs, which sprayed water widely over the women" seated at ground level (quoted by Fabbri, no. 9.29, who connects this text to Don Virginio's chariot instead; but see cat. 79, 83). The broad pedestaled basin, capped by a male figure holding a spouting dolphin, rests on a two-tiered base painted with broad seascape vistas. The satyrs may have cavorted on the wide balustraded lower section.

[83]
Allegorical chariot, Don Virginio Orsini as
    Mars. Orazio Scarabelli.
New York, Metropolitan Museum of Art
    (Harris Brisbane Dick Fund, 1931), no.
    31.72.5(25). London, Victoria and Albert
    Museum, no. E.5221-1907 (without
    border).
Fabbri 1975, 138, no. 9.30; Massar 1975, no.

82

83

11; Blumenthal 1980, no. 12; Blumenthal 1990, 105.
Small engraving, also published with outer
border (see cat. 72). The third element in
the finale (see cat. 81), a tall chariot drawn
by four white horses dressed in cloth of silver. It bore Virginio costumed as Mars, accompanied by satyrs and eight nymphs,
probably wearing costumes borrowed from
the Uffizi theater. The nymphs sang, then
distributed to the women in the audience
flowery baskets filled with love poetry by
Virginio. The float opened to reveal a fountain, but this would have been too small to
spray the audience, lending support to the
identification of cat. 82 as a separate, independent fountain large enough to contain
the necessary hydraulic apparatus and crew.
(Cavallino, 42, makes clear there were multiple fountains.) Following behind cat. 83
came Virginio's companions in arms, then
eight soldiers dressed as women, whom
Cavallino found grotesquely amusing.

[84]
Allegorical chariot, six knights. Orazio
  Scarabelli.
New York, Metropolitan Museum of Art
  (Harris Brisbane Dick Fund, 1931), no.
  31.72.5(23). London, Victoria and Albert
  Museum, no. E.5229-1907 (without border).
Fabbri 1975, 139, no. 9.32; Massar 1975, no.
  5; Blumenthal 1980, 20, no. 10; Blumenthal
  1990, 105.
Small etching-engraving, also published with
  outer border (see cat. 72). The fourth element in Don Virginio's finale (see cat. 81),
  this latticed car (similar to the hermed
  bowers in cat. 27) held six armed and
  plumed knights and, at its front, a singing
  nymph who again recalls Circe or perhaps
  Venus in a garden of love. The two animals
  pulling the wagon resemble wolves or foxes,
  though Cavallino (43) specifies four asses
  disguised with skins as lions and bears. He
  names three of the knights, Antonio Tasso,
  Giovanni Battista Ragonia, and the

84

Marchese di Riano; the latter had been in-
ducted into the Order of Santo Stefano the
previous Sunday.

[85]
Allegorical float, garden before extension.
    Cherubino Alberti (?).
New York, Metropolitan Museum of Art (The
    Elisha Whittelsey Collection, The Elisha
    Whittelsey Fund, 1968), no. 68.681.10.
London, Victoria and Albert Museum, no.
    E.5220-1907.
Massar 1975, no. 12.
Small etching-engraving, no outer border in
    either example (see cat. 72). The fifth ele-
    ment in Don Virginio's finale (see cat. 81),
    this boxy float bore one knight seated in a
    geometric garden, its base decorated with a
    Marslike warrior and river gods and dogs,
    symbols of marital fidelity and fertility. It
    moved without visible cause, probably pro-
    pelled by crew hidden inside along with 18
    nymphs, who did not appear until the float

opened up as in cat. 86 (Pavoni, 38; Cavallino, 44).

[86]
View of garden float extended. Orazio
    Scarabelli.
New York, Metropolitan Museum of Art
    (Harris Brisbane Dick Fund, 1931), no.
    31.72.5(18).
23.9 × 35.6 cm (9⅜ × 14 in.). Engraving.
Fabbri 1975, 139, no. 9.34; Massar 1975, no.
    13; Strong 1984, fig. 95.
The garden float for Don Virginio's finale
    (see cat. 85) is here shown after its sides
    opened up to disclose some 20 sections of
    arbored fencing, which were unfolded to
    the perimeter of the courtyard, engulfing
    the animal float still on the field (cat. 81).
    The resulting enclosed garden, symbolic of
    Paradise and of sacred conjugal love, thus
    overpowered the profane lust symbolized
    by the earlier float. Each section was cov-
    ered with topiary figures of animals, birds,

85

86

ships, humans, and architecture and was attended by a torchbearing nymph who had
emerged from the float. Living birds sang
in these bowers; one near Christine flew
into her lap and was captured and saved as a
memento. Within this enclosure Virginio
and his companions fought the concluding
battle of the evening's first half (Pavoni, 38–
39; Cavallino, 44).

[87]
Naumachia, Pitti courtyard. Orazio Scarabelli
    (signed lower right).
New York, Metropolitan Museum of Art
    (Harris Brisbane Dick Fund, 1931), no.
    31.72.5(11). Florence, Uffizi, GDS no.
    95990 *stampe sciolte*.
24.2 × 35.8 cm (9½ × 14 in.). Engraving.
Nagler 1964, 92; Gaeta Bertelà and Petrioli
    Tofani 1969, 84, no. 42; Strong 1973, 195;
    Fabbri 1975, 139, no. 9.36; Fara 1979, 16,
    no. 108; Blumenthal 1980, 25, no. 13; Borsi

1980, 321, no. 1.52; Strong 1984, fig. 96;
Blumenthal 1990, 105–6.

The second half of the May 11 entertainment
was this mock naval battle between Christian attackers and Turkish defenders of the
castle built against the rear wall of the Pitti
courtyard, with its backdrop of four canvases by Francesco Rosselli and Lorenzo
Francini (see cat. 71). In the rear are visible
the two arched doorways leading to the
grotto, with its Michelangelesque sculptures, from which the attackers entered;
within the flooded arena are visible many of
their small boats, decorated to resemble
seagoing battleships. Male spectators are
visible on two tiers of upper balconies; the
female viewers seated beneath the ground-
level arcade are not shown (Pavoni, 40–43;
Cavallino, 44–46). Detailed specifications
for the courtyard décors are listed in MR
7v–8v, etc.; for sources see Chap. 4, and for
narrative of the battle, Chap. 6.

87

STREET PROCESSION, MAY 28
(Catalogue 88)

[88]
Chariot procession of Neptune. Epifanio
d'Alfiano (signed lower right).
New York, Metropolitan Museum of Art
(Harris Brisbane Dick Fund, 1931), no.
31.72.5(12).
24.3 × 33.7 cm (9½ × 13¼ in.). Engraving.
Massar 1975, 22; Blumenthal 1980, 15, no. 7;
Blumenthal 1990, 104.
Earlier discussions of this print, unable to cite
any written description, were uncertain as
to the event depicted. The scene is, however, recorded by Settimani (155v–156r) in
a previously unnoticed, detailed transcription closely corresponding to this image
(though his original source remains unknown). According to him, this procession
took place during the daytime on Sunday,
May 28, and was staged by a group of costumed young noblemen (*una compagnia di
nobili giovani fiorentini*) who departed from
the grand duke's stables (the Pitti Palace
forecourt is visible in the background).
They represented the sea god Neptune,
shown at rear on a high chariot drawn by
four horses (Settimani says two whales), and
24 bearded equestrian river gods (22 are
visible), with torchbearers and musicians
(Settimani says they were led by three tritons and several nymphs on foot, and gives
each young noble a liveried suite of ten to
twelve servants). The river gods were
wreathed in fruited evergreen branches
(*fronde d'abeti e simili alberi alpestri cinti di
un festone di frutte*) and carried cornucopias
and urns as in the print. The troupe rode
through the streets of Florence, stopping at
the houses of prominent gentlewomen,
where they explained in song that the waters of the earth had come to pay tribute to
the new grand duchess. The masquerade

88

was organized by Niccolò Capponi, Cosimo Ridolfi, Piero Bonsi (Bonti?), Agostino del Nero, Carlo Guidacci, and Francesco del Riccio. For the theatrical activities of adolescent males, see Chap. 6; the impersonation by these legally disenfranchised youth of bearded old men seems ironically humorous.

Appendix: Genealogical Tables

LORRAINE, VALOIS, HABSBURG

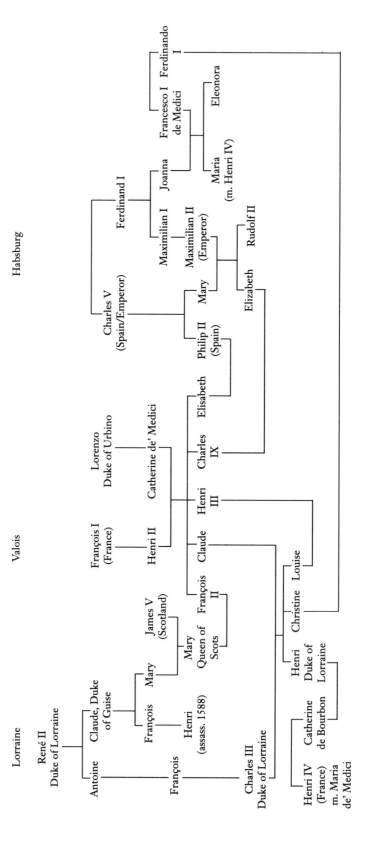

MEDICI AND RELATED ITALIAN FAMILIES

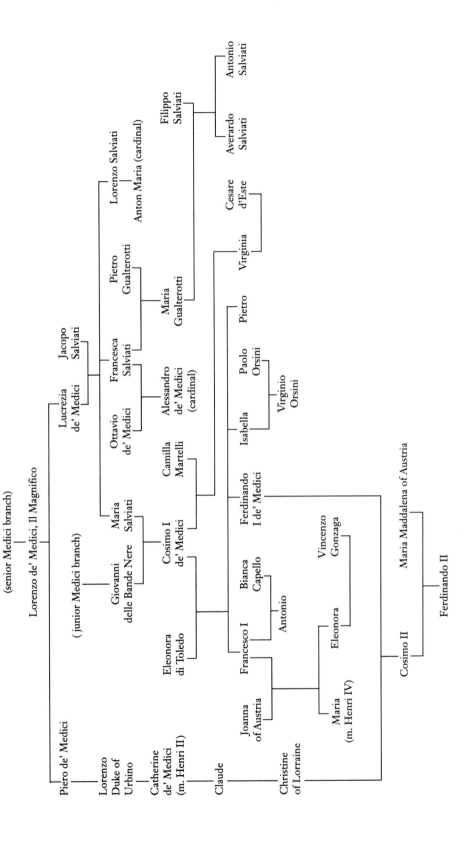

Notes

INTRODUCTION

1. Blumenthal, "Medici Patronage," 97. On the economic position of Tuscany in the late sixteenth century see Braudel, *Mediterranean*, 701–3, who notes several reasons why economic success at this time was shared by the smaller European states rather than by the larger emerging ones that would overwhelm them in the seventeenth century; on economy, culture, and religious conditions see further Eric Cochrane, "The End of the Renaissance in Florence," in *The Late Italian Renaissance, 1525–1630*, ed. Cochrane (London: Macmillan, 1970), 43–76.

2. *Sontuosissimi apparecchi*, 6.

3. Starn and Partridge, *Arts of Power*, 211.

4. Wolff, *Social Production of Art*, 139; her study offers an introduction and overview of recent methodologies in this field, from Marxist to poststructuralist, with bibliography.

5. Wilson, *Transformation of Europe*, 185.

6. All of these mss., which will be referred to in notes below, are in the Archivio di Stato, Florence (hereafter cited as ASF); see Bibliography, *Archival Documents*. Settimani's compilation fills a lengthy series of volumes, ASF, Manoscritti, filze 125–47; the part relevant to the present study is vol. 5 (1587–95), filza 130 (hereafter cited as Settimani, *Memorie*).

7. Berner, "Florentine Society," 224–25, calls that separation "an anachronistic dichotomy." The younger sons of noble families often entered the Church for their careers, as did Ferdinando himself, so that control of church and state were held by what would today be called "interlocking directorates" with shared purposes and loyalties. Ferdinando's cousin, Alessandro de' Medici (later Pope Leo XI) was, for example, archbishop of Florence at the time. A search of the archives of the Opera del Duomo or of the churches of San Marco and San Lorenzo, where the principal religious events were held, might turn up details on some of these events. For the performance of a religious drama by Cecchi which was recorded in a festival book, see Chap. 6.

8. Warburg, "Costumi teatrali," 1895; the version cited herein was reprinted in his *Gesammelte Schriften*, ed. Gertrud Bing (1932; reprint 1969), 259–300, 394–441. Bing, editing after Warburg's death, added extensive though incomplete transcriptions of Seriacopi, cited hereafter as the major printed access to this ms.

9. Starn and Partridge, *Arts of Power*, 166, discuss the increasing complexity of later feste, which depended on "institutional arrangements . . . administered by teams of cultural bureaucrats, designers, and artisans."

10. Braudel, *Mediterranean*, 450. For an overview of current scholarly issues in the methodology of narrative history and discourse studies, see the editor's introduction to Hunt, *New Cultural History*, 1–24, and the essay therein by Lloyd Kramer, "Literature, Criticism, and Historical Imagination: The Literary Challenge of Hayden White and Dominick LaCapra."

11. By "microhistory" I refer to the current mode of historical research that uses detailed analysis of a single event or place to draw broad conclusions about the values, habits, and social structures of a particular milieu. I have been particularly influenced in this direction by the work of Natalie Zemon Davis, Robert Darnton, Carlo Ginzburg, and Emmanuel Le Roy Ladurie.

12. Heinrich Plett, "Aesthetic Constituents in the Courtly Culture of Renaissance England," *New Literary History* 14 (1983): 597; cited by Kerrigan and Braden, *Idea of the Renaissance*, 5.

13. Wisch and Munshower, *All the World's a Stage*, 1: xvi. For a classic statement of the need to approach festival art from the widest spectrum of disciplines, see Jacquot, *Fêtes*, 3: 8–14.

14. Berti, "Alcuni aspetti," is a valuable overview of this text, though focused on narrowly defined issues of context and technique. Some of the most recent New Historicist scholarship on state propaganda arts, notably by Starn and Partridge, has been more explicitly concerned with the interplay between artistic and social forces; their *Arts of Power* deals with Medicean Florence during Cosimo I's generation, but no scholars using this methodology have as yet addressed the 1589 festival itself. This school has produced a large bibliography, beginning in literary studies; for an overview of its relevance to the present topic, with basic sources, see Jean E. Howard, "The New Historicism in Renaissance Studies," *English Literary Renaissance* 16 (1986): 13–43.

15. There is no full-length biography of Ferdinando. For the outlines of his life and career, see Berner, "Florentine Society," with additional bibliography; Hale, *Florence and the Medici*, 144–76; Hibbert, *Rise and Fall*, 279–81. For political and economic developments in his reign, see Diaz, *Granducato*, 85–108, 127–82, 280–336, 342–63. A guide to the historiography of the following discussion may be found in Anthony Molho, "Recent Works on the History of Tuscany: 15th to 18th Centuries," *Journal of Modern History* 62 (1990): 57–77.

16. On Ferdinando's overseas initiatives see Vannucci, *History of Florence*, 184, 208–9; Hale, *Florence and the Medici*, 151–61; Goldthwaite, *Building of Renaissance Florence*, 40–54; Braudel, *Mediterranean*, 106–7. Ferdinando was continuing a policy of Francesco, who hosted a delegation of Japanese in 1585.

17. The bibliography on Medici festivals is enormous; for the precedents set by festival patronage of the earlier grand dukes, see Nagler, *Theatre Festivals*; the series of articles by Eve Borsook on "Art and Politics at the Medici Court," *Mitteilungen des Kunsthistorisches Insti-*

tutes in Florenz, 1965–69, which first accurately documented and analyzed the funeral of Cosimo I, et al.; Andrew C. Minor and Bonner Mitchell, eds., *A Renaissance Entertainment: Festivities for the Marriage of Cosimo I, 1539* (Columbia: University of Missouri Press, 1968); Bonner Mitchell, "Les intermèdes au service de l'état," in Jacquot, *Fêtes*, 3: 117–31; and most recently, the provocative reading of the wedding of Francesco de' Medici in Starn and Partridge, *Arts of Power*.

18. Berner, "Florentine Society," 207–9. On magnificence see Warnke, *Court Artist*, 224–30; Peter Burke, *The Fabrication of Louis XIV* (New Haven: Yale University Press, 1992), 4–8, with further bibliography; and with reference to building, Thomson, *Renaissance Architecture*.

19. On the emergence of the nation-state and its characteristics see Immanuel Wallerstein, *The Modern World-System*, vol. 1, *Capitalist Agriculture and the Origins of the European World-Economy in the Sixteenth Century* (San Diego: Harcourt Brace Jovanovich, 1974), esp. chap. 3. On this and many other aspects of social history relevant to the present study see the magisterial study by John Hale, *The Civilization of the Renaissance in Europe* (New York: Atheneum, 1994), which appeared too late to be cited more fully here. Jacquot, *Fêtes*, 3: 11, notes that a major impact on sixteenth-century festivals was "le renforcement du pouvoir monarchique, la centralisation du pouvoir." Braudel, *Perspective of the World*, emphasizes the parallel growth of capitalist economic structures and the tension between merchants and the state; both centers of power, however, share interests in maximizing efficiency, centralization, and worldwide control. Two further qualifications must be attached to this process of state formation. First, in spite of the increases in technical capabilities and the scale of governmental operations, in practice the power of the emerging monarchical state was not yet fully efficient or widely effective. Second, the relatively small size of Tuscany meant that it ultimately could not compete with the larger

European states in sustained economic development, and fell increasingly behind in the seventeenth century (see Chap. 7). For a summary of the Tuscan situation from the 1580s onward, see Cochrane, *Florence in the Forgotten Centuries*, 95–115; see also Berner, "Florentine Society," 211–21; Goldthwaite, *Building of Renaissance Florence*, 52–53; Hale, *Florence and the Medici*, 150–169.

20. Wilson, *Transformation of Europe*, 2–14, outlines this erratic progress toward mastery of the physical elements. On the development of early capitalist economy, wage-labor, and economic rationalization, and their relationship to artistic processes see Braudel, *Mediterranean*, and Arnold Hauser, *Mannerism: The Crisis of the Renaissance and the Origin of Modern Art* (Cambridge: Harvard University Press, 1965), 55–58.

21. New York, Metropolitan Museum of Art, no. 57.650.364(4). The series of 16 prints was engraved by Callot ca. 1614–17 after designs by Matteo Rosselli and others. For the Livorno print see Lieure, *Jacques Callot*, no. 150.

22. Hale, *Florence and the Medici*, 165. For the judiciary see John K. Brackett, *Criminal Justice and Crime in Late Renaissance Florence, 1537–1609* (Cambridge: Cambridge University Press, 1992).

23. Berner, "Florentine Political Thought," 183–85; on this process in general see further Ronald G. Asch and Adolf M. Birke, eds., *Princes, Patronage, and the Nobility: The Court at the Beginning of the Modern Age, 1450–1650* (Oxford: Oxford University Press, 1991); Berner, "Florentine Society," 231–35, 241–42; R. Burr Litchfield, *Emergence of a Bureaucracy: The Florentine Patricians, 1530–1790* (Princeton: Princeton University Press, 1986); Diaz, *Granducato*, 342–45, who notes that this class nonetheless maintained their commercial and manufacturing activities.

24. On the importance and structures of collective ritual see Trexler, *Public Life*, which unfortunately covers only the period up to the beginning of the grand duchy; and in Europe generally, Wisch and Munshower, *All the World's a Stage*, 1: xv–xix, with further bibliography. Geertz's anthropological theories are set out most explicitly in his *Negara: The Theatre State in 19th-Century Bali* (Princeton: Princeton University Press, 1980), and discussed in Hunt, *New Cultural History*, 77–78. See also Berner, "Florentine Society," 223–25; Jacquot, *Fêtes*, 3: 10; Hale, *Florence and the Medici*, 154.

25. On the concept of *theatrum mundi* see the introduction by Ernst R. Curtius, *European Literature and the Latin Middle Ages*, trans. W. R. Trask (New York: Bollingen/Pantheon, 1953), 138–44; Yates, *Theater of the World*, esp. 162–68, with further bibliography; Anne Righter [Barton], *Shakespeare and the Idea of the Play* (New York: Barnes and Noble, 1962), 64–68, 165–72; Kerrigan and Braden, *Idea of the Renaissance*, 58–59. For an introduction to the concept as developed further in the seventeenth century, see Irving Lavin, *Bernini and the Unity of the Visual Arts* (New York: Oxford University Press, 1980), 1: 146–57, with further bibliography. On the change in consciousness see, e.g., Stephen Greenblatt, *Renaissance Self-Fashioning* (Chicago: University of Chicago Press, 1980).

26. Trexler, *Public Life*, 10; Soldani, in *Prose fiorentine* (Florence, 1716), 1: 313, quoted in Berner, "Florentine Political Thought," 183. For the concept of "theatricalization of space," see Jacquot, *Fêtes*, 3: 15; on its relevance to Florence, Vannucci, *History of Florence*, 184.

27. Cochrane, *Florence in the Forgotten Centuries*, 120–21; the Crusca *Vocabolario*, the first dictionary of Italian, was published in 1612.

28. Dallington, *Survey of the Great Dukes State of Tuscany* (London, 1605), 43, quoted by Berner, "Florentine Society," 208n20.

29. Florence, Galleria degli Uffizi, inv. 1890, no. 4338; Langedijk, *Portraits of the Medici*, 1: 654, no. 5, who observes that this picture seems to depict Christine several years younger than she was at the time, probably in an attempt to please Ferdinando.

30. Gualterotti, *Descrizione*, 4. For funda-

mental information on Christine see *Dizionario biografico degli italiani*, 31: 37–40.

31. On the French political situation see Wilson, *Transformation of Europe*, 52–53; Braudel, *Mediterranean*, 1204–16.

32. Settimani, *Memorie*, 68r, 80r–82v (Dec. 1588) describes in detail the testy negotations between Orazio Rucellai and the French. Rucellai brought home a down payment of 200,000 scudi, the rest to be paid in installments through 1592. Highly paid court administrators received 300 scudi per year, so the dowry amounted to roughly 100–200 million modern dollars. An inventory of the clothes and other goods brought with Christine — including a set of jewels sent as a pledge against the remaining cash due (an indication of the financial straits of the court) — is in ASF, Guardaroba medicea, filza no. 152 (dated 1589). The dowry is discussed by Newman, "Politics of Spectacle," 96–98.

33. The order of events, which still remains partly unclear, is given in most detail at the beginning of Cavallino, *Raccolta* (on which see further Fabbri et al., *Luogo teatrale*, 136, no. 9.20), and by Pavoni, *Diario*, and Settimani, *Memorie*, sometimes inaccurately. The sequence is summarized by Warburg, "Costumi teatrali," 261–62; Nagler, *Theatre Festivals*, 70–72; Gaeta Bertelà and Petrioli Tofani, *Feste e apparati*, 205–7; Strong, *Splendor at Court*, 195.

34. Charles Rosen, "The Ridiculous and Sublime," *New York Review of Books*, Apr. 22, 1993, 15.

I. THE CREATIVE, MANAGEMENT, AND PUBLIC RELATIONS STAFFS

1. Lloyd Kramer, "Literature, Criticism, and Historical Imagination: The Literary Challenge of Hayden White and Dominick LaCapra," in Hunt, *New Cultural History*, 97–98.

2. The identifications are from Gualterotti, whose *Descrizione*, 2: 5, calls Gaddi "cavaliere principalissimo." On Gaddi, see Cristina Acidini Luchinat, "Niccolò Gaddi collezionista e

dilettante del '500," *Paragone* 31 (1980): 141–75, 359–61, with early sources; Turner, *Florentine Drawings*, 197; Blumenthal, "Medici Patronage," 98; for his portrait by Buti, *Primato del disegno*, 91–92. On Angeli see ASF, Depositeria generale, filza 389, 13; an engraved portrait of him ca. 1592 (Bartsch 17.89.116) by Cherubino Alberti is in New York, Metropolitan Museum, no. 51.501.658. For the route and ritual of the 1589 entry, see Chap. 5; for the events of 1539, see Bonner Mitchell, *Italian Civic Pageantry in the High Renaissance*, Biblioteca di bibliografia italiana 89 (Florence: Olschki, 1979), 50–54; Andrew Minor and Bonner Mitchell, *A Renaissance Entertainment: Festivities for the Marriage of Cosimo I, Duke of Florence, 1539* (Columbia: University of Missouri Press, 1968). On 1565, see Vasari, *Vite*, 8: 517–617; Nagler, *Theatre Festivals*, 15–21; Gaeta Bertelà and Petrioli Tofani, *Feste e apparati*, 15–24, 197–98; Fabbri et al., *Luogo teatrale*, 37–39, 109–110, nos. 8.4–5; Borsi et al., *Potere e spazio*, 343–50, nos. 4.26–27. See also Strong, *Art and Power*; Starn and Partridge, *Arts of Power*, part 3.

3. Borghini's letter is published in Michelangelo Gualandi, *Raccolta di lettere sulla pittura . . . dei secoli XV, XVI, e XVII*, ed. Giovanni Bottari and Stefano Ticozzi (Milan, 1822), 1: 140, document LVI. Starn and Patridge, *Arts of Power*, 192–200, discuss Borghini's theories and practices, advisors, the manuscript record, and the preparation of published commentaries, with complete sources.

4. The fundamental source for attributions, iconography, and inscriptions is Gualterotti, *Descrizione*, which illustrates each of the arches and their individual painted scenes in rather crude prints. For additional explanatory texts see discussion of *descrizioni* in this chapter; Bibliography, *Contemporary Printed Sources*; and Chap. 5, with secondary sources.

5. The title page of his *Descrizione*, book 2, claims that it is "di figure adornato da R. Gualterotti." Opinion is divided as to whether a gentleman would have dabbled in the arts himself or whether this implies only that he paid some-

one to produce them. He had earlier published a guide to the Medici Villa at Pratolino, completed by Buontalenti, and the illustrated program book for the 1579 joust celebrating Francesco's marriage to Bianca Cappello. On Gualterotti and the often crude or hasty illustrations, see Blumenthal, *Italian Renaissance Festival Designs*, nos. 27, 28, 32; idem, *Theater Art of the Medici*, 3–4, no. 1.

6. On the history and typical form of the *descrizioni*, see Bonner Mitchell, *A Year of Pageantry in Late Renaissance Ferrara* (Binghamton, N.Y.: CMRS, 1990), 3–11; Wisch and Munshower, *All the World's a Stage*, 1: xv–xvi.

7. For complete bibliographical and codicological data on the two editions, see Solerti, *Musica, ballo, e drammatica*, 12–13. Several variants are held by the Biblioteca Nazionale Centrale, Florence; the complete version cited herein is that in the New York Public Library, Spencer Collection.

8. Daddi Giovannozzi, "Alcune incisioni," 94–97.

9. For Catherine's death, see Chap. 3. Postal service at this time was highly irregular and variable, and dispatches from France could take two or three weeks: Braudel, *Mediterranean*, 1: 355–72.

10. For Bardi's life see *Dizionario biografico degli italiani*, 6: 300–303 (s.v. Bardi); 22: 661 (s.v. Cavalieri); *Enciclopedia dello spettacolo*, 1: 1498; Claude Palisca, "Giovanni de' Bardi," in *New Grove Dictionary*, 2: 150–52. For summary discussions of his work in 1579, 1586, and 1589 see Strong, *Splendor at Court*, 185–87; idem, *Art and Power*, 134–44; Borsi et al., *Potere e spazio*, 357, no. 5.5.

11. On the Camerata see, in addition to biographical sources in n. 10, Claude Palisca, *The Florentine Camerata: Documentary Studies and Translations* (New Haven: Yale University Press, 1989); Pirrotta and Povoledo, *Music and Theatre*, 201–5; Solerti, *Albori del melodramma*, 1: 42–46, vol. 2 (on Rinuccini).

12. Rossi, *Descrizione dell'apparato*, 5–6.

13. ASF, Magistrato de' Nove Conservatori, filza 3679, Seriacopi, *Memoriale e ricordi* (hereafter cited as MR), 3r: "Il Sr. Gio. de bardi ordina che si dia mano al fare li abiti per li intermedi et si protesta che sendovi difficulta nessuna si dica adesso et che se non si sara poi a tempo non ne vuole essere tenuto a mente." Even twenty years later, Bardi was insistent about the primacy of his own concerns: see a letter of 1608 in which Giulio Parigi, designer for the wedding that year of Cosimo II, complains "Signor Giovanni de' Bardi is annoying me all day because he'd like to rehearse the musicians up on the clouds" of the unfinished stage machinery (transcribed in Blumenthal, *Giulio Parigi*, 368–69).

14. On the development of the genre, see *Enciclopedia dello spettacolo*, 6: 572–76 (s.v. Intermezzo); David Nutter, "Intermedio," *New Grove Dictionary*, 9: 258–69; Pirrotta and Povoledo, *Due Orfei*, 173–236; Bonner Mitchell, "Les intermèdes au service de l'état," in Jacquot, *Fêtes*, 3: 117–31; John Shearman, *Mannerism* (Baltimore: Penguin, 1967), 104–12, who treats the genre as one of the most characteristic forms of the mannerist esthetic. For Lasca's comment and his satiric madrigal on the same subject, see Solerti, *Albori del melodramma*, 1: 9; d'Ancona, *Origini del teatro*, 2: 168, 420.

15. Rossi, *Descrizione dell'apparato*, partially reprinted in Solerti, *Albori del melodramma*, 2: 15–42, and in Walker, *Fêtes du mariage*, xxxiii–lviii. Rossi and his book are discussed by Warburg, "Costumi teatrali," 263; Fabbri et al., *Luogo teatrale*, 37, 110, no. 8.7; Blumenthal, *Theater Art of the Medici*, 7–9, no. 3. For Rossi's friendship with Bardi, see *Dizionario biografico degli italiani* (s.v. Bardi); for the forced reprinting, ibid. (s.v. Cavalieri). The several variant editions are held by the Biblioteca Nazionale Centrale, Florence, in the Palatina collection; the version cited herein, from the first printing, is that in the New York Public Library, Performing Arts Library.

16. That Rossi had access to the drawings was suggested by Franco Berti, in Borsi et al.,

Potere e spazio, 363. Such correspondences are not consistent, however; perhaps Rossi saw only some of the drawings, which could have been developed over a period of time. Certainly changes were made after Rossi's text had been prepared: in many drawings some areas are labeled with a color that does not correspond to that of their watercolor washes.

17. Pirrotta and Povoledo, *Due Orfei*, 213, make the latter suggestion, which is certainly plausible given what we know of the rivalries involved, but they do not confront the problem of why, when the grand duke himself ordered the book reprinted to remove its biases, the text changes were not also inserted.

18. The complete texts of the intermedi are available in the edition of the score, ed. D. P. Walker, and in Solerti, *Albori del melodramma*, vol. 2. For the patterns of symbolism see Molinari, *Nozze degli dèi*, 13–34; LeClerc, "Mythe platonicien"; Harry Levin, *The Myth of the Golden Age in the Renaissance* (Bloomington: Indiana University Press, 1969), 38–41 on the Medici. On the golden age theme in the Quattrocento, see *The "Stanze" of Angelo Poliziano*, trans. David Quint (University Park: Pennsylvania State University Press, 1993), 9–11, esp. n. 4. Berner, "Florentine Political Thought," 179–85, discusses the importance of claims to "ancient lineage" in Medici and European statecraft. More summary treatments include Nagler, *Theatre Festivals*, 72; Blumenthal, *Theater Art of the Medici*, 7–9; idem, *Giulio Parigi*, 118–19. For earlier links between court theater and politics see Anthony M. Cummings, *The Politicized Muse: Music for Medici Festivals, 1512–1537* (Princeton: Princeton University Press, 1992). Hanning, "Glorious Apollo," 485–513, perceptively analyzes similar symbolism in a slightly later musical event in Florence (see below, Chap. 7), created by several of the same team that worked on the 1589 intermedi, to which she also devotes some attention. I am also indebted to the unpublished papers on iconography delivered by Professor Hanning at the 1991 Aston-Magna Academy, New Brunswick,

N.J., and, for literary sources and structural interpretation, to the paper delivered by Robert C. Ketterer, "Strange Bedfellows: The Classical Sources for the 1589 Intermedi," at the International Congress of Medieval Studies, Kalamazoo, Mich., 1992.

19. For more detailed summaries of each plot see Rossi, *Descrizione dell'apparato*, and Mamone, *Teatro nella Firenze*.

20. The quotations on court encomium are by Quint, *Poliziano*, xii–xv, xxii.

21. Barrington Moore, Jr., *Social Origins of Dictatorship and Democracy: Lord and Peasant in the Making of the Modern World* (Boston: Beacon, 1966), 522, quoted in Walter Cohen, *Drama of a Nation: Public Theater in Renaissance England and Spain* (Ithaca: Cornell University Press, 1985), 27. See also Berner, "Florentine Political Thought," 177–99; idem, "Florentine Society," 204; and the discussion of this ideological function in architecture in Ackerman, *Villa*, 10.

22. In 1539, Eleonora's entry depicted agricultural productivity, such as wheatfields and the draining of the Maremma marshes (Mitchell, "Intermèdes," 128); Giovanna's in 1565 represented Agriculture on the arch of Florence, figuring Tuscany as the "garden of Europe," and one arch represented Maritime Empire (Starn and Partridge, *Arts of Power*, 185–96). On the political goals and symbolic epistemology of the intermedi and of court encomium generally, see Berner, "Florentine Society," 187, 204; idem, "Florentine Political Thought"; Aletta Biersack, "Local Knowledge, Local History: Geertz and Beyond," in Hunt, *New Cultural History*, 77–81; Starn and Partridge, *Arts of Power*, 184.

23. Newman, "Politics of Spectacle," discusses the plot and alterations in detail, with further bibliography; I thank Paula Elliot for bringing this article to my attention. Newman's thesis develops a more general observation by Frances Yates about the unity of festival components, in Jacquot, *Fêtes*, 1: 422, and depends on the analysis in the modern critical edition of

La pellegrina, ed. Cerreta, esp. 40–43. The amended Bargagli text was published soon after performance (Siena: Bonetti, 1589): see Blumenthal, *Italian Renaissance Festival Designs,* 83, no. 34; Fabbri et al., *Luogo teatrale,* 110, no. 8.6. An English translation is available by Ferraro, *The Female Pilgrim.*

24. These performances are described in most detail by Pavoni (for the mad scene, *Diario,* 46) and Cavallino, and summarized by Settimani, *Memorie,* 132, 149, 150; the relevant excerpts from Settimani are transcribed by Solerti, *Albori del melodramma,* 2: 18. See Fabbri et al., *Luogo teatrale,* 116, no. 8.21, for additional contemporary sources, and below, Chaps. 2, 6. On the content of these plays and the commedia dell'arte tradition in general, see d'Ancona, *Origini del teatro,* 2: 167, 406–95; Warburg, "Costumi teatrali," 261–62; Clubb, *Italian Drama,* 249–80.

25. "Non è così assiduo alla persona, perché ama la libertà; ma possiede assai la grazia di S.A.": published in Eugenio Albèri, *Relazioni veneziane* (Florence, 1863), appendix, 285. For Cavalieri's salary see ASF, Depositeria generale, filza 389, 13; on his life and career see *Dizionario biografico degli italiani,* 22: 659–64; Warren Kirkendale, "Emilio de' Cavalieri, A Roman Gentleman at the Florentine Court," in *Memorie e contributi . . . offerti a Federico Ghisi, Quadrivium* 12, no. 2 (1971): 9–21; Claude Palisca, "Emilio de' Cavalieri," *New Grove Dictionary,* 3: 20–23.

26. For the various composers involved, and the musical issues of the Camerata, see Pirrotta and Povoledo, *Due Orfei,* 211–306; Claude Palisca, "The 'Camera fiorentina': A Reappraisal," *Studi musicali* 1 (1972): 203–36; Federico Ghisi, "Un aspect inédit des intermèdes de 1589 à la cour médicéenne," in Jacquot, *Fêtes,* 1: 145–52; Fabbri et al., *Luogo teatrale,* 116, nos. 8.22, 8.23.

27. Steven Ledbetter and Roland Jackson, "Luca Marenzio," *New Grove Dictionary,* 11: 667–74; Frank D'Accone, "Cristofano Malvezzi," ibid., 11: 590–91; on Malvezzi's edition see Bibliography, *Contemporary Printed Sources.*

Both communicated with Seriacopi about musical instruments and other needs: MR 45r (Apr. 9), 50r (Apr. 23).

28. The first solo for Vittoria Archilei as Harmony is credited to Cavalieri by Rossi but to Antonio Archilei in Malvezzi's edition; this contradiction may be resolved by the suggestion that Archilei composed only the customary vocal embellishments to Cavalieri's setting: Hugh Keyte, "Intermedi for *La pellegrina,*" (liner notes, *Una "stravaganza" dei Medici,* London: EMI, 1988, 18. In addition to sources cited above, for the individual composers and performers I have relied on the biographies in *New Grove Dictionary*: William Porter, "Peri," 14: 401–5; H. Wiley Hitchcock, "Caccini," 2: 576–81; idem, "Archilei, Vittoria," 1: 551–52; Nigel Fortune, "Archilei, Antonio," 1: 551. For additional sources and discussion of musical performers, see Chap. 2.

29. On Guidiccioni see Warren Kirkendale, "L'opera in musica prima del Peri: Le pastorali perdute di Laura Guidiccioni ed Emilio de' Cavalieri," in *Firenze e la Toscana dei Medici,* 2: 365–95. For the differences between the two versions see originally Solerti, *Albori del melodramma,* 2: 34–42, and Solerti's article, "Laura Guidiccioni Lucchesini ed Emilio de' Cavalieri, i primi tentativi del melodramma," *Rivista musicale italiana* 1 (1902): 797. On Cavalieri's role see further Solerti, *Musica, ballo, e drammatica,* 12–19, 235–38.

30. Both versions of the finale are printed by Solerti, *Albori del melodramma,* 2: 34–42. Pirrotta and Povoledo, *Due Orfei,* 213, note that Malvezzi's edition (prepared at Cavalieri's request) does not include Caccini's number, an omission that they interpret as yet another example of spite between the Bardi and Cavalieri circles. On the changes and the probable rivalry see further D. P. Walker, "La Musique des Intermèdes florentins de 1589 et l'humanisme," in Jacquot, *Fêtes,* 1: 137–44, with further bibliography (reprinted in his *Fêtes du mariage*).

31. Rossi, *Descrizione dell'apparato,* 44–45. Some of Malvezzi's dance diagrams and textual

description are reproduced in Solerti, *Musica, ballo, e drammatica*, 17–18; and, in modernized form, in Walker, *Fêtes du mariage*, lvi–lviii. Unfortunately, Walker's projected volume 2, a detailed study of the 1589 performance itself, never appeared.

32. The proclamation of his appointment is partially published in Gaye, *Carteggio inedito*, 3: 484.

33. On the bureaucracy see Arnaldo d'Addario, "Burocrazia, economia e finanze dello stato fiorentino alla metà del Cinquecento," *Archivio storico italiano* 121 (1963): 372; Braudel, *Mediterranean*, 681–92; R. Burr Litchfield, *Emergence of a Bureaucracy: The Florentine Patricians 1530–1790* (Princeton: Princeton University Press, 1986); Berner, "Florentine Political Thought," 193–95; idem, "Florentine Society," 244–45. For the arms-control legislation see ibid., 218, with sources.

34. *Libro di conti relativi alla commedia diritta da Emilio de' Cavalieri*: ASF, Guardaroba medicea, filza 140 (hereafter cited as LC); the entries are written by an unidentified hand. On bookkeeping methods see Braudel, *Perspective of the World*, 128; Goldthwaite, *Building of Renaissance Florence*, 47–49.

35. Pages in the Libro are identified hereafter in the following form: for the Taglio section, T followed by the original page number of the two-page entry; for the later sections, Q or N plus the modern folio numbers that run continuously through these originally unnumbered pages.

36. Braudel, *Mediterranean*, 341–42.

37. Among those who claim (to my mind somewhat overstating the case) that 1589 marked the first time that all visual aspects were under one individual's control, see Mamone, *Teatro nella Firenze*, 72–77; Fabbri et al., *Luogo teatrale*, 42.

38. For basic biographical background see Vasari, *Vite*, 7: 310, 614–17; Baldinucci, *Notizie dei professori*, 2: 490–532; *Dizionario biografico degli italiani*, 15: 280–84; *Enciclopedia dello spett-*

acolo, 2: 1334–35 (s.v. Buontalenti), with additional ms. sources; Daddi Giovannozzi, "Vita di Buontalenti"; Botto, *Mostra di disegni*, introduction. For the continuing uncertainty about his birth date, which has been placed variously between 1523 and 1547, see Fara, *Buontalenti: Architettura e teatro*, 2, 22–23n5. For the situation of court architects in Florence and elsewhere, see Goldthwaite, *Building of Renaissance Florence*, 387–95; Warnke, *Court Artist*, 175–88. Little of his painting or sculpture survives; on his technical works see Casali and Diana, *Buontalenti e la burocrazia*, with archival references and background on the embryonic state of bureaucratization (they suggest, 27–28, that he did not really enjoy this work); Spini, *Architettura e politica*.

39. For the architectural work see Fara, *Buontalenti: Architettura e teatro*; idem, *Buontalenti: Architettura, guerra e l'elemento geometrico*; Botto, *Mostra di disegni*.

40. A College of Engineers was founded in Milan, 1563; on the rising status of the engineer, see Goldthwaite, *Building of Renaissance Florence*, 365–66, with further references. For Hero's text and the treatises, see Gaye, *Carteggio inedito*, 3: 449, and additional sources cited by Warburg, "Costumi teatrali," 266nn5–6; Strong, *Art and Power*, 136. An edition of Hero's work on vacuums was dedicated to Buontalenti: Lazzaro, *Italian Renaissance Garden*, 16–19.

41. On the increasing professional distinction of architects, see Goldthwaite, *Building of Renaissance Florence*, 356–67. Buontalenti's technical expertise is documented by Anna Cerchiai and Coletta Quiriconi, "Relazioni e rapporti all'Ufficio dei Capitani di Parte Guelfa," in Spini, *Architettura e politica*, 208.

42. Blumenthal, *Giulio Parigi*, 28nn22–23, 89–90, 112–13; Daddi Giovannozzi, "Vita di Buontalenti."

43. For Buontalenti's compensation, see ASF, Depositeria generale 389, 11; ASF, Capitani di Parte Guelfa, filza 1471, 139; Daddi Giovannozzi, "Vita di Buontalenti," 522.

44. Rossi, *Descrizione dell'apparato*, 5 (*sovr'u-mana ingegno*); Vasari, *Vite*, 7: 614. On manner-ist theory see generally Shearman, *Mannerism*.

45. On these specific theatricals and others see Gaeta Bertelà and Petrioli Tofani, *Feste e apparati*, and below, Chap. 7.

46. For the occupation of *provveditore*, which was common for most large institutions, see Goldthwaite, *Building of Renaissance Florence*, 159. On Seriacopi's title and job description see Warburg, "Costumi teatrali," 394–97; Nagler, *Theatre Festivals*, 78; and Franco Berti, "Alcuni aspetti," the only study exclusively devoted to Seriacopi. On the similar role of Caccini (not to be confused with the artist of the same name from 1589), see Starn and Partridge, *Arts of Power*, 200–203. Employees who performed similar logistical functions at other Medici sites appear in the records, though less can be gleaned about them: Benedetto Fedini, *guard-aroba del granduca* for the Pitti and the Medici villas; Enea Vaini, *maggiordomo* at the Pitti; and Napoleone Cambi, head of Ferdinando's *Depo-siteria generale*, or treasury (on whom see Diaz, *Granducato*, 317).

47. On the content and structure of the *Me-moriale*, see Warburg, "Costumi teatrali," 394–423 (appendix by Gertrud Bing, with partial transcriptions); Berti, "Alcuni aspetti"; and brief catalogue entries in Fabbri et al., *Luogo teatrale*, 111, no. 8.8, and Borsi et al., *Potere e spazio*, 358, no. 5.12. The log often mentions three principal sites of operations, the Pitti, where Guardaroba matériel is kept; the "Pal-azzo," presumably Palazzo Vecchio; and the "Castello," probably the Fortezza da Basso, the city's major military depot.

48. There were in fact two Seriacopis, Gio-vanni, who died, and his successor Girolamo: see the auditors' report, LC T91, cited in War-burg, "Costumi teatrali," 394–97 (on Gio-vanni's activities June 1587–Feb. 1588, see ASF, Guardaroba medicea, filza 134, 25, 227, 629). On Girolamo's life and letters, see Gaye, *Car-teggio inedito*, 3: 469, 513, 518, 520; Gualandi,

Nuova raccolta di lettere, 1844 ed., nos. 100, 103; Berti, "Alcuni aspetti."

49. The letters cited are ASF, Carteggio mediceo, Principato, filza 802, c. 489 (Dec. 25, 1588), and filza 805, cc. 21 (Mar. 2, 1589) and 874 (Mar. 16). For Borghini's remark, see Starn and Partridge, *Arts of Power*, 201.

2. CASTING, COSTUMES, AND REHEARSALS

1. On the Intronati, see the works on Bar-gagli and *La pellegrina* cited in Chap. 1; Fabbri et al., *Luogo teatrale*, 110, nos. 8.6 and 8.7. The best known of these groups was the Accademia Olimpica in Vicenza, for which Palladio de-signed the theater in 1580.

2. On these performances see Chaps. 1 and 6; d'Ancona, *Origini del teatro*, 2: 167, 466; War-burg, "Costumi teatrali," 261–62; Fabbri et al., *Luogo teatrale*, 110 no. 8.6, 116 no. 8.21, 158; Mamone, *Teatro nella Firenze*, 77. On the An-dreini see *Dizionario biografico degli italiani* (s.v. Andreini); on the family and, more generally, the artistic and professional organization within the commedia dell'arte, see Clubb, *Italian Drama*, 249–80, with further sources, including transcription of Pavoni. Fabbri et al., 45, main-tain that Piissimi, a Roman, headed a rival troupe to the Andreini, who were from Pistoia, and that Piissimi's company performed at the banquet in the Palazzo Vecchio following the *Pellegrina* premiere.

3. The list contains a requests for 82 pairs of shoes, with names so that each performer can be measured: MR 44r–v (Apr. 9). On the person-nel of the granducal chapel see originally R. Gandolfi, "La cappella musicale della corte di Toscana, 1539–1859," *Rivista musicale italiana* 16 (1909): 508 ff.

4. But not for 2 (whose sketches bear no names) or for 4 or 6 (whose drawings are lost). It is beyond my scope here to provide full cast lists, which could readily be reassembled, for

the three intermedi noted, by collating the names on the individual costume drawings (see Catalogue) with the accounts of names and costumes in Cavalieri's and Seriacopi's books: LC Q291–96, N414, 415, 423, 424, 431, 432, 441; MR 44r–v. For summaries and partial transcriptions of the sources on casting see Warburg, "Costumi teatrali," 268, 274–76, 298–300, 406 (including Franciosino's school), citing particularly the household salary records in Archivio di Stato Fiorentino (hereafter ASF), Guardaroba medicea (hereafter GM), filza 389, *Ruolo della casa et familiarii del Ser.mo Ferdinando Medicis . . .* ; see also Nagler, *Theatre Festivals,* 77. Warburg, 268 (and, following him, Nagler) contradicts his own findings in claiming that the accounts detail only singers from the first intermedio. Additional personal identifications of performers appear in Cristofano Malvezzi's printed edition of the score, *Intermedii et concerti,* and the version of Malvezzi edited by Walker, *Fêtes du mariage.*

5. On Alberigo see MR 44r, and Frank D'Accone, "Malvezzi, Cristofano," in *New Grove Dictionary,* 11: 590.

6. On Vittoria Archilei see H. Wiley Hitchcock, "Archilei, Vittoria," in *New Grove Dictionary,* 1: 551–52.

7. On the Caccinis see LC Q291; bibliography cited in Chap. 1nn28, 30; Hugh Keyte, "Intermedi for *La pellegrina*" (liner notes, *Una "stravaganza" dei Medici,* London: EMI, 1988), 18. On Margherita, see ASF, Depositeria generale, filza 389, 17; Warburg, "Costumi teatrali," 299.

8. On Gualfreducci see LC N432; ASF, Depositeria generale 389, 17; Warburg, "Costumi teatrali," 300; and below. On the boys (*ragazzi*), see Rossi, *Descrizione dell'apparato,* 54; MR 66v.

9. ASF, Depositeria generale 389, 17; transcr. Warburg, "Costumi teatrali," 299–300. On orchestral practice see Howard Mayer Brown, *Sixteenth-Century Instrumentation: The Music for the Florentine Intermedii* (Dallas: American Institute of Musicology, 1973); on the Striggio family see articles by Barbara Russano Hanning

and Iain Fenlon, *New Grove Dictionary,* 18: 271–74.

10. Clubb, *Italian Drama,* 261; Keyte, "Intermedi for *La pellegrina,*" 15.

11. On women in the commedia dell'arte see Clubb, *Italian Drama,* 257–63; I am also indebted to unpublished lectures by Nancy Dersofi (Aston-Magna Academy, New Brunswick, N.J., 1991) and Sylvia Dimiziani, "The Emergence of the Diva in the High Renaissance" (International Congress on Medieval Studies, Kalamazoo, Mich., 1992). For issues of women and gender in Renaissance theater and other professions, which have generated a vast bibliography, basic sources include Margaret L. King, *Women of the Renaissance* (Chicago: University of Chicago Press, 1991); Natalie Zemon Davis and Arlette Farge, eds., *A History of Women in the West,* vol. 3, *Renaissance and Enlightenment Paradoxes* (Cambridge: Harvard University Press, 1993); Merry E. Wiesner, *Women and Gender in Early Modern Europe* (Cambridge: Cambridge University Press, 1993).

12. For Gualfreducci see LC N432 (and references above); Pierino, LC N441; Bartolino, ASF, Depositeria generale 389, 17, transcr. Warburg, "Costumi teatrali," 300. On castrati, see Thomas Walker, "Castrato," in *New Grove Dictionary,* 3: 875–76; the somewhat inadequate study by Angus Heriot, *The Castrati in Opera* (London: Secker and Warburg, 1956); Patrick Barber, *Les Castrats* (Paris: Grasset, 1989); Vern Bullough and Bonnie Bullough, *Cross-Dressing, Sex, and Gender* (Philadelphia: University of Pennsylvania Press, 1993), chap. 4.

13. For 24 pairs of *poppe e petti di cartone,* see LC T19, transcr. Warburg, "Costumi teatrali," 279; Nagler, *Theatre Festivals,* 77.

14. For sumptuary laws in Florence, see Settimani, *Memorie,* Aug.–Nov. 1588 passim; and more generally Diane Owen Hughes, "Sumptuary Law and Social Relations in Renaissance Italy," in *Disputes and Settlements: Law and Human Relations in the West,* ed. John Bossy, 69–99 (Cambridge: Cambridge University Press, 1983).

15. The nature of theatrical costume changed radically from the sixteenth through the seventeenth century; before the advent of women, men had taken what has been called "real disguise" — in which the female role was played seriously and the audience expected to accept it as such—whereas after the Restoration travesty became marginalized to "false disguise," in which the audience is expected to enjoy the awareness that the performer is a man. On transvestism in the Renaissance and Baroque theater (more extensively studied for England than elsewhere), see, among important recent studies, Stephen Orgel, "Nobody's Perfect: Or Why Did the English Stage Take Boys for Women?" *South Atlantic Quarterly* 88 (1989): 7–29; Jonathan Goldberg, *Sodometries: Renaissance Texts, Modern Sexualities* (Stanford: Stanford University Press, 1992), chap. 4, "The Transvestite Stage." Contemporary theories are reviewed by Bullough and Bullough, *Cross-Dressing*, 74–82, with references (the terms "real disguise" and "false disguise" are Roger Baker's, cited p. 82); and Jean E. Howard, "Power and Eros: Crossdressing in Dramatic Representation and Theatrical Practice," in her *The Stage and Social Struggle in Early Modern England* (New York: Routledge, 1994), 93–127.

16. On the artistic and philosophical hermaphrodite/androgyne and the conceptual links among these terms and homosexuality, see James M. Saslow, *Ganymede in the Renaissance: Homosexuality in Art and Society* (New Haven: Yale University Press, 1986), chaps. 2, 3; Ann Rosalind Jones and Peter Stallybrass, "Fetishizing Gender: Constructing the Hermaphrodite in Renaissance Europe," in *Body Guards: The Cultural Politics of Gender Ambiguity*, ed. Julia Epstein and Kristina Straub, 80–111 (New York: Routledge, 1991). The many studies of images of Elizabeth are indebted to Yates, *Astraea*, part 2. Andreini's speech is recorded in a printed scenario for her play *La pazzia d'Isabella*, which differs significantly from the action reported by Pavoni in 1589: see Clubb, *Italian Drama*, 265. On the miniature of François,

ca. 1545 (Paris, Bibliothèque Nationale), see *L'Ecole de Fontainebleau* (exh. cat., Paris: Grand Palais, 1972), no. 27, probably by Niccolò da Modena (Nicolas Bellin).

17. For homosexuality in this period and its social structures and relation to the theater, see Saslow, *Ganymede*; idem, "Homosexuality in the Renaissance: Behavior, Identity, Artistic Expression," in *Hidden from History: Reclaiming the Gay and Lesbian Past*, ed. Martin Duberman, Martha Vicinus, and George Chauncey, 90–105 (New York: New American Library, 1989); Guido Ruggiero, *The Boundaries of Eros: Sex Crime and Sexuality in Renaissance Venice* (Oxford: Oxford University Press, 1985); Alan Bray, *Homosexuality in Renaissance England* (London: Gay Men's Press, 1982); Bullough and Bullough, *Cross-Dressing*, 74–78. Michael Rocke, *Friendly Affections, Nefarious Vices: Male Homosexuality in Renaissance Florence* (Oxford: Oxford University Press, 1996), has found detailed evidence of homosexual subcultures for the fifteenth century; for a preliminary survey of sixteenth-century archival sources see Luciano Marcello, "Società maschile e sodomia: dal declino della *polis* al Principato," *Archivio storico italiano* 150 (1992): 115–38. Lisa Jardine maintains that the links between public theater and homosexuality emerged slowly after 1600, and became more prominent after 1700: "'As Boys and Women Are for the Most Part Cattle of this Colour': Female Roles and Elizabethan Eroticism," in *Still Harping on Daughters: Women and Drama in the Age of Shakespeare* (Totowa, N.J.: Barnes and Noble, 1983), 9–36.

18. Testaverde, "Creatività e tradizione," 186.

19. For references to the comedy costumes by character name, costume number (presumably keyed to lost drawings), and materials, see LC N397–402, 425–28. These are summarized by Newman, "Politics of Spectacle," 99. Apparently the granducal workshops also provided some costumes for the Compagnia dei Gelosi performers; a note from one of them to Cavalieri requests certain costumes, perhaps

because their ordinary theatrical stock was considered inadequate to the grandeur of the Uffizi occasion (LC N389).

20. For totals see LC Q191; Warburg, "Costumi teatrali," 268 (see below, Chap. 7 for the subsequent fates of missing drawings). Intermedio 1 is more completely documented than the others; for lists of fabrics by costume number and cast name for this act, see LC Q293, N411–16, 423–24, 431–32, 441. Various additional drawings have been tentatively identified as preparatory sketches by Buontalenti; I have not attempted to catalogue all of these for reasons of space and focus. Some can be connected to specific catalogued drawings, and are noted at the appropriate entry. Others are more generic and uncertain; see, e.g., Blumenthal, *Italian Renaissance Festival Designs*, nos. 35, 36, 38.

21. Besides being misattributed to Giulio Parigi, the drawings in the BNCF folder are assigned modern *carta* numbers that bear little relation to their original order. The folder system and design sequence are suggested by Franco Berti in Borsi et al., *Potere e spazio*, 361–63; idem, "Alcuni aspetti," 166.

22. For background on the theatrical costume tradition, see Warburg, "Costumi teatrali"; Testaverde, "Creatività e tradizione," 178–80; Stella Mary Newton, *Renaissance Theatre Costume and the Sense of the Historic Past* (New York: Theatre Art Books, 1975), chap. 7. De' Sommi describes the conventions for dress of nymphs and other pastoral types, as does Angelo Ingegneri, in his *Discorso della poesia rappresentativa* (Ferrara, 1598). Testaverde provides some excerpts from de' Sommi, Ingegneri, and the anonymous *Il Corago* from the early seventeenth century; for partial transcription of de' Sommi see also d'Ancona, *Origini del teatro*, 2: 581 and passim; and the complete critical edition of de' Sommi, *Quattro dialoghi*. For extensive transcriptions from various other authors see Marotti, *Spettacolo dall'umanesimo*; *Il Corago*, ed. Fabbri and Pontilio.

23. De' Sommi, *Quattro dialoghi*, 48; Tes-

taverde, "Creatività e tradizione," 181. Occasionally the costumes adapt exotic contemporary fashions, such as the Levantine styles for the Delphians of intermedio 3, whom Rossi (*Descrizione dell'apparato*, 42–48) describes as *alla greca*, here in the sense of the (formerly Byzantine) Middle East (see cat. 43, 46, 48).

24. On colors and fabrics see *Il Corago*, chapter 20; Testaverde, "Creatività e tradizione," 176; Reade, *Ballet Designs*, 3, no. 5.

25. De' Sommi, *Quattro dialoghi*, 53; Testaverde, "Creatività e tradizione," 178n10, with further citations.

26. De' Sommi's remark, from *Quattro dialoghi*, day 3, is quoted by Testaverde, "Creatività e tradizione," 182. On the use of velvet in the costumes, see LC T20, T24, Q300–306; Rossi, *Descrizione dell'apparato*, 41, 49; Nagler, *Theatre Festivals*, 84 (intermedio 3, composed largely of mortals, used only a single braccio for hats). The sumptuous texture of the velvet was sometimes enhanced by stamped patterns: beginning on Dec. 2, amounts of it were consigned from the Guardaroba to one Piero di Ruggieri, flagmaker and printer (*banderaio e stampatore*), to be printed (LC Q297, and another such order, N407).

27. Rossi, *Descrizione dell'apparato*, 46–48, similarly describes two of the Delphian couples (cat. 36, 37; pl. 12) with much more detail about trimmings and jewelry than is conveyed by the sketches, suggesting that he must have seen either an intermediate drawing (or these two costumes in a completed stage) far enough in advance to insert them in his text; as he is silent or vague on the other Delphians, they may not yet have been worked up into detail drawings when he was writing. For a uniquely detailed tailor's book that survives from ca. 1540–70, which preserves costume sketches along with the patterns needed to cut and construct them, see *Il libro del sarto della Fondazione Querini Stampalia di Venezia* (Ferrara: Panini, 1987), including reprint of an explanatory essay by Fritz Saxl.

28. "Describo mores hominum" (Rossi, *De-*

scrizione dell'apparato, 12). For these costumes see LC N389–402; on the genre as a whole, Testaverde, "Creatività e tradizione," 181, with sources and quotations.

29. See LC N427–28 for numbered lists and geographical descriptions; Pavoni, *Diario*, 12–14, carefully notes Christine's change from French to Italian fashions (see further below, Chaps. 5–6). See LC N389 for the quoted note: "Che quella fanciulla che finge la pazzia fussi vestita, non di tocchette false, ma di cose sode, d'abiti nobili et apparenti, come tante volte s'è detto; e pure si potrebbono torre in presto senza spese." Testaverde's discussion of this costume, "Creatività e tradizione," 181, misidentifies it as being for Drusilla.

30. For Cambi see MR 6v (Nov. 26), and LC T3, T5, Q8–14 (materials delivered Nov.–Jan.). For materials for which Gorini was responsible see LC Q1–4 and passim. For a breakdown of total materials for each intermedio, listed separately, see LC Q300–306.

31. As in the traditional English pound, 12 denari (pence, abbr. *d*) equal one soldo (shilling, *s*) and 20 soldi equal one lira (£); this money of account was converted to gold coin at a rate of seven lire per ducat. On the number of tailors and pay to the heads of the enterprise, see LC Q188–97; Warburg, "Costumi teatrali," 277–79; Nagler, *Theatre Festivals*, 77. For the weekly records of named tailors, see LC Q87–89. The tailors here are all male, but women were paid for other sewing (see below).

32. For wages in the construction industry see the chart in Goldthwaite, *Building of Renaissance Florence*, 318–19. His chap. 6, "Labor," provides a useful estimate and overview of wages, prices, and living conditions for workers, with data up to 1600, but discussion unfortunately concentrates on the earlier Renaissance.

33. For administrative and artistic salaries see above and Chap. 1; for Seriacopi's and Fedini's roles see LC Q88. For labor history and wages in the sixteenth century see Goldthwaite,

Building of Renaissance Florence, 301–31; Braudel, *Mediterranean*, 458–570; Carlo Cipolla, *La moneta in Firenze nel Cinquecento* (Bologna: Mulino, 1987). Although it is notoriously difficult to compare prices and wages across classes or locales, Braudel (458–59) notes that in Venice at this time 20 ducats per year constituted poverty, and an accountant typically earned 180 annually (15 per month).

34. For references to Tonino see LC T6–8, T18, T23, T27; for headdress costs and details, LC N437–439.

35. Masks: MR 11r–v (*maschera* may also mean an entire costume, but here clearly refers to faces); shoes: MR 44r–v (Apr. 9; as noted above, this list includes most of the total cast), and LC N427–29, with costs; shoes and other accessories: LC Q393.

36. Flemish raw fabrics and tablecloths, GM 128, 93r; GM 148, 5r. English cloth, GM 148, 113r (Jan. 1589); Bavarian swords, MR 54v (May 9). On the international scope of Florentine trade see Diaz, *Granducato*, 343.

37. Francesco Bellori (or Bellotti) reported that, acting on Cavalieri's request, he had paid messer Marenzio for 49 *canne* (rods, i.e., bolts) of "green velvet from Catenzano" bought from "a Jew"; final payment seems to have been characteristically dilatory (see Chap. 7). LC N447–48, 453–54, 463, 467; additional notices and calculations about *velluto verde*, LC T20, N458.

38. On trade growth and the international textile industry see Pounds, *Historical Geography*, 234–45. On the local industry and associated crafts, which began to decline under foreign competition by 1600, see Berner, "Florentine Society," 213; Goldthwaite, *Building of Renaissance Florence*, 42–52, with further bibliography on social organization and production techniques; Diaz, *Granducato*, 350–55.

39. MR 41v–42r (Apr. 7); LC T6, T19. On the industry see Pounds, *Historical Geography*, 237.

40. On women in trades see Jordan Goodman and Judith Brown, "Women and Industry

in Florence," *Journal of Economic History* 40 (1980): 73–80; Goldthwaite, *Building of Renaissance Florence*, 52–54, 201, 225–26, 322; and primarily for northern Europe, Martha C. Howell, *Women, Production, and Patriarchy in Late Medieval Cities* (Chicago: University of Chicago Press, 1986). On the importance of both secular and religious women in this industry see Merry E. Wiesner, "Spinsters and Seamstresses: Women in Cloth and Clothing Production," in *Rewriting the Renaissance: The Discourses of Sexual Difference in Early Modern Europe*, ed. Margaret Ferguson et al., 191–205 (Chicago: University of Chicago Press, 1986).

41. Margherita: ASF, Magistrato de' Nove, filza 3712, 98 (July 2, 1588). On the rapid increase in nuns in the sixteenth century see Trexler, *Public Life*, 33–51; on convent economics see Goldthwaite, *Building of Renaissance Florence*, 225–26; for convent payments see ASF, GM 157, fol. 23r, and further below. Convents were also the site of women's only attempts at all-female theatrical activity; the genre of convent theater — in which, out of necessity, women played male roles as well as female — offers a mirror image of the largely male public stage; see Elissa Weaver, "Spiritual Fun: A Study of Sixteenth-Century Tuscan Convent Theater," in *Women in the Middle Ages and the Renaissance: Literary and Historical Perspectives*, ed. Mary Beth Rose, 173–205 (Syracuse: Syracuse University Press, 1986).

42. Warburg, "Costumi teatrali," 269, describes the costume but misunderstands the sequence of events. Ceserone also played a Delphian in intermedio 3 and a sailor in 5, at a monthly salary of 15 ducats: ASF, Depositeria generale 389, 17; Warburg, 300.

43. The lists, LC Q292 and N416, are partially transcribed in Warburg, "Costumi teatrali," 279.

44. LC T1, Q291; Warburg, "Costumi teatrali," 278–79; Nagler, *Theatre Festivals*, 78.

45. A schematic drawing by Buontalenti on one page of the *Libro di conti* (LC N430) has been suggested as a costume sketch for one of the attendants at the Pitti tournament (see cat. 70).

46. The rich documentation of the granducal household preserved in the ASF would repay a study of its economic and artistic organization beyond the scope of the present work. The principal archival sources on which I have relied for the period 1587–92 are the following (for details see Bibliography): GM, filze nos. 120, 122, 126, 128, 130, 131, 134, 137, 138, 142, 144, 148, 157, 159. Vaini is a "camera" employee, i.e., Ferdinando's personal staff, at 50 ducats a month; Fedini is a "guardaroba," or administrative officer, at 20 per month: ASF, Depositeria generale (parte antica), filza 389, 1–8. GM 120 is Fedini's record of all general liveries in 1588–89; he cites Vaini's responsibilities and authority, 2v; on Cavalieri's involvement with Fedini, see GM 120, 8v; GM 142, 110r, 111r.

47. Testaverde, "Creatività e tradizione," 185–86; the *Libro de' sarti* discussed earlier was from Milan, an important center for embroiderers (*ricamatori*). A letter of Nov. 15, 1588 to Ferdinando recounts the efforts of his agent in Milan, Pirro Malvezzi, to procure cloth of gold and embroidered trimmings there, at Vaini's orders: ASF, Carteggio mediceo, Principato, filza 802, 100.

48. Allori is mentioned frequently, sometimes as an evaluator of other artists' work for payment: see, e.g., GM 144, July 15 1588, Feb. 3 1589. On Allori's and Butteri's arch paintings, see cat. 1; on their ship décor, GM 157, 4, 12; Butteri's designs for the nuns, GM 144, Aug. 28, Nov. 14, 1588; further on them and other artists, see Chap. 3. Additional livery designs were produced by Count Francesco Paciotto, an architect on the court payroll: ASF, Depositeria generale 389, 11.

49. On the tailors see, among many references: GM 120, 7v–10r; GM 144, July 8, 1588, and Mar. 10, 1589 (Marchino); GM 148, 8r, 360r; GM 157, 38; GM 159, 19–112, 120, 138;

Testaverde, "Creatività e tradizione," 183–85 (erroneously citing GM 159, 142); ASF, Depositeria generale 389, 8. On Oreto and Allori, see GM 159, 104. On Oreto, GM 120, part 1, 23r and part 2, 1; GM 128, 11r; GM 144, Sept. 1, Sept. 30, 1588, Jan. 5, 1589; GM 157, 9 ff.; GM 159, 40, 105–6. For his household work, Oreto received 8 ducats a month, separate from his intermedi payments; Domenico, 12 per month.

50. For these costumes see Settimani, *Memorie*, 150r (cited in Berner, "Florentine Society," 226); GM 120, 7r–8r (cited in Testaverde, "Creatività e tradizione," 183). For more detail of individual livery costumes, see Chap. 6.

51. Separate from his general records of everyday livery matters, Fedini kept several notebooks to assist in preparations for the wedding, beginning in November and December; the title of one gives special attention to the "manufacture of liveries," and includes many sheets of names, drawn up on Dec. 17–18 and later, detailing the personages who needed to be outfitted, including Christine's own pages and other attendants. See GM 157, *Libro de' debitori e creditori della guardaroba . . . 1588, 1589, 1590, 1591* (a double-entry ledger, whose earliest notices pertaining to the wedding are dated Dec. 16, fol. 1); GM 142, *Quad.e e note attenenti alle manifatture de livree . . .* (earliest notices for the wedding are dated Nov. 4, fol. 61r). Lists of pages are at GM 142, fols. 196r (visitors from Rome), 198r (Ferdinando's own pages, total 31), and Christine's pages, 202–4 (10 names of pages and staff members, with costume specifications). For Franciosino's musicians, see GM 159, fol. 96r (Dec. 23). Extensive (and somewhat inconsistent) lists and descriptions of the liveries for attendees at Christine's entries are provided by Gualterotti, *Descrizione*, between books 1 and 2, and Cavallino, *Raccolta*, 23–32 (89 individuals plus their staffs).

52. For the numerous women cited, including eleven named convents, see GM 120, 23–77 passim; GM 128, 3 (nuns, sewing and embroidery); GM 144, Aug. 3–Nov. 14, 1588; GM 157 (nuns, clothing and household linens); GM 159, 1 (nuns, embroidery). On Chelini see GM 128, 11r; GM 148, 8r, 11r; GM 157, 19.

53. For these aristocratic suppliers see GM 157, 70–76. Lorenzo Guicciardini, for example, sold the Guardaroba 545 ducats' worth of velvet and other fabrics (on his family see Chaps. 5, 6).

54. For the bridge and painters at Palazzo Vecchio, see MR 14r (Dec. 16); for the committee, Settimani, *Memorie*, 85r. On Nov. 4, even before the "welcoming committee" was officially formed, Fedini was surveying the facilities and bedding available to lodge and feed the wedding guests: GM 142, 61r.

55. MR 3r–11r, 16r–18r, 21v (part transcr. Warburg, "Costumi teatrali," 399); see Chap. 3. (In 1608, Bardi again ordered alternation of rehearsal and painting under time pressure: see Chap. 1.)

56. "Ricordandoli l'importantia delle cose sue e l'interesse del offitio mio, e se quando si antivede i pericoli non si punisce e rimedia, non servono dopo sono seguite le disgratie": ASF, Carteggio mediceo, Principato, filza 802, 489, Dec. 22; transcr. Warburg, "Costumi teatrali," 396–97 (with wrong date of Dec. 25).

57. On the nuns, GM 157, 2–3; musicians, GM 159, 96r; Alfonso's letter, GM 142, 113r; see also Settimani, *Memorie*, 84r–85v, on Livorno preparations. While in Pisa, Ferdinando corresponded with Cavalieri regarding wedding preparations, MR 21v (Dec. 26), transcr. Warburg, "Costumi teatrali," 399. The grand duke's gift of jewels for his fiancée arrived in France on the 23rd, the same day that her cousin, the Duke of Guise, was assassinated by order of King Henri III.

58. For Ferdinando's activities see Settimani, *Memorie*, 78r–87r (entries for November–December 1588, by day); on Chelini, GM 148, 8r, 96r. The ritual of a cardinal putting on armor was later dramatized by the English playwright John Webster in *The Duchess of Malfi*, act 3, scene 4 (1614), loosely based on the lives of

Ferdinando and Francesco de' Medici (as was his earlier tragedy *The White Devil*).

3. THE THEATER, THE SCENERY, THE ARTISTS

1. ASF, Magistrato de' Nove Conservatori 3679, 23v (hereafter cited as MR): negotiations with Francesco di Matteo Calici, who had already been dyeing the red cloth for the theater curtains and the Pitti awning, reached agreement on Feb. 4 on prices for work both past and future (about one lira per braccio). The phrase "in Firenze" is preceded by the year 1588, so it may alternatively indicate the local calendar style (New Year in March); the Guardaroba records are continuous for January and February, indicating that normal operations were not interrupted elsewhere. On Catherine's death and funeral see Settimani, *Memorie*, 91r, 96r; preparations for mourning livery, ASF, Guardaroba medicea (hereafter cited as GM), filza 120, 3r (Feb. 2, pages' livery); GM 159, 108r, black silk ribbons and laces given to the same 29 pages, as well as to Maria de' Medici and the princesses' dwarf Camillo. See also Gaeta Bertelà and Petrioli Tofani, *Feste e apparati*, on the tradition of family ceremonies.

2. Goldthwaite, *Building of Renaissance Florence*, 24. For Vasari's work from 1565 to 1574, see most recently Leon Satkowski, *Giorgio Vasari: Architect and Courtier* (Princeton: Princeton University Press, 1993). For Buontalenti's work at the Uffizi and Palazzo Vecchio, see Daddi Giovannozzi, "Vita di Buontalenti," 509–13; Fara, *Bernardo Buontalenti: Architettura e teatro*; Hale, *Florence and the Medici*, 145–46. Jacopo Ligozzi, Agostino Ciampelli, and other artists who also worked on the wedding assisted in painting the Tribuna in 1588 (on them see below).

3. Goldthwaite, *Building of Renaissance Florence*, 17–25; see further Spini, *Architettura e politica*.

4. The Baldracca was provided with new cloth hangings before Dec. 2, 1588; for pay-

ments, see ASF, Magistrato de' Nove Conservatori, filza 3712, 104 (Jan. 5, 1589); wood for the grand duke's box, 106 (Sept. 3, 1588). On the Baldracca see Roselli et al., *Teatri di Firenze*, 51–57; Mamone, *Teatro nella Firenze*, 78–81 with sources, further bibliography; Fabbri et al., *Luogo teatrale*, 45; for surviving evidence of its appearance, Borsi et al., *Potere e lo spazio*, 370–74. After its owner, the theater was sometimes also called "della Dogana"; it now houses the Biblioteca Magliabecchiana.

5. MR IV; Berti, "Alcuni aspetti," 160. Characteristically, Buontalenti was already concerned over thrift, efficiency, and safety, insisting that the statues be given a coat of gesso before being lifted into place, since doing so afterward would require scaffolding and risk splattering the walls (presumably already painted). Sporadic earlier payments indicate that craftworkers and sculptors were engaged in large-scale interior remodeling work from January through August 1588: ASF, Magistrato de' Nove Conservatori, filza nos. 3712 (1585–88), cc. 86–87, 94–95, 98, 106, and 3713 (1588–93).

6. On the Olimpico and the place of the Uffizi in theater history, see Pevsner, *Building Types*, 63–90, s.v. "Theaters"; Kernodle, *From Art to Theatre*, 177–84; *Enciclopedia dello spettacolo*, 2: 1334–35, s.v. "Buontalenti"; Roselli et al., *Teatri di Firenze*, 38–40; Strong, *Art and Power*, 208n8. Earlier permanent theaters appeared at Ferrara in 1528 and 1577, in Mantua in 1549: see Blumenthal, *Giulio Parigi*, 80.

7. Roselli et al., *Teatri di Firenze*, 38–47; Borsi et al., *Potere e spazio*, 355–56; Fabbri et al., *Luogo teatrale*, 108, no. 8.4, and 105–8; Berti, "Alcuni aspetti," 160; Mamone, *Teatro nella Firenze*, 60–81; Pirrotta and Povoledo, *Music and Theatre*, 365–67. Blumenthal, *Giulio Parigi*, 85–87, 113, figs. 173–75, reproduces the first visual record of a proscenium arch at the theater of the Accademia degli Intronati, Siena (the group that performed *La pellegrina*), in 1560, and discusses the probable temporary proscenium for 1565. For the 1586 performance see Bastiano de' Rossi's printed *descrizione* of

that event (Florence, 1586), discussed by Warburg, "Costumi teatrali," illustrating surviving sketches; Botto, *Mostra di disegni*, viii, 44–46, no. 34.

8. The original entrance door mentioned by Rossi, *Descrizione dell'apparato*, 7, survives as the portal to the Gabinetto Disegni e Stampe, but the balcony over it for musicians has been removed. See the drawings by Buontalenti, Uffizi, GDS, Nos. 2374A, 2379A; Botto, *Mostra di disegni*, 41–43, no. 33, fig. 27.

9. The Callot (London, Victoria and Albert Museum, No. E2387-1962) represents a scene from "La liberazione di Tirreno e d'Arnea," performed for the wedding of Caterina de' Medici and Ferdinando Gonzaga. See Lieure, *Jacques Callot*, no. 185; Fabbri et al., *Luogo teatrale*, 123, no. 8.42; Blumenthal, *Giulio Parigi*, 37n78, 113n54; Roselli et al., *Teatri di Firenze*, 46.

10. Unfortunately, it is impracticable to reproduce here the numerous informative models and diagrams that recreate the space and its accoutrements, which include: Borsi et al., *Potere e spazio*, figs. 69–72; Fabbri et al., *Luogo teatrale*, 105–8; Lucchesini, *Teatri di Firenze*, 51–70, drawings of wall elevation and plan; Sergio Bertelli, *The Courts of the Italian Renaissance* (Milan: Mondadori, 1986), 138–39, color photographs of model. For a good overview of the design, though not illustrated, see Pirrotta and Povoledo, *Music and Theatre*, 364–82.

11. Rossi, *Descrizione dell'apparato*, 6–7, seems to suggest a stage depth of 25 braccia, followed by Mamone, *Teatro nella Firenze*, 116–20, though some modern sources estimate 20. On the theater design and decor see Gaeta Bertelà and Petrioli Tofani, *Feste e apparati*, 74; Mancini et al., *Illusione e pratica*, 42, on palcoscenico; Roselli et al., *Teatri di Firenze*, 39–43; Lucchesini, *Teatri di Firenze*, 59–65; Pirrotta and Povoledo, *Music and Theatre*, 208; Borsi et al., *Potere e spazio*, 355–56; Fabbri et al., *Luogo teatrale*, 36–37, 105–7; Nagler, *Theatre Festivals*, 73; Fara, *Buontalenti: Architettura e teatro*, 13–14.

12. The statues were completed by Dec. 6, when they were evaluated for payment. Giambologna's Roman in military dress, made of a mixture of clay or chalk (*creta pura*) and tow (*stoppa*), was rediscovered in 1972 and displayed at the base of the gallery access stair until the bombing in 1993 and the subsequent restoration; for an illustration see Roselli et al., *Teatri di Firenze*, 49–51. This figure corresponds exactly to one of the ten allegories described by Rossi: Epic Poetry, "a man of kingly majesty, and grandeur, armed, with sword in hand" (12; for description of the ceiling, 14–15).

13. For interior and seating see Rossi, *Descrizione dell'apparato*, 7–17; Pavoni, *Diario*, 14; Mamone, *Teatro nella Firenze*, 68–119; Roselli et al., *Teatri di Firenze*, 60n36. Gendered seating was also practiced in churches (as in synagogues of the period): Trexler, *Public Life*, 117. On Vasari's collapsible seating see Berti, "Alcuni aspetti," 160. Carpenters were ordered to work on new elements or additions to the gradi (small steps, etc.), MR 2v (Oct. 4); Vieri de' Medici, MR 6r.

14. On the proscenium front see Rossi, *Descrizione dell'apparato*, 35; Roselli et al., *Teatri di Firenze*, 43; Kernodle, *From Art to Theatre*, 177–80; Mamone, *Teatro nella Firenze*, 70. Callot's engraving (fig. 6) differs in showing the proscenium opening the full width of the auditorium — an unlikely detail, as this arrangement would leave no backstage area for hiding multiple sets, actors, etc. Although some critics maintain that the stair from auditorium to stage was merely painted on in illusionistic perspective, Rossi clearly says that it was functional and had a balustrade that concealed some of the footlights.

15. For the sixteenth-century history of perspective sets see Elena Povoledo, "Scenography," *Encyclopedia of World Art*, 17 vols. (New York: McGraw Hill, 1959–87), vol. 12, col. 763; idem, "Intermezzi" and "Italia: La scenografia prospettiva," *Enciclopedia dello spettacolo*, vol. 6, cols. 572–76, 649; Blumenthal, *Giulio Parigi*, chap. 3, esp. 80–82; Pirrotta and Povoledo,

Music and Theatre, 311–33 (fixed perspective sets), 335–83 (intermedi and movable sets). On the mathematical and political implications of the system, see originally Panofsky, *Perspective as Symbolic Form;* more recently, Starn and Partridge, *Arts of Power*, esp. 181.

16. The set is described by Rossi, *Descrizione dell'apparato*, 33–34; see Fabbri et al., *Luogo teatrale*, 116, no. 8.21.

17. Both periaktoi and floor shutters are described by various treatise writers on stagecraft; see Sabbattini, *Pratica di fabricar scene*, bk. 2, chaps. 4–9, 13–15; English trans. in Hewitt, *Renaissance Stage*, 100–104, 113–19. Blumenthal, *Giulio Parigi*, 88–89, 112n44, 116n65, traces their earlier development (derived from Vitruvius) with bibliography, and concludes they were probably used in 1589. James Middleton, stage director with the Baroque opera company Ex Machina (St. Paul, Minn.), strongly supports their presence in 1589 (personal communication, February 1993) and has demonstrated the practicability of quadrilateral telari in numerous productions. Inclined against their use are Nagler, *Theatre Festivals*, 79–80, and Pirrotta and Povoledo, *Music and Theatre*, 369–74. Berti, "Alcuni aspetti," 164–65, suggests a mix of flats and rotating pieces. Mancini et al., *Illusione e pratica*, 41–46, no. 9, illustrate a plausible alternative using flat sliding panels, which is close to my own conclusions.

18. Although de' Rossi does say once that "the scene was turned" (*si volta*), the reference is to intermedio 2, in which mobile grottoes were rotated to reveal the performers within. Pavoni uses *mutarsi* (*Diario*, 15, 16, 17, 20, etc.) and *coprirsi* (18); he, too, writes *si volta* only once (15). The term *voltarsi* may simply be used in the metaphoric sense of "turned into" something else: see Pirrotta and Povoledo, *Music and Theatre*, 374; Nagler, *Theatre Festivals*, 75. Seriacopi once refers to *telari* being built by carpenters for painters (MR 2v, Sept. 14), but the context suggests merely wooden frames covered with canvas, which could equally mean flat

shutters or even panels for the wall paintings; moreover, he lists stagehands specifically to operate sliding shutters, but not for *telari* (see below and Chap. 4).

19. MR 16r (Dec. 23): "alla prima nugola verso le stanze delli zanni e comedianti" and "alla seconda nugola verso il corridore riscontro"; Nagler, *Theatre Festivals*, 78, notes this usage but misinterprets "stanze delli zanni" to refer to dressing rooms within the Uffizi itself. Praise for the smooth set changes notwithstanding, the machinery was undoubtedly noisy and irregular by modern standards; Sabbattini, *Pratica di fabricar scene*, bk. 2, chap. 1, suggests ways to distract the audience during scene changes.

20. Reconstructions of the stage area and equipment have been attempted by Nagler, *Theatre Festivals*, 79–80; Mancini et al., *Illusione e pratica*, 41–46 with diagrams; Middleton, personal communication; Blumenthal, *Giulio Parigi*; Zorzi, *Teatro e città*, 109–18, pls. 69–72; Fabbri et al., *Luogo teatrale*, 105. See also Helen Purkis, "La Décoration de la salle et les rapports entre le scène et le public dans les mascarades et les intermèdes florentins, 1539–1608," in Jacquot, *Fêtes*, 3: 239–51. The closest surviving apparatus, though severely damaged, is at the Teatro Farnese, Parma, surviving drawings for which show ropes, pulleys, and telescoping platforms: for reproductions see Nagler, *Theatre Festivals*, figs. 131, 136; Strong, *Splendor at Court*, figs. 141, 168.

21. Rope order, MR 3v (Oct. 29); construction of catwalks or "sky bridges" (*i ponti del cielo*), 39r (Mar. 28); hanging canvas drops, 50v (Apr. 25). Falling curtain, Rossi, *Descrizione dell'apparato*, 15, 17; Pavoni, *Diario*, 21; Sabbattini, *Pratica di fabricar scene*, bk. 1 (trans. Hewitt, *Renaissance Stage*, 90–92); Warburg, "Costumi teatrali," 272; Kernodle, *From Art to Theatre*, 199–200; Nagler, *Theatre Festivals*, 73 (in error); and Strong, *Splendor at Court*, 180 (in error). *Il Corago*, 116–17, reviews methods of curtain movement and mentions Buontalenti's innovations. One backcloth, at least, was sewn

by a woman, Madonna Margherita (see Chap. 2). Cloud machines were already used in 1586, and are visible in the one surviving drawing from that event, Uffizi, GDS, No. 7059F: see Warburg, "Costumi teatrali," fig. 77; Gaeta Bertelà and Petrioli Tofani, *Feste e apparati*, 60, no. 31; Fabbri et al., *Luogo teatrale*, 109, no. 8.5.

22. The list for Dec. 23 is found at MR 16r–18r (part transcr. Warburg, "Costumi teatrali," 399); the second, 30v–34r (Mar. 16). I have used the second list for calculations here, as presumably closer to the final configuration. The latter also lists nearly fifty names for men to light, refill, and watch over the numerous lamps in house and stage areas and indicates constant changes of personnel and their assignments; on the stage crew see further Chap. 4.

23. Alternatively, the "great cloud" (*nugola grande*) of intermedio 4, holding the demons of the air, may have been the central unit, with extensions: it required ten men, one "eel," and five more men to open it when reached the center. On rising and falling clouds, heavenly "paradise" techniques, and horizontal movement through the air, see Sabbattini, *Pratica di fabricar scene*, bk. 2, chaps. 43–54 (trans. Hewitt, *Renaissance Stage*, 153–74). The grid also supported wires for the flight of Apollo: two named men, doubtless standing on the catwalks, launched the cardboard figure from above on an iron wire.

24. Most of these were probably on sliding shutters, though Pavoni, *Diario*, says that the Rome backdrop rose up, so it may have been a single hanging cloth. Moreover, the wooded backdrop of 3 was somewhat altered from that of 2 by being fitted with shutters (*sportelli*) in the center, showing scorched trees around a cave mouth, through which the dragon entered. Additional drops may have modified the *Pellegrina* set away from Pisa for the two later comedies: see cat. 68.

25. MR 32v–33r; Rossi, *Descrizione dell'apparato*, 38; the devil of intermedio 4 utilized only a single *verricello* with four crewmen. On traps and rising platforms, especially for hell scenes,

see Sabbattini, *Pratica di fabricar scene*, bk. 2, chaps. 17–24, illustrating a telescoping platform (trans. Hewitt, *Renaissance Stage*, 119–25); Berti, "Alcuni aspetti," 164–65. A reconstruction diagram of the mountain machine for 1589, based on Sabbattini, is reproduced in Borsi et al., *Potere e spazio*, 340, no. 3.22.

26. Simulated waves had been developed for the 1586 intermedi; because the new wave machine, perhaps merely a restoration of the existing one, was among the first elements to be constructed (MR 1v, Aug. 31), Seriacopi's log contains no further information about it. On wave machines, see Sabbattini, *Pratica di fabricar scene*, bk. 2, chaps. 27–33 (trans. Hewitt, *Renaissance Stage*, 130–43); Nagler, *Theatre Festivals*, 87–88. In addition, the floor was probably painted with a perspective grid to emphasize and measure spatial recession: see Kernodle, *From Art to Theatre*, 180; a sketch by Buontalenti, possibly for the 1586 production, shows such a grid (Uffizi, GDS, No. 2306A; Botto, *Mostra di disegni*, no. 34, fig. 28).

27. The windlass preserved at the Farnese Theater is a massive wooden cylinder about five feet in diameter and two feet thick, not many of which could have fit in the Medici theater on one level (at least four on each side are called for). A drawing by Inigo Jones for an English production of 1640, inspired by Florentine models (see Chap. 7), shows such mechanical equipment placed beneath the floor (illustrated in Strong, *Art and Power*, no. 105). Offstage balconies behind the sets are mentioned by Sabbattini, *Pratica di fabricar scene*, bk. 1, chap. 36 (trans. Hewitt, *Renaissance Stage*, 89–90) as a means to accommodate the musicians — who were here, as Rossi notes (*Descrizione dell'apparato*, 20), scattered through the upper heaven and elsewhere within the stage area.

28. MR 1v (Aug. 31). On Vasari's work for 1565, see Vasari, *Vite*, 8: 520–617. On Buontalenti's creativity in lighting, see Rossi, *Descrizione dell'apparato*, 15–16; *Enciclopedia dello spettacolo*, 2: 1334–35, s.v. "Buontalenti"; Berti, "Alcuni aspetti," 161–62; Blumenthal, *Giulio*

Parigi, 106; Molinari, *Nozze degli dèi*, 48–89; Nagler, *Theatre Festivals*, 79–80. On stage lighting equipment and procedures of the time, see Sabbattini, *Pratica di fabricar scene*, bk. 1, chaps. 38–41; for technical details drawn from the 1586 intermedi, Pirrotta and Povoledo, *Music and Theatre*, 378–79.

29. Rossi, *Descrizione dell'apparato*, 9, 14–15; MR 2v (Oct. 4), 3r (Oct. 12), 25r (Feb. 13); Mamone, *Teatro nella Firenze*, 70, 117–20.

30. On Dec. 23 (MR 19v–20r), Buontalenti listed three types of lanterns and the numbers required: For the comedy, 100 long square ones with four lights each, 220 large round ones with four lights, and 200 small round ones with two lights; for the Pitti tournament, 200 large square, 100 large round, 200 small round. Of these, 268 were on hand, the rest to be manufactured by Salvatore the lampmaker (*lanternaio*).

31. Rossi, *Descrizione dell'apparato*, 33–35; Blumenthal, *Giulio Parigi*, 92; Mamone, *Teatro nella Firenze*, 70–71. On lighting techniques, including shutters and adjustable candle holders, see Sabbattini, *Pratica di fabricar scene*, bk. 1, chaps. 38–41, bk. 2, chaps. 12–16, 55 (trans. Hewitt, *Renaissance Stage*, 92–99, 111–19, 174). That lights were mounted on the comedy houses again supports the contention that these units were fixed, not rotating.

32. For the Pitti lists, MR 5r. The same list calls for 50 large "field lanterns" and unspecified amounts of smaller candles and torches. For further details on Pitti lighting see MR 5r–8v (Nov. 22–29). MR 25r (Mar. 2) records a request to modify the theater lamps so that they can be lit without having to be lowered to the stage floor but does not explain how this is to be arranged. Further details on lighting design and supply recur from March through the date of performance: MR 27r–28v, 37v, 39v, 40v–41r, 43v, 45r, 49r–v, 51v–52v.

33. Rossi, *Descrizione dell'apparato*, 16, 34–35; MR 25v (Mar. 2), Buontalenti requests the perforations in the ceiling to be made "as appears in the model [*mostra*]"; MR 27v (Mar. 14).

34. ASF, Carteggio mediceo, Principato, filza 805, c. 21 (letter to Ferdinando, Mar. 2, 1589). See also MR 9v (Dec. 6), "I've gone to the Pitti."

35. On Ammannati's salary (20 ducats per month) see ASF, Depositeria generale (parte antica), filza 389, 11; for his work as estimator, MR 9v, Dec. 6 (the wording, "per pregiare le statue . . . se ne pigli informazione," is ambiguous, for Giambologna also made one of these statues). For biographical background and sources see Pope-Hennessy, *High Renaissance and Baroque*, 372–77.

36. Cioli: Warburg, "Costumi teatrali," 396, 400, with biographical sources in Baldinucci and Borghini; MR 9v (Dec. 6), Feb. 7; *Primato del disegno*, 107. In the household payroll of 1588, Cioli's salary is 15 ducats per month: ASF, Dep. generale 389, 11. For Giambologna on the granducal payroll, see ASF, Depositeria generale 389, 11 (September 1588, 25 ducats per month), and further below for his work at Palazzo Vecchio. See generally Charles Avery, *Giambologna: The Complete Sculpture* (Mt. Kisco, N.Y.: Moyer Bell, 1987); Pope-Hennessy, *High Renaissance and Baroque*, 380–89.

37. On Allori see Freedberg, *Painting in Italy*, 608–19; *Primato del disegno*, 51–54; as evaluator of Cigoli, ASF, Depositeria generale, Registro 416, c. 42, Nov. 12 (128 scudi). Allori was earlier recorded as approving a craftworker's payment request to Seriacopi at the Uffizi gallery, Aug. 1587: ASF, GM 134, c. 629; he also had an interest in decorative arts, serving as head of the granducal tapestry workshops in 1576.

38. On Santi see Freedberg, *Painting in Italy*, 620–25; the concise biographical summary in *Primato del disegno*, 204–5; Bacou, *Seizième Siècle*, 239. Other artists from this generation who participated in 1589 (for partial listings see Warburg, "Costumi teatrali," 416) include: Giovanni Stradano (Jan van der Straeten, 1523–1605), *Primato del disegno*, 212–13; Girolamo Macchietti (1535–92), ibid., 136; Giovanbattista Naldini (ca. 1537–91), a pupil of Pontormo, 148–52; and Allori's partner Giovanmaria Butteri (1540–1606), 92.

39. For notices of Alfonso, see: MR 16r, 27v, 31r, 32r, 33v, 35v, 46r, 68r (stage crew); ASF, Magistrato dei Nove 3712, c. 86 (Palazzo Vecchio, January–August 1588); ASF, Fabbriche medicee filza 24, c. 83r (Palazzo Vecchio, August 1588). On the Parigi family, see Blumenthal, *Giulio Parigi*, esp. chaps. 1, 2, and appendixes A, B; Elena Povoledo, "Parigi, Giulio" and "Parigi, Alfonso," *Enciclopedia dello spettacolo*, cols. 1675–78. Giulio's son, Alfonso the Younger, continued the family tradition (see Chap. 7).

40. Warburg, "Costumi teatrali," 416, lists various artists involved, with older biographical citations; for biographical summaries of this third generation see, in addition to standard sources (Thieme-Becker; Freedberg, *Painting in Italy*; Baldinucci, *Notizie dei professori*; Pope-Hennessy, *High Renaissance and Baroque*), the concise biographies provided in *Primato del disegno* for Giovanni Balducci (Cosci, 1560–1631), 67; Ludovico Buti (1550–1611), who painted a portrait of the programmer Niccolò Gaddi (see above, Chap. 1), 91–92; sculptor Giovanni Battista Caccini (1559/62–1613), brother of the musician Giulio, 92–93; Agostino Ciampelli (1565–1630, pupil of Santi, collaborated with Ligozzi on the Tribuna), 100; Alessandro del Barbiere Fei (cat. 6; 1543–92), 111; Jacopo Chimenti da Empoli (1551–1640), 112–13; Jacopo Ligozzi (1547–1627), 134–36 (for his salary, see ASF, Depositeria generale 389, 11; ASF, Fabbriche medicee 24, c. 138r; other payment records, ASF, GM 183, 1588 no. 4); Valerio Marucelli (ca. 1563–1620), 139–40; Gregorio (Goro) Pagani (1558–1603), Santi pupil, 152; Passignano (Domenico Cresti, 1559–1638), pupil of Macchietti and Naldini, who at the same time frescoed the new chapel of Saint Antoninus prepared at San Marco for the wedding, 155; Bernardino Poccetti, architectural pupil of Buontalenti (1548–1612), 165; Poppi (Francesco Morandini, 1544–97), 176–79. On other entry arch designers, such as Taddeo Landini (cat. 5), who came from Rome about 1585, see Daddi Giovannozzi, "Alcune inci-

sioni," 100; on Giovanantonio Dosio (cat. 4, 7), who also designed the funerary chapel for Gaddi, at Santa Maria Novella, see Heydenreich and Lotz, *Architecture in Italy*, 324.

41. On Boscoli see Freedberg, *Painting in Italy*, 629–30; *Primato del disegno*, 80. The duomo project, involving various painters, proceeded from the 1570s until Ferdinando hastened its completion; see Miles Chappell, "The Decoration of the Cupola of the Cathedral in Florence for the Wedding of Ferdinando I de' Medici in 1589," *Paragone* 467 (1989): 57–60. The grand duke's involvement with the duomo was illustrated by Callot: Lieure, *Jacques Callot*, no. 149.

42. Matteoli, *Cigoli*, reprints much original source material, including the biography by Baldinucci, and discusses Cigoli's theatrical activity, 274–77, no. 173; payments for the Prato arch, 423. See further Faranda, *Ludovico Cardi*; Chappell, *Disegni di Cigoli*, 6 (duomo), cat. 5 (Petraia); Molinari, "Attività teatrale." On Cigoli as architect, see Heydenreich and Lotz, *Architecture in Italy*, 97–98.

43. Cosimo I, who chartered the Accademia delle arti del disegno, envisioned it as a channel for state patronage. On the Accademia and artists' attempts to raise their intellectual and professional status throughout the century, see Freedberg, *Painting in Italy*, 469; Rossi, *Dalle botteghe alle accademie*; Warnke, *Court Artist*; and generally, on the rise of status based on literature in the wake of the spread of printing, Wolff, *Social Production of Art*, 35–40, with further references.

44. On artists' working conditions and social standing, see Rossi, *Dalle botteghe alle accademie*; Arnold Hauser, *The Social History of Art* (1951), repr. 4 vols. (London: Routledge, 1968), esp. 2: 48–61; M. Wackernagel, *The World of the Florentine Renaissance Artist*, trans. A. Luchi (1938; repr. Princeton: Princeton University Press, 1981), largely on the fifteenth century; Bruce Cole, *The Renaissance Artist at Work from Pisano to Titian* (New York, 1983); Warnke, *Court Artist*, 129–42. For working conditions two gener-

ations earlier, see the exhaustive study by Wallace, *Michelangelo at San Lorenzo.*

45. For payments to Allori: ASF, GM 144, Jan. 21, 26, Feb. 3, 1589; Allori's letter to Fedini regarding Butteri, GM 183, entries for 1588, no. 7. In September 1589 he was receiving 8 ducats a month for services for Emilio de' Cavalieri, that is, for the Uffizi/Galleria fine arts administration: ASF, Depositeria generale 389, c. 11. The fullest accounts for him are in ASF, GM 157 (Jan. 1, 1588/89 through 1590, weekly pay records): Allori received 14 ducats on May 17 "per più lavoranti tenuti à pitti à mettere d'oro uno armadio," c. 12. Butteri himself was credited with amounts of 35 ducats a week in January and February, suggesting that he had his own "sub-crew" of assistants to pay within the larger workshop, whose overall receipts go to Allori. Other named painters received 10–19 ducats a week, raising the further question whether this included amounts for supplies; on such questions see Chap. 4. Cigoli similarly set up an independent workshop about 1588 but also worked on salary for the Medici palace crew.

46. For payments to Giambologna "a spese per la bottegha" who were working on the Cosimo sculpture, as well as on a well and/or fountain at the Palazzo Vecchio, see ASF, Fabbriche medicee, filza 24, cc. 33r–34r (Aug. 13 and Sept. 10, 1588), etc.; two rooms of this bottega were whitewashed at Fabbrica expense (c. 93r). At other points in this log, however, his subordinate workers are accounted for and paid individually (34r). Giambologna himself also received a flat salary of 25 ducats per month for his state work in 1588: ASF, Depositeria generale 389, c. 11. Later, in 1594, among 46 artists on the state payroll, he continued to receive the same salary: Grazilla Silli, *Una corte alla fine del '500* (Florence, 1928), 35, cited in Berner, "Florentine Society," 207. On the Salviati Chapel see Michael E. Flack, "Giambologna's Cappella di Sant'Antonino for the Salviati Family" (Ph.D. diss., Columbia University, 1986); Pope-Hennessy, *High Renaissance and Baroque,*

386–87 (with text of letter citing granducal consent, noting that they had raised his salary to 50 scudi a month); on the statue of Cosimo, ibid., 387–88. The patrons of the chapel were Averardo and Antonio di Filippo Salviati; the cloth manufacturer is named as Filippo d'Antonio. Further complicating the situation was the personal interest in encouraging St. Antoninus' cult by the Archbishop of Florence, Alessandro de' Medici (later Pope Leo XI), a cousin of Ferdinando's.

47. MR 25r–v (Mar. 2); part transcr. Warburg, "Costumi teatrali," 400–401.

48. "Li atterrai con ragioni vive di sorte che penso non li dira più cosi alla libera essendoli da efficaci ragioni ributtati": ASF, Carteggio mediceo, Principato, filza 805, c. 21; part transcr. Warburg, "Costumi teatrali," 397. The letter also mentions that Buontalenti's list still did not cover some items needed for the Pitti joust, but this, at least, was not Buontalenti's fault: decisions were still pending from Cavalieri, on which Seriacopi planned to meet with him the next day.

49. The contracts for the dragon components had been agreed upon on Feb. 7, at Bardi's insistence, but apparently not yet carried out; see MR 24r and Chap. 4. For the specifications and construction method, see cat. 50. Much of this section of the MR is transcribed by Blumenthal, *Giulio Parigi,* 117n72.

50. "Ogni sorte serve": MR, 4r–8v, for preparations from Nov. 22–28; 12v–13v, further orders for Dec. 12–15. The mechanics and setting are also described by Pavoni, *Diario,* 40–42. Fuller's earth (*terra di purgho*), used in cloth processing, was procured from the wool guild (*Arte della Lana*).

51. For the boat search, see MR 14v (Dec. 20), 22v (Jan. 1). As the total cost per used boat, including repairs and elaborate transportation on wagons, averaged about 80 lire, the savings were relatively small; probably they needed both sources of supply to meet the overall requisition.

52. For the Palazzo Vecchio campaign, see

ASF, Scrittoio delle fortezze e fabbriche, Fabbriche medicee, filza no. 24 (*Palazzo Ducale 1588*), a record of continuous construction and decoration from July 1588 to March 1589. For Seriacopi's weekly mention in the pay records, see cc. 113r (Sept. 17), 194 (Jan. 21), etc.; on Ligozzi, 138r; on Giambologna's *fonte di piazza* and *pozzo*, 181v–182r (Jan. 2). For his statue of Cosimo, in progress since late 1587, see the observation in Pope-Hennessy, *High Renaissance and Baroque*, 387, that the sculptor asked the painters Cigoli and Pagani to suggest alternate designs.

53. MR 9v (Dec. 6), 21v (Dec. 25); ASF, Fabbriche medicee 24, cc. 83r (Parigi, August), 116r (*testata*), 127r (Parigi, October), 128r, 138r (Ligozzi), 140r (*testata*, Dec. 10), 230r (*testata*, Mar. 6), 232r (kitchen, Mar. 10, 13).

54. ASF, Depositeria generale, registro 416, c. 42 (Nov. 12); Matteoli, *Cigoli*, 274–77, no. 123; Chappell, *Disegni di Cigoli*, 5, no. 3. For artists and details, see Chap. 1 and cat. 1–7.

55. ASF, GM 142 (Fedini's account book), 155v, 157v, 158r, 159v (Feb. 16), 191r, 192r.

56. On the fleet and ships, see Settimani, *Memorie*, 84r (December), 91r (Jan. 12). On Chelini, GM 148, 5r, 8r, 96r (Dec. 22, 26; Oreto the tailor was also to make two outfits for the ship's crew, Dec. 30, Jan. 24). On musicians: GM 159, 105–6, 112. Butteri worked until mid-February, after which his partner Allori seems to have taken over; payments for work by Butteri (Jan. 7–Feb. 11) and by Allori (Feb. 10–May 26): GM 157, 12. On galley décor, describing sumptuous bedclothes and hangings received from Chelini, starting on Feb. 28: GM 120, 11r–12v.

57. MR 25v (Mar. 2): "Crescer la nuvola del primo intermedio che vada più alta della Sig.ra Vittoria"; MR 27v (Mar. 11, houses blocking clouds). See also Warburg, "Costumi teatrali," 402; Nagler, *Theatre Festivals*, 80.

58. MR 25v: "sendosi provato l'intermedio della nave non ci ha visto novizzi bombardieri che se nessuno di[?] essi[?] ci fussino stati." These added troops were painted figures, not living cast, for he says that "he would like to have them put in operation, and will have them given out to be made (dice che li harebbe messi in opera et harrà dato loro da fare et questo per non traspedire a comandamenti di S.A.S.)". This would resolve a conflict between two accounts of the number of the ship's crew. Rossi (*Descrizione dell'apparato*, 57) claims that there were 40 men, which seems an impossibly large number for the size of the stage, whereas Pavoni (*Diario*, 20) estimates 25; perhaps 15 out of 40 were artificial.

59. MR 25v: "si come più fa dice haver detto al proved.re e ancho per essere sopra il chapo di S.A. vorrebbe fussino gente fidate et pratiche che nascendo inconvenienti il proved.ore possa punire et gastigare d.o."

60. Gualterotti, *Descrizione*, 1: 4; Settimani, *Memorie*, 97r. Gaeta Bertelà and Petrioli Tofani, *Feste e apparati*, 67, usefully summarize the wedding and subsequent events; Strong, *Splendor at Court*, 172, misstates several points.

61. On arms control see Berner, "Florentine Society," 218, with source in Settimani; and above, Introduction.

62. Strong, *Splendor at Court*, 172.

4. ARTISANS, STAGEHANDS, TECHNICAL REHEARSALS; CHRISTINE'S OUTBOUND JOURNEY

1. At the Palazzo Vecchio, as at the theater, the pace was intensifying. On Mar. 11, ten *libbre* of candles were ordered "for working on the palazzo and the fabbrica [Uffizi workshops] and for the piping [*condotti*] of the fountains in the piazza and the palace," suggesting that work was now extended into evening overtime (another ten pounds were requested on Mar. 22): ASF, Scrittoio delle fortezze e fabbriche, Fabbriche medicee, filza 24, 232. A further note on p. 238 refers to "restoring" the piazza fountain, which had been installed earlier; the fountain inside the palace may be Verrocchio's fifteenth-century *Putto with a Dolphin*.

2. ASF, Carteggio mediceo, filza 805, 316.

3. MR 36v; Malvezzi was also consulted on Apr. 5, MR 39v.

4. MR 26r–v; transcr. Warburg, "Costumi teatrali," 402; the date for rehearsal of "all the intermedi" is noted at MR 28r (Mar. 13).

5. For earlier records of these items see MR 24r (Feb. 7), 25r–v (Mar. 2), and above, Chap. 3; preparation of the giant ship for intermedio 5, MR 39r, 43v (Mar. 28, Apr. 9), transcr. Warburg, "Costumi teatrali," 406.

6. Flower orders, MR 26r (Mar. 9), 36r (Mar. 18); transcr. Warburg, "Costumi teatrali," 404. For the nuns' payment in May, see LC Q188 and above, Chap. 2; later orders, MR 39r–v (Mar. 29).

7. Similarly, on Apr. 8 Tornaquinci reported to Gorini that he had calculated a need for 50 artificial flowers of various kinds (*fiorellini*), even after Buontalenti's extensive orders of a few weeks before. On Tornaquinci, see MR 36r (Mar. 18); 43r (Apr. 8); and his cast list for shoes discussed in Chap. 2, 44r (Apr. 9).

8. MR 36r (Mar. 18), 39r (Mar. 28); transcr. Warburg, "Costumi teatrali," 404.

9. On Caccini's nickname and this incident see Baldinucci, *Notizie dei professori*, 2: 490–532; Pirrotta and Povoledo, *Music and Theatre*, 375. Lack of confidence in the machinery's stability was seen in Chap. 3, when Buontalenti placed struts under the risen mountain of intermedio 2; further on such struts and props, MR 39r (Mar. 28).

10. These processes are identified and described for the 1565 entry and theatricals by Starn and Partridge, *Arts of Power*, 206–7, who assert that the theoretical separation of "design and execution coincided with their increasingly common separation in practice because of the large scale and short deadlines of state projects."

11. For Buontalenti's final inventory and will see Blumenthal, *Giulio Parigi*, 100 and n. 93, with sources; and below, Chap. 7.

12. Lanterns, MR 40v (Apr. 5); for work in the theater, the painter-partners Francesco Rosselli and Lorenzo Francini signed an agreement "to perform all the tasks that are in the *modello*" at a preset total rate, MR 14r (Dec. 16). On the importance of drawings to define and enforce a chief artist's conceptions for executants, see Warnke, *Court Artist*, 185–88; Wallace, *Michelangelo at San Lorenzo*, 170–74.

13. For Buontalenti's sketches, see MR 13v (Dec. 15), pulley; 28r (Mar. 13), swag; 40r (Apr. 5), platform. On the dragon: MR 24r (Feb. 7), transcr. Warburg, "Costumi teatrali," 400. On one occasion the log specifies both a *modello* and a *disegno* for Alessandro Pieroni: 41v (Apr. 7).

14. Occasionally related terms are used, such as *saggio* (trial or test-piece), *esemplo* (example or sample), and *campione* (pattern, specimen to be copied); see, e.g., MR 8r–v (Nov. 28–29). For the demonstration, MR 7v (Nov. 28); as shown in Chap. 1, Buontalenti's presence at the three main sites rotated daily. On the similar coordinating role of Vasari in 1565, see Starn and Partridge, *Arts of Power*, 203–12. On the development of architectural drawings and models (three-dimensional models were common), see Goldthwaite, *Building of Renaissance Florence*, 367–85.

15. Awning, MR 20v (Dec. 24); garlands, MR 27r–28r (Mar. 13). Modelli were made for all three central Florentine sites. At the theater, Buontalenti provided modelli or mostre for numerous subsidiary elements, such as costumes (see Chap. 2); lighting fixtures, MR 6v–7r (Nov. 26), 40v (Apr. 5); stairs on the front parapet of the stage, for which Alessandro Pieroni received both a modello and a disegno, 39v (Apr. 4), 41v (Apr. 7); Pieroni also painted an entry arch, cat. 1. Giovanni Mettidoro, a gilder, made two pairs of cardboard wings from Buontalenti's design, as a mostra for putti and devil figures, which were then approved by Buontalenti. Here the term suggests a "sample" of Giovanni's ability to follow instructions; passing the test allowed him to get the job for all 28 pairs: MR 37v, 42r, 45r, 46r ((Mar. 23–Apr. 13). At the Pitti, Buontalenti sketched the joust barricade, etc.: MR 7r–8v (Nov. 27–28), and made

other drawings for Rosselli and Francini. And at the Palazzo Vecchio, Buontalenti, probably working with Alfonso Parigi, provided a modello for the bridge leading from the Uffizi to the banquet hall, and for the platform in the hall, MR 21v (Dec. 25; see above, Chaps. 2, 3).

16. "Quanto prima": MR 38v (Mar. 26), 39v (Mar. 29). Threats to painters: MR 40r (Apr. 5), transcr. Warburg, "Costumi teatrali," 404, ending with "acciò faccia quello che merita loro troppa tardita." Poccetti also painted the coats of arms in the theater, MR 38v, 39v (Apr. 4), and one of the entry arches (cat. 7).

17. Pitti cost comparisons: MR 29r (Mar. 14), 37v (Mar. 18); lists of records, 29v (Mar. 16). To meet changing demands and resources, materials were often shifted from one storehouse or account to another, and equipment, such as scaffolding, that was no longer needed at one work site would be moved to a new one; such transfers were duly noted, as when Seriacopi instructed Gorini, "Get two spruce logs from the workshop at the palace, and arrange with the clerk that the work will be charged to the comedy, for these two and for the others": MR 38r (Mar. 27; on the same page, he orders the leftover lumber advanced to a carpenter for soon-to-be-completed work in the "musicians' rooms" be taken to the workshop for the comedy); see also 49r (Apr. 19). Similarly, when an unnamed painter was engaged to paint final details on the magpies of intermedio 2 and one of the dragons' wings, Seriacopi admonished Gorini, "Each time you give [some of] them out, write them down, and when getting them back see that you've received all of them. And when none are missing, countersign [the record book], because [otherwise] someone will have to pay for them": MR 52r (Apr. 29), transcr. Warburg, "Costumi teatrali," 409.

18. On Nellio, MR 38r (Mar. 27); artists' signatures, Alessandro Pieroni, 44v (Apr. 9), and Rosselli and Francini, below. For additional agreements about prices and materials, see the theater carpenter contracts, MR 2v (Sept. 16); Pitti carpenter contracts, 10r (Dec. 7–9), 23v

(Feb. 4, dyers), etc.; and Berti, "Alcuni aspetti," 159. Artisans sometimes took pains to specify what responsibilities they were *not* undertaking: Andrea di Antonio accepted a commission for Pitti courtyard swags "declaring that he is not to be held responsible for putting them up, but only for fabricating them": MR 28r (Mar. 13). Similar careful record keeping and payment agreements can be glimpsed at the Palazzo Vecchio and the gallery workshops at the Uffizi, where individual craftworkers were required to keep daily logs of their labor on each *cottimo*; some personalized the paper covers of their individual booklets (*quadernaccio*) with small sketches, such as the hammer and anvil drawn by a smith: ASF, Guardaroba medicea (hereafter cited as GM), filza 134, esp. cc. 454–515. This wage-labor system contrasts with the practices under the more independent guilds, which the state gradually co-opted or subsumed in the sixteenth century; see Goldthwaite, *Building of Renaissance Florence*, 252–72.

19. On Orazio and Domenico, see MR 1v (Aug. 31), 2r (Sept. 1), 2v (Sept. 16), 8v (Nov. 29), 21v (Dec. 26), 35v (Mar. 18), 38r (Mar. 23), 42r (Apr. 7), 49r (Apr. 19). Orazio received a commission to make 17 candelabra for the auditorium (MR 2v), but 18 were required (see Chap. 3), so one must have been made previously as the mostra for him to copy. Both men are among a half-dozen carpenters who signed a set of contract clauses (*capitoli*) for the Pitti on Dec. 7 (MR 10r).

20. Palazzo Vecchio, MR 21v (Dec. 26), transcr. Warburg, "Costumi teatrali," 399; dragon, MR 24r (Feb. 7), transcr. Warburg, 400, specifying pieces in clay, probably forms for casting the lighter, final material. For a detailed cottimo for the carpenters, see MR 25r (Mar. 20).

21. Carpenters vs. painters: MR 2v (Sept. 14); ultimatum to Orazio and Atticiato: 28r (Mar. 13): "altrimenti mi incolloreri con detti malamente."

22. Other examples of a cottimo to be executed *a tutta sua spese:* MR 1v (Aug. 31, lathe

worker); 3r (Oct. 12); 10r (Dec. 10, lamp maker); 14r (Dec. 16); 46r (Apr. 13). On Mar. 13, garlands were sent for bids, but a calculation of the cost of required tinsel was made before the bidding and taken into account by all parties (MR 28r).

23. Delli and *festoni*, MR 27r (Mar. 13), 46r (Apr. 13); a carpenter is given materials to make props, MR 28v (Mar. 14). For the hybrid arrangements, see MR 2r (Sept. 2, Domenico), 28v (Mar. 14), 29v (Mar. 16).

24. "Con più vantaggio si puo": MR 2r (Sept. 7). Giovanni agreed to work for 16 lire per figure *a tutte sue spese* for gesso and gold but was warned that if his work was not of good quality the payment would be reduced to 12 lire (Sept. 9). Other bargaining with craftworkers: MR 3r (Oct. 29).

25. Jacopo di Lessandro, MR 27r (Mar. 13), with six names; ironworker, 24v (Feb. 25); swords, 23v (Feb. 6). Additional examples of competitive bids: MR 20r (Dec. 23, lamps for Pitti); 20v (Dec. 24, Pitti awning); 22r (Dec. 29, Pitti lighting); 28r (Mar. 13, Pitti garlands). On bidding and cost concerns in the logbook see generally Berti, "Alcuni aspetti," 159.

26. Piero, MR 40v (Apr. 5); Cioli, 24r (Feb. 7), transcr. Warburg, "Costumi teatrali," 400. On Mar. 16 Orazio the carpenter agreed to make the theater smoke vents, but Seriacopi then took the job away when he found another carpenter willing to work at a lower price (MR 29v). Some indication of administrators' hard-nosed attitude toward the labor force comes from Bardi's counterpart for the 1565 wedding, Vincenzo Borghini, who warned his quartermaster about price negotiations with artists, "Beware of the greed . . . of certain ugly animals": Starn and Partridge, *Arts of Power*, 201.

27. Stefano Pieri, MR 10r–v; Baldinucci, *Notizie dei professori*, 3: 501–2. On the firing, MR 38v (Mar. 26): "Poiche lessandro di casentino ha abbandonato il salone, e io non sono potuto entrare dua o tre volte che ci sono tornato se li dia buona licentia, non havendo bisogno di chi stia tanto assente. . . . E se questo li dispiace

consideri ch'a me molto piu dispiacque in non potere spedire le mia faccende mediante lui." Alessandro Pieroni, behind schedule on the painted stair for the stage parapet, was threatened with a replacement at his expense, MR 44v (Apr. 9).

28. Rossi, *Descrizione dell'apparato*, 8: "Lorenzo Francini, si come, e di lui, e di Francesco Rosselli, artefici, non solamente d'assai speranza, ma di gran prova, è stato tutto 'l carico, e di dipignere, e far dipignere, salvo la Prospettiva, tutto 'l rimanente." On the two painters see also Nagler, *Theatre Festivals*, 73; Gaeta Bertelà and Petrioli Tofani, *Feste e apparati*, 74. The latter repeat Rossi's erroneous statement that the two men did not paint the stage sets: references throughout Seriacopi's log show at least Rosselli's participation in scenic work. In December he had requested that a scaffold be erected on the stage so he could paint the "garden," probably for intermedio 2: MR 11r (Dec. 11), transcr. Warburg, "Costumi teatrali," 398. Rosselli also painted details on costumes for the magpies of intermedio 2, Lucifer for intermedio 4, and the zodiacal animals beneath the planets and Astraea in intermedio 1: MR 42r–v (Apr. 7). Additional references to Rosselli and Francini: MR 3v (Nov. 19), ordering paints from Venice; 8v (Nov. 28); 49r–v (Apr. 19–20). On Rosselli at the Palazzo Vecchio, see Chap. 3.

29. For their work at the Pitti and Buontalenti's creative supervision, see MR 7v (Nov. 28); modello for backdrops, 14r (Dec. 16); garlands, 27r (Mar. 13), 41r (Apr. 7); costume sketches, 48r (Apr. 18) and above, Chap. 2. Although both men painted Pitti costumes, Francini seems to have worked more exclusively at that site than Rosselli, who alone is mentioned at the Palazzo Vecchio. Unlike the principal painters for the entry arches, Rosselli and Francini are not known as members of the Accademia del Disegno or other higher-level artists' groups, another index of their lesser professional status in the widening divide between artists and craftworkers.

30. MR 7v–8v (Nov. 28): "capi di lavori per

l'apparato nel cortile de pitti . . . accio si dieno a fare a stima, o a cottimo secondo si giudichi essere meglio servito con rispiarmo. e percio fara fare d'ogni sorte di detti lavori per mostra, e per esemplo." On the gradi and the courtyard in general, see Chap. 3. The list also speaks of existing modelli or disegni for the balustrades, cartouches, and various painted panels.

31. MR 14r (Dec. 16): "per ultima resolutione. Poiche S.A. ha mala sodisfatione per l'ultimo cottimo dato sicome piu volte hanno sentito i pittori e altri." The four paintings whose medium is disputed form the backdrop to the castle of the naumachia, on the second level of the court, and are visible in cat. 87. For Gorini's list drawn up on Dec. 21, MR 14v–15v; further on their progress, below, Chap. 5.

32. MR 40r (Apr. 5), transcr. Warburg, "Costumi teatrali," 404; 42v (Apr. 7), 43r (Apr. 8).

33. Stage crew, 33r (Mar. 17); stage construction and installation, 25r (Mar. 2), 40v (Apr. 6); lighting, 25r (Mar. 2), 26r (Mar. 9), 41r (Apr. 6); costume storage equipment, 39r (Mar. 28). As noted in Chap. 3, Pagolini also disguised ropes and beams of the clouds with fabric, following a demonstration by Buontalenti: 25r (Mar. 2), 42r–43r (Apr. 7).

34. The dolphin was ordered on Mar. 14 (MR 27v, transcr. Warburg, "Costumi teatrali," 402) and silvered on Apr. 9 (43v); sea monsters, 41r (Apr. 6); coral, 41v (Apr. 7).

35. On Lucifer see MR 25r (Mar. 2), 38r (Mar. 23: Pagolini requests the creature's glass eyes), 40r (Apr. 5: Pagolini, Rosselli), 42r (Apr. 7: Rosselli, Bardi). Rossi's description of Lucifer and the other hell monsters (*Descrizione dell'apparato*, 54) notes many of the characters specified here by Bardi, in the same order and stage positions — another example of Rossi's advance access to Bardi's notes (see Chap. 1). On the Lucifer see also Berti, "Alcuni aspetti," 165.

36. MR 41r–v (Apr. 6–7): he also asks for Oreto Berardi, the head tailor, to send over two tailors immediately — presumably to upholster the stools — and repeats Pagolini's assignment to cover the flyropes.

37. Wings, MR 51r (Apr. 25); Seriacopi's threat, MR 46r: "mi lamenterò di lui" (transcr. Warburg, "Costumi teatrali," 407).

38. As noted in Chap. 3, a first crew list was started on Dec. 10 (MR 11v), but names were recorded only on Dec. 23 (MR 16r–18r). The final roster, from which the analysis here is primarily taken, was drawn up between Mar. 16 and 18 (MR 30v–36r). On Parigi at the Pitti and Palazzo Vecchio, see MR 27v (Mar. 14); additional crew notes, MR 24r (Feb. 7–19). For an overview of stagehands and their tasks, see Berti, "Alcuni aspetti," 164. (His assertion that crew lists go up only through intermedio 4 overlooks that the same machines and crews doubled for both 1 and 6.) The division of labor among the stagehands corresponds closely to the staffing and technical recommendations in Sabbattini's treatise, *Pratica di fabricar scene.* That the numerous crews whose functions are described in detail include no assignments for periaktoi (*telari*) reinforces the conclusion that they were not used on this occasion.

39. Orazio and Domenico appear in the first list, MR 16r–18r (Dec. 23), transcr. Warburg, "Costumi teatrali," 399, and Domenico provides other employees for the crew, 31v. The lighting crew list, 30v, provides more consistent occupational and geographic detail than the larger stagehand list that follows it. Three carpenters are also named for a Feb. 8 rehearsal of intermedio 6, each of whom is to bring along five apprentices (*garzoni*), 24r (Feb. 7).

40. Sleeping in theater, MR 3v (Nov. 12), 51v (Apr. 27); cleaning and water supply, 36v (Mar. 18), 39v (Mar. 30); scribe, MR 25r–v (Mar. 2), 35r–36r (Mar. 18), 39r (Mar. 28), 55r–v, 66r, 69r; Fabbri's role is summarized by Berti, "Alcuni aspetti," 158–59. Fire remained an overriding concern: besides all the stage and auditorium lamps, highly volatile fluids were used for the fumes of hell and the fire-breathing dragon (Buontalenti ordered *acqua vitae* or *acqua arzente finissima* from Apr. 20 through May 1, MR 49v, 50r, 51v, 52v). In Sabbattini's technical treatise, his instructions for smoke and

flames specify cloths soaked in the same chemicals, but he cautions that this is especially dangerous: *Pratica di fabricar scene*, bk. 2, chaps. 11, 22–23; transl. Hewitt, *Renaissance Stage*, 111, 126–27. On the fire that nearly broke out in December, see Chap. 2; other references to fire risk or prevention, MR 30v, 32v (Mar. 16), 36v (Mar. 18).

41. Housing arrangements and theatrical supply: MR 30r–v (Mar. 16), 35v–37v (Mar. 18), transcr. Warburg, "Costumi teatrali," 403–4. Fabbri also traveled to Livorno on Mar. 24 (MR 38r) to deliver an unspecified *modello*. On the Intronati, MR 41r, 42r, 43r (Apr. 7–8): they request white face powder (*polvere di cipri*), a French-style case (*astuccio*), and a large sack "to go in the piazza" onstage, all suggesting that they are well into rehearsals at this point. They also ask for "two clerks who write well," perhaps to transcribe script changes, and for doors to be cut in the Pellegrina set — evidence, as noted in Chap. 3, supporting a fixed set over periaktoi.

42. For the ship supplies, ASF, GM 142, 59r, 146r–149r; this volume, Fedini's account book for the preparation of wedding liveries and lodgings, also includes numerous sketches for flags and other naval decorations, 35–45. On Bortolo, GM 128, 166; for livery disbursements to crew, GM 120, 5r–v (Mar. 15–17).

43. ASF, Carteggio mediceo, Principato, filza 805, 154 (Mar. 8). This volume contains a long series of letters from March 1589 that detail the general weather and social conditions noted, 350–650 passim.

44. Christine's journey and Don Pietro's preparations are recounted by Gualterotti, *Descrizione*, 1: 4–10; Settimani, *Memorie*, 101r–2r, 109r–10r (source of quotation); and summarized by Gaeta Bertelà and Petrioli Tofani, *Feste e apparati*, 67, with further original sources. On her journey and the political situation see further *Dizionario biografico degli italiani*, 31: 38, s.v. "Cristina di Lorena"; Strong, *Art and Power*, 124–30. Don Pietro's letter: ASF, Carteggio mediceo, Principato, filza 805, 562–63 (undated, bound chronologically between letters

written Mar. 24 and Apr. 5). Orazio Rucellai itinerary is uncertain: Settimani reports him sailing from Livorno, but Gualterotti (more authoritatively) implies that he attended the proxy wedding, then traveled south through France in advance of Christine.

45. Gualterotti, *Descrizione*, 1: 12–13; Settimani, *Memorie*, 110r. Christine gave a short but touching and sincere speech, affirming that she had come to marry the grand duke not only at the command of her king, but more of her own free will, out of her hope for an "inviolable friendship" with Ferdinando. Chelini's deliveries and the bedroom: ASF, GM 120, 11r–12r, and above, Chap. 2.

46. ASF, Carteggio mediceo 805, 801 (undated, inserted at Apr. 13 in date-written order): "Je resu tant de ioie et doneur de voir Monsr. vre. frere et vos galerres lesquelles sont si belles e[t] prinsipellemant la miene quant ie i[?] entrisse ie panssois entre en paradise e[t] croies que estant sibele que la mer ne pouroit fair mal tousfois ie nespaleses de me trouver un peu indispossee qui escause que ie crains point par secourie a vre. alletese dont ie vous sublie me le pardonner et croire que ie un extreme deplesir que le ta[n]t et si mou[i/e]s pour avoir lonheur de resevoir vos com[m]andemans les ie garderes ausi sonneusemant que la propre vie de / Vre. tres hu[m]ble et tres obeissa[n]te fiansse e[t] servante, / Chrestienne de Lorraine."

47. Averardo's two letters, ASF, Carteggio mediceo, 805, 654–55, unfortunately do not specify the place from which he is writing.

48. For Uffizi events, MR 43v (Apr. 9): "Nota di robe che erano restate indietro rispetto al guastarsi" (which may imply "problems" or "deterioration" as well as "damage").

5. DRESS REHEARSALS;
CHRISTINE'S INBOUND JOURNEY
AND ENTRY

1. Duomo closing: Settimani, *Memorie*, 103v; Gorini, ASF, Magistrato de' Nove, filza 3679 (hereafter cited as MR), 24r (Feb. 7). On

Ferdinando's relations with the church and Alessandro's career and patronage, see Diaz, *Granducato*, 290–91, 321–26; Pope-Hennessy, *High Renaissance and Baroque*, 387; on the state's need for association with the church's higher ethical order, see Trexler, *Public Life*, 32–39.

2. Vittorio Franchetti Pardo, "Territorio e città nel Cinquecento mediceo," in Borsi et al., *Potere e spazio*, 21–29, outlines these various physical development initiatives. See also Spini, *Architettura e politica*; Francesco Gurrieri et al., eds., *Architettura e interventi territoriale nella Toscana granducale* (Florence: CLUSF, 1972); Goldthwaite, *Building of Renaissance Florence*, 181, 240–41; Hale, *Florence and the Medici*, 157–61. On the development of fortification see generally Martha D. Pollak, *Military Architecture, Cartography, and the Representation of the Early Modern European City* (Chicago: Newberry Library, 1991).

3. Rossi (1586), quoted in Fabbri et al., *Luogo teatrale*, 40. Parallel efforts at systematization and public display included the family's art collections, first brought together by Francesco in the Uffizi, and for whose display Ferdinando had Buontalenti add the Tribuna in 1589: Vannucci, *History of Florence*, 184; Hale, *Florence and the Medici*, 149.

4. Winter: Settimani, *Memorie*, 102v. Wilson, *Transformation of Europe*, xi, 14, discusses how the success of sixteenth-century regimes rested on exploitation of material resources and notes the technical and administrative limitations on that process. For a Pitti monument to animal labor, see Goldthwaite, *Building of Renaissance Florence*, 330, illustrated.

5. Cavalieri's notice, MR 42r (Apr. 7); Gorini was ordered to start readying the theater on Apr. 10 by removing the protective dropcloths around the room, carting off construction rubble, and reattaching lamps that had worked loose: MR 45r. The musician Antonio Naldi (see Chap. 2), now called *guardaroba della musica*, perhaps analogous to a modern chorus master, was charged with scheduling the cast for the rehearsal, 42v.

6. MR 44r–45r (Apr. 7–9). Fabric for decorating the musical instruments as serpents was requested from the granducal Guardaroba, 45r. On Thursday, Apr. 13, Piero Pagolini was relieved of his assignment to make coral branches because of more pressing needs (see Chap. 4), and orders were issued to clean up the costume and property workrooms by Saturday the 15th.

7. Booth: MR 42r (Apr. 7), "per venire coperto allo scrittoio"; see also MR 66v (June 7), "the little room of messer Bernardo where there has to be a small chair," and Berti, "Alcuni aspetti," 161.

8. Palco: MR 25v (Mar. 2), 40v (Apr. 5, sketch), 43v (Apr. 9). This design was very similar to the later recommendations for princely platforms by Sabbattini, *Pratica di fabricar scene*, bk. 1, chap. 34 (trans. Hewitt, *Renaissance Stage*, 87–88). On the platform see also Rossi, *Descrizione*, 15–16; Fabbri et al., *Luogo teatrale*, 111, no. 8.8, who illustrates and discusses the MR page with Buontalenti's sketch; and below, Chap. 6. Pagolini, the master tailor Oreto Berardi, and a crew of upholsterers were admonished to finish the gentlemen's seats, MR 41r–43v (Apr. 6–9).

9. Braudel, *Mediterranean*, 375–77. A letter from Pietro to Ferdinando from Monaco, Apr. 13, describes events and people on board since leaving Marseilles: ASF, Carteggio mediceo, Principato, filza 805, 1021–22. On the difficulties of the mail system, see Braudel, *Mediterranean*, 363–70; on Monaco and supplies, ibid., chapter 11, "Seas and Coasts," esp. 105–14. For narratives of Christine's journey, see Gualterotti, *Descrizione*, 5–17; Strong, *Art and Power*, 129–30; Gaeta Bertelà and Petrioli Tofani, *Feste e apparati*, 67–68.

10. A major Italian economic center along with Venice, Florence, and Milan, the city was at its peak of influence from the 1550s until the first quarter of the seventeenth century. Braudel, *Perspective of the World*, 157–74, and idem, *Mediterranean*, 387–95, 500–508, outlines Genoese supremacy and wide economic reach.

11. For details of the itinerary, Apr. 11–24, see Gualterotti, *Descrizione*, 1: 12–16 (*teatri divenute*, 16); Pavoni, *Diario*, 5–6; Settimani, *Memorie*, 110v–14r. Gualterotti claims the fleet left Genoa on Apr. 21, but Pavoni, who was present in Genoa (p. 5), adds the information about the (vaguely quantified) delay due to wind; both Gualterotti and Settimani imply that the fleet reached Livorno the same day it left Genoa, which seems unlikely given the pace of the rest of the trip.

12. San Marco: Settimani, *Memorie*, 104r–5v (though elsewhere, 116r–v, he seems to date the same event to Apr. 25). Plans for rehearsals and notes afterward: MR 46r–48v (Apr. 14–18), transcr. Warburg, "Costumi teatrali," 407–8; see also Mamone, *Teatro nella Firenze*, 123–25. On this rehearsal, which was attended by many people, see Settimani, 104v (Apr. 16).

13. MR 46v–47r (Apr. 14), transcr. Warburg, "Costumi teatrali," 407–8; see also Chap. 6 on the food served for actual performances.

14. MR 48r–50r (Apr. 18–23); part transcr. Warburg, "Costumi teatrali," 408.

15. Settimani, *Memorie*, 109r–12r; Gualterotti, *Descrizione*, 1: 16 (dating her arrival to April 21, apparently in error). Correspondence between Ferdinando's household officials describes the pages sent from Florence to welcome her (Enea Vaini to Benedetto Fedini, Apr. 11: ASF, Guardaroba medicea [hereafter cited as GM], filza 142, 112r; note from Vaini regarding twelve men on Ferdinando's staff who need an *abito di campagna* to go to Livorno, 191r.)

16. On the history and development of Livorno see the classic study by Braudel and Romano, *Navires et marchandises*; Diaz, *Granducato*, 295–303, 317, 358–60, with sources and further bibliography; Hale, *Florence and the Medici*, 160–63 (comandata). On fortifications and Buontalenti's role, see Goldthwaite, *Building of Renaissance Florence*, 363; J. R. Hale, *Renaissance Fortification: Art or Engineering* (London: Thames and Hudson, 1977); Fara, *Buontalenti: Architettura e teatro*, 3–22. On Cosimo I's celebration of his fort building in the 1565 entry, see Starn and Partridge, *Arts of Power*, 180; and above, Chap. 1.

17. On drainage and reclamation: Braudel, *Mediterranean*, 66–68 with earlier sources; Wilson, *Transformation of Europe*, 2–9; Diaz, *Granducato*, 346–50; Hale, *Florence and the Medici*, 150.

18. Gualterotti, *Descrizione*, 16–17. When Christine arrived in Pisa, Ferdinando's secretary Usimbardi wrote to reassure him that "her beauty will please you much better than in her portrait" (sent before her marriage: fig. 2); cited by Langedijk, *Portraits of the Medici*, 1: 654–55, no. 31.5.

19. Piazza: Pardo, "Territorio e città," in Borsi et al., *Potere e spazio*, 25–27; duomo visit: Gaulterotti, *Descrizione*, 15; Pisan absorption into the Florentine orbit: Diaz, *Granducato*, 308–11. Ferdinando's restoration of the city's aqueduct was commemorated in one of Callot's prints of his life: Lieure, *Jacques Callot*, no. 151.

20. On poverty, banditry, and corruption and the attempts to deal with them through civil administration, see Braudel, *Mediterranean*, 734–54; Berner, "Florentine Society," 216; Diaz, *Granducato*, 303–8. Ferdinando, like Francesco before him, also made use of an extensive network of spies and informants, both at home and abroad, to keep him abreast of potential threats: Berner, 239–41; and above, Introduction.

21. Population estimate: Braudel, *Mediterranean*, 408. On the botanical garden, see Gadoli and Natali, *Luoghi della Toscana*, 65; Francesco had earlier commissioned Jacopo Ligozzi, who worked on the 1589 events (see Chaps. 2, 3), to produce botanical and zoological drawings for similar ends. On granducal support of scientific pursuits, see Elizabeth Cropper, Giovanna Perini, and Francesco Solinas, eds., *Documentary Culture: Florence and Rome from Grand Duke Ferdinand I to Pope Alexander VII* (Baltimore: Johns Hopkins University Press, 1992); Joy Kenseth, ed., *The Age of the Marvelous* (exh. cat., Hanover, N.H.: Dartmouth College Art Museum, 1991).

22. This and a similar report (by Tommaso Contarini, 1588) are quoted at length in Diaz, *Granducato*, 296–97 (from *Relazioni di ambasciatori veneti*, ed. A. Segarizzi, vol. 3, pt. 2, 38–104, 105–17). For a later report (1608) by another Venetian, Francesco Morosini, also praising the judicial system and terming it a compensation for the resultant loss of liberty and economic independence, see Diaz, 320 (Segarizzi, vol. 3, pt. 2, 127). Modern scholars qualify this judgment with the observation that Cosimo I and his successors were at times forced to concede some autonomy to local institutions and social classes; for example, Starn and Partridge, *Arts of Power*, 340, observe the ongoing tension "between the centralization and the dispersion of power."

23. ASF, Carteggio mediceo, Principato, filza 805, 717–18: "tutto a spese di q.a communita, no[n] havendo essa voluto accettar l'offerta sutali da noi fatta di pagarli la spesa de danari di V.A. . . . La spesa d.lla polvere e fuochi lavorati ch[e] percio ci parrebbe di servire di parte di quella gia fatti in forteza come e, d[ic?]o, massime poiche si rispiarmava à V.A. d.lli D 800 che ci promesse, per queste feste tutto il restante da d.ti D 150 in poi." Although the inventor of this program is unknown, it is suggestive of careful government control of even these more distant proceedings that in 1565 the Florence programmer, Borghini, assisted sponsoring groups in other cities: Starn and Partridge, *Arts of Power*, 198. In another example of intertwined private and public efforts, the Intronati gave a public rehearsal of *La pellegrina* in Siena in March (before going to Florence for the premiere), for which the granducal treasury paid to construct a stage: LC T91.

24. For the festivities see Ridolfi's letter, Carteggio mediceo 805, 717–18; Gualterotti, *Descrizione*, 17–18; Settimani, *Memorie*, 113v–17v; Gaeta Bertelà and Petrioli Tofani, *Feste e apparati*, 67–68, with further bibliography, 237. One published souvenir book details the events: *Descrizione delle pompe e feste fatte ne la città di Pisa* (see Bibliography). The city had good rea-son to be grateful to Ferdinando: its population, which had declined precipitously under Francesco to some 8,000, rose again during Ferdinando's reign to about 17,000 (Braudel and Romano, *Navires et marchandises*, 20).

25. MR 48r–v (Apr. 18); Seriacopi notes that Buontalenti has 250 workers to choose from and suggests that if the architect lacks time to make the selection, he might delegate it to his son. This may be the Francesco Buontalenti who ordered some supplies for smoke effects on Apr. 29 (MR 51v); on Bernardo's son and apprentice see Chap. 1. Settimani, *Memorie*, 114v, says the comedy was performed for a second time before a large audience on Apr. 24, but he is often slightly wrong in calculating dates.

26. Cavalieri's threat, "che la farà patire Buontalenti": MR 51v, transcr. Warburg, "Costumi teatrali," 409; and see Berti, "Alcuni aspetti," 159. The four narratives were probably running behind due to the dispute over their medium (see Chap. 4): they are now specified as "narratives in oil," not the faster tempera.

27. Gualterotti, *Descrizione*, 18: "era tutta coperta d'huomini armati, e non pur la strada, ma quasi quanto portava l'occhio d'ogni intorno, certo indizio del molto popolo, e dello studio dell'armi . . . con la virtù del quale si ha procreato stato, e impero, e ricchezze, & onori grandissimi"; see also Settimani, *Memorie*, 117v–18r. On mulberries, see Berner, "Florentine Society," 244; Goldthwaite, *Building of Renaissance Florence*, 52; Diaz, *Granducato*, 346–50. On the traditional format of village entries and roadside salutes, see Trexler, *Public Life*, 293–326.

28. On Ambrogiana, see ASF, GM 143, 16, which includes a plan. On the individual villas, see most comprehensively Mignani, *Medicean Villas*.

29. On the villa as a building type and its social and economic functions, see Ackerman, *Villa*, esp. chap. 3, "The Early Villas of the Medici"; Reinhard Bentmann and Michael Müller, *The Villa as Hegemonic Architecture*, trans. T. Spence and D. Craven (Atlantic High-

lands, N.J.: Humanities Press International, 1993).

30. Fedini's logbook for Christine's travels is ASF, GM 142. On villas, planning, granducal administration, see GM 125; additional household accounts kept by Fedini, GM 126, 128, 157, and above, Chaps. 2, 4. The residential villas were administered by Fedini as part of an even larger network of outlying farm properties, some occupied only by tenant staff; see the inventory of many of these *fattorie*, ca. 1588–96, GM 147; and Zeffiro Ciuffaletti and Leonardo Rombai, eds., *Grandi fattorie in Toscana* (Florence: Vallecchi, 1980), with maps and agricultural history since Roman times.

31. Household goods transported from villas to Florence: GM 144, Sept.–Nov. 1588. Vaini: GM 134, 781 (Jan. 22, 1593/4); this thick compendium of unbound correspondence includes many notes from and to Fedini, including some from Ferdinando to Fedini regarding pictures by Allori, etc., 1587–95.

32. On La Petraia see Mignani, *Medicean Villas*, 71–73; Cochrane, *Florence in the Forgotten Centuries*, 96; on Cigoli's contribution, Chappell, *Disegni di Cigoli*, 9, no. 5.

33. On imitation, Ackerman, *Villa*, 30–31; Buontalenti at the Boboli, Fabbri et al., *Luogo teatrale*, 39. For garden decoration and hydraulics, see Fara, *Buontalenti: Architettura e teatro*; more generally, David R. Coffin, *The Villa in the Life of Renaissance Rome* (Princeton: Princeton University Press, 1979); Lazzaro, *Italian Renaissance Garden*, esp. chap. 8. For an introduction to the mannerist esthetic principles invoked, esp. scenography, see Shearman, *Mannerism*.

34. Fig. 10, by Justus Utens: Florence, Museo di Firenze com'era; for the Artimino series, see most recently Mignani, *Medicean Villas*. On aerial views see Lucia Nuti, "The Perspective Plan in the Sixteenth Century: The Invention of a Representational Language," *Art Bulletin* 76 (1994): 105–28. On maps as a technical and discursive strategy of controlling both nature and politics, see generally: David Buisseret, ed., *Monarchs, Ministers, and Maps: The Emer-*

gence of Cartography as a Tool of Government in Early Modern Europe (Chicago: University of Chicago Press, 1992); J.B. Harley and David Woodward, eds., *The History of Cartography*, vol. 1 (Chicago: University of Chicago Press, 1987). On Caprarola see Clare Robertson, *Il Gran Cardinale: Alessandro Farnese, Patron of the Arts* (New Haven: Yale University Press, 1992), 116–22, pl. VIII, IX; on the Uffizi maps, Fabbri et al., *Luogo teatrale*, 37.

35. On the guests' arrival and suites, Settimani, *Memorie*, 104v–17v, Apr. 17–22; total numbers, 163r–v, citing household account books (clearly Fedini).

36. Arriving guests, Settimani, *Memorie*, 85v, 117v, 129r–v, 131r, 132r, also citing use of the Strozzi palace, and some guests who stayed at public inns at Ferdinando's expense (157v, 163r). Fedini's surveys: GM 142, 61r–81r; similar lists continue through fol. 108, mostly undated, one from Nov. 4, 1588; correspondence between Fedini and Enea Vaini over supplies, 108r, 112r (Apr. 11). Berner, "Florentine Society," 222, cites additional primary sources.

37. GM 142: inventory of mattresses, 82–85 (Ducal Palace in Pisa, 340; Ambrogiana, 258; Poggio, 288; Magia, 73); country lodgings, 114r–v; villas being decorated, and the Pisa palace, 146r–49r. Fedini is clearly the source for Settimani's account (*Memorie*, 85v) of preparations in and beyond the city beginning in December.

38. Settimani, *Memorie*, 117r–18r; Gualterotti, *Descrizione*, 19. On the decoration of the villa see Janet Cox-Rearick, *Dynasty and Destiny in Medici Art: Pontormo, Leo X and the Two Cosimos* (Princeton: Princeton University Press, 1984). Coincidentally, local bridal couples today use the steps of the villa, now open to the public, as a favorite backdrop for wedding photographs.

39. On clothing and travel equipment for Christine and her suite: GM 157, 38 (May 10); GM 120, 21r–22r; GM 142, 114r, 147v (orders from Ferdinando to Fedini), 168v (decoration of her coach), 202–4 (outfits for Christine's

pages); and see above, Chap. 2, for tailors. On Ulino, GM 120, 6r (Apr. 17), 19r (Apr. 29); he also appears in the household payroll, at a salary of 7 ducats per month, ASF, Depositeria generale (parte antica), filza 389, 19.

40. The principal source for the entry is Gualterotti's *Descrizione*, 20–31; see also Settimani, *Memorie*, 119r–23r. Cavallino, *Raccolta*, describes the entry with unique details but is often confused or unreliable; on his chronicle see further Chaps. 6, 7. For narrative overviews of the entry see notes from Chap. 1, esp. Strong, *Splendor at Court*, 174–78; idem, *Art and Power*, 130–33; and Nagler, *Theatre Festivals*.

41. Wilson, *Transformation of Europe*, 68; on the larger urbanistic trend see most recently Martha D. Pollak, *Turin 1564–1690: Urban Design, Military Culture, and the Creation of the Absolutist Capital* (Chicago: University of Chicago Press, 1991). On new theorizations of public ritual, see Trexler, *Public Life*; Susan Zimmerman and Ronald Weissman, eds., *Urban Life in the Renaissance* (Newark: University of Delaware Press, 1989). For the entry, as earlier, costuming and equipage were supervised by Fedini, GM 142, 147v–204r (see costume discussion of these folios above, Chap. 2).

42. On the spectator in criticism, see Moshe Barasch, *Theories of Art: From Plato to Winckelmann* (New York: New York University Press, 1985), 203–70; on ritual, Trexler, *Public Life*, xxiv–xxv. On the entire entry see Gaeta Bertelà and Petrioli Tofani, *Feste e apparati*, 68–72. For the formal typology of triumphal arches and their physical construction, see Zdzislaw Bieniecki, "Quelques remarques sur la composition architecturale des arcs de triomphe à la Renaissance," in Jacquot, *Fêtes*, 3: 201–17. For an introduction to the genre, see Annamaria Petrioli Tofani and Annamaria Testaverde, "Gli ingressi trionfali," in Borsi et al., *Potere e spazio*, 343–54; for references, Robert Baldwin, "A Bibliography of the Literature on Triumph," in Wisch and Munshower, *All the World's a Stage*, 1: 358–85.

43. Gualterotti, *Descrizione*, 1: 24–26 (noting

also knightly orders from France, Spain, and Malta, but giving two different estimates of the number of pages); Settimani, *Memorie*, 119v–21r. Settimani's list of canopy bearers (107r) differs from the numbers given by Gualterotti, Cavallino, and Pavoni. (Pavoni, *Diario*, 9–11, gives the names, which include all the aristocratic clans.) For orders by Fedini (to Oreto Berardi and others) from December 1588 onward for livery for Ferdinando's and Christine's pages and attendants, see ASF, GM 120, 13v–19v; GM 142, 196r–204r; GM 159, 142r; and above, Chap. 2.

44. Gualterotti, *Descrizione*, 2: 4, 23: "il quale le possa fare ora uficio d'interprete de i concetti nuovi, & ora di ridicitore delle storie de' tempi preteriti." On the dates and purposes of his two parts, see Chap. 1. Providing further evidence for the publication sequence, he concludes this guidebook-catalogue, called part 2 in the complete edition, with a statement in contradictory tenses: "And what will happen in the rest of the ceremonies will be described before [*avanti*], in the first book" (176).

45. Gualterotti, *Descrizione*, 1: 23; Pavoni, *Diario*, 12; Cavallino, *Raccolta*, 22. The scene was later included by Callot in his series on the life of Ferdinando: Lieure, *Jacques Callot*, no. 162 (frontispiece).

46. GM 142, 60r. I thank Martha Howell for sharing her thoughts about the symbolic significance of women's personal property (Columbia University, Institute for Research on Women and Gender, Spring 1994).

47. This description follows Gualterotti, *Descrizione*, 1: 27; Cavallino, *Raccolta*, 22–23, lists liveries for some 89 participants and their suites, but his details and names differ from Gualterotti's. On the Marchese of Cetona, who had some of his costumes designed by his own tailors, see Chap. 2. On the 1565 route and its historical associations see Starn and Partridge, *Arts of Power*, 178, 217, 345n65, and their fig. 64. For street maps of Florence at this time, see the many reproductions in Mori and Boffito, *Piante e vedute*.

48. Wolff, *Social Production of Art*, 97; Starn and Partridge, *Arts of Power*, 170. The length and complexity of such processions can be seen in the "strip-map" engraving of the entry for Maria Maddalena of Austria, bride of Ferdinando and Christine's son Cosimo II, in 1608, illustrated in Strong, *Splendor at Court*, 204, and in Molinari, "Attività teatrale," pt. 2, 63.

49. Gualterotti, *Descrizione*, 1: 33–36, describes the liveries; Pavoni, *Diario*, 11. A hymn in praise of Christine written by Orazio's highly literate kinsman Palla Rucellai was sung in the duomo (Gualterotti, 30–31).

50. The classic study of occupationally derived visual habits of mind is Michael Baxandall, *Painting and Experience in Fifteenth-Century Italy* (Oxford: Oxford University Press, 1972), dealing largely with mercantile classes.

51. Even less susceptible to analysis of their subject position as audience are the household dwarves and slaves, some noted as African, who were also costumed for unrecorded roles in the festivities: GM 120, 22r–23r.

52. On the traditions of princely largesse and wedding alms, see Trexler, *Public Life*, 434.

53. Quoted from Gualterotti, *Descrizione*, four unnumbered pages inserted at the end of his book 1, "Ornamento fatto dentro del duomo"; see also Pavoni, *Diario*, 8; Cavallino, *Raccolta*, 21; Settimani, *Memorie*, 122v; and discussion in Solerti, *Albori del melodramma*, 1: 43. On the cupola project see most recently Chappell, *Disegni di Cigoli*, 6; on Christine's platform, ASF, GM 142, 147v.

54. Pisa gift: ASF, GM 159, 23r. Annunziata gift: GM 122, 15; Settimani, *Memorie*, 106v. On economic and artistic interconnections between court and patricians, see Chap. 2. On the Salviati see Appendix, genealogical table; their livery, Gualterotti livery list; their chapel dedication, Chap. 6.

55. Francesca Baglione, whose mother was a Medici, married the Roman Francesco Orsini but returned to Florence to supervise the women's and children's household; on her role in palace affairs see above, and ASF, GM 148, 4 (May 4, 1589). Later, as a wealthy widow, she influenced Roman ecclesiastical building; see Carolyn Valone, "Women on the Quirinal Hill: Patronage in Rome, 1560–1630," *Art Bulletin* 76 (1994): 140–41. On women's patronage at courts generally see Merry E. Wiesner, *Women and Gender in Early Modern Europe* (Cambridge: Cambridge University Press, 1993), 140–43.

56. Gualterotti, *Descrizione*, 1: 31, says she dined alone with the Duchess of Brunswick; Settimani, *Memorie*, 123r. Pavoni, *Diario*, 11, says there was a small banquet, and lists two tables of family and retainers.

6. THE WEDDING AS/IN PERFORMANCE

1. For example, the Genoese ambassador arrived on May 3, that of Bologna on the 4th with "60 mouths": Cavallino, *Raccolta*, 32; Settimani, *Memorie*, 131r.

2. "Fù giudicato per cosa rustica, inventione mirabilissima"; he also reports a concert, banquet and ball in the evening, at which groups took turns dancing by nationality: Pavoni, *Diario*, 12–13. See also Settimani, *Memorie*, 129r–v (the month of May continues to fol. 157).

3. Pavoni and Cavallino were, like Rossi, writing in an official souvenir capacity, but little is known about them and their circumstances; both books were published abroad, probably for distribution in the Papal States. On Pavoni, see Fabbri et al., *Luogo teatrale*, 116, no. 8.21; Borsi et al., *Potere e spazio*, 397, no. 9.32; Pirrotta and Povoledo, *Music and Theatre*, 379n69, noting that Pavoni's account of the intermedi is often so similar to Rossi's that either Pavoni made use of Rossi's draft or both were working from a common source, perhaps Bardi. On Cavallino, see Fabbri et al., 136, no. 9.20; Borsi et al., 397, no. 9.31.

4. Basic sources for the intermedi and comedy include Rossi, *Descrizione*, parts of which are transcribed and discussed in Warburg,

"Costumi teatrali," 271–74, and in Mamone, *Teatro nella Firenze*, 119–20 and passim; Pavoni, *Diario*, 14–23; Cavallino, *Raccolta*, 3–7, who is often confused and unreliable (further on these texts, see below and Chap. 7). On the dimensions of the auditorium (65 × 130 feet) see Rossi, 7–17, and above, Chap. 3; modern theaters require some 6–9 square feet per seat. Cavallino estimated a capacity of 5,000 (3); Michelangelo Buonarroti the Younger, in his *Descrizione delle felicissime nozze della Cristianissima Maestà di Madama Maria Medici* . . . (Florence: Marescotti, 1600), claimed an audience of 3,000 men and 800 women for Caccini's opera on that occasion (but he also wrote that 1,000 people operated the stage machines, an unlikely tenfold multiplication of the staff employed in 1589). The most reasonable contemporary estimate reports that the gradi held upwards of 300 women (perhaps one-third of total capacity): *Sontuosissimi apparecchi*, 7.

5. Berti, "Alcuni aspetti," 163, offers the convincing hypothesis, with examples from slightly later performances, that the entries in Seriacopi's log (ASF, Magistrato de' Nove 3679, hereafter cited as MR) regarding the balconies, MR 46r (Apr. 13) and 50r (Apr. 22), were for clerical seating; compare their segregation at the ensuing banquet on May 7, below. Cavalieri's term, *paradiso*, was also used for any upper zone, including the stage catwalks and actual heavenly setting.

6. Evidence for the Corridoio route: see ASF, Guardaroba medicea no. 120 (hereafter cited as GM), 6v (May 2, Zacharia); Mamone, *Teatro nella Firenze*, 60–61. For Christine's gown, Pavoni, *Diario*, 14.

7. Rossi, *Descrizione*, 16: "Accesi i lumi dell'Apparato, e percotendo negli ornamenti, e nelle preziose gioie, che in testa, in dito, e nelle vesti avevan le gentil donne sedenti, parevano tutti i gradi carichi di stelle, che scintillassero, i quali trassono a se tutti gli occhi de circustanti, che con incredibil piacere, senza vedersi quasi ad alcuno, si può dir giammai battere occhio, e

lo splendor delle gioie, e le bellezze di quelle giovani donne, intentamente, e fisamente non si saziavan di riguardare." Nicola Sabbattini, in his later manual for theater designers, confirmed the custom of seating men and women separately, and advised, in a spirit similar to Rossi's, that the prettier women should be given more prominent locations: *Pratica di fabricar scene*, bk. 1, chap. 40; transl. Hewitt, *Renaissance Stage*, 96–97.

8. Rossi alone reports the Rome scene, which is not attested by visual records or other diarists; Pavoni, *Diario*, 15, says only that a blue backdrop behind Vittoria Archilei masked the heavenly scenery until it was drawn up at her ascent. Possibly Rome was originally planned, but a simpler drop substituted later; alternatively, for a hypothetical explanation of the Rome and Corinthian colonnade sets as done with two drops, see Pirrotta and Povoledo, *Music and Theatre*, 379.

9. MR 32r (Mar. 16). The two men are Battista Bronchoni, identified as a state employee (*nostro lavorante*), and Giovanni di Bartolommeo, from the workshop of the carpenter Domenico Atticiato.

10. Gualterotti, *Descrizione*, 1: 30–31.

11. For the Pisa setting, playwright, and plot, see Rossi, *Descrizione*, 33–36; Nagler, *Theatre Festivals*, 79–80; Mamone, *Teatro nella Firenze*, 71; Pirrotta and Povoledo, *Music and Theatre*, 370–74; and above, Chap. 1. On the interrelation of intermedi and their plays see generally Clubb, *Italian Drama*, 77–80, 176, with references to sixteenth-century theorists; on the political subjugation of Pisa, Chap. 5.

12. Rossi, *Descrizione*, 37–41, 42–48; Pavoni, *Diario*, 15–16. On the dragon see Chaps. 4, 5; on Cosimo see Paul Richelson, *Studies in the Personal Imagery of Cosimo I de' Medici* (New York: Garland, 1978).

13. Rossi, *Descrizione*, 35; he had earlier (16) noted that Buontalenti's method for avoiding any fumes during the initial lamplighting "was something truly remarkable [*considerabile*]," sug-

gesting how exceptional such ability still was. *Sontuosissimi apparecchi*, 7, gives the performance duration. Possibly, as in later opera practice, the audience was free to come and go during the performance.

14. On food at the April rehearsal, see Chap. 5; at a later, presumably typical, performance, MR 66v–67r (June 7), transcr. Mamone, *Teatro nella Firenze*, 121–22. For these crew members see the list of stagehands compiled by Seriacopi (MR 30v–34r), Chap. 4.

15. Rossi, *Descrizione*, 49–54; Pavoni, *Diario*, 18: "furono da molti creduti angioli" (perhaps misconstruing Rossi, 51, "agnoli rassembravan di Paradiso").

16. Rossi, *Descrizione*, 55–59; Pavoni, *Diario*, 20. A similar reference to Philip might inhere in the dragon/serpent of intermedio 3; but as the Delphians are dressed in Levantine style, that creature could equally represent the Turks.

17. On the Order and its activities see Berner, "Florentine Political Thought," 188; Braudel, *Mediterranean*, 876–78; and above, Chaps. 2, 5.

18. Rossi, *Descrizione*, 60–72; Pavoni, *Diario*, 21–23; on this composition see Chap. 1.

19. Similarly, Rossi exclaims (*Descrizione*, 61) that there were so many flowers on the clouds that one would have thought that "all the nymphs ever mentioned in the poets' fables had come together there with full laps, to pour out flowers."

20. Newman, "Politics of Spectacle," 110, citing Cavallino, *Raccolta*, sig. A4r (p. 7 in the edition cited herein), and a report by the papal nuncio for which she cites Cochrane, *Florence in the Forgotten Centuries*, 129, and her personal communication with Cochrane. I have been unable to confirm this citation.

21. The original diagrams and dance descriptions in Malvezzi, *Intermedii e concerti*, are reproduced in Solerti, *Musica, ballo e drammatica*, 16–18, and Walker, *Fêtes du mariage*, lvi–lviii.

22. Painted banners, MR 35r (Mar. 18); Watson, "Sugar Sculpture," describes the process of

sugar casting, suggests particular models, and discusses the prevalence of sugar in Italy from the fifteenth century.

23. Pavoni, *Diario*, 23–24; Cavallino, *Raccolta*, 32. On the candlesticks see Chap. 5.

24. MR 52v–54r (May 3–5), part transcr. Warburg, "Costumi teatrali," 409. The lists include orders for new candles, decorative trimmings, food, and chemicals for the flames.

25. Pavoni, *Diario*, 24–29; Cavallino, *Raccolta*, 33–34. On religious rites, Cavallino, 22 (*alcune cerimonie*), 21 (*le ceremonie [sic] che sogliono fare*). For summary narrative and further references, see Warburg, "Costumi teatrali," 394; Nagler, *Theatre Festivals*, 71; Berner, "Florentine Society," 226–27. For the costumes and livery made by the court tailors, see Chap. 2. For useful background on aristocratic spectacle see most recently Goldthwaite, *Wealth and Demand*, 159–76, with bibliography; on the calcio, Artusi and Gabbrielli, *Feste di Firenze*, 193–217.

26. For the performances on Saturday, May 6 and May 13: Pavoni, *Diario*, 29–30, 46, transcr. Mamone, *Teatro nella Firenze*, 126–27. His account entered the scholarly literature with d'Ancona, *Origini del teatro*, 2: 167, 466, 495, followed by Warburg, "Costumi teatrali," 261–62.

27. MR 52v–53v (May 3–4). On Michele, who was lodged at the Strozzi palace, see Settimani, *Memorie*, 132r, 151r (for comments from both ambassadors on the Florentine political system, see above, Chap. 5); an ambassador from the Marchese del Vasto arrived as late as May 12 (148v).

28. Berti, "Alcuni aspetti," 165–66. The audience at such a private showing would have had very different interests in the stage action from the aristocrats, enjoying the sight of known intimates onstage at least equally to the allegories they represented.

29. MR 52v (May 3); Pavoni, *Diario*, 30–32; Cavallino, *Raccolta*, 35. On the segregated seating of churchmen see also above, May 2.

30. MR 54r–v (May 7–9); Pavoni, *Diario*, 40.

31. Pavoni, *Diario*, 32; Cavallino, *Raccolta*, 35–36; Settimani, *Memorie*, 150r (mistakenly dated May 15); Settimani's summary is translated by Berner, "Florentine Society," 226–27 with further references (erroneously transcribing Settimani's date as May 5). According to Warburg, "Costumi teatrali," 394, this event was also described in *Le ultime feste et apparati . . .* (Bologna: Benacci, 1589), which I have been unable to consult. The animals came from Ferdinando's zoo, itself an indication of the urge to control through classification and display. On livery details (somewhat inconsistent with Pavoni's account) and household tailors for this event see Chap. 2; and ASF, GM 120, 7r–v (May 8), for hunters and musicians; GM 159, 112 (mis-cited by Testaverde as 142), 120 (hunters), 138 (nobles).

32. Pavoni, 33–35 (giving the entire route); Cavallino, 36–38; Settimani, 132r–40v. On required attendance, see Berner, "Florentine Society," 224–25; on the chapel design, ceremonies, and Salviati family, see Chaps. 2–5, and esp. Flack, "Giambologna's Cappella di Sant'Antonino."

33. MR 54v–55r (May 9–10), including haberdashers making costumes, and much concern for procuring enough swords and sheaths of various types, notably rapiers (*stocchi*) from Bavaria, evidently highly prized, to be covered in cloth of gold; this order came from Cavalieri, suggesting that he acted as director at the Pitti as well as the Uffizi.

34. Pavoni, *Diario*, 35; Cavallino, *Raccolta*, 38–40, with rules of the game and costume details (some were dressed in Turkish style, many sported long false beards); Settimani, *Memorie*, 141. For additional costume details see Chap. 2.

35. MR 55v–56r (May 10), part transcr. Warburg, "Costumi teatrali," 409. Notes from the following day show that lighting and costumes were still being brought in and installed on the day of performance, MR 64r. On the use of food and wine to mollify unruly or resistant workers, see Warnke, *Court Artist*, 185.

36. Fara, *Buontalenti: Architettura e teatro*, 1,

16, 21n2; Hale, *Florence and the Medici*, 145; Goldthwaite, *Building of Renaissance Florence*, 53–54; Hibbert, *Rise and Fall*, chap. 21, who credits the founding of this industry, the first in Europe, to the scientifically minded Francesco I.

37. On the awning see MR 4r (Nov. 22), 8r (Nov. 28). For the entire event, see Pavoni, *Diario*, 35–43; Cavallino, *Raccolta*, 40–46 (he says 200 sacks of wheat were hurriedly brought in to absorb the floodwaters).

38. Primary sources for these events are Pavoni, *Diario*, 35–39, and Cavallino, *Raccolta*, 41–46. See further Nagler, *Theatre Festivals*; Massar, "Set of Prints"; catalogue entries in Fabbri et al., *Luogo teatrale*; Fara, *Buontalenti: Architettura e teatro*, 16; Berti, "Alcuni aspetti," 167. The principal study of this event by Massar ordered the floats and illustrated record largely following the account in Pavoni, whereas the treatment in Fabbri et al. relies more heavily on Cavallino; all agree that inconsistencies and gaps make any order somewhat conjectural. The sequence here generally follows Cavallino, who is more useful in detail and corresponds more closely, though still not completely, to the visual survivals. On the 1579 prototype see Leo Schrade, "Les Fêtes du mariage de Francesco de' Medici et de Bianca Cappello," in Jacquot, *Fêtes*, 1: 107–30.

39. MR 55v (May 10), 64v (May 11). On the chariot's design and construction see Chaps. 3–5. Pavoni, *Diario*, 19, describes the furies of intermedio 4 "with wild hair, very misshapen faces, and serpents twined around their hands and arms"; less likely, these borrowed items might have served for Don Virginio's escort, which Cavallino (42) says included eight similarly masked and ugly women.

40. ASF, GM 140 (hereafter cited as LC), N429–30; p. 430 contains the costume sketch by Buontalenti often assigned to the Pitti events, discussed in Chap. 2, and illustrated by Fabbri et al., *Luogo teatrale*, 137, no. 9.21.

41. On the rocks, Rossi, *Descrizione*, 18; Pavoni, *Diario*, 15. Pavoni's vague description

recalls the backstage term for Archilei as simply "una che va in una nugola" (Chap. 4); his identifications of the characters in the sfila are also generic (sorcerer, nymph, siren). Similarly, *Sontuosissimi apparecchi* is often confused or silent on iconography, misidentifying the sorceress of intermedio 4 as Juno and hell as the forge of Vulcan (6).

42. Cavallino, *Raccolta*, 43: "vi era in questo carro la Primavera tutta di fiori ornata con otto ninfe inghirlandate, con canestri di frutti . . . vestite . . . di biancho . . . seguiva un altro carro tutto di verde smaltato, con ninfe parimente"; Pavoni refers briefly to sirens. The patrons of these floats are unnamed.

43. Pavoni, *Diario*, 38–39; Cavallino, *Raccolta*, 42–43. The eight cross-dressed soldiers (Cavallino, "scudieri immascherati villanescamente da donne molto ridiculosi per la bruttezza de loro visi") might have been wearing the eight fury costumes borrowed from the Uffizi on May 10 and 11 (see above); but as those outfits were designated for marchers who were to *governare il carro di S.A.S.* — which seems to refer to actual pullers rather than followers — the borrowed costumes are here identified with the carro of Don Pietro (cat. 73–74).

44. For lists of 18 boats with crews, MR 56v–63v (May 11), in an unknown hand (matching the note on eight furies, above, MR 64v); Pavoni, *Diario*, 40, agrees with this number. Crews varied from three to ten per boat. For the costume colors, MR 54r (May 7).

45. Pavoni, *Diario*, 35–43, part transcr. in Massar, "Set of Prints," and Mamone, *Teatro nella Firenze*, 125–26; Cavallino, *Raccolta*, 40–46, part transcr. in Fabbri et al., *Luogo teatrale*; Settimani, *Memorie*, 143–48. For secondary narratives, see Nagler, *Theatre Festivals*, 91; Strong, *Splendor at Court*, 195–96.

46. MR 66r (May 13); Pavoni, *Diario*, 43–47; Settimani, *Memorie*, 149r, 150v, records both dates, adding that the performance on May 15 was for Venetian ambassadors and other late arrivals.

47. Pavoni, *Diario*, 44–46; Settimani, *Memo-*

rie, 149r. Christine had apparently been studying Italian and could speak it haltingly upon arrival in Tuscany: Newman, "Politics of Spectacle," 107. On this performance see further Molinari, "L'altra faccia del 1589."

48. Settimani, *Memorie*, 151r–53r (May 17–20); MR 66r (May 20).

49. Settimani, *Memorie*, 154r–55r, cites similar events on both May 23 and 24, perhaps misreading his sources. More likely both descriptions refer to the 23rd; Cesare d'Este and Virginia de' Medici left on May 24, and no major event had proceeded without them. On the *saracino*, a tilt at a mannequin of a Moor, see Artusi and Gabbrielli, *Feste di Firenze*, 155–64.

50. Settimani, *Memorie*, 155v–56r; I have not uncovered his original source for this detailed account. Warburg, "Costumi teatrali," 262 (apparently based on the calendar in Cavallino), notes a *mascherata dei fiumi* on this date; Strong, *Splendor at Court*, 195, misinterprets this as a reference to a celebration taking place on the Arno River.

51. On the social position of Florentine youth and attempts at their ritual integration from the fifteenth century onward, see Trexler, *Public Life*, chap. 11, esp. 393–418, 515–21.

52. Cecchi's son Baccio published an account of this event, *Descrizione dell'apparato e de gl'intermedi fatti per la storia dell'esaltazione della croce* (see Bibliography); this text is published fully in d'Ancona, *Sacre rappresentazioni*, 3: 121–38, and partly in Flavio Testi, *La musica italiana nel seicento*, 2 vols. (Milan: Bramante, 1970), 1: 11–19. For description and analysis see Konrad Eisenbichler, "Spazi e luoghi nel teatro fiorentino del Cinquecento: Giovan Maria Cecchi," *Yearbook of Italian Studies* 6 (1987): 51–62; Gaeta Bertelà and Petrioli Tofani, *Feste e apparati*, 73.

53. In their analysis of the 1565 entry, Starn and Partridge invoke Trexler's analysis of public ritual to expose the sexual undertone of these men, who symbolically "harnessed the vitality and sexual energy of youth for the city's regeneration": *Arts of Power*, 185, citing Richard Trexler, "Ritual in Florence: Adolescence and

Salvation in the Renaissance," in *The Pursuit of Holiness in Late Medieval and Renaissance Religion*, ed. C. Trinkhaus and H. Oberman, 200–264 (Leiden, 1974); on youth culture see more broadly Trexler, *Public Life*, chap. 11. On Florentine homosexual networks and links to theater, transvestism, and music, see Chap. 2; on the entire illicit world of young men's sexuality, Guido Ruggiero, "Marriage, Love, Sex, and Civic Morality," in *Sexuality and Gender in Early Modern Europe*, ed. James G. Turner, 10–30 (Cambridge: Cambridge University Press, 1993).

54. Trexler, *Public Life*, 504–15, gives an overview of these performing groups that suggests that further study would be profitable beyond his cutoff date of the early principate. Pavoni did, as noted, record one example of nonelite wedding art, the Peretolan maypole.

7. AFTERMATH AND LATER INFLUENCE

1. "Chi mancha debbe essere molestato dalla iustitia, e con rigore": ASF, Magistrato de' Nove 3679 (hereafter cited as MR), 66v–67r (June 7); transcr. Mamone, *Teatro nella Firenze*, 121–22; discussed by Berti, "Alcuni aspetti," 165–66.

2. MR 67v–68r (June 10); transcr. Warburg, "Costumi teatrali," 410; Berti, "Alcuni aspetti," 165. These pages also contain instructions for fastening and/or locking away the hanging lamps, stage canvases, and the ship of intermedio 5; sealing the vent holes in the auditorium ceiling; and refilling the fire buckets. The chairs were to be locked away to avoid having to pay for any that might be lost or stolen, and the painter Francesco Rosselli was to touch up his chiaroscuro decoration on the gradi for free.

3. ASF, Guardaroba medicea, filza 140 (hereafter cited as LC), T6, T20, etc.; the receipt, or corresponding credit entry, for the velo return is in the Guardaroba records, ASF, Guardaroba medicea (hereafter cited as GM), filza 148, 136.

4. Settimani, *Memorie*, 157v–63v, describes various departures throughout June; on Brunswick, 162r.

5. Pietro's departure: Settimani, *Memorie*, 170r. On Marenzio and Archilei, see household payroll records (*Ruolo*), ASF, Depositeria generale, parte antica, filza 389, 17; on their subsequent careers, see biographical references cited Chaps. 1, 2.

6. ASF, GM 144, Sept. 23–24, 1588, reveals the pay procedures; Ferdinando's guardaroba Benedetto Fedini, acting as paymaster, also countersigned a request made by Gorini, LC Q88. On del Maestro, whose *Ricordanze* cover the wedding period and his administrative role in it, see ASF, Carte Strozziane, ser. 1, vol. 1, nos. 20, 27, 29, 30, 51. His role in organizing the Livorno reception is noted by Settimani, *Memorie*, 106r; his salary of 20 scudi per month plus a horse equals that of Vaini as the highest pay for a household official: ASF, Depositeria generale 389, 5–6.

7. MR 64r, 66r: "Però ne faccia nuovo conto e in buona forma, atteso ch'un altro dato non stava bene non vi essendo il giorno, ne il nome ne sottoscritione, e però sia con le sua circunstantie."

8. ASF, GM 157, 9, lists Oreto's work for household liveries from January to October 1589 and corresponding amounts paid to him between March and November. Cavalieri's *Libro* records payments from June through September to Oreto, Niccolò, and others for the 286 intermedi and *Pellegrina* costumes, LC Q188–97 (on the final reckoning, 191, see Chap. 2); transcr. Warburg, "Costumi teatrali," 268–69, 300–306.

9. Pavoni, *Diario*, 47; Settimani, *Memorie*, 163r–v (June 30). Some of the same figures are cited by Berner, "Florentine Society," 222, with further original sources.

10. A copy of the Monte report, which summarizes the sources and types of matériel lent or expended from the government stores, was inserted into Cavalieri's *Libro* in early June: LC T91, transcr. Warburg, "Costumi teatrali," 269, 394–95; many items in the *Libro* have the

word *riscontro* (checked, audited) written beside them in the margin, perhaps notations made for this audit. The officials' shock followed the expense of 25,000 scudi for the 1586 Uffizi theatricals, which was itself considered stupendous at the time: Strong, *Splendor at Court*, 186–87. The monetary conversion estimates that 300 scudi, the highest annual managerial salary in the household accounts, was perhaps equivalent to at least $30,000–50,000 in 1995 dollars.

11. On Christine's dowry, see Introduction, Chap. 5, and GM 152. For the economy campaign of 1590 see the memoir by Giovanni del Maestro, ASF, Carte strozziane, ser. 1, vol. 1, no. LI, "Quaderno del governo e riforma del governo della casa, 1590."

12. On the causes and trajectory of Tuscan economic decay, and Dallington's comment, see Introduction; on what he calls "the prodrome of decline," already evident in wool by 1587, see further Diaz, *Granducato*, 350–55, 360–63.

13. Even his iconographic section has its shortcomings: he confusingly conflates or misorders arches 4 through 6, and his reproduction of the only arch painting still in existence compresses the original's narrow vertical composition to proportions suitable to book pages, an alteration then copied by Scarabelli (Christine at Marseilles).

14. Most known exempla of these prints are on loose sheets, but the most comprehensive surviving set, 29 prints at the Metropolitan Museum of Art, is gathered in a vellum binding that dates from the late sixteenth or seventeenth century; its prints are in haphazard order, not unexpectedly in a period when books were bound only after receipt of loose sheets. I thank Mindy Dubansky of the museum's book conservation department for sharing her expertise in this area.

15. Problems remain with this hypothetical reconstruction. Although 32 different prints are known, the large-format series includes only 31, because no large framed reprint survives of the small cat. 85; either it has been lost, or this subject was dropped from the larger series and replaced or supplemented by two additional Pitti scenes which exist only in large format (cat. 82, 86; for the latter identification with the Pitti, which is uncertain, see Chap. 6); for details see individual entries. On the series see Gaeta Bertelà and Petrioli Tofani, *Feste e apparati*, 80.

16. Scarabelli's dependence on Gualterotti was first noted by Daddi Giovannozzi, "Alcune incisioni," 87.

17. On the history and creators of *La Dafne* (first performed in a private palace, not a theater), see Hanning, "Glorious Apollo"; idem, "Rinuccini," *New Grove Dictionary*, 16: 46–47; Pirrotta and Povoledo, *Due Orfei*, 276–33; Fabbri et al., *Luogo teatrale*, 87, no. 6.8.1; Blumenthal, *Giulio Parigi*, 101n95.

18. On events of 1600 see Donington, *Rise of Opera*, 130–40; Nagler, *Theatre Festivals*, 93–100; Strong, *Splendor at Court*, 196–202; Blumenthal, *Giulio Parigi*, 100–104, 355; Fabbri et al., *Luogo teatrale*, 116–18 (on Pieroni); Roselli et al., *Teatri di Firenze*, 45–46. Also performed on this occasion, but not in the Uffizi theater, was the opera *L'Euridice* by Rinuccini and Peri, in which Peri and Vittoria Archilei sang the principal roles, and which was designed by Buontalenti or the painter Cigoli: see Blumenthal, *Theater Art of the Medici*, 28–30; Molinari, "Attività teatrale," pt. 1, 62–67. On Buontalenti's inventory, see Blumenthal, *Giulio Parigi*, 73n131, 100n93, and above, Chap. 4.

19. Fig. 12, Metropolitan Museum of Art (Harris Brisbane Dick Fund, 1930), no. 30.58.5(63). On Parigi, his family, and works and the influence of Buontalenti, see Blumenthal, *Giulio Parigi*, chaps. 1–2, esp. 35, 47–54 (calendar of designs from 1608–26), 73, 355–56, 365 (family tree); idem, *Theater Art of the Medici*, 30–86; Elena Povoledo, "Parigi, Giulio," "Parigi, Alfonso," *Enciclopedia dello spettacolo*, vol. 7, cols. 1675–78; Fabbri et al., *Luogo teatrale*, 123–31. For the documents concerning reuse of earlier equipment, see Blumenthal, *Giulio Parigi*, 47n134, 48n146, 368–

69; for Buontalenti's final inventory and will, 73n131, 100n93. On the 1608 performance and commemorative prints, see generally Nagler, *Theatre Festivals*, 101–15; Strong, *Splendor at Court*, 206–11. For an additional example of Parigi's adaptation of Buontalenti motifs, see cat. 73–74. Two further artists associated with the 1589 events also prepared the entry and other works for 1608. On Jacopo Ligozzi, see Blumenthal, *Giulio Parigi*, 47n134. On Cigoli, ibid., 48n146; Blumenthal, *Theater Art of the Medici*, no. 39; idem, *Italian Renaissance Festival Designs*, 104, no. 44; Molinari, "Attività teatrale," pt. 2, 62–69.

20. On the Farnese theater by G. B. Aleotti, and further development of the building type, see Wittkower, *Art and Architecture*, 122–23; Pevsner, *Building Types*, 66–90; Borsi et al., *Potere e spazio*, 368–69.

21. For Giulio's academy and Jones's attendance see Giuliano Pellegrini, "Inigo Jones 'Fiorentino,'" in Borsi et al., *Potere e spazio*, 375–79; Blumenthal, *Giulio Parigi*, 32–33. On Jones see Stephen Orgel and Roy Strong, *Inigo Jones: The Theatre of the Stuart Court*, 2 vols. (Los Angeles: University of California Press, 1973); Strong, *Splendor at Court*, chap. 6. Jones's Indian scene is illustrated by Strong, 220, fig. 161; Orgel and Strong, 2: 599–612, cat. 295.

22. In 1588–89, Servi "fa di stucco" for the workshop in the Uffizi: ASF, Depositeria generale 389, 11; on his portrait of Christine, see Langedijk, *Portraits of the Medici*, 1: 667, no. 27, illustrated. On Servi see Baldinucci, *Notizie dei professori*, 3: 207–29; for his career in England, Pellegrini, "Inigo Jones 'Fiorentino,'" with text of his letter and earlier references; Roy Strong, *Henry Prince of Wales and England's Lost Renaissance* (London: Thames and Hudson, 1986), 88–105. More broadly on the presence of foreign artists and masons in England, see Thomson, *Renaissance Architecture*, 44. On Buontalenti's bequest of the modelli inventoried as

remaining in his possession at his death (others may have been kept in Medici archives from their creation), see above. My hypothesis (not otherwise documented) about the particular drawings sent to Servi may be supported by the fact that all four of the surviving original set designs are now in England (cat. 8, 26, 33, 63), and one of only two costume drawings that survive from int. 6, showing Fortune (cat. 66), was also in an English collection; further research into the early provenance of these drawings might shed light on this suggestion.

23. For an overview of the art and architecture developments after 1590 see Ludwig Heydenreich and Wolfgang Lotz, *Architecture in Italy, 1400–1600* (Harmondsworth: Penguin, 1974), esp. chap. 27, "Tuscany 1550–1600" (on Dosio, 324n24); Wittkower, *Art and Architecture*, who notes (97) that "the role of Florence in Seicento painting is disappointingly but not unexpectedly limited" and devotes only a few pages to architecture, similarly characterized as "limited" (125–26, on Cigoli). On musical events of the 1590s see the survey by Donington, *Rise of Opera*, chaps. 8–9.

24. On Rubens's *Debarkation* (Paris, Louvre, inv. 1774), see Susan Seward, *The Golden Age of Marie de' Medici* (Ann Arbor: UMI Press, 1982), 60–67; Ronald F. Millen and Robert E. Wolf, *Heroic Deeds and Mystic Figures: A New Reading of Rubens' "Life of Maria de' Medici"* (Princeton: Princeton University Press, 1989), 63–72. Neither source comments on the similarity to Cosci.

25. *Dizionario biografico degli italiani*, 31: 37–40 (s.v. Christina di Lorena).

26. On Alfonso Parigi's and later uses of the theater, see Mancini et al., *Illusione e pratica*, 49–52; Fara, *Buontalenti: Architettura e teatro*, 13. The surviving fragment of Giovanni Bologna's statue for the theater interior (see Chap. 3) was removed from display after the 1993 bombing of the Uffizi.

Bibliography

ARCHIVAL DOCUMENTS

Archivio di Stato, Florence (ASF), Carteggio mediceo, Principato, filza 802.

ASF, Carteggio mediceo, Principato, filza 805.

ASF, Carte Strozziane, ser. 1, vol. 1: Giovanni del Maestro, *Relazione della venuta, preparazioni e ricevimento della Ser.ma Gran Duchessa Christina di Loreno, de' personaggi che furono alle nozze, e come furono ricevuti* (1597).

ASF, Depositeria generale (parte antica), filza 389: *Ruolo della casa et familiarii del Ser.mo Ferdinando Medicis, Gran Duca di Toscana, 1588.*

ASF, Fabbriche medicee (Scrittoio delle fortezze e fabbriche), filza 24: *Palazzo Ducale, 1588.*

ASF, Guardaroba medicea (GM), filza 120: *Quaderno di livree e vestiti fatto dall'anno 1587 con seguita.*

ASF, Guardaroba medicea, filza 122: *Libri di donativi diversi* (1587–93).

ASF, Guardaroba medicea, filza 125: *Inventario di oggetti mandati nelle ville granducali* (1587–97).

ASF, Guardaroba medicea, filza 128: *Inventario a capi del taglio, 1587–96.*

ASF, Guardaroba medicea, filza 130: *Libro di debitori e creditori della guardaroba, 1587–91.*

ASF, Guardaroba medicea, filza 131: *Memoriale di manifattori della guardaroba, 1587–88.*

ASF, Guardaroba medicea, filza 134: *Filza d'affari diversi della guardaroba generale (1586–96).*

ASF, Guardaroba medicea, filza 136: *Libro intitolato Magia . . .* (1588–90).

ASF, Guardaroba medicea, filza 137: *Libro d'entrata e uscita della guardaroba, 1588–96.*

ASF, Guardaroba medicea, filza 140 (LC): *Libro di conti relativi alla commedia diritta da Emilio de' Cavalieri.*

ASF, Guardaroba medicea, filza 142: *Quad.e e note attenenti alle manifatture di livree . . . del Sig. Bened.o Fedini, et in occas.e delle nozze del Ser.mo G. Duca.*

ASF, Guardaroba medicea, filza 143: *Filza contenente perizie, disegni di mobili, note, conti, ecc., 1588–94.*

ASF, Guardaroba medicea, filza 144: *Libro di conti diversi e mandati di pagamenti, 1587–94.*

ASF, Guardaroba medicea, filza 147: *Inventari degli oggetti che si trovano nelle fattorie di S.A.S . . . , 1588–96.*

ASF, Guardaroba medicea, filza 148: *Libro del taglio della guardaroba, 1588–89.*

ASF, Guardaroba medicea, filza 152: *Inventario delle gioie portate di Francia dalla Principessa Cristina di Lorena . . .*

ASF, Guardaroba medicea, filza 157: *Libro de debitori e creditori della guardaroba . . . del M.co S.r Benedetto Fedini . . . , 1588–90.*

ASF, Guardaroba medicea, filza 159: *Abiti, o vesti reale per S.A.S.* (1588–91).

ASF, Guardaroba medicea, filza 183: *Filza di conti . . . della galleria, 1588–89.*

ASF, Magistrato de' Nove Conservatori, filza 3679 (MR): Girolamo Seriacopi, *Memoriale e ricordi tenuto da Girolamo Seriacopi Provveditore del Castello di Firenze, 1588–1589.*

ASF, Magistrato de' Nove Conservatori, filza 3712: *Debitori e creditori della fabbrica dei XIII magistrati* (1585–88).

ASF, Magistrato de' Nove Conservatori, filza 3713: *Libro di debitori e creditori della fabbrica, 1588–93.*

ASF, Manoscritti, filza 130: Francesco Settimani, *Memorie fiorentine dell'anno MDXXII . . . infino all'anno MDCCXXXVII . . . ,* vol. 5 (1587–95).

Biblioteca Nazionale Centrale, Florence (BNCF), Sezione manoscritti e libri rari, Palatina C.B.3.53, vols. 1 and 2. *Parigi, Giulio: Disegni originali de' carri e figure . . . aggiuntivi*

i disegni dei personaggi che rappresentarono la
commedia intitolata "La pellegrina" . . .

CONTEMPORARY PRINTED
SOURCES

Li artificiosi e dilettevoli intermedi rappresentati
nella comedia fatta per le nozze della Serenissima
Gran Duchessa di Toscana. Perugia: Pi-
etropaolo Orlando, 1589.

Bargagli, Girolamo. *La pellegrina, commedia di*
M. Girolamo Bargagli rappresentata in Firenze
. . . Siena: Bonetti, 1589, and Florimi, 1589.

———. *La pellegrina.* Ed. Florindo Cerreta.
Florence: Olschki, 1971.

———. *The Female Pilgrim.* Trans. Bruno Ferraro. Carleton Renaissance Plays in Translation, 12. Ottawa: Dovehouse, 1988.

Cardi, Niccola de. *Venuta della serenissima Cri-*
stina di Loreno in Italia al seggio ducale di
Fiorenza del suo serenissimo sposo Don Ferdi-
nando Medici Gran Duca terzo di Toscana rac-
colta in ottava rima. Florence: Marescotti,
1590.

Cavallino, Simone. *Raccolta di tutte le solen-*
nissime feste nel sponsalitio della Serenissima
Gran Duchessa di Toscana fatte in Fiorenza il
mese di maggio 1589. Rome: Blado, 1589.

Cecchi, Baccio. *Descrizione dell'apparato e de*
gl'intermedi fatti per la storia dell'esaltazione del-
la croce con i suoi intermedi ridotto in atto rap-
presentativo . . . recitata in Firenze da' giovani
della Compagnia di San Giovanni Vangelista . . .
Florence: Sermantelli, 1589.

Descrittione della solenissima entrata della Ser.ma
Donna Cristina di Loreno in Fiorenza fatta alli 3
di aprile 1586 [sic]. Bologna: Benacci, 1589.

Descrizione delle pompe e feste fatte ne la città di
Pisa per la venuta de la S. Madama Christierna
de l'Oreno Gran Duchessa di Toscana. Nella
quale si contano l'entrata, la battaglia navale, la
battaglia del ponte, la luminaria, i fuochi arti-
fiziali . . . Florence: Marescotti, 1589.

Discours de la magnifique réception et trionphante
entrée de la Grande Duchesse de Toscane en la
ville de Florence, avec les cérémonies de son cou-

ronnement et esponsailles. Lyons: Benoist Rig-
aud, 1589.

Le feste fatte nelle nozze delli Ser. Granduca e
Granduchessa di Toscana Ferdinando I e Cristina
di Lorena. N.p., n.d.

Gualterotti, Raffaello. *Descrizione del regale ap-*
parato per le nozze della Serenissima Madama
Cristiana di Loreno moglie del Serenissimo Don
Ferdinando Medici III Granduca di Toscana.
Book 2. Florence: Padovani, May 1589.

———. *Della descrizione del regale apparato fatto*
nella nobile città di Firenza per la venuta e per le
nozze della Serenissima Madama Cristina di
Loreno moglie del Serenissimo Don Ferdinando
Medici terzo Gran Duca di Toscana. Books 1
and 2. Florence: Padovani, June 1589.

Malvezzi, Cristofano. *Intermedii e concerti, fatti*
per la commedia rappresentata in Firenze nelle
nozze del Serenissimo Don Ferdinando Medici e
Madama Christiana di Lorena Gran Duchi di
Toscana. Venice: Vincenti, 1591.

Pavoni, Giuseppe. *Diario descritto da Giuseppe*
Pavoni delle feste celebrate nelle solennissime
nozze delli serenissimi sposi . . . nel quale con
brevità si esplica il torneo, la bataglia navale, la
comedia con gli intermedi . . . alli molto illustri
. . . Giasone et Pompeo fratelli de' Vizani. Bologna: Rossi, 1589.

———. *Entrata della serenissima Gran Duchessa*
sposa, nella città di Fiorenza, scritta da Giuseppe
Pavoni. Al molto illustre, e pieno di cortesia si-
gnore, il Signor Gio. Battista Strada Hispano.
Bologna: Rossi, 1589.

Percivalle, Bernardino. *L'orsilia boschereccia*
sdrucciola di M. Bernardino Percivalle esposta
nelle eroiche e suntuosissime nozze del sereniss. ed
invito D. Ferdinando Medici . . . Bologna:
Rossi, 1589.

Rossi, Bastiano de'. *Descrizione dell'apparato e*
degl'intermedi fatti per la commedia rappresen-
tata in Firenze nelle nozze de' Serenissimi Don
Ferdinando Medici e Madama Cristina di Lo-
reno, Gran Duchi di Toscana. Florence: Padovani; Milan: Piccaglia, 1589.

Li sontuosissimi apparecchi, trionfi, e feste, fatti nelle
nozze della Gran Duchessa di Fiorenza: con il

nome, e numero de duchi, precipi, marchesi, baroni, et altri gran personaggi: postovi il modo di vestire, maniere, e livree. Et la descrittione de gl'intermedi. . . . Aggiuntovi l'ordine, e modo che s'è tenuto nel coronare l'Altezza della Serenissima Gran Duchessa. Florence and Ferrara: Baldini; Venice: Larduccio, 1589.

L'ultime feste ed apparati superbissimi fatti in Fiorenza nelle nozze del Ser.mo Granduca di Toscano. Bologna: Alessandro Benacci, 1589.

Vasari, Giorgio. *Le vite de' più eccellenti pittori, scultori, ed architettori.* 1568. Ed. Gaetano Milanesi. 9 vols. Florence: Sansoni, 1878–85.

Walker, D. P., ed. *Les Fêtes du mariage de Ferdinand de Médicis et de Christine de Lorraine, Florence, 1589.* Vol. 1, *Musique des Intermèdes de "La Pellegrina."* Paris: CNRS, 1963.

SECONDARY SOURCES

Ackerman, James. *The Villa: Form and Ideology of Country Houses.* Princeton: Princeton University Press/Bollingen, 1990.

d'Ancona, Alessandro. *Sacre rappresentazioni dei secoli XIV, XV, e XVI raccolte ed illustrate.* 3 vols. Florence: LeMonnier, 1872.

———. *Origini del teatro italiano.* 2 vols. Turin: Loescher, 1891. Reprint, Rome: Bardi, 1971.

Artusi, Luciano, and Silvano Gabbrielli. *Le feste di Firenze.* Rome: Newton Compton, 1991.

Bacou, Roseline. *Le Seizième Siècle européen: Dessins du Louvre.* Exhibition catalogue, Paris: Musée du Louvre, 1965.

Bacou, Roseline, and Jacob Bean. *Dessins florentins de la collection de Filippo Baldinucci.* Exhibition catalogue, Paris: Musée du Louvre, 1958.

———. *Disegni fiorentini del Museo del Louvre.* Exhibition catalogue, Rome: Gabinetto nazionale delle stampe, 1959.

Baldinucci, Filippo. *Notizie dei professori del disegno da Cimabue in qua.* 1681. Ed. F. Ranalli. 5 vols. Florence: Batelli, 1845.

Bartsch, Adam. *Le Peintre-graveur.* 21 vols. Vienna, 1803–21.

Berner, Samuel. "Florentine Political Thought in the Late Cinquecento." *Il pensiero politico: Quaderni dell'Istituto di scienza politica Università di Genova* 3 (1970): 177–99.

———. "Florentine Society in the Late Sixteenth and Early Seventeenth Centuries." *Studies in the Renaissance* 18 (1971): 203–46.

Berti, Franco. "Studi su alcuni aspetti del diario di Girolamo Seriacopi e sui disegni buontalentiani per i costumi del 1589." *Quaderni di teatro* 2, 7 (Mar. 1980): 157–68.

Blumenthal, Arthur. *Italian Renaissance Festival Designs.* Exhibition catalogue, Madison: Elvehjem Art Center/University of Wisconsin Press, 1973.

———. *Theater Art of the Medici.* Exhibition catalogue, Hanover, N.H.: Dartmouth College Museum/University Press of New England, 1980.

———. *Giulio Parigi's Stage Designs: Florence and the Early Baroque Spectacle.* New York: Garland, 1986.

———. "Medici Patronage and the Festival of 1589." In *IL 60: Essays Honoring Irving Lavin on His Sixtieth Birthday*, ed. Marilyn Aronberg Lavin, 97–106. New York: Italica Press, 1990.

Bohlin, Diane DeGrazia. *Prints and Related Drawings by the Carracci Family: A Catalogue Raisonné.* Washington, D.C.: National Gallery, 1979.

Borsi, Franco, et al. *Il potere e lo spazio: La scena del principe.* Exhibition catalogue, Florence: Forte di Belvedere; Milan: Electa, 1980.

Botto, Ida Maria. *Mostra di disegni di Bernardo Buontalenti.* Exhibition catalogue, Florence: Uffizi/Olschki, 1968.

Braudel, Fernand. *The Mediterranean and the Mediterranean World in the Age of Philip II.* Trans. Siân Reynolds. New York: Harper and Row, 1973.

———. *The Perspective of the World.* Civilization and Capitalism, 15th–18th Centuries, vol. 3. Trans. Siân Reynolds. Berkeley: University of California Press, 1984.

Braudel, Fernand, and Ruggiero Romano. *Na-*

vires et marchandises à l'entrée du port de Livourne, 1571–1611. Paris: Colin, 1951.

Bullough, Vern, and Bonnie Bullough. *Cross-Dressing, Sex, and Gender.* Philadelphia: University of Pennsylvania Press, 1993.

Casali, Giovanni, and Ester Diana. *Bernardo Buontalenti e la burocrazia tecnica nella Toscana medicea.* Florence: Alinea, 1983.

Chappell, Miles. *Disegni di Ludovico Cigoli.* Exhibition catalogue, Florence: Uffizi/Olschki, 1992.

Clubb, Louise George. *Italian Drama in Shakespeare's Time.* New Haven: Yale University Press, 1989.

Cochrane, Eric. *Florence in the Forgotten Centuries, 1527–1800.* Chicago: University of Chicago Press, 1973.

Il Corago, o vero alcune osservazioni per metter bene in scena le composizioni drammatiche. Ca. 1628. Ed. Paolo Fabbri and Angelo Pompilio. Florence: Olschki, 1983.

Daddi Giovannozzi, Vera. "La vita di Bernardo Buontalenti scritta da Gherardo Silvani." *Rivista d'arte* 14 (1932): 505–24.

———. *Ricerche su Bernardo Buontalenti.* Florence: Olschki, 1934.

———. "Di alcune incisioni dell'apparato per le nozze di Ferdinando de' Medici e Cristina di Lorena." *Rivista d'arte* 22 (1940): 85–100.

Diaz, Furio. *Il granducato di Toscana: I Medici.* Storia d'Italia, 13. Turin: UTET, 1987.

Dizionario biografico degli italiani. 40 vols. to date. Rome: Istituto della Enciclopedia Italiana, 1960–.

Donington, Robert. *The Rise of Opera.* London: Faber and Faber, 1981.

Enciclopedia dello spettacolo. 11 vols. Rome: Le Maschere, 1954–62.

Fabbri, Mario, Elvira Garbero Zorzi, and Annamaria Petrioli Tofani, eds. *Il luogo teatrale a Firenze: Brunelleschi, Vasari, Buontalenti, Parigi.* Exhibition catalogue, Florence: Palazzo Medici-Riccardi/Electa, 1975.

Fanelli, Giovanni. *Firenze, architettura e città.* Florence: Vallecchi, 1973.

Fara, Amelio. *Bernardo Buontalenti: Architettura e teatro.* Florence: La nuova Italia, 1979.

———. *Bernardo Buontalenti: L'architettura, la guerra e l'elemento geometrico.* Genoa: SAGEP, 1988.

Faranda, Franco. *Ludovico Cardi detto il Cigoli.* Rome: de Luca, 1986.

Firenze e la Toscana dei Medici nell'Europa del '500. 3 vols. Vol. 2, *Musica e spettacolo,* ed. Furio Diaz. Florence: Olschki, 1983.

Flack, Michael E. "Giambologna's Cappella di Sant'Antonino for the Salviati Family: An Ensemble of Architecture, Sculpture, and Painting." Ph.D. diss., Columbia University, 1986.

Freedberg, S. J. *Painting in Italy, 1500–1600.* Harmondsworth: Penguin, 1975.

Gadoli, Antonio, and Antonio Natali, eds. *Luoghi della Toscana medicea.* Florence: Becocci, 1980.

Gaeta Bertelà, Giovanna, and Annamaria Petrioli Tofani. *Feste e apparati medicei da Cosimo I a Cosimo II.* Exhibition catalogue, Florence: Uffizi/Olschki, 1969.

Gaye, Giovanni. *Carteggio inedito d'artisti dei secoli XIV–XVI.* 3 vols. Florence, 1839–40.

Goldthwaite, Richard. *The Building of Renaissance Florence: An Economic and Social History.* Baltimore: Johns Hopkins University Press, 1980.

———. *Wealth and the Demand for Art in Italy, 1300–1600.* Baltimore: Johns Hopkins University Press, 1993.

Gualandi, Michelangelo. *Raccolta di lettere sulla pittura, scultura ed architettura scritte da' più celebri personaggi dei secoli XV, XVI e XVII.* Ed. Giovanni Bottari and Stefano Ticozzi. 2 vols. Milan, 1822.

———. *Nuova raccolta di lettere sulla pittura, scultura, ed architettura scritte da' più celebri personaggi dei secoli XV a XIX.* Rev. ed. Giovanni Bottari and Stefano Ticozzi. 3 vols. Bologna, 1844–56.

Hale, J. R. *Florence and the Medici: The Pattern of Control.* New York: Thames and Hudson, 1977.

Hanning, Barbara Russano. "Glorious Apollo: Poetic and Political Themes in the First Opera." *Renaissance Quarterly* 32 (1980): 485–513.

Heikamp, Detlev. "Il Teatro Mediceo degli Uffizi." *Bollettino del Centro internazionale di studi di architettura Andrea Palladio* 16 (1974): 323–32.

Hewitt, Bernard. *The Renaissance Stage: Documents of Serlio, Sabbattini, and Furttenbach.* Coral Gables: University of Miami Press, 1958.

Heydenreich, Ludwig, and Wolfgang Lotz. *Architecture in Italy, 1400–1600.* Harmondsworth: Penguin, 1974.

Hibbert, Christopher. *The Rise and Fall of the House of Medici.* Harmondsworth: Penguin, 1974.

Howard, Jean E. *The Stage and Social Struggle in Early Modern England.* New York: Routledge, 1994.

Hunt, Lynn, ed. *The New Cultural History.* Berkeley: University of California Press, 1989.

Jacquot, Jean. "Les Fêtes de Florence (1589): Quelques aspects de leur mise-en-scène." *Theatre Research* 3: 6 (1961): 157–76.

———, ed. *Les Fêtes de la Renaissance.* 3 vols. Paris: CNRS, 1956–75.

———, ed. *Le Lieu théâtral à la Renaissance.* Paris: CNRS, 1964.

Kernodle, George. *From Art to Theatre: Form and Convention in the Renaissance.* 1944. Reprint, Chicago: University of Chicago Press, 1970.

Kerrigan, William, and Gordon Braden. *The Idea of the Renaissance.* Baltimore: Johns Hopkins University Press, 1989.

Langedijk, Karla. *The Portraits of the Medici: 15th to 18th Centuries.* 3 vols. Florence: Studio per edizioni scelte, 1981.

Laver, James. "Stage Designs for the Florentine Intermezzi of 1589." *Burlington Magazine* 60 (1932): 294–300.

Lazzaro, Claudia. *The Italian Renaissance Garden.* New Haven: Yale University Press, 1990.

LeClerc, Hélène. "Du Mythe platonicien aux fêtes de la Renaissance: 'L'Harmonie du monde,' incantation et symbolisme." *Revue d'histoire du théâtre* ser. 2, 11 (1952): 106–49.

Libro del sarto della Fondazione Querini Stampalia di Venezia. Ferrara: Panini, 1987.

Lieure, J. L. *Jacques Callot, catalogue de l'oeuvre gravé.* Paris: Gazette des beaux-arts, 1924.

Lucchesini, Paolo. *I teatri di Firenze.* Rome: Newton Compton, 1991.

Mamone, Sara. *Il teatro nella Firenze medicea.* Milan: Mursia, 1981.

Mancini, Franco, Maria Teresa Muraro, and Elena Povoledo, eds. *Illusione e pratica teatrale: Proposti per una lettura dello spazio scenico dagli intermedi fiorentini all'opera comica veneziana.* Exhibition catalogue, Venice: Fondazione Giorgio Cini; Vicenza: Neri Pozza, 1975.

Marotti, Ferruccio. *Lo spettacolo dall'umanesimo al manierismo: Teoria e tecnica.* Storia documentaria del teatro italiano, 10. Milan: Feltrinelli, 1974.

Massar, Phyllis Dearborn. "A Set of Prints and a Drawing for the 1589 Medici Marriage Festival." *Master Drawings* 13 (1975): 12–23.

Matteoli, Anna. *Lodovico Cigoli, pittore e architetto: Fonti biografiche.* Pisa: Giardini, 1980.

Mignani, Daniela. *The Medicean Villas by Giusto Utens.* Trans. Stephanie Johnson. Florence: Arnaud, 1991.

Mitchell, Bonner. *A Year of Pageantry in Late Renaissance Ferrara.* Binghamton, N.Y.: Center for Medieval and Early Renaissance Studies, 1990.

Molinari, Cesare. "L'attività teatrale di Ludovico Cigoli." *Critica d'arte* 8, 47 (1961): 62–67; 8, 48 (1961): 62–69.

———. *Le nozze degli dèi: Un saggio sul grande spettacolo italiano del Seicento.* Rome: Bulzoni, 1968.

———. "L'altra faccia del 1589: Isabella Andreini e la sua *Pazzia.*" In *Firenze e la Toscana dei Medici nell'Europa del '500,* vol. 2, *Musica e spettacolo,* 565–73. Florence: Olschki, 1983.

Mori, Attilio, and Giuseppe Boffito. *Piante e*

vedute di Firenze: Studio storico topografico cartografico. Florence: Giuntina, 1926. Reprint, Rome: Multigrafica, 1973.

Nagler, Alois. *Theatre Festivals of the Medici, 1539–1637.* New Haven: Yale University Press, 1964.

The New Grove Dictionary of Music and Musicians. Ed. Stanley Sadie. 20 vols. London: Macmillan, 1980.

Newman, Karen. "The Politics of Spectacle: *La pellegrina* and the Intermezzi of 1589." *MLN* 101 (1986): 95–113.

Newton, Stella Mary. *Renaissance Theatre Costume and the Sense of the Historic Past.* New York: Theatre Art Books, 1975.

Panofsky, Erwin. *Perspective as Symbolic Form.* 1927. Reprint, New York: Zone, 1991.

Parker, K. T. *Catalogue of the Collection of Drawings in the Ashmolean Museum.* 2 vols. Oxford: Clarendon, 1956.

Pevsner, Nikolaus. *A History of Building Types.* Princeton: Princeton University Press/ Bollingen, 1976.

Pirrotta, Nino, and Elena Povoledo. *Li due Orfei.* Turin: ERI, 1969.

———. *Music and Theatre from Poliziano to Monteverdi.* Trans. Karen Eales. Cambridge: Cambridge University Press, 1982.

Pope-Hennessy, John. *Italian High Renaissance and Baroque Sculpture.* London: Phaidon, 1970.

Pounds, N[orman]. J. G. *An Historical Geography of Europe.* Cambridge: Cambridge University Press, 1990.

Il primato del disegno. Exhibition catalogue, Florence: Palazzo Strozzi/Centro Di, 1980.

Reade, Brian. *Ballet Designs and Illustrations 1581–1940: A Catalogue Raisonné.* Victoria and Albert Museum. London: Her Majesty's Stationery Office, 1967.

Roselli, Piero, Giuseppina Carla Romby, and Osanna Fantozzi Micali. *I teatri di Firenze.* Florence: Bonechi, 1978.

Rossi, Sergio. *Dalle botteghe alle accademie: realtà sociale e teorie artistiche a Firenze dal XIV al XVI secolo.* Milan: Feltrinelli, 1980.

Russell, H. Diane. *Jacques Callot: Prints and Related Drawings.* Exhibition catalogue, Washington, D.C.: National Gallery, 1975.

Sabbattini, Nicola. *Pratica di fabricar scene e machine ne' teatri.* 1638. Ed. Elena Povoledo. Rome: Bestetti, 1955.

Shearman, John. *Mannerism.* Harmondsworth: Penguin, 1967.

Solerti, Angelo. *Gli albori del melodramma.* 3 vols. Milan: Sandron, 1904–5. Reprint, Bologna: Forni, 1976.

———. *Musica, ballo e drammatica alla corte medicea dal 1600 al 1637.* Florence: Bemporad, 1905. Reprint, Bologna: Forni, 1969.

Sommi, Leone de'. *Quattro dialoghi in materia di rappresentationi sceniche.* Ca. 1565. Ed. Ferruccio Marotti. Milan: Il Polifilo, 1968.

Spini, Giorgio, ed. *Architettura e politica da Cosimo I a Ferdinando I.* Florence: Olschki, 1976.

Starn, Randolph, and Loren Partridge. *Arts of Power: Three Halls of State in Italy, 1300–1600.* Berkeley: University of California Press, 1992.

Strong, Roy. *Splendor at Court: Renaissance Spectacle and the Theater of Power.* Boston: Houghton Mifflin, 1973.

———. *Art and Power: Renaissance Festivals, 1450–1650.* Berkeley: University of California Press, 1984.

Testaverde, Anna Maria. "Creatività e tradizione in una 'sartoria teatrale': L'abito scenico per le feste fiorentine del 1589." In *Il costume nell'età del rinascimento,* ed. Dora Liscia Bemporad, 175–99. Florence: Edifir, 1988.

Thomson, David. *Renaissance Architecture: Critics, Patrons, Luxury.* Manchester: Manchester University Press, 1993.

Trexler, Richard C. *Public Life in Renaissance Florence.* Ithaca: Cornell University Press, 1980.

Turner, Nicholas. *Florentine Drawings of the Sixteenth Century.* Exhibition catalogue, London: British Museum; Cambridge: Cambridge University Press, 1986.

Vannucci, Marcello. *The History of Florence.* Rome: Newton Compton, 1986.

Viatte, Françoise. *Dessins italiens du Musée du Louvre I: Dessins toscans XVIe–XVIIe siècles.* Tome 1, *1560–1640.* Inventaire général des dessins italiens, 3. Paris: Réunion des musées nationaux, 1988.

Wallace, William E. *Michelangelo at San Lorenzo: The Genius as Entrepreneur.* Cambridge: Cambridge University Press, 1994.

Warburg, Aby. "I costumi teatrali per gli Intermezzi del 1589: I disegni di Bernardo Buontalenti e il 'Libro di conti' di Emilio de' Cavalieri." 1895. In *Gesammelte Schriften*, ed. Gertrud Bing, 259–300, 394–441. Leipzig: Teubner, 1932. Reprint, Liechtenstein: Kraus, 1969.

Warnke, Martin. *The Court Artist: On the Ancestry of the Modern Artist.* Trans. David McLintock. Cambridge: Cambridge University Press, 1993.

Watson, Katherine J. "Sugar Sculpture for Grand Ducal Weddings from the Giambologna Workshop." *Connoisseur* 199 (Sept. 1978): 20–26.

Wilson, Charles. *The Transformation of Europe, 1558–1648.* Berkeley: University of California Press, 1976.

Wisch, Barbara, and Susan Scott Munshower, eds. *"All the world's a stage . . . ": Art and Pageantry in the Renaissance and Baroque.* Papers in Art History from the Pennsylvania State University, 6. University Park: Pennsylvania State University Press, 1990.

Wittkower, Rudolf. *Art and Architecture in Italy, 1600–1750.* 3d ed. Harmondsworth: Penguin, 1980.

Wolff, Janet. *The Social Production of Art.* New York: New York University Press, 1984.

Yates, Frances. *Theater of the World.* Chicago: University of Chicago Press, 1969.

———. *Astraea: The Imperial Theme in the Sixteenth Century.* London: Routledge, 1975.

Zorzi, Ludovico. *Il teatro e la città: Saggi sulla scena italiana.* Turin: Einaudi, 1977.

SOURCES OF ILLUSTRATIONS

Index

Academy of Design (Florence), 91–92

Accademia degli Intronati, 51, 54, 116, 127, 171, 297*n*23

Accademia della Crusca, 16, 27, 29

Actors, in comedies, 50–51

Agostino (dancer), 51

Alberti, Cherubino, 180

Alessandro del Impruneta, 107

Alfiano, Epifanio d', 180–81

Allori, Alessandro, 2; as artistic adviser, 71; as administrator of Uffizi workshops, 90–93; salary, 92; decoration of Poggio a Caiano, 137; work for Capitana, 289*n*56

Allori, Cristofano, 92

Ambrogiana, 133–35, 137

Ammannati, Bartolommeo, 89, 90

Amphitrite, role of (intermedio 5), 32, 52, 61

Andreini, Francesco, 51

Andreini, Isabella, 37, 51, 54, 56, 76, 169–70

Androgyne, 56

Angeli, Pietro, da Barga, 22, 24

Antoninus, Saint. *See* San Marco

Apollo: role of (intermedio 3), 32, 157; role of (intermedio 6), 33; costumes for, 61; overhead wires for, 95, 115, 154

Archilei, Antonio, 39–40, 52–53, 176

Archilei, Margherita, 52–53, 157

Archilei, Vittoria, 39, 52–53, 62, 152, 157

Architecture, emergence as profession, 44

Arion, role of (intermedio 5), 32–33, 67

Aristocracy: attempts to limit power of, 13–14, 161; manufacturing activities, 72

Artimino (villa), 136

Artists, status and socioeconomic organization of, 91–93

Astraea, role of (intermedio 1), 31

Atticiato, Domenico di Bartolo, 107–10, 115, 128, 301*n*9

Bacchus, role of (intermedio 6), 33, 61

Balbi, Giovanni (tailor), 71

Baldracca Theater (Florence), 76–78, 81

Balducci. *See* Cosci, Giovanni

Bandini, Giovanni, 90

Bardella. *See* Naldi, Antonio

Bardi, Giovanni de': programmer of intermedi, 2, 39–40, 113–14; member of Accademia della Crusca, 16, 27; programmer for *1586* wedding, 25; biographical outline, 27–29; collaboration with Buontalenti, 28, 45; as iconographer at Pitti, 33; disliked by Ferdinando, 40; supervises rehearsals of intermedi, 73; punch lists for theater, 101; family lodges guests, 137; at entry, 143; at Uffizi performance, 152–53; treatise on calcio, 161; work after *1589*, 183

Bargagli, Girolamo, 4, 36

Bargagli, Scipione, 21, 36

Bartolini, Niccolò, 55

Bavaria, 66

Berardi, Oreto, 64–65, 68; work for Guardaroba, 71; late payments, 176–77; work for Capitana, 289*n*56; work on upholstery, 293*n*36

Bologna, Giovanni (Giambologna), 2; sculpture for Medici Theater, 4, 79; work at Pratolino, 81, 89, 135; as cost estimator, 89; sculptures for entry, 89; works at Palazzo Vecchio, 89–90, 92, 97; work at San Marco, 92–93; work at Pisa, 130; sugar sculpture, 159–60

Borghini, Vincenzo, 23–24, 46–47, 292*n*26, 297*n*23

Boscoli, Andrea, 2, 45, 62–63, 90–91, 181

Boys, as performers, 52, 175

Bronzino, Agnolo, 42, 71, 89–90

Brunswick, Duchess of, 141, 160, 175, 300*n*56

Buontalenti, Bernardo: as designer of Uffizi Theater, 2; activities as engineer, 12; rivalry with Dosio, 24; as designer of *1579* and *1586* weddings, 25, 28; collaboration with

Buontalenti, Bernardo (*continued*)
Bardi, 28, 45; biographical outline, 42–45; costume designs for *1589*, 59–60; as supervisor of artists and craftworkers, 88–92; disputes with Seriacopi, 93–96, 99–101; dispute with Cavalieri, 132–33; as decorator of villas, 135; work after *1589*, 182–85
Buontalenti, Francesco, 172, 174, 297n25
Bureaucracy, 12–13, 16, 40, 92–93, 107. *See also* Cavalieri, Emilio de'; Control
Buti, Ludovico, 287n40
Butteri, Giovanmaria, 71, 92, 98

Caccia (animal baiting), 163–64
Caccini, Giovanni (quartermaster), 46
Caccini, Giovanni Battista (sculptor), 39, 287n40
Caccini, Giulio, 28, 39–40, 52–53, 104, 182
Caccini, Lucia, 39, 52, 55
Calcio, giuoco di (football game), 161–62
Callot, Jacques, 12–13, 79, 183–84, 296n19
Cambi, Napoleone, 64, 73, 88, 275n46
Camerata fiorentina, 2, 28, 38
Canto de' Bischeri (Florence), 145–46
Canto de' Carnesecchi (Florence), 144
Canto degli Antellesi (Florence), 146
Capitana (flagship), 71, 74, 92, 97–98, 117–18
Cappello, Bianca, 28, 166
Carracci, Agostino, 180–81
Castrati, 52–55
Catherine de' Medici, Queen of France, 1, 16–18, 25, 75, 97, 100, 142
Catholic Church, 5, 121, 144–45
Cavalieri, Emilio de': organizes *Libro di conti*, 5, 175; as superintendent of fine arts, 5, 16, 37–38, 40–42; administrative role in wedding, 25–27, 176; as musical director of intermedi, 28; as composer, 37–40; rivalry with Bardi, 38–40; supervision of costumes, 70; activities as stage director, 99; mediates labor disputes, 112; dispute with Buontalenti, 132–33; at entry, 143; at Uffizi performance, 152–53; as choreographer, 158–59; career after *1589*, 186

Cavallino, Simone, 4, 33, 149, 161, 166–69, 179
Cavalori, Mirabello, 90
Cecchi, Giovan Maria, 171
Cecchino (dancer), 51
Ceserone (basso), 55, 68
Cetona, Marchese of. *See* Vitelli, Gianvincenzo
Charles III, Duke of Lorraine, 16
Chelini, Alessandro, 72, 74, 98, 118
Chelino, Tonino di (wigmaker), 65
Christine de Lorraine: marriage negotations, 1; biographical outline, 16–20; dowry of, 18, 140, 177; calendar of wedding events, 19; proxy wedding, 75–76, 99; journey to Marseilles, 99–102, 117; departure and sea voyage, 118–20, 124–26; in Livorno, 128–29; in Pisa, 129–32; at Poggio, 137–38; entry to Florence, 138–47; at Uffizi performance, 150–60 *passim*; at *La pazzia*, 170; life after *1589*, 186–88
Ciampelli, Agostino, 90, 287n40
Cigoli, Ludovico, 2; pupil and assistant of Buontalenti, 44–45; paintings for entry, 90; other wedding-related projects, 91, 181; work at villas, 135; work at Duomo, 144; career after *1589*, 183, 185
Cioli, Valerio, 89, 110
Claude de France, 16
Cloth industry, Florentine, 66–67, 72, 178. *See also* Silk industry
Commedia dell'arte, 37, 54, 76
Compagnia dei Gelosi, 37, 51, 54, 162, 169
Contarini, Francesco, 131, 142
Contarini, Michele, 162, 170
Contarini, Tommaso, 297n22
Contracts, with craftworkers, 108–10
Control, technological and social, by government, 11–12, 122–26, 128–29, 133–37
Convents, 67–68. *See also* Nuns
Cosci, Giovanni, 25, 100, 118, 142–43, 287n40
Cosimo I de' Medici, Grand Duke of Florence, 10, 13, 76, 154
Cosimo II de' Medici, 178, 183

Costumes: design process, 29–30, 50; for intermedi and comedies, 55–70; drawings for, 59–60; for public events, 70–72; revisions to, 103; for Pitti events, 127, 166–67. *See also* Livery

Craftworkers, socioeconomic organization of, 106–10

Dafne, La, (1598), 2, 182
Dallington, Robert, 16, 178
Dance, 40, 51, 157–59
Dante, 32, 156
Descrizioni. See Festival books
Dolphin (intermedio 5), 32
Domenico (carpenter). *See* Atticiato, Domenico di Bartolo
Doric Harmony, role of (intermedio 1), 31, 62, 69
Dosio, Giovannantonio, 23–24, 185–86
Drawings, 50, 59–60, 62–63, 95, 105–6, 185
Drusilla *(La pellegrina)*, 36–37, 56, 60, 63, 66, 153
Duomo (Florence), 51, 121–22, 144–45

Effeminacy, 58
Eleonora of Toledo, 13, 22
Elizabeth I, Queen of England, 56
Empoli, Jacopo Chimenti da, 287*n*40
Engineering, emergence as profession, 43–44
England, 66, 184–85
Entry to Florence, 138–47; creative staff, 22–25, 73; iconography, 35; arch construction, 97; symbolism of date, 121
Este, Cesare d', 25, 71, 137, 140, 180

Fabbri, Cialle, 102, 114–16, 170
Farnese Theater (Parma), 81, 84, 184
Fedini, Benedetto, 64–65, 70, 74, 275*n*46; attends planning meeting, 98; organizes Livorno activities, 117; supervises villas and lodging, 134–35, 137, 143
Fei, Alessandro del Barbiere, 287*n*40
Ferdinando I de' Medici: marriage negotiations, 1; biographical outline, 10–16; final authority for wedding decisions, 27; brings Cavalieri to Florence, 38; appoints festival overseers, 72–73; receives complaints from staff, 93–94; intervenes in intermedi design, 99; gifts to churches, 122; attends rehearsals, 123–24; encourages economic and scientific development, 130–31; meets Christine at Poggio, 138; role at entry, 140–41; at Uffizi performance, 150–60 *passim*; death of, 185
Ferrara, 54, 179–80
Festival books, 4, 140, 178–81
Festivals, history of, 14–16
Fire, 73, 116, 293*n*40
Flanders, 66
Florence, urban reconstruction of, 76–78, 139
Flowers, artificial, 103
Food: for theater workers, 126–27, 155; at banquet, 158–60; at Piazza Santa Croce, 162–63
Fortezza da Basso, 275*n*47
Francesco I de' Medici, 10, 28, 31, 78–79
Francini, Lorenzo, 111–13; paints costumes, 65, 127; paints stage sets, 89, 132; work at Pitti, 106, 133; work at Palazzo Vecchio, 108
Franciosino, Bernardo: music school, 51, 58, 172; salary, 53; supplies musicians, 53, 98; costumes for musicians, 73, 117
François I, King of France, 56–57

Gaddi, Niccolò, 22–24, 138, 143, 287*n*40
Galilei, Galileo, 10, 91, 130
Galilei, Vincenzo, 28
Gender: in costumes, 53–58; in theater seating, 79–81, 151, 165; in food distribution, 126–27; in public, 144; in spectatorship, 161
Genoa, 70, 117, 126, 169
Ghottardo (tailor), 71, 138
Giambologna. *See* Bologna, Giovanni
Giovani (youths), 161, 171–73
Giuoco di calcio (football game), 161–62
Golden Age, myth of, 31–35

Gonzaga, Vincenzo, Duke of Mantua: at Pitti *sfila*, 45, 166; costumes for *caccia*, 71; lodgings in Florence, 137; at entry, 140; at jousts, 164, 171

Gorini, Francesco, 46–47, 64, 69, 103, 113, 186

Graziadio, Orazio, 95, 107–10, 115, 128, 132, 160

Gualfreducci, Onofrio, 52, 55

Gualterotti, Raffaello, 4; festival book for *1579*, 23; festival book for *1589*, 23–24, 140, 178–81; as artist, 161

Guardaroba (state agency), 41, 47, 176; economic reach of, 71–72; role in lodging guests, 137; livery production, 138, 163; construction in Duomo, 144; goods reconsigned to, 175

Guicciardini family, 45; as cloth manufacturers, 72; livery of, 140; float for Pitti, 168

Guidiccioni Lucchesini, Laura, 28, 39, 54, 157, 186

Guise, Henri, Duke of, 18, 100, 281*n*57

Hamadryads, role of (intermedio 2), 32, 54, 61

Henri II, King of France, 16

Henri III, King of France, 1, 16, 56, 100, 175–76

Henri IV, King of France, 176, 182, 186

Hermaphrodite, 56

Homosexuality, 58, 172

Intermedi: history of genre, 1, 29; libretto of, 4; music of, 4; plot and characters of, 30–33; allegorical language of, 33–36; in performance, 151–58

Intronati. *See* Accademia degli Intronati

Jacomelli, Giovanni Battista, 53

Jews, 43, 129, 279*n*37

Joanna (Giovanna) of Austria, 22–23, 146

Jones, Inigo, 184–85

Julius Pollux, 32

Landini, Taddeo, 23

Lapi, Giovanni, 68–69

Lasca, Il (A. F. Grazzini), 29, 36

Leo XI, Pope. *See* Medici, Alessandro de'

Lepida (character in *La pellegrina*), 63

Libro di conti (LC), 5; transcribed by Warburg, 6, 9; structure of, 41; costume information in, 59; accounts closed, 175–77

Lighting: onstage, 86–88, 103, 115, 120, 127; in Uffizi auditorium, 87, 99; at Pitti Palace, 88, 96

Ligozzi, Jacopo, 90, 287*n*40, 296*n*21

Livery, 70–72, 97–98, 117, 138–41

Livorno: fortification of, 12; preparations for fleet and welcome, 117; Christine's arrival in, 128–29

Lodging, of guests and performers, 116, 137

London, 58

Loreto, 51, 175

Lorraine, Christine de. *See* Christine de Lorraine

Louise, Queen of France, 17

Lucchesini, Laura. *See* Guidiccioni Lucchesini, Laura

Lucifer (intermedio 4), 32, 52, 86; design for, 91; construction of, 95, 102, 113–14; in performance, 156; print of, 181

Lyons, France, 18, 118, 179

Macchietti, Girolamo, 286*n*38

Maestro, Giovanni del, 176, 178

Magnificence, 11

Magpies, role of (intermedio 2), 32

Malvezzi, Alberigo, 52

Malvezzi, Cristofano, 39–40, 52, 102, 123

Mantua, Duke of. *See* Gonzaga, Vincenzo

Maps, 135–37

Marchino (tailor), 71

Marenzio, Luca, 38–39, 52–53, 176

Margherita (singer). *See* Archilei, Margherita

Marlowe, Christopher, 58

Marseilles, France, 118

Marucelli, Valerio, 287*n*40

Masks, 55, 65

Medici, Alessandro de' (Pope Leo XI), 122, 144, 164, 267*n*7

Medici, Antonio de', 134

Medici, Averardo de', 120

Medici, Catherine de'. *See* Catherine de' Medici

Medici, Cosimo de'. *See* Cosimo I de' Medici

Medici, Eleonora de' (Duchess of Mantua), 137

Medici, Ferdinando de'. *See* Ferdinando I de' Medici

Medici, Francesco de'. *See* Francesco I de' Medici

Medici, Isabella de', 134

Medici, Lorenzo de', 31, 49, 137

Medici, Maria de', 182, 186

Medici, Pietro de': chariot for Pitti, 45, 166; livery for, 71; attended planning meeting, 98; northbound voyage on Capitana, 117–20; at entry, 140; at Uffizi performance, 156; at calcio, 161; at Pitti, 166; departure for Spain, 176

Medici, Virginia de', 25, 137

Medici Theater. *See* Uffizi Theater

Memoriale e ricordi (MR), 5–6, 9, 46–47, 75, 106. *See also* Seriacopi, Girolamo

Mercury, 61

Monaco, 125–26

Monarchy: growth of, 11; as performance, 15; divine right theory of, 34–35, 39; visualized by stage perspective, 82

Money, 42

Muses, role of (intermedio 2), 31–32

Musical instruments, decoration of, 62, 103, 295*n*6

Musicians, 50–53, 176

Naldi, Antonio, 52–53, 295*n*5

Naldini, Giovanbattista, 286*n*38

Naumachia, 35, 96–97, 127, 168–69

Necessity, role of (in intermedio 1), 8, 31, 55, 63

Needlework, 67–68, 144

Neptune, procession of, 171–73

Nuns, 67–68, 71–73

Orazio (carpenter). *See* Graziadio, Orazio

Oreto (tailor). *See* Berardi, Oreto

Orsini, Francesca, 117, 140, 147, 156

Orsini, Virginio, 117, 134, 140, 161, 168, 171

Paciotto, Francesco, 280*n*48

Pagani, Gregorio, 90, 287*n*40

Pagolini, Piero, 95, 113–15, 154, 156, 160

Palazzo Medici, 81, 137

Palazzo Vecchio: Salone dei Cinquecento, 72–73, 97, 112; renovations and additions, 76, 97; payroll and labor, 97, 107; lodging of guests in, 137; activities for entry, 146–47; banquet in, 158–60

Paper industry, 67

Parcae (Fates), role of (intermedio 1), 31

Parigi, Alfonso the Elder, 89–90, 97, 115, 155, 175

Parigi, Alfonso the Younger, 188

Parigi, Giulio, 44, 90, 172, 182–88

Passignano (Domenico Cresti), 287*n*40

Pavoni, Giuseppe, 4, 33, 149, 161–71 *passim*, 179

Pazzia, La, 37, 162, 169–70

Pellegrina, La: text, 4; symbolic relation to Christine, 18; plot and revisions, 36–37, 82; cast of, 54; costumes for, 58–59; stage set for, 82–83, 94, 99; in performance at Uffizi, 153; performance in Siena, 297*n*23

Peretola, 149

Peri, Jacopo, 2, 28, 39, 52, 156, 174, 182

Periaktoi, 82–83, 94

Perspective, in stage sets, 81–84, 98–99

Petraia, La (villa), 135

Philip II, King of Spain, 145–46, 156

Piazza Santa Croce (Florence), 36, 70, 161–65, 171

Piccolomini, Alfonso, 130, 142

Pieri, Stefano, 110

Pierides, role of (intermedio 2), 31–32

Pierino (castrato), 55

Pieroni, Alessandro, 124, 182, 185, 290*n*15, 291*n*18, 292*n*27

Piissimi, Vittoria, 37, 51, 162

Pisa, 63, 74, 128–32, 153, 169

Pitti Palace, 4; site for events of May 11, 33, 35; construction by Buontalenti, 43; Boboli Gardens, 43, 135; preparations for entertainments, 73, 96–97, 106, 127, 133, 165; contracts and labor, 112–13; lodging of guests in, 137; performance at, 165–69

Plato, 33, 56

Poccetti, Bernardino, 107, 287*n*40

Poggio a Caiano (villa), 133–38, 169

Poliziano, Angelo, 29, 60

Ponte alla Carraia (Florence), 141–44

Poppi (Francesco Morandini), 90, 287*n*40

Porcelain industry, 36, 165

Porta al Prato (Florence), 139–141

Potenze, 172–73

Pratolino (villa), 43, 81, 135

Proscenium, 81–82

Puteo, Carlo Antonio, Archbishop of Pisa, 140–41, 145, 160

Python (intermedio 3), 32, 95, 102, 108, 153–54, 175, 182

Rehearsals, of intermedi, 73, 98–99, 102, 114–16, 126–28, 132–33

Ridolfi, Ruberto, 131–32

Rinuccini, Ottavio, 28, 39–40, 182

Rosselli, Francesco, 111–13; paints costumes, 65, 127; paints stage sets, 73, 89, 95, 114, 132; paints at Pitti, 97, 133; work at Palazzo Vecchio, 108

Rossi, Bastiano de', 4; on magnificence, 11; member of Accademia della Crusca, 16, 29; texts for *1579* and *1586* weddings, 28, 49, 123; working procedures for *1589* festival book, 29–30, 179; text revised by Ferdinando, 40; at Uffizi performance, 152–53

Rubens, Peter Paul, 186–87

Rucellai, Camilla, 64, 147

Rucellai, Orazio, 1, 73, 117, 142, 147, 156, 176–77

Sailors, in naumachia, 163, 169

Salaries: of administrators, 38; of artists, 44, 92–93; of musicians, 53; of tailors, 64–65

Salviati family: as cloth manufacturers, 72; as patrons at San Marco, 72, 92–93, 145, 164; at entry, 145; at Santissima Annunziata, 160; in Order of Santo Stefano, 163

San Lorenzo (Florence), 51, 75, 160, 162–63, 185

San Marco (Florence), chapel of St. Antoninus, 72, 92–93, 126, 145, 164

Santa Croce (Florence), 51, 115

Santa Felicità (Florence), 78

Santi di Tito, 90

Santissima Annunziata (Florence), 51, 145, 160

Santo Stefano, Order of, 74, 117, 129, 130, 157, 163

Scarabelli, Orazio, 180–81

Seriacopi, Girolamo, 5; administrative role in wedding, 27, 45–48; treatment of workers, 73, 160, 174–75; as labor supervisor, 89; disputes with Buontalenti, 93–94, 99–101; after *1589*, 186

Serlori, Niccolò, 64–65, 176–77

Servi, Costantino de', 185

Settimani, Francesco, 5

Siena, 51, 102, 131, 297*n*23

Silk industry, 66, 133–34

Sirens, role of (intermedio 1), 8, 31, 55, 61, 68–69

Sixtus V, Pope, 15, 122

Sodomy, 58

Sommi, Leone de', 60–61, 153

Sorceress, role of (intermedio 4), 32

Spain, Tuscan rivalry with, 10. *See also* Philip II

Spectator response, 139, 141–44, 148–49, 150–60 *passim*, 167–69, 172

Stage crew, 85, 89, 114–16, 127, 174–75

Stage machinery, 84–86

Stage sets, 93–96, 104, 127. *See also* Perspective

Stradano, Giovanni, 286*n*38

Striggio, Alessandro, 53

Strozzi, Giovanni Battista, 28, 63, 79, 152–53, 183

Strozzi, Piero, 28

Tailors: for Pellegrina, 64–65; for livery, 70–72; for intermedi, 132; for Pitti, 163–64. *See also* Berardi, Oreto

Theatrum mundi, 14–15, 19–20, 128, 139, 151–52, 158

Tornaquinci, Benedetto, 52, 65–66, 103–4

Transvestism, 53–58, 64, 168

Turks, 129, 132, 157, 169

Tuscany: economy of, 41–42; winter in, 123; population of, 130; decline of, 178

Uffizi Palace, 13; gallery (museum), 16, 76; tribune, 76, 156; workshops, 107; map room, 136–37
Uffizi Theater: remodeling for wedding, 2, 21, 44; dimensions and design, 78–81, 150; stage space and mechanical equipment, 84–87; décor, 94; use after *1589*, 181–88 *passim*
Utens, Justus, 136

Vaini, Enea, 64, 70, 73, 134, 143, 175–76, 280*n*46
Vasari, Giorgio: *1565* wedding activities, 23, 42, 45; as court architect, 43, 76–79; light-ing designs, 87; as educator, 89–91; work in Pisa, 130
Velvet, green, 61–62, 66, 175
Venice, 51, 66, 292*n*28
Villas, 91, 133–38. *See also* Poggio a Caiano; Pratolino
Virgil, 31, 33
Vitelli, Gianvincenzo, Marchese of Cetona, 71, 73, 141, 163

Wave machinery, 44, 86
Webster, John, 281*n*58
Women: as authors, 54; in theater, 54–58, 157; in needlework, 67–68, 144

Zingara, La, 37, 162